2001 EDITION

MUSICAL INSTRUMENT
AUCTION PRICE GUIDE

D1714064

STRING LETTER PUBLISHING

String Letter Publishing, Inc.
PO Box 767
San Anselmo, California 94960
(415) 485-6946

Editor: Jessamyn Reeves-Brown
Associate Editor: Heather K. Scott
Book Editor: Stacey Lynn
Managing Editor: Paul Kotapish

Design Director: Trpti Todd

Production Director: Ellen Richman
Production Coordinator: Judy Zimola
Production Assistant: Donna Yuen

The publishers wish to thank Peter Horner of Bonhams, Kerry Keane and Genevieve Wheeler of Christie's, Philip Scott and Mary Jane Potter of Phillips, David Bonsey of Skinner, and Tim Ingles of Sotheby's for their kind assistance in providing information and photographs for this guide. Photos on pages 93–96, courtesy of Christie's; pages 97–99, courtesy of Phillips; pages 199–202, courtesy of Skinner; and pages 93, 100, 197, 198, 203, and 204, courtesy of Sotheby's. Front cover photos: top and middle rows courtesy of Sotheby's; bottom row left, courtesy of Skinner; center, courtesy of Christie's; right, courtesy of Sotheby's. Back cover photos: top, courtesy of Sotheby's; bottom, courtesy of Christie's.

The Publishers assume no responsibility for errors or omissions in the material contained in this guide.

ISBN 1-890490-42-3

TABLE OF CONTENTS

INTRODUCTION

This guide offers descriptions and prices of musical instruments and bows offered at auction by identifiable makers at 23 sales held in the United States and Great Britain during 2000. (For a complete list of sales, see page 6.) It is emphatically not a guide to the playing qualities of these instruments, nor to their physical condition. Nor does the guide generally reflect "retail prices," since many items bought at auction are subsequently resold.

The guide is divided into three sections. The first section presents a report on stringed-instrument sales in 2000, reprinted from *Strings* magazine. The second section contains auction results in the Item-by-Item Listing. It provides the details on each item: where it was offered, lot number, where and when it was made, low and high estimated prices, the specifics of the most recent certificate—if any—with which the item was offered, and the actual selling price shown in two currencies. The first currency is U.S. dollars, followed by pounds sterling. The order of currencies is fixed, regardless of the currency in which the sale was conducted.

The third section contains the Summary by Item and Maker, which briefly encapsulates the offerings of the last five years in two currencies. Limiting the currencies to two has allowed us to reduce the number of pages in this Guide—so instead of a price increase this year we have been able to bring the price down. The summary is subdivided alphabetically by item, from Accordion to Zither-Banjo. Within each subdivision, you will find an alphabetical list of makers whose work appeared at auction, along with the barest of facts: how many items by that maker were offered, how many sold, and what were the lowest, highest, and average selling prices. If no items were sold, you will find no price information. If no items were offered by a particular maker, you will simply not find that maker's name.

Please note that all the basic information in this guide was supplied by the auction houses themselves, and it mirrors whatever inconsistencies or ambiguities you will find in the catalogs and the salesrooms. To cite one such example, you may find bows stamped "A. Vigneron," with no attempt to lump them with bows by Joseph Arthur Vigneron or his son, André. Although authorities may tell us that it was the father who used this stamp, while his son used a stamp reading "André Vigneron," we are not prepared to second-guess the auction houses who offered these bows under the sobriquet "A. Vigneron."

At the same time, we have attempted to clear up merely stylistic inconsistencies. For example, Italian forms of proper names are used rather than Latin forms; thus Hieronymus Amati II is listed as Amati, Girolamo (II).

Let the reader then be wary. When in doubt, first refer, if possible, to the catalog of the auction house itself. If the catalog is unavailable to you, contact the auction house directly, using the directory of names and addresses on page 7 of this guide, and request further clarification.

MARKET FORCES
Will the limited supply of big-name instruments keep up prices in an uncertain economy?

Heather K. Scott

Although the strength of high-quality instruments is still driving auction sales, the year 2000 fostered a rather conservative market. "Second- and third-tier makers are more prevalent in the market, but they really have gone soft," says Kerry Keane, head of the Musical Instruments department at Christie's. "The great masters of the 18th, the 19th, and even the 20th century still prevail."

"The master makers are always in demand," agrees Tom Metzler, a dealer based in Glendale, California, "but we have recently had trouble finding them for players."

Musicians seeking out the high-quality, bigger-name instruments is a trend verified by dealer Michael Selman at J. & A. Beare. "It is a little frustrating, but to get a really good-sounding instrument costs so much. Artists' tools are just out of reach for a lot of players, and that is so unfortunate. There just seem to be more players in the world right now, and more and more salaried positions available to musicians. Put that together with fewer instruments, and the prices go up," he says. Selman sees musicians leaning toward 17th- and 18th-century Cremonese makers. "I feel that many musicians are returning to the instruments regarded more for the depth and range of tone and color, such as the Amati, Ruggeri, and early Guarneri makers."

The highlight of Christie's year was the sale of the "Taft" Stradivari violin at a May 5 auction. The first successful sale of a Strad at a U.S. auction in more than 16 years, it was also the most expensive instrument ever to be sold at auction ($1,326,000). "It is a wonderful violin," notes Keane. "Its patronage has always been as a loan instrument to various high-level musicians, and, appropriately, the new buyer was another American collector who plans to continue lending out the instrument. It sent chills up my spine to know that it would continue that kind of patronage."

For those players not lucky enough to get on the loaner list for such an instrument, there is always the option of trying your hand at a little bidding. Keane feels strongly that there is a preponderance of musicians in the market—this year more than in years past. "Players are learning and feeling confident with using the expertise of auction specialists to make informed purchases. I think musicians are buying more on their own."

One of Tim Ingles of Sotheby's favorite lots shows this trend. "We sold a rare Mathias Hofmans viola, a fabulous playing instrument with its original label, for a record £25,800 ($38,958)—to a player," Ingles reveals. "We had really good working instruments this year rather than clean collectors' instruments."

"We had several record sales, but all in all it was an opportunity for good, lesser-known makers to come up in value," agrees David Bonsey of Skinner. "For example, some of them were from private sources and came from their original owners." One from the November sale was a particular favorite for Bonsey: a Gaetano Pollastri violin, dated 1935, that was commissioned by its original and only owner when he was a 15-year-old student in Bologna. It sold for $33,350, a record. "It was in near-mint condition, with a lot of layers of rosin on it but minimal wear to the varnish, and such a wonderful history.

"I think that this venue is not just for dealers and collectors anymore," Bonsey sums up. "It is open to everyone, and specialists are provided to help people with questions. I think players are becoming more aware of the auctions and more willing to check them out. Especially with bows, which are a little bit easier to buy, sell, and collect. And the trend in bows has been that the better-quality French bows have retained the highest value as investments, so they are a good initial investment, easy to buy—and most players own more than one. If I were a buyer, I would definitely recommend looking at masters like Thomassin, Lamy, Tubbs, and Hill." A viola bow by Thomassin sold at Skinner for $9,775, well up from the previous record for a Thomassin ($4,025 in 1995). Says Bonsey, "Because of the dearth of viola bows, they are an especially good buy."

"I think the better names in bows are still undervalued," agrees Bonhams' Peter Horner. "Sartory, for example. We will certainly catch up with some of the older French makers."

"Bows really were particularly strong for us this year," concurs Christopher Reuning of Reuning & Sons in Boston. "And new instruments sold more and more. But the really great old violins are more in demand than ever. We do very little any more with student and lower-cost instruments, and we sold a lot of violins to musicians."

All the big names were present in Sotheby's bow sales, too, although for some reason Tourtes just didn't sell well. "We had great success with our sales this year," says Ingles. "And it is still instruments by the well-known makers which are setting the records."

Fine instruments and bows generally did well at Bonhams, with highlights including a record-breaking sale of a Rocca violin for £132,250 ($189,120) and an "exceptional" Vuillaume for £63,250 ($94,875), the highest price paid for a Vuillaume violin. But the house's specialist, Peter Horner, doesn't feel that sales were as strong as some believe. "There were just too many instruments and not quite enough money," he declares. "We had a sale in London [in November] that just proved to be too much. There were four other sales scheduled over a four-day period. And with what is going on with the American economy, the coming year should be interesting. You know the saying, 'When America sneezes, Europe gets the cold.' We are going to skip our March sale in 2001, and focus on just two good sales a year—you simply can't put together a good catalog with three sales a year."

Dealer Thomas Metzler has noticed an increased level of return this past year, but tends to agree with Horner. "The year was stronger than previous years—but not dramatically. We always sell a really diverse lot of instruments. But this past December was particularly strong for us. Part of this may be the Italian Exhibition and Sale we had; we also saw a much larger number of modern Italian instruments being sold." Metzler's shop hosted the third annual traveling exhibition of the Violin Makers of Cremona November 26–December 9, 2000, and also held supplementary discussions and demonstrations. The exhibit traveled across the country throughout the fall.

With the U.S. economy in flux, the question of how it will affect the European trade market is a concern for the auction houses, most of which are based in London. Then there's the Internet, where the American on-line instrument company Tarisio built on last year's shakeup of the status quo. The new firm pulled in impressive sales this year. "Business has been very strong. We've experienced a continuation of growth that has been both gratifying and satisfying," says Reuning, who is a partner at Tarisio. "It is definitely developing into a bigger [auction venue] than we had originally anticipated. We've had three auctions thus far, and have been selling an average of 80 percent, with 100 percent Internet sales." No doubt fueling this success is Tarisio's flat 12.5 percent buying and selling commissions, lower than those of brick-and-mortar auction houses, which can reach 20 percent.

Phillips jumped into the on-line fray by incorporating Web-based viewing and bidding this year; the house launched its first simultaneous real-world–on-line sale in London in November. And it went very well, according to Philip Scott. "It was quite satisfying to bring the sale to a wider number of people around the world," he says. The auction recorded more than £700,000 ($1,035,700) in sales (premium included). "We had a Scottish collection [this year] that brought over £300,000 ($443,830) and a beautiful Panormo violin that sold for £26,450 ($39,675). So this was just a really good year for us."

Other houses are coping with the competition by holding sales in the States. Christie's opened a musical-instrument department in New York, where it held a sale in May, and Sotheby's hosted its first sale in Chicago in more than 15 years in October. Both houses considered the sales successful and plan to repeat them in 2001.

As musicians become more important players in the market, auction houses are looking for alternative ways to reach them. On-line sales and a concentration on "working" instruments are some of the answers birthed in 2000. Will they be enough to offset budding economic concerns? Sotheby's thinks so. "The market is getting smaller. What can be sold, the amount of instruments being turned over in the market, is smaller," says Ingles. It will be interesting to see what the 21st century brings.

Auction Activity

2001
instrument
sales

SALES INCLUDED IN THIS GUIDE

The bracketed code is shorthand that consists of a letter (or letters) denoting the auction house, followed by a number for the month in which the sale took place. If a particular house held two sales in the same month, the code consists of the letter for that house and a four-digit code for both the month and day. You will find these codes used throughout the detailed item-by-item listings later in the guide.

House	Place	Code	Date	Rate of Exchange
Phillips	London	[P2]	2/14/00	$1.59
Bonhams	Knightsbridge	[B2]	2/16/00	$1.60
Phillips	London	[P3]	3/13/00	$1.58
Sotheby's	London	[S3]	3/14/00	$1.57
Christie's	South Kensington	[C3]	3/15/00	$1.57
Butterfields'	Los Angeles	[Bf3]	3/21/00	$1.00
Skinner	Bolton, Massachussetts	[Sk4]	4/1/00	$1.00
Christie's	New York	[C5]	5/5/00	$1.00
Skinner	Boston	[Sk5]	5/7/00	$1.00
Bonhams	Knightsbridge	[B5]	5/31/00	$1.50
Phillips	London	[P6]	6/2/00	$1.51
Sotheby's	London	[S7]	7/12/00	$1.51
Bonhams	Knightsbridge	[B7]	7/13/00	$1.50
Phillips	London	[P9]	9/11/00	$1.41
Bonhams	Knightsbridge	[B9]	9/27/00	$1.46
Sotheby's	Chicago	[S10]	10/6/00	$1.00
Skinner	Boston	[Sk11]	11/5/00	$1.00
Phillips	London	[P11]	11/13/00	$1.43
Bonhams	Knightsbridge	[B11]	11/13/00	$1.43
Sotheby's	London	[S1114]	11/14/00	$1.43
Christie's	London	[C11]	11/15/00	$1.43
Sotheby's	London	[S1116]	11/16/00	$1.42
Sotheby's	Billingshurst	[S12]	12/7/00	$1.44

DIRECTORY OF AUCTION HOUSES

These are the firms in the United States and England that regularly conduct major sales of musical instruments, particularly stringed instruments and bows.

Bonhams
Montpelier St.
Knightsbridge
London SW7 1HH, England
Telephone: (44) 171-393113900
Fax: (44) 171-393113905
Web site: www.bonhams.com
Specialist: Peter Horner

Butterfield & Butterfield
7601 Sunset Blvd.
Los Angeles, CA 90046
Telephone: (323) 850-7500
Fax: (323) 850-5843
Web site: www.butterfields.com
Note: Butterfields' no longer holds musical instrument auctions. Results from the March 2000 auction are included in this book, but the musical-instrument department has been closed.

Christie's
85 Old Brompton Rd.
London SW7 3LD, England
Telephone: (44) 207-321-3470
Fax: (44) 207-321-3321
Web site: www.christies.com
Specialist: Kerry K. Keane

219 E. 67th St.
New York, NY 10021
Telephone: (212) 606-0562
Fax: (212) 744-9946
Specialist: Kerry K. Keane
Consultant: Frederick Oster

Phillips
101 New Bond St.
London W1Y 0AS, England
Telephone: (44) 207-465-0223
Fax: (44) 207-465-0223
Web site: www.phillips-auctions.com
Specialist: Philip Scott

406 E. 79th St.
New York, NY 10021
Telephone: (212) 570-4830
Fax: (212) 570-2207

Skinner
357 Main St.
Bolton, MA 01740
Telephone: (978) 779-6241
Fax: (978) 779-5144
Web site: www.skinnerinc.com
Specialist: David Bonsey

Sotheby's
34-35 New Bond St.
London W1A 2AA, England
Telephone: (44) 207-293-5034
Fax: (44) 207-293-5942
Web site: www.sothebys.com
Specialist: Tim Ingles

1334 York Ave.
New York, NY 10021
Telephone: (212) 606-7938
Fax: (212) 774-5310
Consultant: Charles Rudig

A KEY TO THE ITEM-BY-ITEM LISTINGS

1. Name of Maker   2. Sale/Lot   3. Item   4. Where/When Made

GUADAGNINI, LORENZO [P11/154] Fine and Handsome Violin w/case: Piacenza, 1742 (W. E. Hill & Sons, London, June 1933)   122,960/184,440
$304,326   £198,000

5. Certificate   7. Selling Prices   6. Estimated Prices ($)

1. Name. An "attributed" work is stated to be by the maker named, usually in accompanying documentation; an "ascribed" work is traditionally associated with the maker named. The auction house may or may not concur that an attribution or ascription is correct. Each house has its own definition of these terms; please refer directly to the auctioneers for clarification.

2. The lot number assigned by the auctioneer is preceded by an initial to identify the house (B Bonhams; Bf Butterfields'; C Christie's; P Phillips; S Sotheby's; Sk Skinner) followed by a number for the sale. If there were two sales at one house during the same month, the numbers for the month and day are both used to identify the sale.

3. A description of the item as it appears in the sale catalog. When the item is sold with accessories or when additional items are part of the same lot, a brief itemization appears here. This is also the place where defects or repairs, as reported in the sale catalog, are noted.

4. Place and date of manufacture, if known.

5. If sold with a certificate attesting to its provenance or identity, the most recent issuer is indicated in parentheses, along with the place and date of issuance.

6. Low and high estimated prices (in dollars) are separated by a slash (/). This is the price range within which the item was expected to sell, in the opinion of the auctioneers. On occasion, no estimate is made—most often involving an important instrument by a famous maker. In these cases, only the selling price appears in the tables.

7. The actual selling price includes the buyer's premium, at Bonhams, Christie's, Phillips, and Sotheby's: 15 percent on the first £30,000 of the hammer price and 10 percent on the amount above; and at Butterfields' and Skinner, 15 percent on the first $50,000 plus 10 percent on the amount above. Prices are given in two currencies, converted from local currency at their value on the day sold. You may determine the auction house at which the sale took place from the "Sale" information in "2" above. An unsold item is recorded as "NS." These listings do not provide details on size, weight, color, etc., which often help to identify or distinguish particular items. You are advised to consult the catalogs published prior to the sales, which may be obtained directly from the auctioneers.

———

ACCORDION

BUSSON [B2/15] Antique Accordion   192/240
$405   £253

TANZBAR [Sk4/63] Twenty-Eight-Note Automatic
Accordion in walnut case   700/1,000
$1,955   £1,232

ÆOLIAN HARP

PROWSE & CO., KEITH [S1116/295] Æolian Harp:
England, c. 1835   426/710
$648   £456

BAGPIPES

HENDERSON, PETER [S1116/306] Great Highland
Bagpipes w/case, goose, books: Glasgow, 1903
          4,260/5,680
$4,260   £3,000

BANJO

ESSEX, CLIFFORD [B5/68] Five-Stringed Zither, The
"Paragon" Banjo   450/750
$1,121   £748

ESSEX, CLIFFORD [B9/64] Special XX Banjo
          584/730
$504   £345

GRAY [B5/67] Four-Stringed Tenor Banjo   300/450
$500   £334

GREY & SONS, JOHN [B5/65] Four-Stringed Tenor
Banjo: London   75/105
$52   £35

LANGE, WILLIAM L. [Sk5/6] Paramount Aristocrat
Tenor Banjo, w/case: New York, c. 1926   800/1,200
$575   £374

SCHALL, J.B. [Sk11/22] American Five-String Banjo:
Chicago, c. 1900   100/200
$115   £81

STROMBERG, CHARLES & ELMER [Sk11/6]
Tenor Banjo w/case: Boston, c. 1920   600/800
$403   £282

VEGA COMPANY [B5/66] Four-Stringed Senator
Banjo   600/900 NS

VEGA COMPANY [B9/61] Four-Stringed Banjo
          730/1,022 NS

VEGA COMPANY [B9/62] Good Four-Stringed
Tenor Banjo   219/292
$285   £196

VEGA COMPANY [Sk5/3] Peter Seeger Model
Plectrum Banjo, w/stand: Boston   1,000/1,200
$1,725   £1,121

VEGA COMPANY [Sk5/20] Style M Tenor Banjo,
w/case: Boston   400/600
$403   £262

VEGA COMPANY [Sk11/2] American Tubaphone
No. 9 Model Five-String Banjo w/case: Boston, 1926
          2,000/3,000
$4,600   £3,220

VEGA COMPANY [Sk11/23] Whyte Laydie No. 7
Five-String Banjo w/case: Boston, 1921   300/400
$4,600   £3,220

WASHBURN [B5/64] Five-Stringed Zither Banjo
w/case   300/600
$380   £253

WEYMANN CO. [Sk5/4] Tenor Banjo w/case:
Philadelphia   200/300
$173   £112

BANJOLELE

STEWART, S.S. [Sk5/5] Banjolele   200/300
$144   £93

BASSOON

BILTON [B2/26] Nine-Keyed Bassoon   800/1,280
$773   £483

BUFFET [B9/28] Bassoon   2,190/2,628 NS

HOWARTH [B9/29] Bassoon   438/730
$403   £276

MAHILLON, C. [B5/28] Bassoon   450/750 NS

MAHILLON, C. [B9/30] Bassoon   219/292
$201   £138

METZLER & CO., G. [S1116/311] Eight-Keyed
Maple Bassoon: London, c. 1840   852/1,136 NS

MILHOUSE, WILLIAM [S1116/265] Six-Keyed
Maple Bassoon: London, c. 1800   852/1,136 NS

SCHREIBER & SOHN [B9/31] Bassoon   584/876
$604   £414

BUGLE

CURTIS & SON, RICHARD [S1116/282] Eight-
Keyed Bugle: London, 1825   3,550/4,970 NS

CLARINET

BASSI, LUCIAN [B2/25] Boehm-System Clarinet
          160/240
$147   £92

BESSON [B5/21] Boehm-System Clarinet   120/180
$121   £81

BESSON [B9/26] Clarinet   88/117
$76   £52

BOOSEY & HAWKES [B5/19] C-Model Clarinet
          450/750 NS

BOOSEY & HAWKES [B5/20] Boehm-System
Clarinet   600/900 NS

BOOSEY & HAWKES [B5/25] Boehm-System
Clarinet   120/180 NS

BOOSEY & HAWKES [B9/22] Boehm-System
Clarinet   88/117
$109   £75

BOOSEY & HAWKES [B9/23] C-Model Clarinet
219/292 NS

BOOSEY & HAWKES [B9/25] Boehm-System
Clarinet   117/175
$185   £127

BOOSEY & HAWKES [B9/27] Emperor Clarinet
117/175
$143   £98

CHIBONVILLE FRERES [Sk5/189] French Boxwood
Clarinet   400/600
$575   £374

COWLAN, MICHAEL [B2/23] Six-Keyed Boxwood
Clarinet: c. 1840   160/320
$221   £138

D'ALMAINE & CO. [B5/26] Six-Keyed Boxwood
Clarinet   150/225
$276   £184

DUVAL, RENE [B9/20] Boehm-System Clarinet
292/365 NS

GRANDJON, J. [Sk5/197] French Boxwood Clarinet:
Paris   400/600
$374   £243

HAWKES & SON [B5/23] Boehm-System Clarinet
150/225
$121   £81

MILLER, GEORGE [C3/2] Five-Keyed Boxwood and
Ivory Clarinet: London   157/314
$469   £299

NOBLET [B5/22] Boehm-System Clarinet: France
120/180 NS

NOBLET [B9/21] Boehm-System Clarinet   44/73
$84   £58

RUDALL, CARTE & CO. [B5/24] Boehm-System
Clarinet   120/180
$104   £69

SELMER [B2/24] Rosewood Boehm-System Clarinet:
London   240/320
$248   £155

WOLF & CO., ROBERT [C3/4] Six-Keyed Clarinet
314/471
$181   £115

WREDE, H. [Sk5/201] English Boxwood Five-Key
Clarinet: London, 19th C.   300/500
$518   £337

CLAVICHORD

GOFF, THOMAS [S1116/331] Unfretted Clavichord:
London, 1948   1,704/2,272
$1,704   £1,200

SONDERMANN, MARCUS GABRIEL [S1116/328]
Bundfrei Clavichord: Rendsberg, 1805 14,200/21,300
$29,288   £20,625

CONCERTINA

CASE, GEORGE [P2/2] Concertina w/matching walnut box: London   477/636
$695   £437

EBBLEWHITE [C11/15] Forty-Eight-Button English-
System Concertina in fitted box   501/644 NS

JEFFRIES [B9/44] Thirty-Button Anglo-System
Concertina w/case   1,460/2,190
$3,862   £2,645

JEFFRIES, C. [C11/16] English Duet-System
Concertina in original box   429/715
$2,184   £1,527

JEFFRIES, CHARLES [S1116/317] Thirty-Seven-
Button Anglo-German System Concertina w/case:
London, early 20th C.   1,704/2,272
$3,749   £2,640

JEFFRIES BROS. [S1116/316] Forty-Nine-Button
Duet-System Concertina w/case: London, c. 1900
2,556/3,550 NS

JONES, C. [B5/41] Forty-Button Concertina   45/75
$173   £115

LACHENAL [B9/46] Thirty-Three-Button Anglo-
System Concertina w/case   292/438
$1,427   £978

LACHENAL & CO. [C5/32] Forty-Eight-Button
English Concertina w/fitted case: c. 1915 800/1,200
$705   £458

LACHENAL & CO. [S1116/315] Forty-Eight-Button
English Concertina w/case: London, early 20th C.
568/852
$596   £420

LACHENAL & CO. [S1116/319] Thirty-Seven-
Button Anglo-German System Concertina w/case:
London, c. 1925   852/1,136
$1,704   £1,200

LACHENAL & CO. [C3/13] English Concertina
w/fitted box   393/550
$361   £230

LACHENAL & CO. [C3/14] Anglo-System English
Concertina w/leather box   314/471
$271   £173

LACHENAL & CO. [C11/242] English-system
Concertina in fitted box   501/644 NS

LACHENAL & CO. [C11/243] Thirty-Two-Button
Anglo-Chromatic-System Concertina w/case 286/429
$839   £587

PROWSE & CO., KEITH [B5/42] Forty-Eight-Button
English-System Concertina w/fitted case   270/375
$345   £230

WHEATSTONE, C. [B5/40] Duet-System Concertina
450/750
$690   £460

WHEATSTONE, C. [C3/12] English Concertina
w/wooden box   471/628
$451   £288

WHEATSTONE, C. [C11/14] Good Forty-Eight-
Button English-System Concertina w/original case
501/644
$588   £411

WHEATSTONE & CO., C. [C11/13] Sixty-Four-
Button English-System Concertina w/original leather
case   501/644
$2,016   £1,410

WHEATSTONE & CO., C. [S1116/318] Forty-Eight-
Button English Concertina w/case: London, 1921
426/710
$1,022   £720

CORNET

COURTOIS, ANTOINE [C11/255] Silver-Plated
Cornet w/period mouthpiece, 2 extra crooks 215/286
$202   £141

HILLYARD, W. [P9/2] Silver-Plated Cylinder-Valve
Military Band Cornet w/case: London   423/564
$405   £288

PACE & SON, CHARLES [S1116/287] Cornet
w/case, 2 mouthpieces: London, c. 1860   426/710
$477   £336

DOUBLE BASS

FRAMUS [Sk5/368] German Rockabilly Model
Double Bass   500/800
$2,185   £1,420

PRESCOTT, ABRAHAM [Sk11/387] American
Double Bass with one replacement tuning key, loss to
scroll: Concord, c. 1840   1,500/1,800
$8,050   £5,635

DOUBLE BASS BOW

BRYANT, P.W. [P9/137] Good Silver Double Bass
Bow   846/987
$1,216   £863

FETIQUE, VICTOR [S3/147] Silver Double Bass Bow
with repaired head: Paris, c. 1900   1,099/1,884
$2,347   £1,495

MORIZOT, L. [C3/136] Silver Double Bass Bow
1,570/2,355
$1,986   £1,265

MORIZOT, L. [P11/221] Good Nickel Double Bass
Bow with full hair, w/bow box   1,144/1,287
$1,316   £920

NURNBERGER (workshop of) [Sk11/115] German
Silver Double Bass Bow with repair   600/800
$1,380   £966

NURNBERGER, KARL ALBERT [S7/109] Nickel
Double Bass Bow w/double bass bow:
Markneukirchen, mid 20th C.   1,208/1,812 NS

TUBBS, JAMES [P2/110] Part-Silver Double Bass
Bow   1,590/1,908
$1,317   £828

WINKLER, F. [Sk5/181] Silver German Double Bass
Bow   400/600
$345   £224

ENGLISH HORN

CABART [B9/19] Black Wood English Horn w/origi-
nal double case   438/730
$1,007   £690

TRIEBERT & SONS, GUILLAUME [S1116/271]
Ten-Keyed Curved English Horn: Paris, early 19th C.
4,260/7,100
$11,928   £8,400

FIFE

CAHUSAC [B5/29] Boxwood Fife w/boxwood fife
120/180
$483   £322

FLAGEOLET

BAINBRIDGE [B5/14] Double Flageolet   150/225
$414   £276

BAINBRIDGE & WOOD [Sk5/192] English
Boxwood Double Flageolet: London, 19th C.
1,200/1,500
$1,265   £822

GARRETT, R. [C3/3] Ivory Boxwood Flageolet
$217   £138

SIMPSON [C11/8] Ivory and Boxwood Flageolet:
c. 1826   429/715
$807   £564

FLAGEOLET-FLUTE

BAINBRIDGE [B5/15] Double Flageolet-Flute
450/750
$587   £391

FLUTE

ASTOR & CO. [Sk5/193] English Boxwood
Transverse Flute: London, 19th C.   200/300
$575   £374

ASTOR & CO., GEORGE [C3/6] Baroque Flute
628/942 NS

BEYER [B9/13] Six-Keyed Rosewood Flute w/original
case   146/219
$537   £368

BOOSEY & CO. [B2/17] Eight-Keyed Rosewood
Flute w/case, piccolo   128/160
$515   £322

BUFFET [B5/7] Silver-Plated Flute   120/180
$104   £69

BUNDY [B2/18] Silver Boehm-System Flute w/case
128/192
$147   £92

CLEMENTI & CO. [S1116/266] Four-Keyed Boxwood Third Flute w/flute, clarinet: London, early 19th C. 568/852
$682   £480

CLEMENTI & CO. [C11/10] Eight-Keyed Silver and Cocuswood Flute 572/858
$503   £352

CLEMENTI & CO. [C11/11] Eight-Keyed Boxwood and Ivory Flute 215/286 NS

CORONET [B5/12] Silver Flute: c. 1964 600/750 NS

CRONE, JOHANN AUGUST [S1116/309] One-Keyed Boxwood Flute w/case: Leipzig, last quarter 18th C. 8,520/11,360 NS

DAWKINS & CO., THOMAS [S1116/303A] Eight-Keyed Rosewood Flute w/case: London, c. 1850 994/1,420
$1,108   £780

DELUSSE, CHRISTOPHER [S1116/310] One-Keyed Boxwood Flute w/case: Paris, c. 1785   4,260/7,100
$4,771   £3,360

EISENBRANDT, HEINRICH CHRISTIAN [Sk5/200] Rare American Four-Keyed Ivory and Silver Flute: Philadelphia, c. 1814 400/600
$6,325   £4,111

FREYER, JOHANN GOTTLIEB [S1116/267] Six-Keyed/Four-Keyed Ebony Flute w/case: Potsdam, late 18th C.
11,360/17,040 $13,632   £9,600

GEROCK, CHRISTOPHER [S1116/303] One-Keyed Boxwood Flute w/case: London, first quarter 19th C. 568/852 NS

GRENSER, JOHANN HEINRICH [S1116/268] Four-Keyed Ebony Flute: Dreseden, c. 1800 3,550/4,970
$8,861   £6,240

HIRSCHSTEIN, MATHAUS [S1116/264] One-Keyed Ivory Flute w/case: Leipzig, mid 18th C. 1,136/1,704
$1,704   £1,200

HOPKINS, A. [Sk5/205] American Boxwood Transverse Flute missing cap: Litchfield, Connecticut, 19th C. 300/500
$1,265   £822

KAUFFMANN, ANDREW [S1116/308] Eight-Keyed Ivory Flute w/case: London, c. 1820   1,136/1,704
$1,193   £840

MONZANI & CO. [C11/12] Eight-Keyed Silver and Rosewood Flute w/case 1,430/2,002 NS

MONZANI & CO. [S1116/269] Eight-Keyed Blackwood Flute w/case: London, 1821 1,136/1,704
$2,215   £1,560

PEARL [B2/19] Silver Boehm-System Flute w/case 800/1,120 NS

PEARL [B5/10] Silver Boehm-System Flute w/original case 450/750 NS

PEARL [B9/11] Silver Boehm-System Flute w/original case: Japan 292/438
$470   £322

POND & CO., WM. A. [Sk5/202] American Boxwood Transverse Flute: New York, 19th C. 400/800
$518   £337

POTTER [B2/16] Six-Keyed English Boxwood Flute with one broken key 240/400
$221   £138

POTTER [B9/12] Wooden Flute w/flute 73/102
$84   £58

POTTER [C11/9] Six-Keyed Boxwood and Ivory Flute w/case, 2 cocuswood flutes 429/572 NS

RUDALL, CARTE & CO. [B5/9] Silver-Plated Flute 900/1,200 NS

RUDALL, CARTE & CO. [B9/10] Silver Boehm-System Flute 438/730 NS

RUDALL, CARTE & CO. [B9/9] Silver-Plated Flute 219/438
$369   £253

RUDALL, CARTE & CO. [C3/18] Boehm-System Ebony and Silver Flute: c. 1890 314/628 NS

RUDALL, ROSE, CARTE & CO. [P9/3] Eight-Nickel-Keyed Rosewood Flute w/box: London 564/705
$973   £690

YAMAHA [B5/11] Flute 105/135
$121   £81

FRENCH HORN

GREY & SONS, JOHN [B9/32] French Horn w/original case 146/292
$151   £104

PAXMAN [B5/33] French Horn w/original case 225/375
$449   £29

GUITAR

BARTON, PETER [B2/36] Guitar w/case 2,080/2,400
$2,392   £1,495

BAZZOLO, THOMAS [Sk11/31] Classical Guitar w/case: Lebanon, CT, 1994 2,000/4,000 NS

BELLIDO, JOSE LOPEZ [B5/44] Spanish Classical Guitar 750/1,050
$863   £575

BOHLIN, GEORG [P6/15] Good Eight-String Guitar in immediate playing condition, w/case: Stockholm, 1986 1,208/1,359 NS

BOULLANGIER, G. [P3/6] Fine and Handsome Guitar w/case: c. 1870 948/1,264
$1,508   £955

14

D'ANGELICO, JOHN [Sk5/10] Fine, Rare, American New Yorker Model Archtop Guitar, w/case: New York, 1937   20,000/30,000
$21,850   £14,203

D'ANGELICO, JOHN [Sk11/9] Fine American Archtop Model Excel Guitar with sunburst finish, w/case: New York, 1947   12,000/15,000 NS

D'ANGELICO, JOHN [Sk11/10] Fine Rare American Archtop New Yorker Model Guitar with cutaway body and natural finish, w/case: New York, 1953
                                        25,000/30,000
$25,300   £17,710

DOBRO [Sk5/8] Resonator Guitar w/case, steel, fingerpicks: c. 1970   400/600
$489   £318

DUBOIS [S1116/293] Guitar w/case: Mirecourt, c. 1810   1,704/2,272

$2,215   £1,560

EPIPHONE [S10/133] Electric Guitar w/case, amplifier: Kalamazoo, late 20th C.   600/700
$720   £497

FABRICATORE, GENNARO [P11/16] Fine Italian Guitar requiring some restorations and missing one fret: Napoli, 1826   2,145/2,860
$3,125   £2,185

FABRICATORE, GENNARO [S1116/294] Guitar w/case: Naples, 1815   4,260/7,100 NS

GALLINOTTI, PIETRO [S1116/300] Guitar w/case: Solero, 1971   4,260/7,100 NS

GIBSON CO. [B5/50] Guitar   750/1,050
$2,933   £1,955

GIBSON CO. [B5/53A] Guitar   1,500/2,250 NS

GIBSON CO. [Sk5/2] Fine American Guitar w/original hardshell case: Kalamazoo, 1929   3,500/4,500
$6,325   £4,111

GIBSON CO. [Sk5/9] TG-0 Model Tenor Guitar, Serial No. 241260, w/case   300/350
$288   £187

GIBSON CO. [Sk5/12] American Guitar w/original hardshell case: Kalamazoo, 1964   1,800/2,200
$1,840   £1,196

GIBSON CO. [Sk5/15] American L-7 Style Archtop Guitar, w/case: Kalamazoo, c. 1935   800/1,000
$1,150   £748

GIBSON CO. [Sk5/16] American L-Century Model Guitar, w/case: Kalamazoo, c. 1933   800/1,200
$1,955   £1,271

GIBSON CO. [Sk5/18] American J-40 Model Guitar, w/case: Kalamazoo, 1973   300/500
$1,035   £673

GIBSON CO. [Sk11/7] Rare American Model Nick Lucas Special Guitar w/case: Kalamazoo, 1928
                                        5,000/7,000
$14,950   £10,465

GIBSON CO. [Sk11/15] Good American Archtop Model Super 400 Guitar: Kalamazoo, 1957
                                        7,000/9,000 NS

GIBSON CO. [Sk11/26] American Model ES-175 Guitar: Kalamazoo, 1960   1,000/1,500
$2,760   £1,932

GUTIERREZ, MANUEL [S1116/302] Guitar: Seville, 1836   2,130/3,550
$2,386   £1,680

HARMONY [B2/39] Guitar   160/240
$221   £138

HASHIMOTO [B5/53] Classical Guitar   300/450
$293   £196

HAUSER, HERMANN [C5/1] Fine Classical Guitar w/period case: Reisbach, 1947   18,000/22,000
$49,350   £32,078

HAUSER, HERMANN [C5/2] Classical Guitar w/period case: Reisbach, 1947   8,000/12,000
$25,850   £16,803

HERNANDEZ, SANTOS [S1116/301] Guitar w/case: Madrid, 1925   2,840/4,260
$7,668   £5,400

KRINER, SIMON [Sk11/24] German Guitar w/case: Mittenwald, 1804   600/800 NS

LACOTE [P3/4] Fine and Handsome Guitar w/case: 1821   1,580/2,370
$3,452   £2,185

LACOTE [P3/5] Handsome Guitar with some restorable blemishes, w/case: 1825   1,580/2,370
$4,088   £2,588

MARTIN & CO., C.F. [C5/3] Rare American Guitar w/original wood case: Nazareth, c. 1870 1,200/1,600
$1,645   £1,069

MARTIN & CO., C.F. [C5/4] American Guitar w/case: Nazareth, 1939   1,800/2,200
$1,998   £1,299

MARTIN & CO., C.F. [C5/7] Fine American Guitar w/case: Nazareth, 1936   5,500/7,500
$7,638   £4,965

MARTIN & CO., C.F. [C11/6] D-18 Model Mahogany Guitar w/original case: Nazareth, Pennsylvania, 1971   715/1,144
$1,344   £940

MARTIN & CO., C.F. [Sk5/13] American 00-17 Model Guitar, w/case: Nazareth, 1938   1,000/1,300
$1,495   £972

MARTIN & CO., C.F. [Sk5/14] American D-28 Model Guitar, w/original hardshell case: Nazareth, 1969   2,500/3,500
$2,415   £1,570

MARTIN & CO., C.F. [Sk5/17] American Archtop Electric Guitar Model GT-75, w/case: Nazareth, 1965   600/800

$805   £523

MARTIN & CO., C.F. [Sk11/19] American Style 000-18 Guitar w/case: Nazareth, 1926   3,000/3,500
$3,335   £2,335

MARTIN & CO., C.F. [Sk11/29] American Style D-41 Guitar w/case: Nazareth, 1971   1,200/1,400
$2,300   £1,610

NATIONAL [Sk5/11] Good Style 1 Tricone Resonator Guitar, w/case, steel, fingerpicks, music: 1929   2,500/3,000 NS

NATIONAL DOBRO CORP. [Sk11/18] Resonator Guitar w/case: c. 1931   1,000/14,000
$1,265   £886

PANORMO, LOUIS [B5/45] Guitar   1,500/2,250
$1,984   £1,323

PANORMO, LOUIS [B5/46] Guitar with later head
    750/1,050
$1,001   £667

PANORMO, LOUIS [B5/47] Guitar   1,500/2,250
$2,588   £1,725

PANORMO, LOUIS [C3/10] English Guitar: London, 1829   1,256/1,884
$1,354   £863

PANORMO, LOUIS [C3/8] English Guitar w/case
    1,884/2,198
$3,972   £2,530

PANORMO, LOUIS [P6/12] Guitar with some back restoration: London, 1849   604/680
$903   £598

RAMIREZ, JOSE [B5/51] Classical Guitar
    2,250/3,750 NS

RAMIREZ, JOSE [B5/55] Classical Guitar
    3,750/5,250
$4,485   £2,990

RAMIREZ, JOSE [B9/71] Classical Guitar
    1,460/2,190 NS

RAMIREZ, MANUEL (workshop of) [Sk11/11] Fine Spanish Guitar attributed to Manuel Borroquero, w/case: Madrid, 1917   10,000/12,000
$9,200   £6,440

RAY, R. [B9/69] Classical Guitar   438/730
$437   £299

RODRIGUEZ, MIGUEL [C3/9] Spanish Guitar w/case: Cordoba, 1987   6,280/9,420 NS

SANAVIA, LEONE [Sk11/5] Venetian Guitar: Venice, 1955   800/1,000
$489   £342

SPAIN, ROY [B5/52] Classical Guitar 750/1,050 NS

STROMBERG, CHARLES & ELMER [Sk11/8] Fine, Rare American Archtop Guitar with natural finish, w/case: Boston, 1947   50,000/60,000 NS

STROMBERG, CHARLES & ELMER [Sk11/12] Fine, Rare American Archtop Guitar with sunburst finish, w/case: Boston, 1954   50,000/60,000 NS

VELASQUEZ, MANUEL [Sk11/14] Flamenco Guitar w/case: New York, 1963   4,000/6,000 NS

VELASQUEZ, MANUEL [Sk11/16] Classical Guitar w/case: New York, 1957   4,000/6,000 NS

HARP

EGAN, JOHN [P11/9] Attractive Grecian Harp with some restorations, missing swell doors and pedal: Dublin, c. 1820   1,430/1,716 NS

ERARD, SEBASTIAN & PIERRE [P11/7] Attractive Gothic Patent Harp with later table, missing swell doors and pedal, w/cover: London   2,860/4,290
$6,414   £4,485

ERARD, SEBASTIAN & PIERRE [P11/8] Attractive Gothic Patent Harp with later table, missing swell doors and pedal: London   2,145/2,860
$2,960   £2,070

ERARD, SEBASTIAN [P11/10] Regency Harp with some restorations and without swell doors: London
    1,144/1,430
$1,316   £920

ERAT, J. & J. [P9/6] Attractive Gothic Patent Harp: London   2,115/2,820
$7,297   £5,175

LIGHT, EDWARD [P6/13] Fine and Handsome Freestanding Dital Harp: London, c. 1810
    1,510/2,265
$4,168   £2,760

HARPSICHORD

BRITSEN, JORIS [S1116/279] Two-Manual Harpsichord: Antwerp, 1680   56,800/85,200 NS

KIRCKMAN, ABRAHAM & JOSEPH [P6/16] Single-Manual Harpsichord: London, 1793
    15,100/22,650
$36,467   £24,150

KIRCKMAN, JACOB [S1116/327] Two-Manual Harpsichord: London, 1758   85,200/113,600 NS

HORN

BOSTON MUSICAL INSTRUMENT MANUFAC-TURER [Sk5/199] American Brass Baritone Horn
    200/300
$259   £168

KIT

JAY, HENRY [S1116/297] Dancing Master's Kit: London, 1774   2,840/4,260 NS

LUTE

BAUER, MATTHAUS [B9/67] Lute   292/584
$705   £483

MANDOLA

HOWE CO., ELIAS [Sk11/21] American Mandola: Boston, 1905   300/400
$316   £221

MANDOLIN

CALACE [B9/50] Good Mandolin: Naples, 1894
438/730
$504   £345

CALACE [B9/55] Mandolin w/case   117/175
$1,209   £828

CALACE, NICOLA & RAFFAELLE [S1116/290]
Neapolitan Mandolin w/case, cover: Naples, 1897
3,550/4,970
$3,749   £2,640

CALACE & SON, RAFFAELE [C11/258] Neapolitan
Mandolin   286/572
$1,008   £705

DE MUREDA [B5/57] Mandolin   120/180
$129   £86

EMBERGHER, LUIGI [S1116/288] Roman
Mandolin w/case: Rome, 1926   1,136/1,704
$2,215   £1,560

FILANO, DONATO [S1116/291] Mandolin w/case:
Naples, 1763   2,840/4,260
$2,897   £2,040

GIBSON CO. [B9/57] Rare Early Mandolin w/origi-
nal case: c. 1914   1,460/2,190
$1,511   £1,035

GIBSON CO. [Sk5/7] American Mandolin w/case
1,200/1,400
$690   £449

GIBSON CO. [Sk11/4] American Model A4
Mandolin w/case: Kalamazoo, 1916   1,200/1,400
$1,610   £1,127

GIBSON CO. [Sk11/17] American Model F4
Mandolin w/case: Kalamazoo, 1916   1,800/2,000
$2,300   £1,610

MARTIN & CO., C.F. [C5/5] Good American
Mandolin w/original leather case: Nazareth, 1912
1,200/1,600 NS

MARTIN & CO., C.F. [Sk11/1] American Mandolin
w/case: 400/500
$403   £282

MARTIN & CO., C.F. [Sk11/20] Neapolitan-Style
Mandolin: Nazareth, 1908   300/400
$288   £202

RINALDI, CARLO [C11/7] Neapolitan Mandolin
286/429
$419   £293

TONELLI, PIETRO [B5/62] Mandolin   300/450 NS

TONELLI, PIETRO [B9/51] Mandolin   146/219
$201   £138

VINACCIA, GENNARO & ACHILLE [S1116/296]
Neapolitan Mandolin: Naples, 1891   852/1,136
$2,215   £1,560

VINACCIA BROS. [B2/33] Mandolin w/case
800/1,120
$1,380   £863

OBOE

DUVAL, RENE [B5/17] Wooden Oboe: Italy
300/450 NS

DUVAL, RENE [B9/17] Wooden Oboe   146/219
$151   £104

GAUTROT-MARQUET [S1116/272] Boehm-System
Rosewood Oboe w/case, cover: Paris, c. 1875
426/710
$477   £336

GOLDE [Sk5/195] German Boxwood Oboe:
Dresden, 19th C.   300/500
$4,600   £2,990

GOULDING & CO. [S1116/314] Two-Keyed
Boxwood Oboe: London, c. 1800   2,840/4,260
$5,112   £3,600

GRENSER, JOHANN HEINRICH [S1116/313] Ten-
Keyed Boxwood Oboe w/case: Dresden, c. 1810
7,100/9,940 NS

GRUNDMANN, JAKOB FREDERICH [S1116/312]
Two-Keyed Boxwood Oboe w/case: Dresden, 1774
14,200/21,300
$28,471   £20,050

KREUL, HANS [C3/22] Modern Oboe w/case, cover
1,256/1,884 NS

LOREE, F. [B9/18] Blackwood Oboe w/original case
365/584
$705   £483

MILHOUSE, WILLIAM [S1116/263] Seven-Keyed
Boxwood Oboe w/case: London, early 19th C.
710/994
$818   £576

NOBLET [C3/20] Modern French Oboe w/case
236/314
$289   £184

SCHUCK, M. [Sk5/196] Austrian Maple Oboe:
Vienna, c. 1900   200/300
$575   £374

ORGAN

GREEN, SAMUEL [S1116/329] Chamber Organ:
London, 1796   5,680/8,520 NS

PISTOR, EDWARD & JOHN [S1116/277] Bureau
Chamber Organ: England, last quarter 18th C.
14,200/21,300 NS

PIANO

BROADWOOD, JOHN [S1116/322] Square Piano:
London, 1787   1,420/2,130 NS

CLEMENTI & CO. [S1116/332] Square Piano:
London, c. 1820   1,704/2,272
$1,874   £1,320

HEINTZMAN & CO. [Sk4/79] Welte-Mignon
Reproducing Semi-Grand Piano in walnut Jacobean
case, w/bench, 26 Welte and other rolls   6,000/8,000
$3,450   £2,174

LONGMAN & BRODERIP [S1116/323] Square
Piano: London, c. 1784   2,130/3,550
$2,556   £1,800

ROLOFF, H. [S1116/280] Obliquely Strung "Dog
Kennel" Piano: Neubrandenburg, c. 1840
                                  7,100/9,940 NS

SEEBURG [Sk4/102] Style B Coin-Operated Piano
w/mandolin attachment   2,000/3,000
$1,725   £1,087

SEEBURG [Sk4/103] Style E Piano in oak case,
w/mandolin attachment, violin pipes, automatic
accordion   700/900
$2,530   £1,594

STEINWAY & SONS [Bf3/6269] Ebonized Grand
Piano w/bench   10,000/15,000 NS

STEWART, NEIL & MALCOLM [S1116/324]
Square Piano: Edinburgh, c. 1800   1,136/1,704
$1,193   £840

WACHTL, JOSEPH & JACOB BLEYER
[S1116/276] Double Giraffe Piano: Vienna, c. 1805
                                     4,260/7,100
$15,336   £10,800

PIANOFORTE

BROADWOOD, JOHN & SONS [S1116/278]
Grand Pianoforte: London, c. 1795   14,200/21,300
$20,306   £14,300

BROADWOOD, JOHN & SONS [S1116/326]
Grand Pianoforte: London, 1804   8,520/11,360
$11,076   £7,800

PICCOLO

D'ALMAINE & CO. [S1116/270] One-Keyed
Boxwood Piccolo: London, c. 1840   568/710
$511   £360

KOHLER & SON [C11/254] Four-Keyed Boxwood
and Ivory Piccolo   143/215 NS

MAHILLON & CO., C. [B5/6] Six-Keyed Wooden
Piccolo   90/120
$86   £58

RECORDER

ADLER, JOHANNES [Sk5/198] Modern German
Tenor Recorder   40/75
$46   £30

DOLMETSCH [B5/27] Tenor Recorder: 1955
                                     150/225 NS

DOLMETSCH [B9/16] Tenor Recorder: 1955 88/117
$285   £196

GOBLE, ROBERT [C3/15] Alto Recorder
                                     314/628 NS

GOBLE, ROBERT [C3/7] Modern Sopranino
Recorder w/modern alto recorder   628/942 NS

MOECK [Sk5/208] Modern Tenor Recorder 75/100
$173   £112

SAXOPHONE

BUESCHER [B2/27] Straight Soprano Saxophone
w/case   320/480
$1,012   £633

BUESCHER [B5/38] Tenor Saxophone w/fitted case
                                     900/1,200 NS

BUESCHER [B9/36] Tenor Saxophone w/case
                                       584/876
$638   £437

BUESCHER [B9/43] Alto Saxophone w/case 365/584
$470   £322

BUESCHER [Sk5/207] Baritone Saxophone w/case,
stand: Elkhart, Indiana   300/500
$920   £598

BUFFET, CRAMPON & CO. [B5/36] Tenor
Saxophone w/fitted case   450/750 NS

BUFFET, CRAMPON & CO. [B9/38] Tenor
Saxophone w/case   292/438
$285   £196

CONN, C.G. [B2/31] Tenor Saxophone w/case
                                     800/1,120 NS

CONN, C.G. [B5/35] Alto Saxophone w/fitted case
                                     600/900 NS

CONN, C.G. [B5/37] Tenor Saxophone w/fitted case
                                     450/750 NS

CONN, C.G. [B9/35] Alto Saxophone w/case
                                       438/730
$873   £598

CONN, C.G. [B9/40] Tenor Saxophone w/case
                                       292/438
$638   £437

CONN, C.G. [B9/41] Alto Saxophone   365/584 NS

DOLNET, HENRI [B9/39] Alto Saxophone 219/292
$252   £173

DORE [B2/29] Alto Saxophone w/case: Paris, early
20th C.   640/960 NS

GRAFTON [C11/253] Brass and Lucite Alto
Saxophone w/case   572/858

GRASS [B2/32] Alto Saxophone w/case   400/560
$331   £207

LECOMTE & CO., A. [Sk5/209] Alto Saxophone
w/case: Paris, c. 1920   600/800
$1,495   £972

SELMER [C5/33] French Mark VI Model Tenor
Saxophone, w/case: c. 1960   1,800/2,200
$3,525   £2,291

SIOMA [B2/30] Tenor Saxophone w/case
                                     640/960 NS

SIOMA [B5/39] Tenor Saxophone w/case, 2 mouthpieces   300/600 NS

SERPENT

GOULDING & D'ALMAINE [S10/130] Four-Keyed
English Serpent: London, c. 1830   3,000/5,000
$3,360   £2,318

JORDAN, JAMES [S1116/286] Five-Keyed Serpent
w/case: Liverpool, c. 1840   2,556/3,550
$3,749   £2,640

SPINET

BARTON (ascribed to) [P6/17] Attractive English
Spinet: c. 1730   6,040/7,550 NS

HAXBY, THOMAS [C11/1] English Spinet on trestle
stand: c. 1770   8,580/11,440
$12,601   £8,812

TROMPE DE CHASSE

RAOUX, MARCEL-AUGUSTE [S1116/281] Helical
Trompe de Chasse: Paris, second quarter 19th C.
2,130/2,840 NS

TRUMPET

COURTOIS, ANTOINE (FILS) [S1116/284] Slide
Trumpet w/case: Paris, 1872   1,420/2,130
$3,749   £2,640

VICKERS [B5/30] Silver-Plated Trumpet 225/300 NS

VICKERS [B9/33] Silver-Plated Trumpet   117/175
$151   £104

UKULELE

MARTIN & CO., C.F. [Sk5/1] Good Style 1 Ukulele,
w/case: Nazareth, c. 1950   300/500
$863   £561

VIOL

CARLETTI, NATALE [Sk5/43] Viola d'Amore
w/case, English bow: Bologna, 1965   2,500/3,500
$2,645   £1,719

CARLETTI, NATALE [Sk11/36] Contemporary
Italian Viola d'Amore w/case: Bologna, 1969
2,500/3,500
$1,955   £1,369

COLETTI, A. [B7/101] Viola d'Amore: Vienna, 1918
1,500/2,250
$1,898   £1,265

COULY, JEAN [B7/111] Viola d'Amore: Nancy, 1746
4,500/7,500 NS

COULY, JEAN [B11/114] Viola d'Amore: Nancy,
1746   2,860/4,290
$2,302   £1,610

GUGGENBERGER, ANTON [P6/19] Fine and
Handsome Viola d'Amore in immediate playing condition, w/case: Vienna, 1961   1,208/1,359
$1,737   £1,150

STIEBER, ERNST [C11/97] German Bass Viola da
Gamba: 1958   2,860/4,290
$4,033   £2,820

TIELKE (workshop of) [S1116/292] Bass Viola da
Gamba w/case, bow: Hamburg, late 17th C.
11,360/17,040
$12,780   £9,000

UEBEL, WOLFGANG [Sk11/424] Contemporary
Bass Viola da Gamba w/case, bow: 1967
1,800/2,400
$1,495   £1,047

VIOLA

ANTONIAZZI, ROMEO [S1114/159] Viola w/case:
Cremona, 1914 (Josef Blum, Stuttgart, February 6,
1982)   14,300/21,450 NS

ASCHAUER, LEO [S7/142] Viola w/case, cover:
Mittenwald, 1958   2,265/3,020
$2,356   £1,560

ASTORI, GIOVANNI [Bf3/6228] Good Modern
Viola: Cremona, 1982   3,000/5,000
$2,587   £1,656

ATTERMATT, JAN [B11/105] Rare Italian Viola:
Turin, 1829   8,580/14,300 NS

BAILLY, PAUL [P6/92] Good French Viola in immediate playing condition, w/case: Paris, 1890 (Etienne
Vatelot, Paris, March 28, 1996)   6,040/6,795 NS

BAILLY, PAUL [P11/117] Good French Viola in good
condition, w/case: Paris, 1890 (Etienne Vatelot, Paris,
March 28, 1996)   5,005/5,720
$5,427   £3,795

BANKS, JAMES & HENRY [B11/112] Very Fine
English Viola in an extremely fine state of preservation: Salisbury   7,150/10,010
$10,689   £7,475

BASTON, VICTOR [S3/113] Viola w/case: Southall,
1948   4,396/5,495 NS

BATELLI, ALFIO [Sk5/47] Good Viola w/case: 1973
5,000/8,000 NS

BERNARDEL, GUSTAVE [C5/143] Good French
Viola: Paris, 1986 (Bernard Millant, Paris, June 17,
1998)   12,000/16,000
$11,750   £7,638

BERTELLI, ENZO [S7/141] Viola: Verona, 1955
3,775/5,285 NS

BETTS, JOHN [P9/74] Fine and Handsome Viola in
good condition, w/case: London, c. 1800   846/987
$4,216   £2,990

BIANCHI, ROBERTO [S1114/162] Viola w/case:
Cremona, 1986   5,005/7,150
$6,006   £4,200

BISSOLOTTI, FRANCESCO [Sk11/46]
Contemporary Italian Viola w/case: Cremona, 1972
2,000/4,000
$4,600   £3,220

BLITZ, LOUIS [P11/33] Good Viola in immediate playing condition, w/case: Rotterdam, 1942
1,001/1,144
$740   £518

BONETTE, MAURICE K. [C5/155] Contemporary Viola: London, 1970   3,000/4,000 NS

BOULANGEOT, EMILE [B7/106] Viola: Mirecourt, 1877   2,250/3,000 NS

BOURGUIGNON, MAURICE [S7/129] Viola: Brussels, 1935 (Willi-Paul Balsereit, Cologne, January 15, 1998)   6,040/9,060 NS

BRADSHAW, B.L. [C11/99] English Viola w/case, bow stamped Knoll   715/1,144 NS

CAPELA, ANTONIO [B7/100] Viola: Portugal, 1978 (D. & A. Capela, Portugal, 1979)   9,000/12,000 NS

CAPICCHIONI, MARINO [B7/104] Italian Viola: Rimini, 1962 (maker's, Rimini, 1962)   21,000/27,000
$24,150   £16,100

CAPICCHIONI, MARINO [C5/140] Good Modern Italian Viola: Rimini, 1965 (Igor Moroder, Verona, June 1995)   18,000/26,000
$19,975   £12,984

CARESSA & FRANCAIS [B7/105] Viola: Paris, 1926
4,500/7,500
$5,175   £3,450

CARLETTI, CARLO [C5/142] Modern Italian Viola: Pieve Di Cento, 1939   18,000/24,000 NS

CARLETTI, CARLO (attributed to) [P9/82] Good Contemporary Viola in immediate playing condition: 1991   1,692/2,115
$1,946   £1,380

CARLETTI, GENUZIO & JOSEPH SETTIN [C5/148] Modern Italian Viola w/case: 1962
6,000/8,000 NS

CARLETTI FAMILY [S10/83] Viola w/case: Pieve di Cento, mid 20th C. (Dario D'Attili, Dumont, New Jersey, September 16, 1991)   9,000/12,000 NS

CAVANI, VINCENZO [S10/80] Viola w/case: Spilamberto, 1967 (Chorberg String Instruments, New York, September 15, 1994)   9,000/12,000
$10,200   £7,038

CE, GIORGIO [S10/82] Viola w/case: Cremona, 1977 (maker's, Cremona)   7,000/10,000 NS

CHANOT, FRANCOIS [P11/17] French Viola in good condition   858/1,001
$1,283   £897

CHAPPUY, NICOLAS AUGUSTIN [P6/123] Good French Viola with old minor restorations: Paris, 1780   4,530/6,040 NS

CHAPPUY, NICOLAS AUGUSTIN [P9/86] Good French Viola with old minor restorations: Paris, 1780   2,538/3,102 NS

CHAPPUY, NICOLAS AUGUSTIN [P11/130] Good French Viola in good condition: Paris, 1780
2,145/2,574
$2,302   £1,610

CHEVRIER, A. [S1114/153] Viola w/case: Paris, 1960   1,716/2,288 NS

COCKER, LAWRENCE [B9/159] Viola   876/1,168
$1,007   £690

COCKER, LAWRENCE [P6/156] Viola in immediate playing condition, w/case: Derby, 1955   1,057/1,208
$1,216   £805

COLLIN-MEZIN, CH.J.B. (III) [S1114/156] Viola: Mirecourt, 1931   3,575/5,005 NS

CONIA, STEFANO [S3/123] Viola: Cremona, 1974
4,710/6,280
$6,319   £4,025

DECONET, MICHELE [C11/102] Fine and Rare Italian Viola w/case, bow: Venice, 1753 (Hamma & Co., Stuttgart, June 17, 1931)   114,400/171,600 NS

DERAZEY, HONORE [P11/82] Fine and Handsome French Viola in good condition, w/case: Mirecourt, c. 1860   17,160/21,450 NS

DILWORTH, JOHN [B7/103] English Viola
7,500/10,500 NS

DOBBS, HARRY [P6/341] Viola in good condition, w/case: Peopleton, Worcester, 1974   1,057/1,208 NS

DOBBS, HARRY [P9/318] Viola in good condition, w/violin, 2 cases: Peopleton, Worcester, 1974 564/635
$568   £403

DUKE, RICHARD [P11/61] Good Viola in good condition, w/case: London, 1782   1,430/2,145
$2,302   £1,610

DUREN, WILHELM [B11/116] Good Viola: Köln, 1880   2,860/4,290
$5,262   £3,680

ENEL, CHARLES (attributed to) [P6/111] French Viola with minor restored table blemishes: Paris, c. 1920   7,550/8,305 NS

FAGNOLA, ANNIBALE [C5/104] Good Italian Viola: Turin, 1933 (Jean Werro, Bern, September 12, 1978)   20,000/30,000 NS

FAIRFAX, ANNELEEN [P6/183] Good Viola in immediate playing condition: Newark, 1983
1,208/1,359
$1,389   £920

FERRONI, FERNANDO [Sk11/39] Modern Italian Viola w/case: Florence, 1926   3,000/5,000
$4,025   £2,818

FICKER, JOHANN GOTTLOB [S3/120] Viola w/case: Markneukirchen, 1785   2,355/3,925
$3,972   £2,530

FIELDING, A. [B11/110] Viola   1,430/2,145 NS

FORSTER, WILLIAM (II) [S10/81] Viola after Amati, w/case: London, 1775   10,000/15,000
$10,200   £7,038

FURBER, HENRY [P11/103] Fine and Handsome English Viola in immediate playing condition: London, 1886   7,150/8,580 NS

GAGLIANO, RAFFAELE & ANTONIO (II) (attributed to) [Sk11/43] Interesting Viola w/case (O.H.
Bryant, Boston, March 2, 1937)   18,000/20,000 NS

GAND & BERNARDEL [C5/92] Good French Viola:
Paris, 1879 (Jacques Français, New York)
15,000/20,000 NS

GAND & BERNARDEL [S3/114] Viola w/case:
Paris, 1888   15,700/23,550 NS

GAND & BERNARDEL [S1114/152] Viola w/case:
Paris, 1888   10,010/14,300 NS

GRANCINO, GIOVANNI (attributed to) [Sk11/42]
Milanese Viola (Association des Maitres Luthiers
Suisses, Zurich, August 28, 1971)   60,000/80,000 NS

GRANDJON, J. [B11/101] Viola   2,860/4,290 NS

GUERRA, ALBERTO [C5/144] Contemporary
Italian Viola: Modena, 1967 (Igor Moroder, Verona,
June 1995)   6,000/8,000
$7,050   £4,583

GUTH, AUGUST [C5/158] Belgian Viola: 1894
1,800/2,200 NS

HANSON, H.E. [Sk11/40] Good American Viola
w/case: New York, 1951   3,200/4,200
$3,450   £2,415

HILL, JOSEPH [C5/146] English Viola: London,
1779 (John & Arthur Beare, London, November 22,
1995)   6,000/8,000
$7,050   £4,583

HOFMANS, MATHIAS [S7/145] Viola w/case, cover,
bow: Antwerp, 1690   22,650/30,200
$38,958   £25,800

HOFNER & VICKERS [P6/325] Viola in immediate
playing condition, w/bow   906/1,057 NS

HOFNER & VICKERS [P9/344] Viola in immediate
playing condition, w/case, bow   564/635 NS

IGNESTI, ROBERTO [Sk11/44] Contemporary
Italian Viola w/case: Florence, 1975   6,000/8,000 NS

JACQUOT, CHARLES [P11/91] Fine and Handsome
French Viola in immediate playing condition, w/case:
Paris, c. 1860   4,290/5,005
$5,427   £3,795

JUNG, CURT [S7/138] Viola: Berlin, 1960
3,775/5,285
$3,986   £2,640

KENNEDY, THOMAS [B11/115] Fine English Viola:
London, 1841   10,010/14,300 NS

KERSCHENSTEINER, XAVER [S3/112] Viola
w/case, bow: Regensburg, 1889   3,925/5,495 NS

KERSCHENSTEINER, XAVER [S1114/150] Viola
w/case, bow: Regensburg, 1889   2,145/3,575
$2,059   £1,440

KLOTZ, AEGIDIUS (I) (attributed to) [S1114/141]
Viola: Germany, 19th C.   1,430/2,145
$3,089   £2,160

KLOTZ, JOHANN CARL [S3/116] Viola w/case:
Mittenwald, 1786   1,884/2,512
$2,889   £1,840

KLOTZ, MATTHIAS [B2/74] Viola   2,400/4,000 NS

KONIG, RUDOLF [B7/93] Viola: Zurich, 1930
1,200/1,800 NS

KONIG, RUDOLF [B11/102] Viola: Zurich, 1930
715/1,001 NS

KRENN, JOSEF [S3/122] Viola w/case, 2 bows:
Vienna, 1931   1,884/2,512
$2,347   £1,495

KRUMBHOLZ, LORENZ [S1114/151] Viola: The
Hague, c. 1930   1,716/2,288
$3,260   £2,280

KUSTER, FREDERICK [Sk5/365] American Viola:
Montpelier   1,000/1,200 NS

LAMB, JOHN [B7/110] English Viola: 1904
1,200/1,800 NS

LAMB, JOHN [B11/113] English Viola: 1904
858/1,144
$987   £690

LANARO, UMBERTO [S7/136] Viola: Padua, second half 20th C.   3,020/4,530
$4,711   £3,120

LAVAZZA, SANTINO (ascribed to) [Sk5/40] Viola
w/case (Paul V. Siebem, Washington, September 7,
1955)   800/1,600
$2,300   £1,495

LE FEBVRE, JEAN BAPTISTE (attributed to)
[S3/124] Viola w/case: mid 18th C.   2,355/3,140
$6,861   £4,370

LONGMAN, LUKEY & CO. [P11/24] Good English
Viola with some restorable blemishes, w/case:
London, c. 1790   1,430/2,145
$3,289   £2,300

LORANGE, PAUL [P6/177] Good French Viola with
minor blemishes: Marseilles, 1933   755/906
$2,257   £1,495

MANGENOT, P. (attributed to) [P6/40] Viola:
c. 1890   1,208/1,359
$1,563   £1,035

MARCHINI, RUDOLFO [Bf3/6229] Fine Modern
Italian Viola: Rome, 1982   5,000/8,000
$4,025   £2,576

MASTERS, JOHN [Sk11/378] American Viola:
Columbus, Ohio, 1977   2,000/4,000 NS

MATSUDA, TETSUO [Sk11/37] Good Contemporary Viola w/case: Chicago, 1996   6,000/8,000
$6,900   £4,830

MATTIUZZI, BRUNO [S3/111] Viola: Udine, 1982
7,065/8,635 NS

MCGRATH, DAVID [P2/231] Viola w/violin: Dublin,
1989   636/795
$1,006   £633

MERMILLOT, MAURICE [S3/115] Viola: Paris,
1900   3,140/4,710
$3,611   £2,300

MILLANT, MAX [Sk5/38] French Viola w/case:
Paris, 1976   7,000/9,000
$6,325   £4,111

MOCKEL, OTTO [S7/130] Viola w/case: Berlin,
1936   2,265/3,020 NS

MOINEL & CHERPITEL [S3/118] Viola: Paris,
1930   2,826/3,925
$3,430   £2,185

MONZETTI, JULIO [S7/143] Viola w/case: Rome,
1994   2,265/3,020 NS

MOUGENOT, GEORGES [S7/131] Viola w/case:
Brussels, 1894   3,775/5,285 $4,349
£2,880

MOZZANI, LUIGI (workshop of) [C11/104] Italian
Viola: Rovereto, 1927   2,860/4,290
$3,361   £2,350

NEUNER & HORNSTEINER [B5/109] Viola:
c. 1880   600/900
$863   £575

NEUNER & HORNSTEINER [B9/154] Viola
                          438/730 NS

NUPIERI, GIUSEPPE [C5/154] Contemporary Italian
Viola: 1979   1,200/1,600
$1,175   £764

NUPIERI, GIUSEPPE [C5/157] Contemporary Italian
Viola: 1976   1,800/2,200 NS

NUPIERI, GIUSEPPE [C5/160] Contemporary Italian
Viola: 1978   1,200/1,600
$1,175   £764

OWEN, JOHN W. [S3/121] Viola w/case, 2 bows:
Leeds, 1906   1,884/2,512 NS

OZAKI, YUKIO [Bf3/6227] Modern Italian Viola:
Cremona, 1974   2,000/3,500 $1,150
£736

PANORMO, GEORGE [B7/108] Fine and Rare Viola
in a near-perfect state of preservation: London, 1812
                          10,500/15,000
$10,868   £7,245

PAOLOTTO, GIO. BATTA. (attributed to) [P6/37]
Good Contemporary Viola in immediate playing condition, w/case: Monza, 1975   1,359/1,510
$1,563   £1,035

PARESCHI, GAETANO [Sk5/45] Modern Italian
Viola w/case: Ferrara, 1965   7,000/8,000
$8,050   £5,233

PILAT, PAUL [B11/111] Viola: 1925   2,860/4,290
$3,618   £2,530

PISTONI, PRIMO [S1114/140] Viola: Cremona,
1986   7,150/10,010 NS

PISTUCCI, GIOVANNI [S10/78] Viola w/case:
Naples, 1923 (John L. Rossi, New York, February 26,
1996)   15,000/20,000 NS

PRELL, JULIUS HERMANN [B2/73] German Viola:
1943   640/960 NS

PRELL, JULIUS HERMANN [B5/108] German Viola
                          375/525
$518   £345

PROKOP, LADISLAV [S7/139] Viola: Chrudim, 1913
                          1,812/2,416 NS

RAMIREZ, MANUEL [P3/62] Fine and Handsome
Spanish Viola in good condition, w/case: Madrid,
1910   4,740/5,530
$12,719   £8,050

RASTELLI, LODOVICO [C5/150] Italian Viola
w/case: Genoa, c. 1825   12,000/16,000 NS

REGAZZONI, DANTE [B7/107] Italian Viola:
Como, 1968 (maker's, Como)   6,000/9,000 NS

REGGAZZONI, DANTE (attributed to) [C11/106]
Contemporary Viola   5,005/6,435 NS

RENDERR, THEODOR [S12/42] Viola: late 19th C.
                          144/288
$265   £184

RINALDI, GIOFREDO BENEDETTO (ascribed to)
[P2/22] Interesting Viola in immediate playing condition, w/case (Hans Schmidta, Mittenwald, February
10, 1971)   6,360/7,950
$5,486   £3,450

ROBINSON, WILLIAM [S7/149] Viola w/case:
London, 1947   3,020/4,530
$3,262   £2,160

ROCCA, GIUSEPPE (attributed to) [P11/86]
Interesting Viola in good condition, w/case: Turin,
1858   4,290/5,720
$19,734   £13,800

ROCCHI, SESTO [S10/84] Viola w/case: San Polo
d'Enza, 1973   10,000/15,000 NS

ROSADONI, GIOVANNI [C5/151] Contemporary
Italian Viola w/case: Como, 1978   2,000/3,000
$2,350   £1,528

ROTH, ERNST HEINRICH [Sk5/46] Modern Viola
w/case: 1960   1,400/1,600 NS

ROTH, ERNST HEINRICH (workshop of) [C11/98]
German Viola   1,144/1,716 NS

SANNINO, VINCENZO [S1114/148] Viola: Naples,
1913   21,450/28,600 NS

SCOLARI, GIORGIO [S7/144] Viola w/case:
Cremona, 1975 (maker's, March 17, 1975)
                          3,322/4,228 NS

SDERCI, IGINO [S1114/142] Viola w/case, cover:
Florence, 1977   8,580/11,440 NS

SIMONAZZI, AMADEO [P6/131] Fine and
Handsome Italian Viola in immediate playing condition, w/case: 1958   3,322/3,775 NS

SIMPSON, THOMAS [B7/96] Viola: Birmingham,
1900   1,050/1,500
$1,035   £690

SMITH, THOMAS [B2/71] Baroque Viola
                          1,280/1,920
$1,840   £1,150

SMITH, THOMAS [S1114/161] Viola w/case:
London, 1801   3,575/5,005
$7,722   £5,400

STOSS, JOHANN MARTIN [S1114/154] Viola
w/case: Vienna, 1837   2,002/2,574
$2,059   £1,440

THIBOUVILLE-LAMY, J. [P2/235] Mirecourt Viola
w/case, 2 bows: c. 1930   477/636
$658   £414

THIBOUVILLE-LAMY, J. [P9/305] French Viola
w/violin: c. 1900   635/776 NS

THIR, JOHANN GEORG [S1114/143] Viola w/case:
Vienna, 1772   3,575/5,005
$8,237   £5,760

TYE, J. [B2/68] Viola   800/1,120
$1,564   £978

VIDOUDEZ, PIERRE [Sk5/42] Contemporary Viola
w/case: Geneva, 1967   3,000/5,000
$4,600   £2,990

VUILLAUME, GUSTAVE [C3/102] French Viola:
1943   2,198/2,512
$3,611   £2,300

WAGNER, SEBASTIAN [S10/79] Viola with later
head, w/case, cover: Meersbourg, second half 18th C.
(Rudolph Wulitzer Co., New York, March 13, 1947)
                            8,000/12,000
$12,000   £8,280

WHITMARSH, EDWIN [B11/106] English Viola:
London, 1908   1,144/1,430
$1,233   £863

WHITMARSH, EMANUEL [B7/98] English Viola:
London, 1908   2,250/3,000 NS

WINTER, ANTON [S7/135] Viola w/case: Berlin,
1984   1,510/2,265 NS

WINTER, ANTON [S7/137] Viola w/case: Berlin,
late 20th C.   2,114/2,718 NS

WITTY, E.T. [B7/97] Viola: Nottingham, 1964
                            1,200/1,800 NS

WITTY, E.T. [B11/107] Viola: Nottingham, 1964
                            715/1,001 NS

WORLE, JOHANN PAUL (attributed to) [P2/27]
Good Viola with minor blemishes only: Pressburg,
c. 1870   3,180/3,975 NS

ZACH, CARL [S3/119] Viola w/case, bow: Vienna,
1890   9,420/12,560 NS

ZACH, CARL [S1114/155] Viola w/case, bow:
Vienna, 1890   6,435/9,295 NS

VIOLA BOW

AUDINOT, JACQUES [Sk11/136] French Gold Viola
Bow   5,000/7,000
$5,750   £4,025

BAUSCH, LUDWIG CHRISTIAN AUGUST
[S1114/99] Chased Silver Viola Bow: Leipzig, c. 1860
                            5,720/8,580 NS

BAZIN, LOUIS [S3/146] Silver Viola Bow:
Mirecourt, c. 1950 (Jean-François Raffin, Paris,
March 28, 1999)   1,570/2,355
$1,806   £1,150

BULTITUDE, ARTHUR RICHARD [S7/66] Gold
and Tortoiseshell Viola Bow: Hawkhurst, 1957
                            2,265/3,020
$4,349   £2,880

BUTHOD, CHARLES [B9/121] Nickel Viola Bow
(Jean-François Raffin)   584/876 NS

CLUTTERBUCK, JOHN [P9/133] Gold Viola Bow
                            846/987
$1,054   £748

COLTMAN, M. [B7/41] Silver Viola Bow
                            1,200/1,800 NS

CUNIOT-HURY, EUGENE [C5/67] Silver Viola Bow
(Jean-François Raffin, Paris, October 16, 1996)
                            2,800/3,200
$4,113   £2,673

CUNIOT-HURY, EUGENE [S7/125] Silver Viola
Bow: Mirecourt, c. 1900   755/1,057
$815   £540

DODD (attributed to) [P6/218] Interesting Old
English Viola Bow: c. 1790   1,133/1,208
$1,216   £805

DUPUY [B11/35] Silver Viola Bow: Paris
                            2,145/2,860 NS

FETIQUE, MARCEL [S1114/204] Silver Viola Bow:
Paris, c. 1920   5,720/7,150
$6,178   £4,320

FETIQUE, VICTOR [S7/243] Silver Viola Bow with
minor damage to head: Paris, c. 1920 6,040/7,550 NS

FINKEL, SIEGFRIED [Sk5/95] Silver Viola Bow for
Rembert Wurlitzer   1,000/1,500
$1,150   £748

FINKEL, SIEGFRIED [C5/65] Silver Viola Bow
                            1,800/2,200 NS

FONCLAUSE, JOSEPH [C5/57] Silver Viola Bow
with tinsel wrap (Bernard Millant, Paris, March 6,
1998)   18,000/22,000
$19,975   £12,984

FRITSCH, JEAN [C3/125] Silver Viola Bow
                            942/1,256
$1,083   £690

GAULARD [C5/66] Ivory Viola Bow with tinsel wrap
(Bernard Millant, Paris, January 16, 1993)
                            12,000/14,000 NS

GAULARD (attributed to) [S3/163] Silver Viola Bow:
Troyes, mid 19th C.   1,884/2,512
$1,986   £1,265

GILLET, LOUIS [Sk11/132] French Silver Viola Bow
without hair   1,800/2,600
$2,415   £1,691

GOTZ, CONRAD [S7/225] Silver and Tortoiseshell
Viola Bow   1,057/1,359 NS

GRANDCHAMP, ERIC [Sk5/152] Silver Viola Bow
1,500/2,000
$2,990   £1,944

GRUNKE, RICHARD [Sk11/103] Silver Viola Bow
1,500/2,000
$1,093   £765

HILL, W.E. & SONS [B7/43] Silver and Ivory Viola
Bow with repaired head   900/1,500
$1,035   £690

HILL, W.E. & SONS [B7/44] Silver Viola Bow
3,750/5,250
$4,313   £2,875

HILL, W.E. & SONS [B9/82A] Good Silver Viola
Bow   2,920/4,380
$3,022   £2,070

HILL, W.E. & SONS [B11/25] Silver Viola Bow
3,575/5,005
$4,605   £3,220

HILL, W.E. & SONS [C5/68] Gold Viola Bow
1,500/2,500
$2,820   £1,833

HILL, W.E. & SONS [P3/158] Good Viola Bow with
full hair: London   1,580/1,896
$2,180   £1,380

HILL, W.E. & SONS [P6/195] Silver Viola Bow with
later adjuster and minor head blemish: London
604/755
$1,042   £690

HILL, W.E. & SONS [P11/181] Good Silver Viola
Bow with full hair: London   1,716/2,145
$3,782   £2,645

HILL, W.E. & SONS [P11/182] Silver Viola Bow
with full hair: London   2,145/2,860
$3,947   £2,760

HILL, W.E. & SONS [S1114/181] Silver Viola Bow:
London, c. 1910   2,145/2,860
$5,148   £3,600

HILL, W.E. & SONS [S1114/58] Silver Viola Bow:
London, 1947   1,716/2,288
$2,746   £1,920

HILL, W.E. & SONS [S1114/62] Gold and Tortoiseshell Fleur-de-Lys Viola Bow: London, c. 1920
2,145/2,860 NS

HILL, W.E. & SONS [Sk5/141] Silver Viola Bow
2,500/3,500
$2,990   £1,944

LABERTE [C11/45A] Good Silver Viola Bow with
tinsel wrap (Jean-François Raffin, Paris, January 2,
2000)   2,288/2,574
$3,024   £2,115

LABERTE, MARC [P2/104] Silver Viola Bow with
full hair (Jean-François Raffin, Paris, June 10, 1998)
1,113/1,272 NS

LAPIERRE, MARCEL [Sk11/133] French Silver
Viola Bow   1,800/2,000 NS

LAPIERRE, MARCEL [S1114/211] Silver Viola Bow:
Mirecourt, mid 20th C.   1,001/2,288
$2,746   £1,920

LENOBLE, AUGUSTE [Sk5/170] French Silver Viola
Bow (G. Houfflack, Paris, March 13, 1958)
2,500/3,500
$2,300   £1,495

LOTTE, FRANCOIS [S7/94] Nickel Viola Bow
w/viola bow   906/1,208 NS

LOTTE, FRANCOIS [Sk5/72] Silver Viola Bow
1,000/1,500
$1,150   £748

LOTTE, ROGER-FRANCOIS [S7/237] Silver Viola
Bow: Mirecourt, c. 1960   906/1,208
$997   £660

LOTTE, ROGER-FRANCOIS [S1114/212] Silver
Viola Bow   572/858
$601   £420

MALINE, GUILLAUME [B7/45] Fine Silver Viola
Bow with cloth lapping (Jean-François Raffin)
7,500/10,500 NS

MALINE, GUILLAUME [C11/50] Silver Viola Bow
5,720/8,580
$6,385   £4,465

MILLANT, BERNARD [S10/67] Ivory Viola Bow:
Paris, c. 1950   2,500/3,500
$2,700   £1,863

MILLANT, JEAN-JACQUES [Sk5/63] Gold Viola
Bow without hair   1,800/2,500
$3,450   £2,243

MORIZOT [B11/51] Silver Viola Bow with later
nickel button   1,430/2,145
$1,809   £1,265

MORIZOT, ANDRE [C11/46] Gold Viola Bow
(Jean-François Raffin, Paris, April 28, 1998)
1,144/1,716
$1,344   £940

MORIZOT, LOUIS [S3/153] Silver Viola Bow:
Mirecourt, c. 1930   1,570/2,355
$1,625   £1,035

MORIZOT, LOUIS [S7/256] Silver and Ivory Viola
Bow: Mirecourt, c. 1930   1,510/2,265
$1,812   £1,200

NURNBERGER, ALBERT [Sk5/75] Silver Viola Bow
600/800
$2,070   £1,346

NURNBERGER, ALBERT [B11/55] Silver Viola Bow
2,145/2,860 NS

NURNBERGER, KARL ALBERT [S1114/200] Silver
Viola Bow: Markneukirchen, mid 20th C.
1,001/1,430
$1,888   £1,320

OUCHARD, EMILE [B5/92] Silver Viola Bow with
later frog and button   600/900
$638   £426

OUCHARD, EMILE A. [S7/103] Silver Viola Bow:
Paris, 1960   4,530/7,550
$6,886   £4,560

OUCHARD, EMILE A. [S10/56] Gold Viola Bow:
Illinois, c. 1955   5,000/7,000
$8,400   £5,796

OUCHARD, EMILE A. [S10/95] Silver Viola Bow:
Paris, c. 1945   4,000/5,000
$8,400   £5,796

PAJEOT, ETIENNE [S7/102] Silver Viola Bow: Paris,
c. 1830   4,530/6,040
$7,248   £4,800

PAULUS, OTTO [Sk11/139] Silver Viola Bow
                                400/600
$115   £81

PECCATTE, CHARLES (attributed to) [S3/181]
Silver Viola Bow: France, early 20th C.   4,710/7,850
$5,055   £3,220

PECCATTE, DOMINIQUE [S7/101] Silver Viola
Bow w/canvas sheath: Paris, c. 1845 (Bernard
Millant, Paris, July 17, 1999)   27,180/37,750
$42,431   £28,100

PENZEL, K. GERHARD [S7/255] Silver Viola Bow:
third quarter 20th C.   604/906
$725   £480

PFRETZSCHNER (workshop of) [Sk11/137] Nickel
Viola Bow without hair   300/400
$173   £121

PFRETZSCHNER, H.R. [S7/226] Silver Viola Bow
w/viola bow: Markneukirchen   906/1,208
$906   £600

PFRETZSCHNER, H.R. [S1114/169] Nickel Viola
Bow: Markneukirchen, early 20th C.   858/1,144 NS

SARTORY, EUGENE [S7/244] Silver Viola Bow with
damaged stick: Paris, c. 1920   6,040/9,060
$10,872   £7,200

SCHICKER, HORST [S7/68] Gold Viola Bow:
Baiersdorf, late 20th C.   604/906
$870   £576

SCHUSTER, ALBERT [Sk5/150] Silver Viola Bow
                                800/1,200 NS

SIMPSON [B7/46] Silver Viola Bow 2,250/3,750 NS

SIMPSON [B11/27] Silver Viola Bow 1,001/1,430 NS

TEPHO, GEORGES [Sk11/112] French Silver Viola
Bow   1,800/2,400
$2,300   £1,610

THIBOUVILLE-LAMY, J. [B11/26] Silver Viola Bow
w/double bow case   715/1,001 NS

THOMASSIN, CLAUDE [B11/37] Very Fine Silver
Viola Bow: Paris, c. 1900   5,720/8,580
$6,578   £4,600

THOMASSIN, CLAUDE [Sk11/130] French Silver
Viola Bow with baleen wrap   6,000/8,000
$9,775   £6,843

TUBBS, JAMES [S3/158] Silver Viola Bow with
minor damage to head: London, c. 1890 (Wm. Lewis
& Son, Lincolnwood, January 26, 1970)
                                6,280/9,420 NS

TUBBS, JAMES [S10/103] Silver Viola Bow: London,
c. 1890   4,000/6,000 NS

TUBBS, JAMES (attributed to) [P3/146] Silver Viola
Bow of quality   2,844/3,160 NS

TUBBS, WILLIAM [C5/64] Fine Silver Viola Bow
                                5,000/8,000 NS

UEBEL, K. WERNER [Sk5/93] Gold Viola Bow
                                1,800/2,000 NS

VIGNERON, A. [C3/124] Silver Viola Bow without
hair   2,826/3,454
$3,430   £2,185

VOIRIN, F.N. [P11/172] Fine and Rare Silver Viola
Bow with full hair: Paris   6,435/7,150 NS

VUILLAUME, JEAN BAPTISTE [Sk11/105] French
Silver Viola Bow converted from self-rehairing style:
c. 1845   8,000/12,000
$18,400   £12,880

VUILLAUME, JEAN BAPTISTE [Sk11/135] Silver
Viola Bow with repair   1,000/1,200
$2,300   £1,610

WEICHOLD, RICHARD [C5/69] Silver Viola Bow
with slightly damaged head   400/600
$940   £611

WEIDHAAS, PAUL [S1114/60] Silver Viola Bow:
Markneukirchen, early 20th C.   858/1,144
$944   £660

WILSON, GARNER [Sk5/100] Silver Viola Bow
                                800/1,200
$1,495   £972

VIOLIN

ACHNER, PHILIP [S10/116] Violin w/case, cover:
Mittenwald, late 18th C. (Dykes & Son, London,
September 3, 1927)   6,000/8,000 NS

ALBANI, JOSEPH [P11/52] Violin with restorations,
w/case, bow: Bolzano, c. 1710 (W.E. Hill & Sons,
London, December 10, 1919)   2,145/2,860
$987   £690

ALBANI, JOSEPH [P11/55] Violin in playing condition, w/case, bow: Bolzano, c. 1710 (W.E. Hill &
Sons, London, December 10, 1919)   2,145/2,860
$4,605   £3,220

ALBANI, MATTHIAS [S7/273] Violin w/case:
Bolzano, 1694   6,040/9,060
$8,154   £5,400

ALOISI, G. (attributed to) [C5/298] Modern Italian
Violin   8,000/12,000 NS
$108,100   £75,670

AMATI, ANTONIO & GIROLAMO [P9/146] Violin
w/case: Cremona, c. 1620 (Hug & Co., Zurich,
November 14, 1942)   84,600/98,700
$91,615   £64,975

AMATI, ANTONIO & GIROLAMO [P9/217]
Violin: Cremona, c. 1624   28,200/42,300
$29,836   £21,160

AMATI, ANTONIO & GIROLAMO [Sk11/84] Fine,
Rare Italian Violin from the collection of Joseph
Wechsberg, w/case: Cremona, 1608   80,000/100,000

AMATI, ANTONIO & GIROLAMO (workshop of)
[Sk11/70] Italian Violin w/case   12,000/15,000
$11,213   £7,849

AMATI, GIROLAMO (II) [C5/88] Good Cremonese
Violin known as the "ex–Benito Mussolini," w/case
(Kenneth Warren & Son, Chicago, January 12, 1979)
          80,000/120,000 NS

AMATI, NICOLO [S1114/26] Violin w/double case:
Cremona, 1676 (Hart & Son, London, October 23,
1928)   100,100/128,700
$107,250   £75,000

AMATI, NICOLO (ascribed to) [S7/61] Violin
w/case: 18th C. (Hamma & Co., Stuttgart, July 29,
1949)   7,550/10,570
$33,749   £22,350

ANTONIAZZI (workshop of) [S7/164] Violin:
Milan, early 20th C.   7,550/10,570
$8,154   £5,400

ANTONIAZZI, RICCARDO [S3/49] Violin w/case:
Milan, c. 1910   18,840/25,120
$39,721   £25,300

ANTONIAZZI, ROMEO [S1114/17] Violin w/case:
Milan, c. 1910   10,010/14,300
$15,444   £10,800

APPARUT, G. [B9/309] Violin   292/438
$336   £230

APPARUT, G. [C3/235] Violin   1,413/1,884
$2,167   £1,380

APPARUT, G. (workshop of) [C11/199] French
Violin   1,716/2,002 NS

APPARUT, GEORGES [B7/211] Violin: 1933
          2,250/3,000
$1,725   £1,150

ARASSI, ENZO [B11/120] Italian Violin: Tergestinus,
1930   4,290/7,150
$4,111   £2,875

ARASSI, ENZO [Sk5/410] Italian Violin w/case:
Milan, 1932   2,000/3,000
$4,370   £2,841

AREZIO, CLAUDIO [Sk5/382] Contemporary
Italian Violin: Florence, 1983   2,500/3,500 NS

ASPINALL, JAMES [P9/299] Violin w/violin, 2 bows:
Sheffield, 1896   564/705 NS

ATKINSON, WILLIAM [B7/212] Violin: Tottenham,
1902   1,500/2,250 NS

ATKINSON, WILLIAM [P3/96] Good Violin in
immediate playing condition: Tottenham, 1908
          2,844/3,476
$3,816   £2,415

AUDINOT, NESTOR [S3/194] Violin: Paris, 1897
          6,280/9,420 NS

AUDINOT, NESTOR [S7/171] Violin: Paris, 1905
          6,040/9,060 NS

AUDINOT, VICTOR [S7/151] Violin w/case: Paris,
1927   2,265/3,020 NS

AUDINOT, VICTOR [S12/181] Violin w/case: Paris,
1927   1,440/2,160
$3,643   £2,530

AUDINOT-MOUROT, V. [B7/213] Violin: Paris,
1929   3,000/4,500 NS

AUDINOT-MOUROT, V. (workshop of) [C11/144]
French Violin   2,145/2,860
$3,192   £2,232

AZZOLA, LUIGI [C5/45] Italian Violin: Turin, 1926
(Igor Moroder, Verona, June 1995)   6,000/8,000 NS

AZZOLA, LUIGI (attributed to) [Sk5/396] Violin
          4,000/6,000
$4,485   £2,915

BAADER, J.A. [Sk5/400] Mittenwald Violin: 1927
          1,500/1,800
$2,300   £1,495

BADALASSI, PIERO (attributed to) [P6/63] Good
Contemporary Violin in immediate playing condition:
Pisa, 1954   2,718/3,322
$3,473   £2,300

BAILLY (workshop of) [S1114/46] Violin: Mirecourt,
early 20th C.   2,145/2,860 NS

BAILLY, CHARLES [B2/113] Violin   800/1,120
$1,748   £1,093

BAILLY, CHARLES [C5/300] French Violin: 1912
          2,000/3,000
$3,055   £1,986

BAILLY, CHARLES [S3/204] Violin: Mirecourt, 1936
          3,140/4,710
$4,694   £2,990

BAILLY, CHARLES [S7/41] Violin: Mirecourt, 1943
          2,265/3,020 NS

BAILLY, CHARLES [Sk5/389] Modern French Violin:
Paris, 1922   2,500/3,500 NS

BAILLY, CHARLES (workshop of) [C3/214] French
Violin   1,256/1,884
$1,264   £805

BAILLY, JENNY [P2/14] Good Violin in immediate
playing condition, w/case, cover: Paris, c. 1920
          1,352/1,511
$2,286   £1,438

BAILLY, PAUL [B7/189] Violin: c. 1880
          2,250/3,000 NS

BAILLY, PAUL [S3/233] Violin w/case: Paris, 1890
          3,140/6,280
$5,778   £3,680

BAILLY, PAUL [Sk11/78] Good French Violin: Paris,
1903   4,500/5,000
$5,520   £3,864

BAILLY, PAUL (attributed to) [P2/7] French Violin in immediate playing condition: c. 1880   1,590/1,908
$4,388   £2,760

BAILLY, PAUL (attributed to) [P6/51] Good French Violin w/case, bow: c. 1900   2,265/2,718 NS

BAILLY, PAUL (attributed to) [P6/89] Good French Violin in immediate playing condition: Paris, 1907
3,322/3,926 NS

BAILLY, PAUL (attributed to) [P9/92] Good French Violin w/violin, case, bow: c. 1900   1,269/1,410
$1,703   £1,208

BAILLY, PAUL (attributed to) [P11/79] Good French Violin in good condition, w/case, 2 bows: 1896
3,575/4,290
$4,111   £2,875

BAILLY, PAUL (attributed to) [P11/89] Good French Violin in good condition: Paris, 1907   3,146/3,718
$1,973   £1,380

BALESTRIERI, TOMMASO [S1114/40] Violin after Pietro Guarneri, w/case: Mantua, 1767 (Roland Baumgartner, Basel, April 16, 1997)
114,400/143,000 NS

BANKS, BENJAMIN [S3/64] Violin w/case: Salisbury, 1794 (J. & A. Beare, London, October 23, 1925)   7,065/8,635
$9,930   £6,325

BARBE, F. [P9/304] French Violin with some old restoration, w/violin: c. 1850   564/705
$892   £633

BARRETT, JOHN (ascribed to) [P9/41] Interesting Violin with some old restorations: London, c. 1740
2,820/4,230 NS

BARRETT, JOHN (ascribed to) [P11/120] Interesting Violin with some old restorations: London, c. 1740
1,716/2,145 NS

BARROWMAN, DAN [P2/66] Violin with minor restorable blemishes only: Bruess, N.B., 1889
1,272/1,431 NS

BARROWMAN, DAN [P6/172] Violin with minor restorable blemishes: 1889   906/1,057 NS

BARTON, J.E. [C11/281] Welsh Violin 858/1,144 NS

BARZONI, FRANCOIS [P2/39] Good French Violin in good condition, w/bow, case: 1892   1,272/1,431
$1,371   £863

BARZONI, FRANCOIS [P2/51] Good French Violin in good condition, w/case, bow: c. 1900   1,272/1,431
$1,554   £978

BARZONI, FRANCOIS [P6/328] French Violin with restorable blemishes, w/case, bow: 1899   604/755
$1,476   £978

BATELLI, ALFIO [S10/40] Violin w/case: Florence, 1977   5,000/7,000 NS

BAZIN, GUSTAVE [C3/94] French Violin: Mirecourt
2,355/3,140 NS

BAZIN, GUSTAVE [P6/114] French Violin with minor restorable blemishes: 1894   1,812/2,265 NS

BAZIN, GUSTAVE [P9/15] French Violin with minor restorable blemishes: 1894   1,128/1,269
$2,108   £1,495

BAZIN, GUSTAVE [S12/180] Violin: Mirecourt, early 20th C.   720/1,008
$662   £460

BAZIN, GUSTAVE (attributed to) [P11/134] Good French Violin with minor table blemish: c. 1910
858/1,001
$987   £690

BEARE & SON [B5/167] Violin   750/1,050
$690   £460

BECKER, CARL [S10/16] Violin w/case, 2 bows: Chicago, 1927   18,000/25,000
$26,625   £18,371

BEEBE, E.W. [Sk11/82] American Violin w/case: Philadelphia, 1937   1,500/2,000
$3,795   £2,657

BELLINGHAM, THOMAS J. [P6/32] Violin in good condition, w/case, bow: Leeds, 1906   906/1,057 NS

BELLINGHAM, THOMAS J. [P9/111] Violin in good condition, w/case, bow: Leeds, 1906   564/705
$973   £690

BELTRAMI, GIUSEPPE [C5/40] Italian Violin: Cremona, 1872 (Carlson Cacciatori Neumann, Cremona, January 5, 1995)   5,000/6,000
$5,875   £3,819

BENEDEK, JOANNES [B7/151] Violin: 1944
2,250/3,000 NS

BENEDEK, JOANNES [B11/151] Violin: 1944
11,440/17,160 NS

BERGER & CO., JOSEPH [S12/94] Violin: Berlin
144/288
$149   £104

BERGER, KARL AUGUST [C5/170] Good American Violin w/case, bow: New York, c. 1935   4,000/6,000
$4,113   £2,673

BERGONZI, LORENZO [S3/72] Violin: Italy, 1990
2,826/3,454
$2,708   £1,725

BERNARDEL (workshop of) [C11/329] French Violin   858/1,144 NS

BERNARDEL (PERE) (attributed to) [P11/28] French Violin in good condition: Paris, 1836 6,435/7,865 NS

BERNARDEL, AUGUST SEBASTIEN PHILIPPE [S3/63] Violin w/case: Paris, 1864   28,260/39,250
$32,499   £20,700

BERNARDEL, GUSTAVE ADOLPHE [S10/28] Violin w/case, 2 bows: Paris, 1901   12,000/15,000
$14,400   £9,936

BERNARDEL, GUSTAVE ADOLPHE [S1114/248] Violin: Paris, 1897   11,440/14,300
$22,094   £15,450

BERNARDEL, GUSTAVE ADOLPHE (attributed to) [S7/286] Violin w/case: France, late 19th C.
4,530/7,550
$9,060   £6,000

BERNARDEL, LEON [B7/173] Very Fine Violin: Paris, 1900   5,250/8,250
$5,175   £3,450

BERNARDEL, LEON (workshop of) [C5/301] French Violin w/case   500/600
$470   £306

BERNARDEL, LEON (workshop of) [C3/239] French Violin   1,256/1,884 NS

BERNARDEL, LEON (workshop of) [C11/220] French Violin   858/1,144 NS

BERTHOLINI, NICOLAS [P2/250] Mirecourt Violin in good condition: c. 1900   636/716
$549   £345

BETTS, JOHN [S3/187] Violin w/case, bow: London, c. 1810   7,850/10,990
$8,125   £5,175

BEUSCHER, PAUL [B7/113] Violin: Paris, 1924
1,800/2,250 NS

BEUSCHER, PAUL [P2/77] Good Mirecourt Violin in good condition: Paris, 1927   954/1,034
$951   £598

BEUSCHER, PAUL [C3/99] French Violin
1,884/2,198
$2,347   £1,495

BIGNAMI, OTELLO [Sk11/65] Contemporary Italian Violin: Bologna, 1982   10,000/12,000
$8,050   £5,635

BINI, LUCIANO [Bf3/6233] Modern Italian Violin w/case: Cremona, 1988   1,500/2,500
$1,265   £810

BISIACH (workshop of) [C5/173] Modern Italian Violin w/case, bow (Jacques Français, New York, December 2, 1997)   15,000/20,000 NS

BISIACH, CARLO [C5/95] Fine Modern Italian Violin: Florence, 1946 (Jacques Français, New York)
18,000/22,000
$22,325   £14,511

BISIACH, LEANDRO [B7/185] Italian Violin: Milan, 1919   22,500/27,000 NS

BISIACH, LEANDRO [B7/207] Italian Violin: Milan, c. 1920   27,000/37,500
$25,875   £17,250

BISIACH, LEANDRO [C11/42] Fine Modern Italian Violin w/wooden case, bow: Milan, 1921
28,600/35,750 NS

BISIACH, LEANDRO [S1114/25] Violin w/case: Milan, 1912   28,600/42,900
$33,605   £23,500

BISIACH, LEANDRO (attributed to) [B7/150] Violin
7,500/10,500 NS

BISIACH, LEANDRO (attributed to) [P3/55] Italian Violin of quality, w/case: Milan, 1910 18,960/23,700
$18,170   £11,500

BISIACH, LEANDRO & GIACOMO [C5/86] Modern Italian Violin: Milan, 1962 (William Moennig & Son, Philadelphia, October 9, 1986)
18,000/22,000
$24,675   £16,039

BISIACH, LEANDRO (II) & GIACOMO [S7/56] Violin w/case: Milan, mid 20th C.   15,100/22,650
$16,308   £10,800

BLANCHARD, PAUL [B7/175] Violin: Lyon, 1888
6,000/9,000 NS

BLANCHARD, PAUL [S7/270] Violin w/case, cover: Lyon, 1898   9,060/12,080 NS

BLONDELET, EMILE [C11/200] French Violin w/case: 1928   1,430/2,145
$1,848   £1,292

BLONDELET, H. EMILE [P3/85] Good French Violin with minor restored table blemishes, w/case: 1929 (maker's)   1,264/1,422
$1,454   £920

BLONDELET, H. EMILE [P6/181] Good French Violin in immediate playing condition, w/case: Paris, 1928   1,057/1,208
$1,042   £690

BLONDELET, H. EMILE [S3/207] Violin w/case: Paris, 1928 (maker's)   3,140/4,710 NS

BLONDELET, H. EMILE [S1114/51] Violin w/case: Paris, 1928   2,002/2,574 NS

BOCQUAY, JACQUES (attributed to) [P2/9] Old French Violin of quality: c. 1750   1,431/1,590
$1,646   £1,035

BOCQUAY, JACQUES (attributed to) [P6/22] Old French Violin: c. 1750   1,359/1,510
$868   £575

BOFILL, SALVATORE (attributed to) [C5/312] Violin: Barcelona, 18th C.   8,000/12,000 NS

BONNEL, EMILE (workshop of) [C5/257] Child's French Violin   1,500/2,000
$2,115   £1,375

BOULLANGIER, CHARLES [P11/139] Good Violin in good condition: London, 1881   4,290/5,720
$6,578   £4,600

BOULLANGIER, CHARLES [S1114/32] Violin w/case: London, 1877   5,720/8,580
$8,237   £5,760

BOURLIER [P3/125] Mirecourt Violin in good condition: c. 1770   948/1,106
$1,090   £690

BRAUND, FREDERICK T. [B2/126] Violin (maker's, Colchester)   480/800
$552   £345

BRETON (workshop of) [C3/187] French Violin
393/550
$686   £437

BREUT, KARL WERNER [B11/123A] Fine Violin: Schonbach, 1928   1,430/2,145 $3,289   £2,300

BRIGGS, JAMES WILLIAM [B11/119] Very Fine Violin: Glasgow, 1921   5,720/8,580 $6,578   £4,600

BRIGGS, JAMES WILLIAM [B11/135] Good Violin 5,720/8,580 NS

BRUET, NICOLAS [B2/167] French Violin: Mirecourt, c. 1850   640/960 $736   £460

BRUSSEAU, ALFRED [Sk5/387] Sunburst Violin w/case: 1960   1,400/2,000 NS

BRYANT, GEORGE E. [Sk5/255] American Violin w/case: Lowell, 1926   2,000/4,000 NS

BRYANT, OLE H. [C5/303] Good American Violin w/case, bow: Boston, 1914   1,400/1,600 $1,645   £1,069

BRYANT, OLE H. [Sk5/362] Good American Violin: Boston, 1921   2,500/3,500 $6,325   £4,111

BUCHSTETTER, GABRIEL DAVID [Bf3/6254] German Violin   4,000/5,000 NS

BUCHSTETTER, GABRIEL DAVID [C11/225] German Violin w/case: Stadtamhof, c. 1760 2,002/2,574 $2,856   £1,997

BUTHOD, CHARLES LOUIS [B7/128] Violin: Mirecourt, 1810   900/1,500 $1,725   £1,150

CALACE, RAFFAELE [P3/110] Violin with post-crack on back, w/case, 2 bows: Naples   948/1,106 $1,181   £748

CALCAGNI, BERNARDO (workshop of) [S7/168] Violin w/case, cover: Genoa, early 18th C. 15,100/22,650 $26,803   £17,750

CAMILLI, CAMILLO [C5/99] Good Italian Violin: Mantua (Max Möller & Zoon, Amsterdam, August 30, 1956)   45,000/65,000 $52,875   £34,369

CAMILLI, CAMILLO [S10/34] Violin w/case, bow: Mantua, 1745 (Wm. Moennig & Son, Philadelphia, November 18, 1950)   90,000/120,000 NS

CANDI, CESARE [P11/111] Fine and Handsome Italian Violin in good condition: Genoa, 1912 (Carlson Cacciatori Neumann, Cremona, May 26, 1997)   25,740/31,460 NS

CANDI, ORESTE [C5/138] Italian Violin w/case: Genoa, 1913   14,000/16,000 NS

CANDI, ORESTE [C11/27] Good Modern Italian Violin w/case: Genoa, 1930   17,160/21,450 NS

CAPICCHIONI, MARINO [C5/42] Good Modern Italian Violin w/case, 2 bows: Rimini, 1961 16,000/18,000 $28,200   £18,330

CAPICCHIONI, MARIO [S7/33] Violin w/case: Rimini, 1972   9,060/12,080 NS

CAPPICHIONI, MARINO (attributed to) [Sk5/126] Italian Violin w/case   4,000/6,000 $5,750   £3,738

CARCASSI, LORENZO (attributed to) [P6/66] Violin with old skillful restorations, w/case: Florence, 1756   12,080/12,835 NS

CARCASSI, LORENZO (attributed to) [P9/55] Violin with old skillful restorations, w/case: Florence, 1756   5,640/6,345 $7,783   £5,520

CARCASSI, LORENZO & TOMMASO [C5/85] Italian Violin: Florence, 18th C. (Rembert Wurlitzer, New York, June 3, 1957)   55,000/65,000 NS

CARCASSI, LORENZO & TOMMASO [C5/97] Good Italian Violin (Jacques Français, New York) 40,000/60,000 NS

CARCASSI, LORENZO & TOMMASO [C11/140] 18th-C. Italian Violin (Rembert Wurlitzer, New York, June 3, 1957)   31,460/37,180 $33,605   £23,500

CARCASSI, LORENZO & TOMMASO (ascribed to) [C5/324] Violin w/case, bow: 18th C. (Eric Lachmann, Los Angeles, December 2, 1952) 6,000/8,000 $9,400   £6,110

CARDI, LUIGI (ascribed to) [Bf3/6248] Modern Italian Violin w/case, 2 bows: Verona, c. 1897 1,800/2,500 $3,163   £2,024

CARESSA, ALBERT [B7/194] Violin: Nice, 1866 3,000/4,500 NS

CARESSA & FRANCAIS [S1114/20] Violin: Paris, 1923   4,290/7,150 $6,521   £4,560

CARLETTI, CARLO (attributed to) [P6/72] Violin in immediate playing condition, w/case: 1937 7,550/9,060 NS

CARLETTI, CARLO (attributed to) [P9/30] Violin in immediate playing condition, w/case: 1937 4,230/4,935 $4,054   £2,875

CARLETTI, GENUZIO & JOSEPH SETTIN [C5/38] Modern Italian Violin w/case: 1961   6,000/800 $9,400   £6,110

CARLONI, ASSUNTO [S1114/242] Violin: Forli, 1994   2,574/3,575 $2,917   £2,040

CASTAGNERI, ANDREA (ascribed to) [Sk11/371] Violin   5,000/6,000 NS

CASTELLO, PAOLO [P6/116] Italian Violin in immediate playing condition, w/case: Genoa, c. 1770 (W.E. Hill & Sons, London, December 19, 1960) 52,850/67,950 $62,514   £41,400

CASTELLO, PAOLO [Sk5/409] Italian Violin:
Genoa, 1780 (Fridolin Hamma, August 31, 1957)
18,000/20,000
$18,400   £11,960

CASTELLO, PAOLO (attributed to) [P11/95]
Interesting Italian Violin in good condition: Genoa,
c. 1780 (Fridolin Hamma, August 31, 1951)
17,160/21,450 NS

CASTURELLI, ANTONIO (ascribed to) [S10/111]
Violin w/case: Rome, mid 19th C. 15,000/20,000 NS

CATENARI, ENRICO [C5/184] Early Italian Violin:
Turin, c. 1670 (John & Arthur Beare, London, June
10, 1987)   55,000/75,000 NS

CAUSSIN, FRANCOIS (attributed to) [P11/42] Good
French Violin in good condition: c. 1860
1,144/1,287 NS

CAVALAZZI, ANTONIO [Bf3/6246] Good Modern
Italian Violin: Ravenna, 1940   3,000/5,000 NS

CAVALLI, ARISTIDE [B7/202] Violin: Cremona
1,800/2,250
$3,105   £2,070

CAVANI, VINCENZO [Sk11/403] Modern Italian
Violin: Modena, 1936   4,000/6,000
$2,300   £1,610

CELANI, EMEDIO (attributed to) [S10/108] Violin:
Ascoli Piceno, 1891   8,000/12,000 NS

CERUTI, ENRICO (ascribed to) [C5/80] Good
Modern Italian Violin w/case: Cremona, 1860 (W.R.
Ford Co., New York, December 12, 1961)
8,000/12,000
$14,100   £9,165

CHANOT, FRANCOIS [P11/18] French Violin missing some inlay decoration: 1818   858/1,001 NS

CHANOT, FREDERICK WILLIAM [B11/129]
Violin: London, 1897   2,860/4,290
$6,578   £4,600

CHANOT, FREDERICK WILLIAM [S3/189] Violin
w/case, 2 bows: London, 1895   3,925/5,495
$10,833   £6,900

CHANOT, FREDERICK WILLIAM (attributed to)
[P6/126] Violin without final coat of varnish, w/case,
bow: London, 1895   1,510/2,265
$2,952   £1,955

CHANOT, GEORGES [B7/219] Fine Violin: Paris,
c. 1850   18,000/22,500 $27,600
£18,400

CHANOT, GEORGES [P9/53] Good French Violin in
good condition, w/case, bow: Paris, 1840
4,230/5,640
$5,513   £3,910

CHANOT, JOSEPH ANTHONY [P6/67] Good
Violin with minor blemishes, w/case: London, 1899
4,530/6,040
$4,341   £2,875

CHAPMAN [B5/179] Violin   450/750 NS

CHAPMAN [B9/192] Violin   292/438
$537   £368

CHAPPUY [P9/209] French Violin in playing condition, w/double case: Paris, c. 1770   987/1,128
$5,189   £3,680

CHAPPUY, AUGUSTIN [Sk11/405] French Violin
w/case, bow: Paris, 1750   3,000/5,000 NS

CHAPPUY, NICOLAS AUGUSTIN [S12/151] Violin:
Mirecourt, c. 1765   576/864
$696   £483

CHAROTTE [C3/156] French Violin: Mirecourt
785/942
$867   £552

CHAROTTE, CLAUDE (attributed to) [P9/64] Old
French Violin with some old restored blemishes:
c. 1770   776/917
$1,297   £920

CHAROTTE-MILLOT, JOSEPH [C5/182] French
Violin (J. van der Wijk de Bries, Groningen,
September 7, 1996)   2,800/3,400
$3,290   £2,139

CHAROTTE-MILLOT, JOSEPH [S7/52] Violin:
Mirecourt, c.1830   3,775/5,285 NS

CHERPITEL, GEORGE [C11/174] French Violin
w/case   858/1,144 NS

CHERPITEL, LOUIS [Bf3/6230] Good French Violin
w/case: Mirecourt, 1925   4,000/5,500
$3,335   £2,134

CHERPITEL, LOUIS [C3/179] French Violin
1,256/1,884
$3,250   £2,070

CHIPOT-VUILLAUME [C11/31] French Violin
w/case, bow   1,716/2,002 NS

CHIPOT-VUILLAUME [Sk5/358] French Violin
w/case   2,000/3,000
$920   £598

CIOAMI, LASANO [S7/190] Violin w/case: Catania,
1996   2,114/2,718
$2,537   £1,680

CLAUDOT, CHARLES (workshop of) [C5/290]
French Violin   1,600/2,200 NS

CLEMENT, JEAN LAURENT [S10/35] Violin
w/case, cover: Paris, 1825 (Thomas Metzler Violin
Shop, Glendale, California, April 1, 1998)
8,000/12,000

COLIN, JEAN BAPTISTE [B7/186] Violin: Mirecourt
1,500/2,250
$1,725   £1,150

COLLENOT, LOUIS [S12/122] Violin: Rouvres-la-
Chétive, early 20th C.   259/360
$364   £253

COLLIN-MEZIN, CH.J.B. [B7/209] Violin:
Mirecourt, 1841   750/1,050 NS

COLLIN-MEZIN, CH.J.B. [B9/320] Violin: 1924
730/1,022
$806   £552

COLLIN-MEZIN, CH.J.B. [B11/126] Violin: Paris,
1892   2,860/4,290
$3,947   £2,760

COLLIN-MEZIN, CH.J.B. [B11/187] Violin: 1902
                                       2,860/4,290 NS

COLLIN-MEZIN, CH.J.B. [B11/194] Good Violin:
1889   5,005/7,150
$5,262   £3,680

COLLIN-MEZIN, CH.J.B. [C3/38] Mirecourt Violin
w/case, bow: 1886   2,826/3,454
$5,055   £3,220

COLLIN-MEZIN, CH.J.B. [C3/93] Violin
                                        2,512/3,140
$3,069   £1,955

COLLIN-MEZIN, CH.J.B. [C5/299] French Violin
w/case: Mirecourt, 1889   1,800/2,200
$1,880   £1,222

COLLIN-MEZIN, CH.J.B. [P2/15] Good French
Violin with minor varnish scratches on back: Paris
                                        1,590/1,908
$3,657   £2,300

COLLIN-MEZIN, CH.J.B. [P2/25] Fine and Handsome French Violin in immediate playing condition,
w/case, bow: Paris, 1879   3,180/3,975
$4,754   £2,990

COLLIN-MEZIN, CH.J.B. [P6/82] Good French
Violin in immediate playing condition: Paris, 1907
(Etienne Vatelot, Paris, August 29, 1996) 4,530/5,285
$4,862   £3,220

COLLIN-MEZIN, CH.J.B. [P9/87] French Violin
requiring some restoration and cleaning: Paris, 1896
                                        1,128/1,269
$2,432   £1,725

COLLIN-MEZIN, CH.J.B. [P11/127] Good French
Violin with very minor table blemishes: 1891
                                        3,575/4,290
$4,769   £3,335

COLLIN-MEZIN, CH.J.B. [P11/69] Good French
Violin in good condition, w/case, 2 bows: Paris, 1884
                                        2,860/4,290
$5,262   £3,680

COLLIN-MEZIN, CH.J.B. [S3/217] Violin: Paris,
1898   2,198/2,826
$3,611   £2,300

COLLIN-MEZIN, CH.J.B. [S3/46] Violin w/case, 2
bows, cover: Mirecourt, 1928   2,355/3,140 NS

COLLIN-MEZIN, CH.J.B. [S7/58] Violin w/case,
bow: Paris, 1884   3,322/3,926 NS

COLLIN-MEZIN, CH.J.B. (attributed to) [P6/48]
Fine and Handsome Violin in immediate playing condition: Mirecourt, c. 1900   3,775/4,530 NS

COLLIN-MEZIN, CH.J.B. (FILS) [P11/57] Good
French Violin in immediate playing condition, w/case:
1935   2,145/2,574 NS

COLLIN-MEZIN, CH.J.B. (II) [S7/152] Violin
w/case: Mirecourt, 1904   1,510/2,265
$1,631   £1,080

COLLIN-MEZIN, CH.J.B. (II) [S1114/244] Violin:
Mirecourt, 1928   1,430/2,145
$2,231   £1,560

COLLIN-MEZIN, CH.J.B. (II) [S1114/47] Violin:
Mirecourt, 1922   1,430/2,145 NS

COLLIN-MEZIN, CH.J.B. (III) [S1114/56] Violin
w/case: Mirecourt, 1936   1,430/2,145 NS

COLLIN-MEZIN, CH.J.B. (III) [S1114/236] Violin:
Mirecourt, 1929   1,716/2,288 NS

COLLIN-MEZIN, CH.J.B. (workshop of) [C3/222]
French Violin   942/1,256
$1,444   £920

COLLIN-MEZIN, CH.J.B. (workshop of) [C3/245]
French Violin   2,355/3,140
$3,972   £2,530

COLLIN-MEZIN, CH.J.B. (workshop of) [C11/26]
French Violin w/case: c. 1890   1,430/2,145
$1,512   £1,057

COLLIN-MEZIN, CH.J.B. (workshop of) [C11/142]
French Violin   1,430/2,145 NS

COLLIN-MEZIN, CH.J.B. (workshop of) [C11/163]
French Violin   2,145/2,431

COLLIN-MEZIN, CH.J.B. (workshop of) [C11/171]
French Violin   858/1,144 NS

COLLIN-MEZIN, CH.J.B. (workshop of) [C11/181]
French Violin   1,144/1,716
$2,016   £1,410

COLLIN-MEZIN, CH.J.B. (workshop of) [C11/214]
Mirecourt Violin: c. 1900   1,430/1,716 NS

COLLIN-MEZIN, CH.J.B. (workshop of) [C11/227]
French Violin   1,144/1,716 NS

COLLINS, GLEN [S7/36] Violin after the "Lord
Wilton" Guarneri del Gesù, w/case, cover, 2 bows:
London, 1995   6,040/9,060
$5,436   £3,600

COMUNI, ANTONIO (ascribed to) [S7/59] Violin
w/case: 19th C. (Hamma & Co., Stuttgart, August
21, 1953)   4,530/6,040
$8,698   £5,760

CONANT, WILLIAM A. [C5/180] American Violin
w/case: Brattleboro, 1882   1,200/1,400
$1,175   £764

CONE, GEORGES [B2/131] Violin   640/960
$1,196   £748

CONE, GEORGES [C11/32] Good French Violin
w/case   5,005/7,865
$6,721   £4,700

CONIA, STEFANO [S7/170] Violin w/case:
Cremona, 1993   4,228/5,285 NS

CONTINO, ALFREDO [C3/28] Italian Violin:
Naples, 1921   7,850/12,560
$13,541   £8,625

COOPER, HUGH W. [P3/119] Violin with some
restorable blemishes: 1904   1,896/2,370
$636   £403

31

COSTA, FELIX MORI [S3/195] Violin: Parma, 1809
15,700/23,550
$43,332   £27,600

COSTA, FELIX MORI (attributed to) [Sk11/410]
Italian Violin w/case: c. 1800   6,000/8,000
$5,463   £3,824

COSTARDI, BRUNO [Bf3/6232] Modern Italian
Violin: Cremona, 1996   1,000/1,500
$2,070   £1,325

COURTIER, LOUIS [C5/165] French Violin w/case
(maker's)   1,600/1,800
$2,350   £1,528

COURTIER, LOUIS [C5/305] French Violin: 1937
2,000/2,500
$2,115   £1,375

COUTURIEUX, M. [B5/155] Violin   375/525
$518   £345

CRAMMOND, CHARLES [P11/297] Violin with
restorable table blemishes: Aberdeen, c. 1840
715/858
$987   £690

CRASKE, G. [B7/160] Violin: London, c. 1870
3,000/4,500 NS

CRASKE, GEORGE [B7/124] Violin: England, 1795
6,000/9,000
$8,280   £5,520

CRASKE, GEORGE [B7/195] English Violin
3,750/5,250
$6,900   £4,600

CRASKE, GEORGE [B11/171] Violin: London,
c .1870   2,860/4,290 NS

CRASKE, GEORGE [S1114/237] Violin w/case, bow:
Stockport, c. 1860   3,575/5,005
$6,521   £4,560

CRASKE, GEORGE [S1114/29] Violin w/case:
Stockport, c. 1860   3,575/5,005
$6,521   £4,560

CROWTHER (attributed to) [P2/223] English Violin
with table restorations, w/case, bow: London, 1803
477/636
$1,006   £633

CUNAULT, GEORGES [Sk5/406] Modern French
Violin: Paris, 1931   5,500/6,500 NS

CUNE, RENE (workshop of) [C5/323] French Violin
1,600/2,200
$2,115   £1,375

CUNY (attributed to) [S7/63] Violin w/case, bow:
France, late 18th C.   3,775/5,285
$3,986   £2,640

CUYPERS, JOHANNES [P3/39] Good Violin in
immediate playing condition, w/case, 3 bows: The
Hague, 1805   15,800/18,960
$16,353   £10,350

CUYPERS, JOHANNES [C11/41] Good Dutch
Violin w/case: The Hague, 1787   20,020/22,880
$23,524   £16,450

CUYPERS, JOHANNES BERNARD [S7/158] Violin
w/double case: first half 19th C. (Josef Vedral, The
Hague, June 5, 1981)   12,080/18,120
$14,496   £9,600

DALINGER, SEBASTIAN (attributed to) [P6/84]
Good Austrian Violin with some restored blemishes:
Vienna, 1772   2,265/2,718 NS

DALL'AGLIO, GIUSEPPE [S1114/42] Violin w/case:
Mantua, c. 1830   21,450/28,600
$22,094   £15,450

DALLINGER, SEBASTIAN [P9/49] Good Violin
with modest table restoration: Vienna, 1790
2,820/4,230 NS

DANIELS, SAMUEL WESLEY [S10/15] Violin:
Jerome, 1979   500/800
$240   £166

DARCHE, HILAIRE [P11/93] Good Violin in good
condition, w/case: Brussels, 1920   4,290/5,720 NS

DARCHE, HILAIRE [S1114/36] Violin after G.B.
Guadagnini: Brussels, 1925   4,290/7,150 NS

DARCHE, NICHOLAS [S7/281] Violin w/case, 2
bows: France, second half 19th C.   1,812/2,416 NS

DAY, W.S. [C11/308] English Violin w/case   286/572
$336   £235

DE BARBIERI, PAOLO [S7/48] Violin w/case:
Genoa, 1956 (maker's, Genoa, April 18, 1957)
9,060/12,080 NS

DE BARBIERI, PAOLO (attributed to) [P3/78] Fine
and Handsome Italian Violin in immediate playing
condition, w/case: Genoa, 1949   12,640/15,800
$12,719   £8,050

DEBLAYE, ALBERT [B7/142] Violin: Mirecourt,
1874   1,500/2,250
$1,725   £1,150

DEBLAYE, ALBERT [C3/26] French Violin (Jean-
Jacques Rampal, Paris, July 20, 1999)   1,884/2,198
$2,347   £1,495

DEBLAYE, ALBERT [P11/67] Good French Violin in
good condition, w/case: c. 1910   2,145/2,860
$2,631   £1,840

DEBLAYE, ALBERT JOSEPH [S12/88] Violin:
Mirecourt, 1922   864/1,152
$1,242   £863

DEBLAYE, ALBERT JOSEPH (workshop of)
[C11/165] Good French Violin: Mirecourt
1,430/2,145
$1,680   £1,175

DECONET, MICHAEL [S7/283] Violin: mid 18th C.
12,080/18,120
$12,684   £8,400

DECONET, MICHAEL (attributed to) [S3/70] Violin:
mid 18th C.   18,840/25,120 NS

DECONET, MICHELE [S1114/38] Violin w/case:
Venice, 1780   21,450/28,600
$36,894   £25,800

DECONET, MICHELE [C11/137] Good Italian
Violin w/case, bow: Venice, 1764 85,800/128,700 NS

DEGANI, DOMENICO [Sk11/60] Good Italian
Violin w/case: Montagnana, 1886 (Rembert
Wurlitzer, New York, August 6, 1945) 8,000/12,000
$19,550   £13,685

DEGANI, EUGENIO [S7/155] Violin: Venice, 1899
                        27,180/37,750 NS

DEGANI, GIULIO [B7/214] Italian Violin: Venice,
1892   12,000/18,000
$18,975   £12,650

DEGANI, GIULIO [P3/69] Good Italian Violin in
immediate playing condition, w/case: Venice, 1893
                        18,960/23,700
$21,804   £13,800

DEGANI, GIULIO [P3/76] Fine and Handsome
Violin in immediate playing condition, w/double case:
Venice, 1904 (Peter Biddulph, London, November 29,
1991)   18,960/23,700
$29,072   £18,400

DEGANI, GIULIO [P11/122] Good Italian Violin in
good condition, w/case, bow: Venice, 1893
                        11,440/12,870
$13,156   £9,200

DEL FREDE, ANTONIO (attributed to) [B11/195]
Interesting Violin   3,575/5,005
$4,111   £2,875

DELIGNON, LOUIS (attributed to) [P11/44] Good
French Violin in good condition   1,001/1,144
$1,151   £805

DENTI, ALBERTO [Bf3/6231] Modern Italian
Violin: Cremona, 1998   1,000/1,500
$1,955   £1,251

DERAZEY (workshop of) [S12/128] Violin: France
                        720/1,008
$1,159   £805

DERAZEY, HONORE [B7/120] Violin: Mirecourt,
c. 1855   3,000/3,750
$4,313   £2,875

DERAZEY, HONORE [B7/201] French Violin
                        6,000/9,000 NS

DERAZEY, HONORE [C3/80] French Violin:
Mirecourt, c. 1860 (Jean-Jacques Rampal, Paris,
November 23, 1999)   10,990/14,130 NS

DERAZEY, HONORE [C5/304] French Violin
w/case: Mirecourt, c. 1860   3,000/5,000
$8,225   £5,346

DERAZEY, HONORE [P3/64] Good French Violin
in good condition: c. 1855 (Jean-Jacques Rampal,
Paris, November 23, 1999)   7,900/9,480
$9,085   £5,750

DERAZEY, HONORE [P11/83] Fine and Handsome
French Violin in immediate playing condition, w/case,
bow: Mirecourt, c. 1860   12,870/14,300
$13,978   £9,775

DERAZEY, HONORE (attributed to) [C5/176]
French Violin w/case   4,000/6,000
$4,465   £2,902

DERAZEY, HONORE (workshop of) [C3/101]
French Violin   2,826/3,454
$3,250   £2,070

DERAZEY, HONORE (workshop of) [C11/143]
French Violin   1,144/1,716
$2,016   £1,410

DERAZEY, HONORE (workshop of) [C11/210]
French Violin: c. 1880   5,005/6,435 NS

DERAZEY, JUSTIN [C11/30] French Violin w/case,
bow: Mirecourt, 1877   5,720/8,580 NS

DERAZEY, JUSTIN [S3/202] Violin: Mirecourt,
c. 1880   2,355/3,140
$2,528   £1,610

DERAZEY, JUSTIN (attributed to) [P6/118] Good
French Violin in immediate playing condition, w/case:
Mirecourt, c. 1890   2,265/3,020
$2,257   £1,495

DERAZEY, JUSTIN (attributed to) [P11/125] Good
French Violin in good condition: c. 1880
                        3,575/5,005 NS

DERAZEY, JUSTIN (workshop of) [C5/234] French
Violin   800/1,200
$705   £458

DERAZEY, JUSTIN (workshop of) [C11/236] French
Violin   858/1,144
$1,427   £998

DE RUB, ANGELO [P6/79] Italian Violin in immediate playing condition: Viterbo, c. 1750
                        12,080/15,100
$13,892   £9,200

DEVEAU, JOHN G. [Sk5/303] Modern Violin: New
York, 1936   1,000/1,200
$1,495   £972

DEVONEY, FRANK [P9/48] Good Violin with some
restored blemishes: 1895   1,692/2,115 NS

DE ZORZI, VALENTINO [Bf3/6239] Fine Italian
Violin: Florence, 1906   16,000/20,000
$14,950   £9,568

DIDCZENKO, DIMITRO [S10/128] Decorated
Violin after Stradivari, w/case, cover, bow: New York,
1944   3,000/5,000
$9,600   £6,624

DIDELOT, J. [C11/293] Mirecourt Violin
                        858/1,144 NS

DIDION, G. [B5/227] Violin   900/1,500 NS

DIEUDONNE (workshop of) [S1114/241] Violin:
Mirecourt, c. 1930   1,430/2,145 NS

DIEUDONNE, AMEDEE [P11/101] Good French
Violin in good condition, w/case: Mirecourt, 1950
                        3,575/4,290 NS

DIEUDONNE, AMEDEE [C3/39] French Violin
                        2,826/3,454
$3,611   £2,300

DIEUDONNE, AMEDEE [C5/46] French Violin:
1929   2,200/2,600
$2,820   £1,833

DIEUDONNE, AMEDEE [S3/60] Violin w/case,
child's violin bow: Mirecourt, 1937   2,355/3,140
$2,347   £1,495

DIEUDONNE, AMEDEE [S7/163] Violin w/case:
France, 1937   3,020/4,530 NS

DIEUDONNE, AMEDEE [S1114/34] Violin after the
"King Joseph" Guarneri del Gesù: Mirecourt, 1932
                                3,575/5,005 NS

DIEUDONNE, AMEDEE (workshop of) [C11/25]
French Violin   1,430/1,716
$2,688   £1,880

DOBRESOVITCH, MARCO (attributed to)
[B7/171A] Violin   1,500/2,250
$2,070   £1,380

DOLLENZ, GIOVANNI (attributed to) [P6/91]
Violin with minor restorations: Trieste, 1834
                                7,550/9,060 NS

DOLLENZ, GIOVANNI (attributed to) [P9/42]
Violin needing minor restorations and cleaning:
Trieste, 1834   4,935/5,640
$4,865   £3,450

DOLLING, HERMANN (JR.) [Sk5/223]
Markneukirchen Violin w/case   1,200/1,500
$1,610   £1,047

DOLLING, ROBERT A. [C5/285] German Violin
w/case: Markneukirchen, 1925   800/1,200
$1,116   £725

DORFEL, ADOLF PAUL [S7/269] Violin after
Amati, w/case: Markneukirchen, 1937   2,718/3,775
$3,080   £2,040

DORFEL, ADOLF PAUL [S7/292] Violin:
Markneukirchen, 1940   2,718/3,775
$3,986   £2,640

DUKE (workshop of) [S7/191] Violin w/case, bow:
London, second half 18th C.   1,812/2,416 NS

DUKE, RICHARD [B7/177] Violin: London
                                2,250/3,000 NS

DUKE, RICHARD [B11/193] Violin: London
                                    715/1,001
$493   £345

DUKE, RICHARD [C11/139] Good English Violin
                                8,580/10,010 NS

DUKE, RICHARD [P3/88] Violin London, c. 1780:
London, c. 1780   2,370/3,160 NS

DUKE, RICHARD [P6/149] Violin with restorable
table blemishes: London, c. 1780   1,510/1,812
$1,737   £1,150

DUKE, RICHARD [P6/34] Violin with old restorations, w/case, bow: London, c. 1770   2,265/3,020
$2,605   £1,725

DUKE, RICHARD [S1114/30] Violin w/case:
London, c. 1770   5,720/8,580 NS

DUKE, RICHARD (attributed to) [P2/50] English
Violin: London, c. 1800   1,272/1,431 NS

DUKE, RICHARD (attributed to) [P6/168] English
Violin: London, c. 1800   1,057/1,208 NS

DUKE, RICHARD (JR.) (attributed to) [P3/42]
English Violin with restorable table blemishes, w/case:
c. 1790   1,106/1,264
$1,181   £748

DUMAS, HENRY [B7/138] French Violin
                                1,800/2,250 NS

DUNCAN, GEORGE [P6/41] Good Violin with
lower rip repair required, w/case: Glasgow, 1882
                                1,359/1,510
$2,605   £1,725

DUNCAN, ROBERT [B5/147] Scottish Violin:
Aberdeen, 1758   900/1,500
$1,294   £863

DUWAER, H.G. [P3/77] Good Dutch Violin in immediate playing condition, w/case: Utrecht, 1894
                                3,160/3,950 NS

DUWAER, H.G. [P6/33] Good Dutch Violin in immediate playing condition, w/case: Utrecht, 1894
                                2,265/3,020
$3,473   £2,300

DVORAK, JAN BAPTISTA [P2/36] Fine and
Handsome Violin in immediate playing condition,
w/case: Prague, 1876   2,385/2,862
$3,657   £2,300

DYKES, GEORGE [S7/287] Violin after Guarneri del
Gesù, w/case: Leeds, 1899   1,812/2,416 NS

EBERLE, TOMASO [B11/161] Italian Violin: Naples,
c. 1770   21,450/28,600 NS

EKLID, ARNDT O. [C5/245] American Violin
w/case: Chicago, 1907   600/800
$411   £267

EMERY, JULIAN [B5/171] Violin   1,200/1,800 NS

EMERY, JULIAN [B9/217] Violin   730/1,022
$840   £575

ESPOSTI, PIERGIUSEPPE [Bf3/6244] Good Modern
Violin: Cremona, 1981   3,000/5,000
$2,875   £1,840

FAGNOLA, ANNIBALE [C3/40] Fine Modern
Italian Violin w/case: Turin, 1928   31,400/47,100
$64,998   £41,400

FALISSE, AUGUSTE & GEORGES [B7/206] Violin:
Brussels, 1907   3,000/4,500
$3,450   £2,300

FAROTTI, CELESTE [C5/90] Good Italian Violin:
Milan, 1925   20,000/25,000
$23,500   £15,275

FAROTTI, CELESTE (ascribed to) [C3/42] Modern
Italian Violin w/case   2,826/3,454 NS

FAROTTO, CELESTE (attributed to) [Sk5/412]
Italian Violin w/case   10,000/12,000
$10,925   £7,101

34

FENDT, BERNARD SIMON [B7/130] Very Fine English Violin in a near-perfect state of preservation: London, c. 1830 (W.E. Hill & Sons, London, January 15, 1907) 18,000/22,500
$29,325 £19,550

FENDT, BERNARD SIMON [B11/190] Fine English Violin: London, c. 1825 11,440/17,160 NS

FENT, FRANCOIS [P11/141] Good French Violin with some old restorations: Paris, c. 1770
4,290/5,720
$8,223 £5,750

FERENCZY-TOMASOWSKY, CHARLES [P11/97] Violin in immediate playing condition, w/case: Rotterdam, 1899 2,145/2,860
$4,934 £3,450

FERRARI, LUIGI [S1114/246] Violin: Castelvetro, 1988 2,860/4,290 NS

FETIQUE, VICTOR [S3/167] Silver Violin with repaired head: Paris, c. 1910 1,099/1,570 NS

FICKER, JOHANN CHRISTIAN [C11/178] Violin w/case, 2 bows 858/1,144
$5,041 £3,525

FIORINI, PAOLO [B11/178] Violin 1,430/2,145
$2,138 £1,495

FISCHER, A.E. [P6/350] German Violin in good condition, w/case, bow: Bremen, 1913 755/906
$781 £518

FISCHER, CARL [B5/127] Violin: 1925 900/1,200
$1,035 £690

FISCHER, LORENZ [Sk11/417] Good American Violin w/case: Milwaukee, 1930 2,000/4,000 NS

FLEURY, BENOIT [P6/59] Violin with restorable table blemishes, w/case: Paris, c. 1760 1,510/2,265
$1,563 £1,035

FORSTER, W. (attributed to) [B7/200] English Violin: London, 1773 1,800/2,250
$2,933 £1,955

FORSTER, WILLIAM [Sk5/125] Good English Violin w/case: c. 1780 4,000/5,000 NS

FORSTER, WILLIAM [Sk11/396] Good English Violin w/case: c. 1780 2,000/4,000
$1,725 £1,208

FORSTER, WILLIAM (III) [S7/26] Violin w/case, cover: London, c. 1810 (Josef Vedral, The Hague, October 5, 1987) 3,020/4,530
$5,436 £3,600

FOSCHINI, GIOVANNI [S7/300] Violin w/case: Bagnacavallo, 1979 4,228/5,285 NS

FRANK, MEINRADUS (attributed to) [P11/119] Good Violin with some restorations, w/case: Linz, 1831 (Hug & Co., Zurich, March 22, 1944)
3,575/5,005 NS

FREDI, RODOLFO [B11/154] Very Fine Italian Violin: 1904 25,740/35,750 NS

FRIEDL, GUSTAVE [S12/145] Violin w/case, bow: Mirecourt, 1894 864/1,152
$994 £690

FRIEDL, GUSTAVE [S12/162] Violin: Bohemia, late 19th C. 144/288
$298 £207

FURBER, MATTHEW [S7/64] Violin w/case: London, 1817 4,228/5,285 NS

FUREY, WILLIAM [Bf3/6253] Good American Violin w/case, bow: Coldwater, Michigan, 1891
800/1,200 NS

GABBITAS, EDWIN [P11/313] Violin in good condition, w/case, 2 bows: Sheffield, 1967 572/715 NS

GADDA, GAETANO (workshop of) [C5/326] Good Modern Italian Violin: Mantova, 1944
14,000/16,000 NS

GADDA, MARIO [S7/44] Violin: Mantua, 1980
6,040/9,060
$8,154 £5,400

GAGLIANO, FERDINAND [Sk5/135] Fine Neapolitan Violin: 1769 (Jacques Français, New York, November 24, 1982) 50,000/70,000
$68,500 £44,525

GAGLIANO, FERDINAND [Sk11/68] Fine Italian Violin formerly in the collection of Nathan Fiedler, w/case: Naples, 1767 (Rembert Wurlitzer, July 17, 1968) 120,000/140,000 NS

GAGLIANO, FERDINAND (attributed to) [C5/82] Good Neapolitan Violin 35,000/45,000
$41,125 £26,731

GAGLIANO, GENNARO [B11/141] Fine Italian Violin with table showing signs of retouching: Naples, c. 1750 57,200/71,500 NS

GAGLIANO, GIUSEPPE [S7/55] Violin w/case: Naples, c. 1780 (Arnaldo Morano, Alessandria)
27,180/37,750 NS

GAGLIANO, GIUSEPPE [S10/33] Violin with later head: Naples, late 18th C. (Rudolph Wurlitzer, New York, March 13, 1945) 40,000/60,000
$46,750 £32,257

GAGLIANO, GIUSEPPE [S1114/261] Violin w/case: Naples, 1797 (Hamma & Co., Stuttgart, January 30, 1979) 57,200/85,800 NS

GAGLIANO, JOSEPH & ANTONIO [B7/156] Fine Italian Violin: Naples, c. 1763 52,500/67,500 NS

GAGLIANO, JOSEPH & ANTONIO [C5/183] Neapolitan Violin w/case (Dario D'Attili, Sumont, September 28, 1976) 20,000/30,000
$21,150 £13,748

GAGLIANO, JOSEPH & ANTONIO (ascribed to) [Sk5/120] Neapolitan Violin w/case: c. 1770 (Lyon & Healy, Chicago, August 25, 1898) 25,000/30,000 NS

GAGLIANO, NICOLA [B7/181] Fine Italian Violin: Naples, 1718 52,500/112,500 NS

GAGLIANO, NICOLA [C5/103] Italian Violin: Naples, c. 1735 (Jacques Français, New York, July 28, 1982) 100,000/150,000 NS

GAGLIANO, NICOLA [C5/327] Neapolitan Violin w/case (Dario D'Attili, Dumont, May 15, 1985) 20,000/25,000
$21,150 £13,748

GAGLIANO, NICOLA [C5/79] Italian Violin w/case, bow: Naples, c. 1755 (W.E. Hill & Sons, London, September 7, 1938) 35,000/55,000
$44,650 £29,023

GAGLIANO, NICOLA [P6/103] Italian Violin with some restorations, w/case: Naples, c. 1750 (Jean-Jacques Rampal, Paris, March 21, 2000) 40,770/48,320 NS

GAGLIANO, NICOLA [S3/197] Violin w/case, bow: Naples, c. 1760 (J. & A. Beare, London, September 30, 1965) 109,900/141,300 NS

GAGLIANO, NICOLA [S1114/253] Violin after Amati: Naples, 1739 (W.E. Hill & Sons, February 9, 1893) 85,800/114,400
$99,385 £69,500

GAGLIANO, NICOLA [S1114/37] Violin w/case, cover: Naples, c. 1735 (Etienne Vatelot, Paris, October 26, 1988) 57,200/85,800 NS

GAGLIANO, NICOLA (I) (attributed to) [C3/30] Neapolitan Violin w/case, bow (Lyon and Healy, Chicago, November 27, 1903) 14,130/17,270
$86,664 £55,200

GAGLIANO FAMILY (MEMBER OF) [C5/314] Neapolitan Violin w/case: c. 1820 12,000/16,000
$20,563 £13,366

GAIBISSO, GIOVANNI BATTISTA (attributed to) [P11/62] Good Italian Violin with restorable table blemish, w/case 8,580/10,010
$9,867 £6,900

GAIDA, GIOVANNI [B7/155] Violin: Ivrea, c. 1900 7,500/10,500
$8,280 £5,520

GAIDA, GIOVANNI [B7/192] Violin: Ivrea, 1929 9,000/15,000
$9,488 £6,325

GALEO [B7/161] Violin 1,200/1,800
$1,294 £863

GALLINOTTI, PIETRO [B7/196] Fine Violin: Solero (Alessandria), 1924 (Roland Baumgartner, Basel, 1998) 12,000/18,000 NS

GALLINOTTI, PIETRO [B11/150] Fine Italian Violin: Solero, Alessandria, 1924 (Roland Baumgartner, Basel, 1998) 8,580/11,440
$9,867 £6,900

GALRAM, J.J. [B7/145A] Fine and Rare Violin: Portugal, 1780 (W.E. Hill & Sons, London, October 31, 1990) 10,500/15,000 NS

GAND, CHARLES ADOLPHE [S3/55] Violin w/case: Paris, 1829 9,420/12,560 NS

GAND, CHARLES ADOLPHE [S1114/27] Violin w/case: Paris, 1829 5,720/8,580 NS

GAND & BERNARDEL [C5/36] French Violin: Paris, 1881 (Bein & Fushi Inc., Chicago, March 31, 1988) 12,000/14,000
$19,975 £12,984

GAND & BERNARDEL FRERES [S10/20] Violin w/case, bow: Paris, 1877 (R. & M. Millant-Deroux, Paris, November 20, 1952) 8,000/12,000
$14,400 £9,936

GEIPEL, HERMANN [C5/235] German Violin 400/600
$1,175 £764

GEMUNDER, AUGUST (workshop of) [C5/169] American Violin w/case 1,000/1,500 NS

GENOVESE, RICCARDO [P9/100] Good Italian Violin in immediate playing condition, w/case: Lecco, 1927 28,200/35,250 NS

GENOVESE, RICCARDO [P11/96] Fine and Handsome Italian Violin in good condition: Montiglio, 1925 (Etienne Vatelot, Paris, May 16, 1974) 20,020/22,880 NS

GIBBONS, ARTHUR W. [B5/159] Violin 450/750 NS

GIBSON CO. [Sk5/297] American Violin w/case: Kalamazoo 800/1,000
$978 £636

GIGLI, GIULIO CESARE [P6/80] Violin with old back restorations, w/case: Rome, c. 1760 (W.E. Hill & Sons, London, November 30, 1922) 12,080/15,100
$13,024 £8,625

GILBERT, JEFFREY J. [B5/152] Violin 1,200/1,800 NS

GILBERT, JEFFREY J. [B9/195] Violin: 1920 584/876
$638 £437

GILBERT, JEFFREY J. [B11/179] Violin: Peterborough, 1922 2,145/2,860
$2,138 £1,495

GILBERT, JEFFREY JAMES [S12/144] Violin w/case: Peterborough, 1933 1,152/1,728
$1,822 £1,265

GILBERT, JEFFREY JAMES [S12/189] Violin w/case, cover: Peterborough, 1933 864/1,152
$1,490 £1,035

GLIER, AUGUST CLEMENS [S12/150] Violin: Markneukirchen, late 19th C. 259/360 NS

GLIER, ROBERT [S10/43] Violin w/case, 2 bows: Cincinnati, 1922 1,500/2,500
$2,400 £1,656

GOBETTI, FRANCESCO [S1114/247] Violin: Venice, c. 1715 (W.E. Hill & Sons, London, December 15, 1910) 42,900/71,500
$79,651 £55,700

GOFFRILLER, MATTEO [S7/280] Violin w/case: Venice, c. 1730 22,650/30,200 NS

GONZALEZ, FERNANDO SOLAR [S7/272] Violin
w/case: Madrid, 1968   3,775/5,285 NS

GOSS, WALTER S. [Sk11/284] American Violin
w/case, bow: Boston, 1912   800/1,200
$3,335   £2,335

GOSS, WALTER S. [Sk11/286] American Violin
w/case, bow: Boston, 1907   800/1,200
$2,070   £1,449

GOSS, WALTER S. [Sk11/325] American Violin:
Boston, 1924   800/1,200
$575   £403

GRAGNANI, ANTONIO [S3/50] Violin w/case:
Leghorn, c. 1780 (The Rudolph Wurlitzer Co., New
York)   18,840/25,120
$43,332   £27,600

GRAGNANI, ANTONIO [S1114/256] Violin w/case:
Livorno, 1782 (W.E. Hill & Sons, London, September
2, 1943)   35,750/42,900 NS

GRAGNANI, ANTONIO [Sk5/121] Fine Italian
Violin w/case: Livorno, 1770   30,000/38,000 NS

GRAHAM, ROBERT [P9/293] Violin w/violin:
Glamorgan, 1913   423/564 NS

GRANCINO, GIOVANNI [C5/98] Good Italian
Violin: Milan, 1720 (Rembert Wurlitzer Inc., New
York, October 22, 1969)   80,000/120,000 NS

GRANCINO, GIOVANNI (II) (attributed to) [C3/79]
Early Milanese Violin: 1699   31,400/47,100
$32,499   £20,700

GRANCINO FAMILY (ascribed to) [P6/98] Violin
with some old restorations: c. 1700   2,265/2,718
$2,605   £1,725

GRANDINI, GERONIMO [B5/169] French Violin
900/1,500
$1,380   £920

GRANDJON, J. (workshop of) [C5/265] Child's
Violin   400/600
$470   £306

GRANDJON, JULES (attributed to) [P6/26] Good
French Violin with restorable table blemishes, w/case:
c. 1870   1,208/1,359
$1,389   £920

GRANDJON, JULES (FILS) [P3/126] Good French
Violin with table to be reglued, w/case: Mirecourt,
1874   948/1,106
$3,271   £2,070

GRANDJON, JULES (FILS) [S7/30] Violin after
Guarneri del Gesù, w/case: Mirecourt, c. 1870
(Etienne Vatelot, Paris, October 3, 1986) 6,040/9,060
$7,248   £4,800

GUADAGNINI, FRANCESCO (ascribed to)
[C5/107] Good Violin: 1921 (Jacques Français, New
York)   20,000/30,000
$21,150   £13,748

GUADAGNINI, GIOVANNI BATTISTA [C11/36]
Good Italian Violin w/case: Turin, c. 1780
107,250/178,750 NS

GUADAGNINI, GIOVANNI BATTISTA [S10/114]
Violin w/case, bow: Milan, 1753 (Erich Lachmann,
Berlin/New York, July 15, 1933)   150,000/200,000
$161,750   £111,607

GUADAGNINI, GIOVANNI BATTISTA [S3/218]
Violin w/case, bow: Turin, c. 1773 (Rembert
Wurlitzer, New York, February 8, 1957)
314,000/471,000
$339,120   £216,000

GUADAGNINI, GIOVANNI BATTISTA [Sk5/128]
Fine Italian Violin w/case: Parma, c. 1770 (Rembert
Wurlitzer, June 13, 1950)   240,000/280,000
$288,500   £187,525

GUADAGNINI, GIUSEPPE [S7/39] Violin w/case,
cover, bow: Pavia, c. 1780 (Hamma & Co., January
24, 1942)   42,280/52,850
$63,269   £41,900

GUADAGNINI BROTHERS (ascribed to) [C11/241]
Fine Italian Violin w/case: Turin, c. 1845 (W. E. Hill
& Sons, London, November 26, 1947)
71,500/85,800 NS

GUARNERI, ANDREA [B7/203] Fine Italian Violin:
Cremona, 1674 (Peter Biddulph, London, June 1999)
37,500/52,500
$43,125   £28,750

GUARNERI, ANDREA [C3/96] Cremonese Violin
w/case: c. 1680 (W.E. Hill & Sons, London, May 30,
1894)   94,200/125,600 NS

GUARNERI, ANDREA [S7/167] Violin w/case:
Cremona, c. 1650 (J. & A. Beare, London, August 3,
1998)   60,400/90,600 NS

GUARNERI, ANDREA [S10/45] Violin w/case:
Cremona, c. 1680 (W.E. Hill & Sons, London, May
30, 1894)   60,000/80,000
$69,750   £48,127

GUARNERI, JOSEPH (DEL GESU) [S1114/262]
Violin w/case: Cremona, c. 1735 (Carl Mächler,
Zurich, December 8, 1979)   429,000/715,000
$444,730   £311,000

GUARNERI, PIETRO (OF MANTUA) [S7/174]
Violin w/case, cover: Mantua, c. 1690 (Hart & Son,
London, April 18, 1900)   18,120/27,180
$26,803   £17,750

GUARNERI, PIETRO (OF VENICE) [B11/184] "Ex-
Prof. Flesch" Violin: 1757 (R. Wurlitzer, November 5,
1973)   NS

GUARNERI, PIETRO (OF VENICE) [S7/278] Violin
w/case, cover: mid 18th C. (Georg Rauer, Vienna,
August 22, 1918)   9,060/12,080 NS

GUARNERI, PIETRO (OF VENICE) [S10/39] Violin
w/case: Venice, c. 1750 (Rudoph Wurlitzer Co., New
York, May 9, 1938)   250,000/350,000 NS

GUASTALLA, ALFREDO (attributed to) [P6/74]
Good Violin in immediate playing condition, w/case:
Reggiolo, 1934   755/9,060 NS

GUASTALLA, ALFREDO (attributed to) [P9/45]
Good Violin in immediate playing condition, w/case:
Reggiolo, 1934   3,525/4,230
$5,837   £4,140

GUERRA, EVASIO EMILE [C5/84] Italian Violin:
Turin, 1934 (Jacques Français, New York, September
14, 1992)   18,000/22,000
$22,325   £14,511

GUERSAN, LOUIS [B11/74] Fine French Violin:
Paris, 1755   5,720/8,580
$11,512   £8,050

GUERSAN, LOUIS [B11/132] Violin with decorated
scroll: Paris, 1798   2,574/3,575 NS

GUERSAN, LOUIS [S10/32] Violin w/case: Paris,
1749   2,000/3,000 NS

GUTH, AUGUST [C5/287] Belgian Violin w/case:
Antwerp, 1894   1,800/2,200 NS

GUTH, AUGUST [C5/288] Belgian Violin w/case:
Antwerp, 1894   1,800/2,200 NS

HAKKERT, JACQUES [C11/223] Modern Dutch
Violin   4,004/4,576 NS

HALL, R.G. [Sk5/256] American Violin w/case:
Portland, Maine, 1916   400/600
$431   £280

HARDIE (attributed to) [P3/90] Violin with raised
original neck: Edinburgh, c. 1810   1,896/2,370
$727   £460

HARDIE, JOHN [B9/252] Violin   584/876
$537   £368

HARDIE, JOHN [C11/167] Scottish Violin w/fitted
walnut case: Edinburgh, 1882   2,574/3,146 NS

HARDIE, MATTHEW (attributed to) [P6/121]
Violin: c. 1810   1,208/1,359
$695   £460

HARRIS, CHARLES [C11/188] English Violin
w/case: 1803   2,860/5,720 NS

HARRIS, J.E. [Sk5/139] English Violin w/case: 1924
                                       4,000/5,000
$3,220   £2,093

HAUSMANN, OTTOMAR [Sk5/237] Mittenwald
Violin w/case, bow   800/1,000
$1,093   £710

HAWKES & SON [S12/65] Child's Violin: Mirecourt,
c. 1900   288/432
$580   £403

HAWKES & SONS [C5/175] Violin: London, 1889
                                       2,200/2,600 NS

HEBERLEIN (workshop of) [S7/274] Violin w/case:
Markneukirchen, 1926   1,510/2,265 NS

HEBERLEIN, ALBERT AUGUST (JR.) [Sk5/232]
German Violin w/case: Markneukirchen   800/1,000
$575   £374

HEBERLEIN, HEINRICH TH. (JR.) [Sk5/284]
German Violin w/case, bow   600/800
$2,875   £1,869

HEL, JOSEPH [B7/226] French Violin: Lille, c. 1880
                                       7,500/10,500
$18,975   £12,650

HEL, JOSEPH [P11/140] Fine and Handsome French
Violin: Lille, 1894 (W.E. Hill & Sons, London,
October 27, 1944)   4,290/5,720
$9,867   £6,900

HELLMER, JOHANN GEORG [B11/138] Fine
Bohemian Violin: Prague, 1755   2,860/4,290
$4,605   £3,220

HENRY, EUGENE [S7/35] Violin after Guarneri del
Gesù, w/case: France, c. 1870   3,775/5,285 NS

HERCLIK, FR. [B7/204] Interesting Violin
                                       3,000/4,500 NS

HERCLIK, JOSEF BOHUMIL [B11/147] Violin
                                       2,574/3,575
$2,960   £2,070

HEROLD, RICHARD [S12/67] Violin: Brunndöbra
                                       144/288
$132   £92

HERRMANN, EMIL (workshop of) [C5/39] Good
German Violin w/case: Berlin, c. 1920   1,200/1,400
$2,350   £1,528

HERTL, ANTON [B9/215] Violin   438/730
$571   £391

HESKETH, THOMAS EARLE [C11/224] English
Violin: 1942   3,575/5,005
$3,697   £2,585

HESKETH, THOMAS EARLE [P2/53] Violin
w/viola, 3 bows, 2 cases: Manchester, 1938
                                       1,590/1,908
$2,926   £1,840

HESKETH, THOMAS EARLE [P6/94] Good Violin
in immediate playing condition, w/case, bow:
Manchester, 1897   6,040/6,795 NS

HESKETH, THOMAS EARLE [P9/17] Good Violin
in immediate playing condition, w/case, bow:
Manchester, 1897   4,230/4,935
$6,000   £4,255

HESKETH, THOMAS EARLE [S1114/14] Violin
after Nicolà Gagliano, w/case, 2 bows: Manchester,
1913   4,290/7,150
$8,580   £6,000

HEYLIGERS, MATHIJS [Bf3/6245] Good Modern
Violin: Cremona, 1984   5,000/7,000 NS

HILL, JOSEPH [P11/68] Handsome Violin in good
condition: London, c. 1770   5,720/7,150
$6,578   £4,600

HILL, JOSEPH (ascribed to) [P9/32] English Violin
w/violin: c. 1770   987/1,128
$811   £575

HILL, W.E. & SONS [B11/156] Fine English Violin:
London, c. 1880   5,720/8,580
$9,045   £6,325

HILL, W.E. & SONS [P11/74] Good Violin with tiny repair on lower back, w/case, 2 bows: London, 1895
5,720/6,435
$13,978   £9,775

HILL FAMILY (MEMBER OF) [B9/218] Violin
2,920/4,380
$3,358   £2,300

HJORTH, A. [B7/126] Danish Violin: Copenhagen, 1819   1,500/2,250 NS

HJORTH, A. [B11/146] Danish Violin retaining its original neck: Copenhagen, 1819   1,144/1,716
$1,398   £978

HOFMANN, GEORG PHILIP [P11/48] Good German Violin with some restorations, w/case: Markneukirchen, 1928   1,144/1,287 NS

HOMENICK BROTHERS [C11/187] American Violin: 1928   1,144/1,716
$1,175   £822

HOPF [B5/145] Violin   1,200/1,800 NS

HOPF [B9/227] Violin   730/1,022
$873   £598

HOPF FAMILY (MEMBER OF) [B7/149] Violin: c. 1850   600/900 NS

HOPF FAMILY (MEMBER OF) [B11/137] Violin
572/858 NS

HOPF FAMILY (MEMBER OF) [S7/294] Violin: Klingenthal, first half 18th C.   2,114/2,718 NS

HOPF FAMILY (MEMBER OF) [Sk11/279] Saxon Violin w/case   2,000/4,000 NS

JACOBS, HENDRIK [C5/106] Dutch Violin (Jacques Français, New York)   8,000/12,000
$14,100   £9,165

JACOBS, HENDRIK [Sk5/133] Fine Dutch Violin with possibly later scroll: Amsterdam, 1690
26,000/30,000 NS

JACQUOT, CHARLES [S3/188] Violin w/case, bow: Paris, c. 1860   4,396/5,495
$8,666   £5,520

JACQUOT, CHARLES [S7/175] Violin w/case: Nancy, c. 1870   5,285/6,795
$7,610   £5,040

JAEGER, HANS [S12/98] Violin after Maggini: Markneukirchen, 1886   144/288
$182   £127

JAIS, ANDREAS [S3/48] Violin: Tölz, c. 1740 (Etienne Vatelot, Paris, March 7, 1973)   4,710/7,850
$4,694   £2,990

JAIS, JOHANNES [S10/41] Violin w/case, bow: Bolzano, 1779 (Rudolph Wurlitzer Co., New York, February 25, 1935)   5,000/7,000
$13,200   £9,108

JAY, HENRY (attributed to) [P3/106] English Violin with table restorations: c. 1760   1,580/2,370
$2,544   £1,610

JIROWSKY, HANS [P2/228] Violin in immediate playing condition, w/violin: Vienna, 1935   954/1,113
$914   £575

JOHN, WILLIAM [S3/73] Violin after the "Heifetz, ex-David" Guarneri del Gesù, w/case: London, 1996
7,850/10,990
$9,028   £5,750

JOHNSON, JOHN [P3/50] Fine and Handsome English Violin in immediate playing condition, w/double violin case: London, 1764   4,740/5,530 NS

JOHNSON, JOHN [P6/130] Fine and Handsome English Violin in immediate playing condition, w/case: London, 1764   3,020/3,775
$4,862   £3,220

JOHNSON, JOHN [S7/268] Violin in original Baroque setup, w/case, bow: London, 1750
1,510/2,265
$4,711   £3,120

JOHNSON, PETER ANDREAS [Sk11/225] American Violin w/case, 2 bows: Aurora, Illinois, 1913   1,000/2,000
$1,265   £886

JOMBAR, PAUL [C3/44] Violin   2,512/2,826
$2,889   £1,840

JOMBAR, PAUL [S7/279] Violin: Paris, 1932
4,530/6,040 NS

JORIO, VINCENZO (attributed to) [B11/133] Violin
11,440/17,160
$13,156   £9,200

JORIO, VINCENZO (attributed to) [P11/78] Interesting Violin in immediate playing condition: c. 1850   17,160/21,450 NS

JORIO, VINCENZO (attributed to) [Bf3/6237] Fine Violin w/case: Naples, c. 1860   10,000/15,000
$8,050   £5,152

JUZEK, JOHN [Sk5/210] Violin w/violin, 2 cases
500/600
$1,093   £710

KAMPFFE, AUGUST [Sk5/325] Markneukirchen Violin w/case, 2 bows: 1803   900/1,000 NS

KAUL, PAUL [P3/51] Violin in immediate playing condition, w/case: Paris, 1933   3,950/5,530
$7,813   £4,945

KAUL, PAUL [P6/105] Fine and Handsome French Violin in immediate playing condition, w/case: Nantes, 1923   7,550/9,060
$7,814   £5,175

KEANE [P2/82] Violin in good condition: Dublin, c. 1920   636/795
$1,097   £690

KEMPTER, ANDREAS [Sk11/64] German Violin w/case, bow: Dillingen, 1776   4,000/6,000 NS

KENNEDY, THOMAS [P2/32] Handsome Violin with restorable table blemish, w/case, 2 bows: London, c. 1825   3,975/4,770
$6,583   £4,140

KERSCHENSTEINER, XAVER [S3/192] Violin
w/case, bow: Regensburg, 1888   3,925/5,495 NS

KERSCHENSTEINER, XAVER [S1114/238] Violin
w/case, bow: Regensburg, 1888   2,145/3,575
$2,059   £1,440

KINGMAN, GORDON MAURY [S10/120] Violin
w/case, cover: Santa Barbara, 1988 (maker's,
California, October 19, 1993)   800/1,200
$840   £580

KINGMAN, GORDON MAURY [S10/23] Violin
w/case: Santa Barbara, 1986   1,000/1,500
$1,080   £745

KLEIN & CIE., A. [S12/109] Violin: Rouen, 1885
                                                   360/504
$497   £345

KLEINMAN, CORNELIUS (attributed to) [Sk5/124]
Dutch Violin w/case: c. 1680   3,000/5,000 NS

KLOTZ [B2/162] Good German Violin   1,600/2,400
$1,693   £1,058

KLOTZ, AEGIDIUS (I) [S7/302] Child's Violin
w/case, bow: Mittenwald, 1790   2,265/3,020 NS

KLOTZ, GEORG (attributed to) [P11/102] Good
Violin with minor restored blemishes, w/case, bow:
Mittenwald, c. 1750   4,290/5,005
$4,934   £3,450

KLOTZ, JOHANN CARL [B7/167] Violin
                                                2,700/3,750
$2,933   £1,955

KLOTZ, JOSEPH [C11/213] Good Mittenwald
Violin: c. 1780   5,005/7,865 NS

KLOTZ, SEBASTIAN [C5/318] Good South German
Violin: Mittenwald, 1793   6,000/8,000
$7,638   £4,965

KLOTZ, SEBASTIAN [S3/234] Violin w/double case:
Mittenwald, 1751 (L.P. Balmforth & Son, Leeds,
September 10, 1955)   2,355/3,140
$3,611   £2,300

KLOTZ, SEBASTIAN [S7/181] Violin: Mittenwald,
c. 1750   1,812/2,416
$2,174   £1,440

KLOTZ FAMILY (MEMBER OF) [B7/132]
Interesting Violin: Mittenwald, c. 1770
                                                1,200/1,800 NS

KLOTZ FAMILY (MEMBER OF) [B7/164] Violin
                                                5,250/8,250 NS

KLOTZ FAMILY (MEMBER OF) [B7/225] Violin:
c. 1780   2,250/3,000 NS

KLOTZ FAMILY (MEMBER OF) [B11/131] Violin
                                                5,005/7,865 NS

KLOTZ FAMILY (MEMBER OF) [B11/143] Violin:
c. 1770   1,430/2,145
$1,480   £1,035

KLOTZ FAMILY (MEMBER OF) [B11/177] Violin:
c. 1780   1,144/1,716
$1,316   £920

KLOTZ FAMILY (MEMBER OF) [Bf3/6256]
Bohemian Violin   700/1,200
$1,035   £662

KLOTZ FAMILY (MEMBER OF) [C11/176]
Mittenwald Violin w/case, 2 bows   4,290/7,150 NS

KLOTZ FAMILY (MEMBER OF) [P11/76] Good
Violin in good condition: Mittenwald, c. 1760
                                                7,150/8,580 NS

KLOTZ FAMILY (MEMBER OF) [S7/184] Violin
w/case: Mittenwald, mid 18th C.   2,265/3,020
$2,537   £1,680

KLOTZ FAMILY (MEMBER OF) [Sk11/80] Violin
w/case: Mittenwald   2,500/3,000
$2,415   £1,691

KNILLING, JOHANN [P11/22] Violin with minor
restorations, w/case, cover: Mittenwald, 1832
(Geigenbau Machold, Zurich, May 3, 1989)
                                                2,145/2,860
$2,796   £1,955

KNORR, P. [C3/34] Good German Violin w/case,
bow: Markneukirchen, c. 1925   2,826/3,454
$5,417   £3,450

KONYA, ISTVAN [S10/29] Violin w/case: Hungary,
1986 (maker's, Heged´készitö, 1986)   2,000/3,000
$2,400   £1,656

KOSTLER, WILLY [S12/163] Violin: Graslitz, early
20th C.   144/288
$265   £184

KRELL, ALBERT [Sk5/331] American Violin
                                                   600/800
$1,380   £897

KREUZINGER II, JOSEPH [S12/185] Violin w/case:
Schönbach, 1911   864/1,152
$1,325   £920

KROGH, CHRISTIAN [B9/274] Violin   365/511 NS

KRUMBHOLZ, LORENZ [C3/246] Dutch Violin
w/case   2,826/3,925
$4,333   £2,760

KUGLER, FERDINAND [C11/203] Good
Contemporary Violin: Vienna, 1988   3,575/5,005
$4,369   £3,055

KULIK, JAN [S1114/22] Violin after Guarneri:
Prague, 1862   5,005/7,150
$8,237   £5,760

KULIK, JAN [Sk5/392] Good Czech Violin w/case:
Prague, 1848   3,000/5,000
$6,555   £4,261

LABERTE [P2/208] Mirecourt Violin in good condition: c. 1910   875/954
$1,042   £656

LABERTE [P2/209] Good French Violin in immediate
playing condition, w/case, 2 bows: c. 1900   557/636
$475   £299

LABERTE [P3/212] Good Small-Size French Violin:
c. 1920   474/553
$654   £414

LABERTE [P3/231] French Violin in good condition, w/violin: c. 1910   790/948
$1,363   £863

LABERTE, MARC [B7/216] Violin: Mirecourt
2,250/3,000 NS

LABERTE, MARC [C3/241] French Violin
1,570/2,355
$1,806   £1,150

LABERTE, MARC (workshop of) [C5/237]
Mirecourt Violin   1,000/1,500
$940   £611

LABERTE, MARC (workshop of) [C5/315] French
Violin w/case   600/800 NS

LABERTE-HUMBERT BROS. [S7/31] Violin w/case,
bow: Mirecourt, 1918   1,510/2,265 NS

LABERTE-HUMBERT BROS. [S12/124] Violin
w/case, bow: Mirecourt, 1918   864/1,152
$911   £633

LANDOLFI, CARLO FERDINANDO [P6/128] Fine
and Handsome Italian Violin in immediate playing
condition, w/case: Milan, 1759 (Hans Edler, Munich,
June 20, 1965)   67,950/75,500 NS

LANDOLFI, CARLO FERDINANDO [C5/87]
Milanese Violin w/case: c. 1758 (Wm. Moennig &
Son, Philadelphia, December 28, 1961)
70,000/120,000 NS

LANDOLFI, CARLO FERDINANDO [P6/129]
Interesting Italian Violin with old restored blemishes,
w/case: c. 1770   9,060/10,570 NS

LANDOLFI, CARLO FERDINANDO [S1114/251]
Violin w/case, cover: Milan, c. 1760 (W.E. Hill &
Sons, London, October 28, 1960)   28,600/42,900
$31,961   £22,350

LANDOLFI, CARLO FERDINANDO (attributed to)
[C5/320] Violin w/case, bow   5,000/6,000 NS

LANDOLFI, CARLO FERDINANDO (attributed to)
[P3/65] Interesting Italian Violin with old restored
blemishes, w/case, cover: c. 1770   15,800/23,700 NS

LANDOLFI, PIETRO ANTONIO (ascribed to)
[Sk11/69] Italian Violin w/case: c. 1780
25,000/30,000
$35,650   £24,955

LANDON, CHRISTOPHE [B7/220] Violin
15,000/22,500 NS

LANGONET, EUGENE [P3/32] Good French Violin
in good condition: Nantes, 1930   3,160/4,740 NS

LANGONET, EUGENE [S7/277] Violin: Nantes,
1930   2,265/3,020 NS

LARCHER, JEAN (attributed to) [P2/61] French
Violin of quality: 1930   636/795
$805   £506

LAVEST, J. (attributed to) [P6/159] French Violin:
1913   1,057/1,208 NS

LAVEST, J. (attributed to) [P11/23] Good French
Violin in good condition: 1926   1,430/1,716 NS

LEAR, M.D. [B9/236] American Violin   584/876 NS

LEEB, ANDREAS CARL [S7/51] Violin w/case, bow:
Vienna, 1778   1,812/2,416
$2,356   £1,560

LEEB, JOHANN GEORG [Sk5/390] Austrian Violin
w/case: Pressburg, 1860   1,200/1,800 NS

LEIDOLFF, JOHANN CHRISTOPH [Sk11/344]
Viennese Violin w/case   800/1,000
$920   £644

LE LYONNAIS, CHARLES [B9/322] Violin
2,190/2,920 NS

LENTZ, JOHANN NICOLAUS [P9/39] Rare English
Violin with old table restorations: c. 1820
1,128/1,269
$973   £690

LIESSEM, REMERUS [S7/267] Violin w/case:
London, 1750   1,510/2,265 NS

LONGSON, F.H. [P2/13] Good Violin with restored
scroll, w/case: Stockport, 1880   1,272/1,431 NS

LONGSON, F.H. [P9/27] Good Violin with restored
scroll, w/case: Stockport, 1880   846/987
$3,243   £2,300

LORANGE, PAUL [B2/150] Violin   640/960
$1,380   £863

LORANGE, PAUL [P3/102] Good French Violin with
minor blemishes: Marseilles, 1933   1,896/2,844 NS

LORANGE, PAUL (attributed to) [P11/47] Good
French Violin in good condition: Marseille, 1927
2,145/2,574
$2,467   £1,725

LOTT, JOHN [P3/63] Good Violin in immediate
playing condition, w/case: London, c. 1850
23,700/28,440
$23,621   £14,950

LOWENDALL, LOUIS [B2/159] German Violin
320/480
$846   £529

LOWENDALL, LOUIS [B5/148] Violin   600/900 NS

LOWENDALL, LOUIS [B9/231] Violin   292/438
$319   £219

LOWENDALL, LOUIS [P3/10] Good Violin in good
condition: Dresden, 1883   790/948
$1,054   £667

LOWENDALL, LOUIS [P3/12] Good German Violin
in immediate playing condition, w/case, bow:
Dresden, 1886   632/790
$1,054   £667

LUCCI, GIUSEPPE [S3/215] Violin: Rome, 1967
9,420/12,560
$16,250   £10,350

LUPOT, NICOLAS (attributed to) [P3/56] French
Violin with skillful table restorations, w/case: c. 1820
(Max Moller N.V., Antwerp, April 3, 1939)
14,220/15,800 NS

LYON, U. [C3/192] American Violin: 1894   314/471
$578   £368

MAGGINI, GIOVANNI PAOLO [P11/107]
Important Violin with back and front restorations:
c. 1600 (L.P. Balmforth & Son, Leeds, November 20,
1952)   42,900/50,050 NS

MAGGINI, GIOVANNI PAOLO [S10/121] Violin
with later head, w/case: Brescia, c. 1620 (Hamma &
Co., Stuttgart, June 15, 1915)   40,000/60,000
$55,950   £38,606

MAGNIERE, GABRIEL [S3/45] Violin: Mirecourt,
1885   3,140/4,710
$4,694   £2,990

MAINARDI, GIOVANNI [Bf3/6249] Modern Violin:
Cremona, 1997   3,000/4,000 NS

MANGENOT, AMATI [P11/100] Good French
Violin in good condition, w/case: Bordeaux, 1928
                               2,860/3,575 NS

MANGENOT, AMATI (workshop of) [C5/317]
French Violin: 1920   1,500/2,500
$2,233   £1,451

MANGENOT, P. [P6/161] Good French Violin with
some varnish restoration: c. 1900   906/1,057
$1,216   £805

MANTEGAZZA, PIETRO GIOVANNI [C3/95]
Good Italian Violin: Milan, late 18th C.
                               54,950/70,650
$68,609   £43,700

MARCHETTI, EDUARDO [C5/109] Italian Violin:
Turin, 1926 (Jacques Français, New York)
                               10,000/15,000 NS

MARCHETTI, EDUARDO (ascribed to) [C5/93]
Italian Violin: Turin, 1905 (Jacques Français, New
York)   10,000/15,000 NS

MARCHETTI, ENRICO (attributed to) [P6/120]
Violin in immediate playing condition, w/case: Turin,
1916   6,040/6,795 NS

MARCHETTI, ENRICO (attributed to) [P9/35]
Violin in immediate playing condition, w/case: Turin,
1916   2,820/3,525 NS

MARCHETTI, ENRICO (workshop of) [C5/105]
Modern Italian Violin: c. 1929 (Jacques Français,
New York)   15,000/20,000 NS

MARCHETTI, ENRICO (attributed to) [C5/306]
Modern Italian Violin w/case: Turin, 1918
                               8,000/12,000 NS

MARCHINI, RUDOLFO [Bf3/6238] Modern Italian
Violin: Rome, 1984   5,000/8,000
$4,025   £2,576

MARCONCINI, JOSEPH (attributed to) [P3/45]
Italian Violin in immediate playing condition, w/case:
Ferrara, 1817 (Eric Blot, Cremona, December 17,
1996)   47,400/55,300 NS

MARGINI, RENZO [C5/319] Contemporary Violin
w/case: Soliera, 1982   2,200/2,600 NS

MARIANI, ANTONIO (ascribed to) [S3/219] Violin:
late 17th C. (Dario D'Attili, New Jersey, October 22,
1991)   12,560/15,700 NS

MARTIN, E. (workshop of) [C5/289] German Violin
w/case: c. 1910   800/1,200
$705   £458

MARTINI, ORESTE [P3/91] Good Violin in immediate playing condition: 1950 (Kenneth Warren & Son,
Chicago, November 30, 1998)   9,480/12,640
$10,902   £6,900

MAST, JOSEPH LAURENT [S3/229] Violin w/case,
bow: Toulouse, c. 1830   3,140/4,710 NS

MAST, JOSEPH LAURENT [S1114/44] Violin
w/case: Toulouse, c. 1830   1,716/2,288 NS

MAYSON, WALTER H. [B7/183] English Violin:
Manchester, 1883   2,250/3,000 NS

MAYSON, WALTER H. [B11/168] English Violin:
Manchester, 1883   1,430/2,145
$2,631   £1,840

MAYSON, WALTER H. [P2/35] Good Violin in
immediate playing condition, w/case, bow:
Manchester, 1902   795/954
$914   £575

MAYSON, WALTER H. [P3/118] Good Violin in
immediate playing condition: Manchester, 1897
                               1,264/1,422
$1,454   £920

MAYSON, WALTER H. [S1114/33] Violin:
Manchester, 1889   1,430/2,145 NS

MCCALLUM, ALEX [S12/90] Violin: Glasgow, 1904
                               216/360
$232   £161

MCLAREN, JOHN (attributed to) [P6/315] Violin
with restorable blemishes: Leith, 1886   604/76
$1,216   £805

MEARES, RICHARD (attributed to) [P11/126]
Interesting English Violin with restorable blemishes,
w/case, bow: London, c. 1740   1,144/1,287
$822   £575

MENNESSON, EMILE [S1114/34] Violin: Reims,
1878   2,002/2,574
$3,775   £2,640

MERIOTTE, CHARLES [Bf3/6251] French Violin
w/case, bow: Lyon, c. 1750 (Hans Weisshaar,
September 14, 1990)   10,000/14,000 NS

MERMILLOT, MAURICE [C5/307] French Violin:
Paris, 1900   4,000/5,000
$4,700   £3,055

MERMILLOT, MAURICE [S7/25] Violin w/case:
Paris, 1897   3,020/4,530
$4,349   £2,880

MERMILLOT, MAURICE (attributed to) [P3/97]
Good French Violin in good condition: Paris, 1890
                               2,370/3,160
$3,452   £2,185

MEUCCI, ENZO [S1114/11] Violin: Como, 1946
2,860/4,290
$3,432   £2,400

MILTON, LOUIS [B11/166] Violin: 1925   715/1,001
$2,631   £1,840

MIRAUCOURT, N. [S3/64A] Violin w/case: France,
1932   1,884/2,512
$1,806   £1,150

MIREMONT, CLAUDE AUGUSTIN [C5/166] Good
French Violin: Paris, c. 1866   6,000/8,000
$7,638   £4,965

MIREMONT, CLAUDE AUGUSTIN [S7/38] Violin
after Guarneri del Gesù, w/case, 2 bows: Paris, 1872
6,040/9,060
$7,248   £4,800

MOINEL & CHERPITEL (workshop of) [C11/135]
French Violin   2,002/2,288
$2,184   £1,527

MOLLER, MAX [C11/28] Good Dutch Violin: 1930
5,005/6,435
$5,041   £3,525

MONK, JOHN KING [B9/234] Violin   438/730
$1,091   £748

MONK, JOHN KING [P2/72] Violin: Surrey, 1892
954/1,113 NS

MONK, JOHN KING [P6/165] Violin: Surrey, 1892
604/755 NS

MONK, JOHN KING [P9/308] Violin: Merton,
Surrey, 1892   564/705 NS

MONTAGNANA, DOMENICO [B11/191] Highly
Important Violin: Venice, c. 1725 (W.E. Hill & Sons)
NS

MONTAGNANA, DOMENICO (attributed to)
[Bf3/6253A] Interesting Violin w/case: c. 1750
2,000/3,000
$2,300   £1,472

MONTANARI, LUIGI (attributed to) [P11/65] Good
Italian Violin in playing condition, w/case, cover
10,010/11,440
$13,978   £9,775

MONTERUMICI, ARMANDO (ascribed to)
[C3/238] Good Modern Italian Violin
6,280/9,420 NS

MOUGENOT [C3/27] Violin   1,884/2,355
$2,167   £1,380

MOUGENOT, GEORGES [S3/61] Violin w/case:
Brussels, 1883   3,925/5,495
$8,125   £5,175

MOUGENOT, GEORGES [P6/99] Good Violin with
minor pegbox repair, w/case: Brussels, 1909
7,550/9,060
$6,599   £4,370

MOUGENOT, GEORGES (attributed to) [P6/124]
Good French Violin with minor restorable blemishes
2,265/2,718 NS

MOUGENOT, LEON [B11/122] Violin   1,716/2,145
$2,138   £1,495

MOUGENOT, LEON [B11/134] Violin   1,144/1,716
$1,316   £920

MOUGENOT, LEON [S3/201] Violin w/case:
Mirecourt, 1903   2,355/3,140
$7,222   £4,600

MOUGENOT, LEON [S7/28] Violin w/case:
Mirecourt, 1909   1,812/2,416
$1,993   £1,320

MOUGENOT, LEON [S1114/12] Violin Mirecourt,
1924   2,145/2,860 NS

MOUGENOT, LEON [S1114/49] Violin after the
"King Joseph" Guarneri del Gesù: Paris or London,
1898   2,574/3,575
$2,746   £1,920

MOUGENOT, LEON [S12/127] Violin: France, early
20th C.   1,008/1,440
$1,242   £863

MOUGENOT, LEON (attributed to) [P6/163] French
Violin in good condition   906/1,057
$1,650   £1,093

MOUGENOT, LEON (workshop of) [C5/162]
French Violin: Mirecourt, 1925   2,200/2,600
$2,350   £1,528

MOUGENOT, LEON (workshop of) [S7/154] Violin
w/case, cover, bow: Mirecourt, 1924   1,812/2,416 NS

MOUGENOT, P. & L. PRONIER [C3/37] French
Violin   2,826/3,454
$4,694   £2,990

MOZZANI, LUIGI [C5/308] Italian Violin: Bologna,
1938   4,500/6,500 NS

MOZZANI, LUIGI [S3/57] Violin w/case: Pieve di
Cento, 1916   3,140/4,710
$5,417   £3,450

MURDOCH & CO. [B5/177] Violin   150/225 NS

MURDOCH & CO. [B9/241] Violin   88/117
$143   £98

NELSON FAMILY [S12/143] Violin w/case: 1929
432/576 NS

NEMESSANYI, SAMUEL FELIX [S10/21] Violin
w/case: Budapest, 1871   14,000/18,000
$35,250   £24,322

NEUNER, MATHIAS [B2/144] Violin   640/960
$699   £437

NEUNER & HORNSTEINER [B2/93] Violin
480/800
$883   £552

NEUNER & HORNSTEINER [B2/146] German
Violin   160/240
$478   £299

NEUNER & HORNSTEINER [B2/157] German
Violin   320/480
$552   £345

NEUNER & HORNSTEINER [B5/170] Violin:
Mittenwald, c. 1880   450/750
$725   £483

NEUNER & HORNSTEINER [B5/201] Violin
                                    300/450 NS

NEUNER & HORNSTEINER [B9/306] Violin
                                    146/219
$134   £92

NEUNER & HORNSTEINER [B11/153] Violin:
c. 1890   572/858
$691   £483

NEUNER & HORNSTEINER [P2/23] Good
Mittenwald Violin in good condition, w/case: c. 1880
                                    795/954
$768   £483

NEUNER & HORNSTEINER [P2/42] Good
Mittenwald Violin in immediate playing condition,
w/case: c. 1880   954/1,113
$1,097   £690

NEUNER & HORNSTEINER [P2/227] Mittenwald
Violin: c. 1880   636/795
$823   £518

NEUNER & HORNSTEINER [P6/298] Good Small-
Size Violin in immediate playing condition, w/case:
Mittenwald, c. 1880   906/1,057
$1,181   £782

NEUNER & HORNSTEINER [P6/300] Small-Size
Violin with minor table restorations, w/case:
Mittenwald, c. 1880   906/1,057
$868   £575

NEUNER & HORNSTEINER [P6/346] Good
Mittenwald Violin w/case, bow: c. 1880   604/755
$1,077   £713

NEUNER & HORNSTEINER [P6/355] Mittenwald
Violin with minor restorable blemishes: c. 1880
                                    604/755
$660   £437

NEUNER & HORNSTEINER [S1114/235]
Miniature Violin: Mittenwald, late 19th C. 858/1,144
$1,287   £900

NICHOLLS, COLIN [B5/204] Violin: 1992
                                    2,250/3,000
$2,070   £1,380

NICHOLLS, COLIN [C11/173] Contemporary
English Violin w/case (Colin Nicholls, August 21,
1995)   5,005/5,720
$5,880   £4,112

NICOLAS, DIDIER (L'AINE) [B2/94] Violin
                                    1,280/1,920 NS

NICOLAS, DIDIER (L'AINE) [B9/254] Fine Violin
                                    730/1,022
$940   £644

NICOLAS, DIDIER (L'AINE) [P6/95] Good French
Violin w/case: Mirecourt, c. 1790   1,208/1,359
$1,389   £920

NICOLAS, DIDIER (L'AINE) [P6/150] Good French
Violin: Mirecourt, c. 1820 (Jean-Jacques Rampal,
Paris, December 10, 1998)   1,208/1,359
$1,389   £920

NICOLAS, DIDIER (L'AINE) [P6/167] Good French
Violin in immediate playing condition: Mirecourt,
c. 1790   1,208/1,359
$1,389   £920

NICOLAS, DIDIER (L'AINE) [P11/135] French
Violin needing cleaning: Mirecourt, c. 1800
                                    1,144/1,287
$1,645   £1,150

NICOLAS, DIDIER (L'AINE) [S3/191] Violin w/case,
violin: Mirecourt, c. 1830   1,884/2,512
$1,806   £1,150

NICOLAS, DIDIER (L'AINE) [S12/52] Violin:
Mirecourt, mid 19th C.   576/864
$745   £518

NICOLAS, DIDIER (L'AINE) [S12/86] Violin:
Mirecourt, mid 19th C.   432/720 NS

NICOLAS FAMILY (MEMBER OF) [S3/47] Violin:
Paris, 1800   3,925/5,495
$9,930   £6,325

ODOARDI, GIUSEPPE [S7/62] Violin w/case, cover,
bow: Ascoli, 1780 (Lewis L. Main, Long Beach, April
26, 1968)   18,120/24,160
$21,593   £14,300

OLIVER, BARRY [C3/236] Contemporary English
Violin   157/1,884
$2,528   £1,610

OMOND, JAMES [P2/58] Violin in immediate playing condition: Stromness, Scotland, 1905
                                    159/1,908 NS

ORLANDINI, ARCHIMEDE [S10/36] Violin:
Parma, 1944 (Peter Biddulph, London, September 11,
1997)   6,000/8,000
$9,000   £6,210

ORMOND, JAMES [Sk11/401] Scottish Violin
w/case: Stromness, 1906   1,000/1,500
$805   £564

ORNATI, GIUSEPPE [C5/81] Fine Modern Italian
Violin: Milan, 1919   18,000/22,000
$21,150   £13,748

ORNATI, GIUSEPPE [C11/136] Fine Modern Italian
Violin w/case: Milan, 1924 (Wm. Lewis & Son,
Illinois, April 9, 1975)   20,020/22,880
$21,843   £15,275

OTTO, LOUIS [C5/274] German Violin
                                    1,600/1,800 NS

OWEN, JOHN W. [S3/68] Violin w/case, 2 bows:
Leeds, 1920   1,884/2,512
$2,347   £1,495

PACHERELE, PIERRE (ascribed to) [C5/139] Fine
French Violin: Nice, c. 1849 (Michael A. Baumgartner, Basel, July 14, 1995)   18,000/22,000 NS

PAINE, THOMAS D. [Sk5/264] American Violin: Woonsocket, Rhode Island, 1878   600/800
$431   £280

PAMPHILON, EDWARD [B7/112] Very Fine Violin: London, c. 1690   6,000/9,000
$13,800   £9,200

PAMPHILON, EDWARD [S3/196] Violin with later head, w/case: London, c. 1680 (C.F. Langonet & Son, London, Janaury 26, 1959)   3,925/5,495
$4,333   £2,760

PAMPHILON, EDWARD [S1114/16] Violin w/case: London, 1670 (W.E. Hill & Sons, London, March 6, 1964)   3,575/5,005
$7,207   £5,040

PANORMO, JOSEPH (attributed to) [B11/145] Interesting Violin   4,290/7,150
$4,111   £2,875

PANORMO, VINCENZO [B7/123] Fine Violin after Nicolo Amati: London, 1797 (W.E. Hill & Sons, London, 1938)   37,500/52,500
$39,675   £26,450

PANORMO, VINCENZO [S7/160] Violin after Nicolo Amati, w/case, cover: Paris, 1762 (W.E. Hill & Sons, London, March 13, 1973)   37,750/45,300
$66,742   £44,200

PANORMO, VINCENZO (attributed to) [P3/34] Violin with post repair and other restorations, w/case: London, c. 1800   3,160/3,950
$1,817   £1,150

PANORMO, VINCENZO (attributed to) [P3/70] Handsome English Violin with restorations: London, c. 1810   2,370/3,160 NS

PANORMO, VINCENZO (attributed to) [P6/108] Handsome English Violin with restorations: London, c. 1810   1,510/2,265
$1,737   £1,150

PANORMO, VINCENZO (attributed to) [S7/53] Violin: London, early 19th C.   15,100/22,650
$25,066   £16,600

PANORMO FAMILY (MEMBER OF) (ascribed to) [Sk11/74] Fine Violin w/case   22,000/25,000 NS

PASSAU, SIMON SCHODLER [P11/29] Good German Violin in good condition, w/case, bow: c. 1770   1,144/1,287
$1,151   £805

PATERSON, J.B. [C11/301] Violin w/case: 1958   572/858 NS

PEDRAZZINI, GIUSEPPE [B7/163] Fine Violin: Milan, 1932   27,000/37,500
$29,325   £19,550

PEDRAZZINI, GIUSEPPE [C5/178] Fine Modern Italian Violin: Milan, 1910 (W.E. Hill & Sons, London, September 21, 1964)   35,000/45,000 NS

PEDRAZZINI, GIUSEPPE [S7/40] Violin w/case: Milan, 1914 (Hawkes & Son, London, March 30, 1914)   21,140/27,180
$33,749   £22,350

PEDRAZZINI, GIUSEPPE [S7/276] Violin w/double case: Milan, 1920   10,570/15,100
$10,872   £7,200

PEDRAZZINI, GIUSEPPE (workshop of) [Bf3/6241] Very Fine Italian Violin in a very fine state of preservation: Milan, c. 1950 (Giuseppe Ornati, August 22, 1963)   10,000/15,000
$8,625   £5,520

PEDRAZZINI, GIUSEPPE (workshop of) [Sk5/405] Good Violin, w/case   8,000/10,000
$4,025   £2,616

PELLACANI, GIUSEPPE [Sk11/71] Italian Violin: Modena, 1949 (Horacio Pineiro, New York, April 25, 1999)   8,000/10,000
$6,440   £4,508

PELLACANI, GIUSEPPE [Bf3/6242] Fine Modern Italian Violin: Modena, 1960 (Rudolfo Marchini, May 11, 1994)   5,000/8,000 NS

PEREGO, FLAVIO [Bf3/6236] Modern Violin: Cremona, 1998   3,000/4,000 NS

PERRIN, E.J. (FILS) [S12/116] Violin: Mirecourt, c. 1860   288/432
$397   £276

PERRIN, ETIENNE [S7/54] Violin w/2 violins: Mirecourt, c. 1840   1,510/2,265 NS

PERRY, THOMAS & WM. WILKINSON [S7/288] Violin w/case: Dublin, 1823   2,265/3,775
$4,711   £3,120

PERRY, WILLIAM (attributed to) [P2/70] Violin in playing condition: Dublin, c. 1800   477/636
$731   £460

PERRY & WILKINSON [P3/38] Violin w/case, 2 bows: Dublin, 1801   1,264/1,422
$2,035   £1,288

PETERNELLA, JAGO [B7/122] Italian Violin: Venice, 1944   6,000/9,000 NS

PETERNELLA, JAGO [B11/155] Violin: Venice, 1944   4,290/7,150
$6,907   £4,830

PETERSON, P.A. [C3/193] American Violin: Chicago, 1914   314/471
$578   £368

PETZOLD, PAUL [P11/308] Violin in playing condition, w/case, bow: c. 1890   715/858 NS

PILAR, KAREL [P2/63] Good Violin in immediate playing condition, w/case: 1927 (Thomas Pilar, Kralove, September 5, 1999)   3,180/3,975
$4,388   £2,760

PILAR, VLADIMIR [P3/92] Good Violin in playing condition, w/case: Hradec Kralove II, 1977   1,896/2,370
$2,907   £1,840

PILLEMENT [P6/35] Good French Violin with some restored blemishes, w/case, bow: Mirecourt, c. 1790   906/1,057
$1,302   £863

PIQUE (ascribed to) [P11/73] Interesting Violin in good condition, w/case: Paris, 1807
17,160/21,450 NS

PIQUE, F. (attributed to) [B7/152] Fine French Violin: Paris, c. 1820　　　　37,500/52,500 NS

PIQUE, FRANCOIS LOUIS (ascribed to) [P6/93] Interesting Old French Violin in immediate playing condition, w/case, bow: c. 1790　　　2,265/3,020
$3,473　　　　£2,300

PIROT, CLAUDE [S7/159] Violin after Stradivari's long pattern, w/case, bow: Paris, 1810
4,530/7,550 NS

PLIVERICS, EMIL [S7/27] Violin w/case, bow: Berlin, 1937　　　　　　4,530/6,040
$6,523　　　　£4,320

POIRSON [B7/139] Violin: Lyon, 1899
3,000/4,500 NS

POLITI, ENRICO & RAUL (attributed to) [C5/295] Contemporary Violin: Rome, 1960 (Roland Baumgartner, Basel, April 10, 1995)　　3,000/5,000
$3,290　　　　£2,139

POLLASTRI, GAETANO [C5/172] Modern Italian Violin: Bologna, 1954 (Kenneth Warren & Son, Chicago, April 15, 1996)　　16,000/20,000 NS

POLLASTRI, GAETANO [Sk11/75] Fine Modern Italian Violin w/case: Bologna, 1935　20,000/30,000
$33,350　　　£23,345

POLLASTRI, GAETANO (attributed to) [Sk11/392] Modern Italian Violin (Dario D'Attili, Dumont, New Jersey, July 8, 1975)　　　　　　3,000/5,000
$6,900　　　　£4,830

POSTACCHINI, ANDREA [C5/100] Good Italian Violin: Fermo, early 19th C. (Jacques Français, New York)　　　　　　50,000/75,000 NS

POSTACCHINI, ANDREA (attributed to) [S1114/41] Violin w/case: Italy, mid 19th C.
11,440/17,160
$20,449　　　£14,300

POSTIGLIONE, VINCENZO [S10/117] Violin: Naples, 1898　　　　　35,000/45,000
$41,000　　　£28,290

POSTIGLIONE, VINCENZO (attributed to) [S10/27] Violin w/case: early 20th C.　5,000/7,000
$7,800　　　　£5,382

PRAGA, EUGENIO (workshop of) [Sk5/408] Italian Violin w/case: Genoa, 1878　　3,000/4,000
$9,775　　　　£6,354

PRAGER, AUGUST EDWIN [C3/127] Silver Violin with original wrap and partial hair　550/707 NS

PRATT, ARTHUR [C5/276] American Violin w/case, 2 bows: Yonkers, 1914　　　　800/1,200
$705　　　　£458

PRIER, PETER PAUL [S10/18] Violin w/case, bow: Salt Lake City, 1980　　　　800/1,200
$840　　　　£580

PROKOP, LADISLAV (attributed to) [P6/180] Good Violin in immediate playing condition, w/case: 1908
604/755
$695　　　　£460

PUGLISI (attributed to) [P6/176] Violin of the Italian School, w/violin: Catania, 1923　906/1,208
$2,952　　　　£1,955

PUGLISI, MICHELANGELO [S10/124] Violin w/case: Catania, 1919　　　　3,000/5,000
$5,700　　　　£3,933

PUGLISI, REALE [C3/41] Modern Italian Violin: c. 1915　　　　　　3,140/4,710 NS

PYNE, GEORGE [P11/56] Good Violin in immediate playing condition, w/case: London, 1916 1,716/2,145
$1,809　　　　£1,265

PYNE, GEORGE [S7/34] Violin w/case: London, 1918　　　　　　　2,265/3,020
$2,718　　　　£1,800

RABASSINI, MASSIMO [Bf3/6243] Good Modern Italian Violin w/case: Cremona, 1989　2,000/4,000
$1,725　　　　£1,104

RAMBAUX, CLAUDE VICTOR (attributed to) [P2/20] Violin with minor old restorations, w/case: Paris, 1848　　　　　　1,272/1,431
$4,754　　　　£2,990

RASTELLI, LODOVICO [C5/102] Good Italian Violin: Genoa, c. 1845 (Jacques Français, New York)
24,000/28,000 NS

RAUTENBERG, NICOLE [Bf3/6247] Modern Italian Violin: Cremona, 1995　　2,500/3,250
$2,588　　　　£1,656

REGAZZONI, DANTE [P6/90] Good Italian Violin in immediate playing condition (maker's)
5,285/6,040 NS

REGAZZONI, DANTE [P11/124] Good Italian Violin belonging to the Regazzoni family: 1984 (maker's)　　　　　　　3,575/4,290
$5,591　　　　£3,910

REGAZZONI, DANTE PAOLO [P3/37] Good Italian Violin in immediate playing condition: (maker's)　　　　　　　5,530/6,320
$8,177　　　　£5,175

REMY (FILS) [C3/197] French Violin w/case, bow
1,256/1,884
$1,354　　　　£863

RENAUDIN, LEOPOLD [S3/203] Violin: Paris, c. 1780　　　　　　　4,710/7,850
$5,055　　　　£3,220

RENAUDIN, LEOPOLD (ascribed to) [C11/216] French Violin w/case: Paris, 1780　2,860/4,290 NS

RENAULT & CHATELAIN (attributed to) [P6/83] French Violin with old table restorations: c. 1760
3,775/4,530 NS

RENAULT & CHATELAIN (attributed to) [P9/77] French Violin with old table restorations: c. 1760
2,115/2,538 NS

RICARD, ALEXANDER [Sk5/357] Modern Violin:
Springfield, Massachusetts, 1917   1,000/1,200
$920   £598

RICHARDSON, ARTHUR [B7/144A] Fine Violin:
Devon, 1923   3,000/6,000
$3,278   £2,185

RICHARDSON, ARTHUR [Bf3/6250] Fine English
Violin: Devon, 1927 (Violin Shop Pte. Ltd., July 1,
1990)   5,000/8,000 NS

RICHARDSON, ARTHUR [S3/52] Violin w/case:
Crediton, 1940   4,710/6,280
$6,319   £4,025

RICHARDSON, ARTHUR [S3/212] Violin:
Crediton, 1936   5,495/7,065
$8,666   £5,520

RICHELME, ANTOINE MARIUS [P2/65] Good
French Violin in immediate playing condition, w/case,
2 bows: Marseilles, 1870   1,908/2,385 NS

ROBIN, M. [B9/280] French Violin 1,168/1,752 NS

ROBINSON, WILLIAM [B2/114] Violin 2,400/3,200
$2,760   £1,725

ROBINSON, WILLIAM [B7/158] Violin: Liverpool,
1929   2,250/3,000 NS

ROBINSON, WILLIAM [B9/203] Violin 1,168/1,752
$1,259   £863

ROBINSON, WILLIAM [B11/172] Violin: Liverpool,
1929   2,145/2,860 NS

ROCCA, ENRICO [Sk11/59] Fine Modern Italian
Violin w/case: Genoa, 1914 (Kenneth Warren & Son,
Chicago, October 25, 1998)   25,000/35,000
$29,900   £20,930

ROCCA, ENRICO (ascribed to) [S10/126] Violin
w/case: 20th C. (Wm. Lewis & Son, Chicago,
October 22, 1960)   1,000/1,500
$2,700   £1,863

ROCCA, GIUSEPPE [C5/101] Good Italian Violin:
Turin, c. 1858 (Jacques Français, New York)
                        140,000/160,000 NS

ROCCA, GIUSEPPE [S3/54] Violin after Guarneri del
Gesù, w/case, bow: Turin, 1849 (Hamma & Co.,
Stuttgart, November 23, 1964)   157,000/219,800
$209,595   £133,500

ROCCA, GIUSEPPE [S1114/31] Violin: Turin, 1845
(John & Arthur Beare, London, March 4, 1916)
                        100,100/143,000 NS

ROCCA, GIUSEPPE [S1114/257] Violin after
Stradivari: Turin, c. 1845 (W.E. Hill & Sons, London,
December 24, 1946)   114,400/171,600
$130,845   £91,500

ROCCA, JOSEPH [B11/175] Important Violin:
Turin, 1851 $189,118   £132,250

ROCCHI, SESTO [S10/42] Violin w/case: San Polo
d'Enza, 1972   10,000/15,000
$12,000   £8,280

ROMBOUTS, PIETER [P3/101] Good Dutch Violin
in immediate Baroque playing condition, w/case:
c. 1700   7,110/8,690
$16,353   £10,350

ROMBOUTS, PIETER [C3/240] Dutch Violin
w/case, bow: Amsterdam, c. 1701   3,140/3,925
$9,930   £6,325

ROPE, ALFRED JAMES [P6/352] Violin in immediate playing condition, w/case, 2 bows: London, 1911
                              604/755
$608   £403

ROSSI, GIOVANNI [P11/137] Italian Violin with old
restored table blemishes: Perugia, 1829
                        21,450/28,600
$39,468   £27,600

ROTH (ascribed to) [P9/47] Violin in immediate
playing condition, w/case: c. 1920   3,525/3,948 NS

ROTH (ascribed to) [P11/123] Violin in good condition, w/case: c. 1920   3,146/3,432 NS

ROTH, ERNST HEINRICH [C5/167] Good
Markneukirchen Violin: 1925   1,800/2,200
$3,525   £2,291

ROTH, ERNST HEINRICH [P11/46] Fine and
Handsome German Violin in good condition, w/case,
bow: Markneukirchen, 1934   1,716/2,145
$4,440   £3,105

ROTH, ERNST HEINRICH [S1114/50] Violin:
Markneukirchen, 1927   1,716/2,288
$3,432   £2,400

ROTH, ERNST HEINRICH [Sk5/238]
Markneukirchen Violin w/case, 2 bows: 1924
                          1,000/1,200
$2,415   £1,570

ROTH, ERNST HEINRICH [Sk5/280] German
Violin w/case: 1928   800/1,000
$1,955   £1,271

ROTH, ERNST HEINRICH (workshop of)
[Sk11/242] German Violin w/case, bow: 1930
                            800/1,200
$2,645   £1,851

ROVESCALLI, AZZO (ascribed to) [C5/171]
Interesting Violin (Igor Moroder, Verona, April 1995)
                          3,000/5,000
$3,290   £2,139

ROVESCALLI, TULLIO [C5/164] Modern Italian
Violin: Milan, 1931 (Carlson Cacciatori Neumann,
Cremona, March 4, 1999)   5,000/7,000
$9,400   £6,110

RUGGIERI, FRANCESCO [S3/225] Violin w/case,
bow: Cremona, c. 1650 (Hamma & Co., Stuttgart,
June 20, 1940)   54,950/78,500
$62,800   £40,000

RUGGIERI, FRANCESCO [S1114/43] Violin:
Cremona, 1694 (W.E. Hill & Sons, London, May 2,
1939)   42,900/57,200
$74,718   £52,250

SALOMON, JEAN BAPTISTE DESHAYES [S7/42]
Violin w/case, cover: Paris, c. 1750   6,040/9,060 NS

SALOMON, JEAN BAPTISTE DESHAYES [S10/26]
Violin: Paris, mid 18th C.   3,000/5,000
$3,600   £2,484

SALSEDO, LUIGI [B9/250] Violin   2,920/4,380 NS

SAUNDERS, ERNEST [C11/298] English Violin
w/case, bow   572/858
$588   £411

SCARAMPELLA, STEFANO [C3/31] Modern Italian
Violin w/case, bow: Mantua, 1922   18,840/25,120
$50,554   £32,200

SCHIRMER, HANS (workshop of) [C5/153] German
Violin w/case, bow: c. 1925   800/1,200
$1,410   £917

SCHMIDT, ERNST REINHOLD [C5/41] Good
Markneukirchen Violin: c. 1925   1,200/1,400 NS

SCHMIDT, MAX WILLIBALD [S10/17] Violin
w/case: Seattle, 1931   600/800
$1,560   £1,076

SCHMITT, LUCIEN [P11/115] Good Violin with use
and wear: Grenoble, 1924   2,145/2,860
$2,631   £1,840

SCHMITT, LUCIEN [C11/133] French Violin
                                       2,574/3,575 NS

SCHOENFELDER, JOHANN GEORG [P11/34]
Good Saxon Violin in good condition, w/case:
Markneukirchen, c. 1800   1,430/2,145
$3,125   £2,185

SCHOENFELDER, JOHANN GEORG [Sk5/251]
Markneukirchen Violin w/case   600/800
$575   £374

SCHONFELDER, JOHANN GEORG (II) [P6/71]
Good Violin with restorable blemishes, w/case:
Markneukirchen, c. 1790   106/1,208
$781   £518

SCHUSTER, EDOUARD [S3/44] Violin after
Guarneri del Gesù, w/case, bow: Brussels, 1925
                                       3,925/5,495
$6,319   £4,025

SCHUSTER, MAX [Sk5/323] Good German Violin:
Markneukirchen, 1922   1,000/1,200
$1,955   £1,271

SDERCI, IGINO [C5/43] Modern Italian Violin:
Florence, 1975   10,000/15,000
$14,100   £9,165

SEBASTIEN, JEAN [Bf3/6255] French Violin in need
of some restoration   600/900
$748   £478

SEITZ, JOHANNES [S7/172] Violin w/case:
Heidelberg, 1944   2,265/3,020 NS

SERAPHIN, SANCTUS [C3/97] Italian Violin: Venice
(Henry Werro, Bern, January 17, 1940)
                                      31,400/47,100
$43,332   £27,600

SERDET, PAUL [B7/166] Violin: Paris, 1902
                                       1,800/2,250
$2,933   £1,955

SERDET, PAUL [S7/285] Violin w/case: Paris, 1903
                                       4,530/6,040
$6,886   £4,560

SERDET, PAUL (workshop of) [C3/35] French Violin:
1897 (Jean-Jacques Rampal, July 20, 1999)
                                       2,198/2,512
$2,167   £1,380

SGARABOTTO, PIETRO [Sk5/134] Fine Italian
Violin w/case: Parma, 1932   18,000/24,000
$23,000   £14,950

SGARBI, GIUSEPPE [P11/110] Good Violin in good
condition, case, original fingerboard: Modena, 1852
(D.R. Hill & Son, Great Missenden, February 24,
1997)   17,160/21,450 NS

SHELMERDINE, ANTHONY [P6/88] Good Violin
in immediate playing condition, w/case, bow:
Liverpool, 1918   1,208/1,359 NS

SHELMERDINE, ANTHONY [P9/18] Good Violin
in immediate playing condition, w/case, bow:
Liverpool, 1918   846/917
$1,054   £748

SHELTON, JOHN F. [B9/243] American Violin
                                          584/876 NS

SILVESTRE, HIPPOLYTE CHRETIEN [P3/104]
Good French Violin in immediate playing condition,
w/case: Neveau a Lyon, 1877   11,850/13,430
$13,628   £8,625

SILVESTRE, HIPPOLYTE CHRETIEN (attributed
to) [P11/72] Fine and Handsome French Violin in
immediate playing condition: Paris, 1887 (Roger
Lanne, Paris, November 13, 1989)   20,020/25,740
$21,379   £14,950

SILVESTRE, PIERRE [S7/24] Violin w/bow: Lyon,
1856   7,550/10,570
$9,060   £6,000

SILVESTRE, PIERRE & HIPPOLYTE [Sk5/383]
Good French Violin: Lyon, 1837   8,000/10,000
$8,050   £5,233

SILVESTRE & MAUCOTEL (workshop of) [C5/174]
French Violin w/case   5,000/7,000
$4,113   £2,673

SILVESTRE & MAUCOTEL (attributed to workshop
of) [C5/309] French Violin w/case   5,000/7,000 NS

SIMONAZZI, AMADEO (ascribed to) [S10/115]
Violin w/case: 20th C. (Dario D'Attili, Dumont, New
Jersey, August 13, 1981)   6,000/8,000
$6,000   £4,140

SIMONAZZI, AMADEO (attributed to) [S3/235]
Violin: Italy, mid 20th C.   2,826/3,925
$5,055   £3,220

SIMPSON, JAMES & JOHN [P9/78] English Violin
with some old restorations, w/case, cover: London,
c. 1790   846/1,128 NS

SINCLAIR, WILLIAM [B9/239] Violin
1,168/1,752 NS

SIVORI [B2/128] Violin 640/960
$1,104 £690

SMILLIE, ALEXANDER [C11/193] Scottish Violin:
Glasgow, 1911 3,575/5,005
$4,705 £3,290

SMILLIE, ANDREW Y. (attributed to) [P2/34] Good
Violin: Glasgow, 1923 1,590/1,908 NS

SMILLIE, ANDREW Y. (attributed to) [P6/29] Good
Violin: Glasgow, 1923 1,057/1,208 NS

SMILLIE, ANDREW Y. (attributed to) [P9/113]
Good Violin: Glasgow, 1923 705/846
$1,054 £748

SMITH, BERT [B7/179] English Violin: Coniston,
1951 1,500/2,250
$2,070 £1,380

SMITH, BERT [B9/179] Violin: 1965 876/1,168
$923 £633

SMITH, JOHN [B5/217] Violin 900/1,050
$1,242 £828

SMITH, JOHN [P3/221] Violin with minor table
blemish: 1920 790/948 NS

SMITH, JOHN [P9/291] Violin with minor table
blemish: 1920 423/564 NS

SOLIANI, ANGELO [C5/96] Fine Italian Violin:
Modena, c. 1800 (Jacques Français, New York)
30,000/40,000 NS

SOLIANI, ANGELO [S7/161] Violin w/case:
Modena, 1791 (Wm. Lewis & Son, Chicago, March
30, 1970) 37,750/45,300 NS

SOLZI, ANDREA [Bf3/6234] Modern Violin:
Cremona, 1998 3,250/4,250
$3,738 £2,392

SOMNY, JOSEPH MAURICE [S12/186] Violin
w/case: London, 1896 1,152/1,728
$1,159 £805

SOUBEYRAN, MARC [P3/111] Good Violin in
Baroque playing condition, w/case, bow: 1982
1,264/1,580
$1,454 £920

SPIDLEN, FRANTISEK F. [P2/76] Good Violin in
immediate playing condition, w/case: Prague, 1913
5,565/6,360 NS

SPIELMANN, RUDOLF [S1114/45] Violin:
Reichenberg, 1934 1,430/2,145

SQUIER, JEROME BONAPARTE [Sk5/257]
American Violin w/case, bow: Boston, 1890 600/800
$1,093 £710

SQUIER, VICTOR CARROLL [S10/30] Violin
w/case: Battle Creek, 1946 800/1,200
$1,560 £1,076

STADLMANN, JOHANN JOSEPH [S3/221] Violin:
Vienna, 1751 4,710/7,850 NS

STADLMANN, JOHANN JOSEPH [S1114/18]
Violin: Vienna, 1751 2,860/4,290 NS

STADLMANN, JOHANN JOSEPH (attributed to)
[P6/127] Good Violin in good condition: c. 1800
2,114/2,718 NS

STAINER, JACOB [S7/282] Violin with later head,
w/case, bow: Absam, 1659 52,850/75,500 NS

STANLEY, ROBERT A. [B5/164] Violin
750/1,050 NS

STANLEY, ROBERT A. [B9/226] Violin 511/803
$470 £322

STAUFFER, JOHANN GEORG [S7/43] Violin of
unusual model: Vienna, 1826 3,020/4,530 NS

STEFANINI, GIUSEPPE [S1114/23] Violin for the
Brothers Bisiach, w/case: Milan, 1949 8,580/11,440
$10,296 £7,200

STIRRAT, DAVID [S3/59] Violin: Edinburgh, 1813
3,925/5,495
$4,514 £2,875

STIRRAT, DAVID (attributed to) [P3/61] Violin in
good condition, w/case: Edinburgh, c. 1810
4,740/5,530
$2,726 £1,725

STRADIVARI, ANTONIO [C5/48] Fine Italian
Violin known as the "Taft, ex–Emil Heermann":
Cremona, 1700 (Jacques Français, New York, July
11, 1994) 1,000,000/1,500,000
$1,326,000 £861,900

STRADIVARI, ANTONIO [S3/69] Violin w/double
case: Cremona, c. 1666 (Chardon & Fils, Paris,
October 15, 1958) 345,400/439,600 NS

STRADIVARI, ANTONIO [S10/118] Violin w/case:
Cremona, 1679 (Dietmar Machold, New York, April
28, 1998) NS

STRIEBIG, JEAN [B2/119] Violin 640/960
$1,196 £748

STRIEBIG, JEAN [B9/315] Violin 584/876
$604 £414

STROBL, MICHAEL [S7/29] Violin after Guarneri
del Gesù, w/case, cover: Berlin, 1948 3,775/5,285 NS

STROBL, MICHAEL [S7/266] Violin w/case, cover:
Berlin, c. 1940 3,020/4,530 NS

STUBER, JOHANN [S1114/10] Violin after Guarneri
del Gesù, w/case: The Hague, 1927 4,290/5,720 NS

SYSKA, JACEK [S3/210] Violin: Nowy Targ, 1993
1,570/2,355 NS

SZEPESSY, BELA [S3/53] Violin w/case, bow:
London, 1888 3,925/5,495
$6,861 £4,370

SZEPESSY, BELA [P3/44] Fine and Handsome Violin
in immediate playing condition, w/case: London,
1885 7,900/9,480
$9,085 £5,750

TARR, SHELLEY [Sk11/395] English Violin w/case:
Manchester, 1892 2,000/3,000 NS

TECCHLER, DAVID [B11/162] Italian Violin: Rome, 1743 (J. & A. Beare)   35,750/50,050 NS

TERRANA, GERLANDO [B7/178] Violin: Naples, 1951   9,000/12,000
$2,243   £1,495

TESTORE, CARLO ANTONIO [Sk5/122] Fine Italian Violin: Milan, 1721   70,000/80,000
$79,500   £51,675

TESTORE, CARLO GIUSEPPE [P11/121] Fine and Handsome Italian Violin in immediate playing condition, w/case, cover, bow: Milan, c. 1710 (W.E. Hill & Sons, London, March 24, 1925)   35,750/42,900
$37,824   £26,450

TESTORE, PAOLO ANTONIO [P3/86] Good Violin in immediate playing condition, w/case: Milan, c. 1740 (J. & A. Beare, London, June 24, 1994)   47,400/55,300 NS

TESTORE, PAOLO ANTONIO [P11/66] Violin in playing condition: c. 1760 (Rene A. Morel, New York, June 14, 1944)   5,005/5,720
$7,565   £5,290

THEODORAN, JACOB [C5/278] Interesting American Violin w/case, bow: 1944   600/800
$646   £420

THIBOUT, JACQUES PIERRE (attributed to) [S1114/13] Violin: France, mid 19th C.   2,574/3,575
$4,462   £3,120

THIBOUVILLE-LAMY, J. [B5/206] Violin   900/1,500 NS

THIBOUVILLE-LAMY, J. [B7/176] Violin   1,050/1,500
$2,243   £1,495

THIBOUVILLE-LAMY, J. [B9/283] Violin   438/730
$756   £518

THIBOUVILLE-LAMY, J. [P2/243] Mirecourt Violin w/violin: c. 1900   636/716
$1,280   £805

THIBOUVILLE-LAMY, J. [P3/11] Good French Violin with table blemishes, w/case: c. 1910   711/790
$1,090   £690

THIBOUVILLE-LAMY, J. [P3/124] Mirecourt Violin in immediate playing condition, w/case: c. 1910   1,106/1,264
$1,363   £863

THIBOUVILLE-LAMY, J. [P3/211] Good Small-Size French Violin with minor restorable blemishes, w/small-size violin: c. 1910   948/1,106 NS

THIBOUVILLE-LAMY, J. [P3/253] French Violin in good condition, w/violin, 2 bows, 2 cases: c. 1900   790/948
$727   £460

THIBOUVILLE-LAMY, J. [P9/201] Good Small-Size Violin in good condition: c. 1900   564/705 NS

THIBOUVILLE-LAMY, J. [P9/205] Good Small-Size French Violin with minor restorable blemishes, w/small-size violin: c. 1910   564/635
$568   £403

THIBOUVILLE-LAMY, J. [P9/241] Good Mirecourt Violin in good condition, w/violin: c. 1900   846/987
$649   £460

THIBOUVILLE-LAMY, J. [P9/243] Mirecourt Violin with some table restorations, w/case, 2 bows: c. 1900   705/846 NS

THIBOUVILLE-LAMY, J. [P9/285] French Violin in good condition, w/violin: c. 1900   705/846
$486   £345

THIBOUVILLE-LAMY, J. [P9/294] French Violin in good condition, w/violin: c. 1900   56/705
$892   £633

THIBOUVILLE-LAMY, J. (workshop of) [C5/267] Child's Violin   150/250
$470   £306

THIBOUVILLE-LAMY, J. (workshop of) [C11/287] French Violin w/case, bow   429/572 NS

THIBOUVILLE-LAMY, J. (workshop of) [C11/292] French Violin w/case   429/572 NS

THIBOUVILLE-LAMY, JEROME [C3/173] Child's French Violin   471/785
$542   £345

THIBOUVILLE-LAMY, JEROME [C3/183] French Violin   471/785
$632   £403

THIBOUVILLE-LAMY, JEROME [C3/184] Child's French Violin   471/785
$578   £368

THIBOUVILLE-LAMY, JEROME [C3/188] Child's French Violin   393/550
$469   £299

THIBOUVILLE-LAMY, JEROME [S12/102] Violin: Mirecourt, late 19th C.   360/504 NS

THIBOUVILLE-LAMY, JEROME [S12/53] Violin: Mirecourt, late 19th C.   288/432
$431   £299

THIBOUVILLE-LAMY, JEROME [S12/62] Violin: Mirecourt, late 19th C.   288/432
$248   £173

THIBOUVILLE-LAMY, JEROME [S12/66] Child's Violin: Mirecourt, late 19th C.   144/288
$182   £127

THIBOUVILLE-LAMY, JEROME [S12/103] Violin: Mirecourt, late 19th C.   288/432
$431   £299

THIBOUVILLE-LAMY, JEROME [S12/130] Child's Violin w/case, bow: Mirecourt, early 20th C. 288/432
$497   £345

THIBOUVILLE-LAMY, JEROME [S12/138] Violin: Mirecourt   432/720
$464   £322

THIBOUVILLE-LAMY, JEROME [S12/159] Violin: Mirecourt, late 19th C.   216/360
$166   £115

THIBOUVILLE-LAMY, JEROME [S12/176] Violin: Mirecourt, late 19th C.   432/720
$580   £403

THIBOUVILLE-LAMY, JEROME [S12/187] Violin w/case, 2 bows: Mirecourt, late 19th C.   432/720
$911   £633

THIBOUVILLE-LAMY, JEROME [S1114/9] Violin: Mirecourt, late 19th C.   1,716/2,288
$2,231   £1,560

THIR, ANTON (attributed to) [P11/30] Good Violin with minor restorable blemishes: Pressburg, 1765
    1,144/1,287
$1,398   £978

THIR, MATHIAS (attributed to) [P6/170] Violin: c. 1770   604/755
$781   £518

THIR, MATHIAS (attributed to) [P6/64] Old Violin in immediate playing condition, w/case, bow: Vienna, 1780   4,530/6,040 NS

THOMPSON, CHARLES & SAMUEL [B5/129] Violin   1,200/1,800
$1,466   £978

THOMPSON, CHARLES & SAMUEL [P2/225] English Violin w/violin: London, c. 1770   636/795
$1,646   £1,035

THOMPSON, CHARLES & SAMUEL [P3/58] Good English Violin with restored table blemishes, w/case: London, c. 1780   1,896/2,370
$2,180   £1,380

THOMPSON & SON [P2/38] Good English Violin in good restored condition, w/case: London, 1764
    1,272/1,431 NS

THOMPSON & SON [P6/106] Good English Violin with minor blemishes only, w/case: c. 1760
    1,057/1,208
$1,216   £805

THOMPSON & SON [P6/147] Good English Violin in good restored condition, w/case: London, 1764
    604/755
$1,302   £863

TIM [P2/84] Mittenwald Violin in immediate playing condition, w/case, bow: 1913   954/1,113
$1,280   £805

TOBIN, RICHARD [C3/155] English Violin
    1,256/1,884 NS

TOBIN, RICHARD [P3/52] Fine and Handsome Violin in immediate playing condition, w/case: London, c. 1820   18,960/23,700 NS

TOBIN, RICHARD [S7/32] Violin w/case: London, c. 1820   18,120/24,160 NS

TONONI, CARLO [C5/91] Violin w/double case: Venice, c. 1720   50,000/70,000
$58,750   £38,188

TONONI, CARLO [S10/24] Violin w/case, cover: Venice, 1725 (W.E. Hill & Sons, London, December 1, 1967)   150,000/200,000
$173,250   £119,542

TOTH, A. [B2/103] Violin   480/800
$589   £368

TUA, SILVIO [Bf3/6235] Modern Italian Violin: c. 1933   6,500/7,500 NS

TUBBS, C.E. [S3/105] Silver Violin: London, early 20th C.   3,925/5,495 NS

TURNER, W. (attributed to) [P6/166] English Violin with minor restorable blemishes: c. 1810   76/906 NS

VANGELISTI, PIER LORENZO (ascribed to) [S10/37] Violin w/case: Florence, first half 18th C. (Harry A. Duffy Violins, Del Mar, California, May 8, 1989)   15,000/25,000
$14,400   £9,936

VAROTTO, GIAMPIETRO (attributed to) [P6/61] Italian Violin with minor table blemish: Padua, 1991
    1,510/181 NS

VATELOT, MARCEL [S7/165] Violin w/case: Paris, 1942   2,114/2,718 NS

VAUTRIN, JOSEPH [C3/158] Violin: 1908
    1,570/2,355
$3,069   £1,955

VAUTRIN, JOSEPH (attributed to) [P6/175] French Violin of some quality: c. 1900   982/1,057
$868   £575

VEDRAL, JOSEPH [P11/32] Fine and Handsome Violin in immediate playing condition: The Hague, 1936   4,576/5,434 NS

VENTAPANE, LORENZO [Bf3/6240] Very Fine Italian Violin in near-perfect state of preservation, w/case: Naples, c. 1850 (Rudolph Wurlitzer Co., January 15, 1946)   45,000/60,000 NS

VENTAPANE, LORENZO [S3/200] Violin w/case, 2 bows: Naples, c. 1820 (W.E. Hill & Sons, London, June 15, 1956)   18,840/25,120
$39,721   £25,300

VIEDENHOFER, BERNHARD [C5/177] Hungarian Violin w/case, 2 bows: Pesth   2,000/2,500
$2,585   £1,680

VIGNALI, GIUSEPPE [P6/97] Good Violin in good condition, w/case, 2 bows: Veruccio, 1915
    2,265/3,020
$4,689   £3,105

VILLAUME, GUSTAVE EUGENE [S3/213] Violin w/case, bow: Nancy, 1946   1,884/2,512
$2,889   £1,840

VILLAUME, GUSTAVE EUGENE [S7/284] Violin w/case: Mirecourt, early 20th C.   1,812/2,416
$1,812   £1,200

VINACCIA FAMILY (MEMBER OF) [Sk11/67] Neapolitan Violin w/case: c. 1800 (Dario D'Attili, Dumont, New Jersey, February 18, 1985)
    6,000/8,000
$5,175   £3,622

VINACCIA FAMILY (MEMBER OF) (ascribed to) [C5/47] Good Neapolitan Violin (Paul Jombar, Paris, June 9, 1914)   30,000/40,000
$32,900   £21,385

VINCENT, ALFRED [P6/86] Good English Violin in immediate playing condition, w/case: 1924
3,020/3,775
$4,341   £2,875

VINCENT, ALFRED [P11/64] Good English Violin with restored blemishes, w/case: London, 1929
3,575/4,290 NS

VUILLAUME, F.N. (attributed to) [P3/46] Violin of quality: c. 1860   5,372/6,004
$8,722   £5,520

VUILLAUME, JEAN BAPTISTE [B7/134] Fine French Violin in a very fine state of preservation: Paris, 1869   52,500/67,500
$94,875   £63,250

VUILLAUME, JEAN BAPTISTE [Bf3/6252] French Violin   35,000/45,000 NS

VUILLAUME, JEAN BAPTISTE [P6/115] Good French Violin with some skillful old table restorations, w/case, bow: Paris, c. 1860   45,300/52,850 NS

VUILLAUME, JEAN BAPTISTE [P11/70] Good French Violin with skillful old repairs, w/buffalo-hide case, cover: Paris, 1848 (W.H. Tibbalds & Sons, Brighton)   50,050/57,200 NS

VUILLAUME, JEAN BAPTISTE [S1114/39] Violin after Maggini, w/case: Paris, 1832   35,750/50,050 NS

VUILLAUME, JEAN BAPTISTE (attributed to) [P3/89] French Violin of quality, w/case: Paris, 1827
6,320/7,110 NS

VUILLAUME, JEAN BAPTISTE (workshop of) [C5/83] Good French Violin: Paris, c. 1827
25,000/35,000
$23,500   £15,275

VUILLAUME, N. (attributed to) [P3/43] Violin: c. 1860   3,160/3,950 NS

VUILLAUME, NICOLAS [P9/40] Good French Violin with restorable table blemishes: Mirecourt, c. 1860   2,115/2,820
$1,784   £1,265

VUILLAUME, NICOLAS (attributed to) [P6/125] Fine and Handsome French Violin with minor restored blemishes, w/case: c. 1860 (Max Moller B.V., Amsterdam, June 15, 1978)   4,530/5,285
$5,383   £3,565

VUILLAUME, NICOLAS (attributed to) [P6/143] Violin after Guarneri: c. 1860   1,812/2,265
$2,084   £1,380

WAHLBERG, LEIF [P6/113] Good Violin with minor restorable table blemish, w/case, bow: Stockholm, 1942   2,265/3,020
$2,778   £1,840

WALKER, WILLIAM [P2/216] Violin in good condition, w/case, bow: Beith, Scotland, 1885   636/795 NS

WAMSLEY, PETER [S7/46] Violin w/case, 2 bows: London, 1749   1,812/2,416
$2,718   £1,800

WARRICK, A. [P3/60] Good Violin in playing condition, w/case: Leeds, 1909   2,370/3,160
$3,634   £2,300

WEICHOLD, RICHARD [B2/51] Silver Violin without hair   640/960
$828   £518

WEISS, EUGENIO [B7/169] Violin: Trieste, 1920 (Daniele Scalfi, Milan, October 10, 1995)
1,050/1,500 NS

WEISS, EUGENIO [B7/205] Violin: Trieste, 1920 (Daniele Scalfi, Milan, October 10, 1995)1,050/1,500
$1,121   £748

WELLER, F.W. [P2/19] Good Violin in immediate playing condition, w/case, 2 bows: Surrey, 1945
1,272/1,431
$1,463   £920

WERRO, JEAN [B11/165] Good Violin: Berne, 1922
2,860/4,290
$4,605   £3,220

WHITE, ASA WARREN [Sk11/251] American Violin w/case: 1879   800/1,200
$1,150   £805

WHITMARSH, EMANUEL [B9/176] Violin
1,460/2,190
$2,183   £1,495

WIDHALM, LEOPOLD [S10/22] Violin w/case: Nuremberg, mid 18th C.   2,500/3,000 NS

WIDHALM, LEOPOLD [S10/25] Violin w/case, cover, bow: Nuremburg, c. 1775   5,000/7,000
$5,400   £3,726

WIDHALM, MARTIN LEOPOLD [S10/109] Violin w/case, bow: Nuremberg, c. 1790   5,000/7,000
$9,000   £6,210

WILD, FRANZ ANTON (attributed to) [P9/297] Violin with minor table-edge repair: 1952
564/705 NS

WILDSTEINBONER, HERMANN [B2/141] Violin
320/480
$258   £161

WILKANOWSKI, W. [C5/268] American Violin w/case   350/550
$588   £382

WILKANOWSKI, W. [Sk5/292] Modern American Violin w/case: Brooklyn, 1936   1,000/1,200
$1,035   £673

WILSON [B9/224] Violin   292/584
$336   £230

WINDER, J. [B7/131A] English Violin: London, 1907
900/1,500 NS

WINDER, J. [B11/188] English Violin: London, 1907
572/858
$1,151   £805

WOLFF BROS. [P6/373] German Violin w/violin: 1891   604/755
$521   £345

WORLE, MATHIAS [S12/78] Violin: Mittenwald,
1921   720/1,008
$1,159   £805

WULME-HUDSON, GEORGE [P3/94] Violin in
good condition   2,212/2,528 NS

WULME-HUDSON, GEORGE [P6/145] Violin in
good condition   1,812/211
$1,737   £1,150

WULME-HUDSON, GEORGE (ascribed to)
[Sk5/397] Good Modern Violin   8,000/12,000
$8,050   £5,233

WURLITZER, REMBERT [S10/14] Violin w/case
                                   1,800/2,500
$4,500   £3,105

ZANISI, FILIPPO (ascribed to) [C5/294]
Contemporary Violin   2,000/3,000
$2,115   £1,375

ZANOLI, GIACOMO (ascribed to) [S10/19] Violin
w/double case: late 18th C. (Lyon & Healy, Chicago,
April 20, 1912)   3,000/5,000
$16,800   £11,592

ZIMMER, K. OTTO [C3/91] Good Hungarian
Violin w/case   4,710/6,280
$10,833   £6,900

ZUST, J.E. [B7/145] Violin: Zurich, 1906
                                   3,000/4,500
$4,313   £2,875

VIOLIN BOW

ADAM (attributed to) [C11/154] Silver Violin Bow
                                   2,860/4,290 NS

ADAM, JEAN [C5/54] Silver Violin Bow with later
adjuster (Etienne Vatelot, Paris, December 28,
1987)   5,000/7,000
$11,163   £7,256

ADAM, JEAN DOMINIQUE [C11/49] Silver French
Violin Bow without hair or wrap (Jean-François
Raffin, Paris, June 7, 2000)   3,575/5,005 NS

ALLEN, SAMUEL [B7/7] Silver Violin Bow: c. 1885
                                   3,000/4,500 NS

ALLEN, SAMUEL [B11/28] Silver Violin Bow for
W.E. Hill & Sons: c. 1885   2,145/2,860 NS

ALLEN, SAMUEL [P11/144] Rare Silver Violin Bow
without lapping: London, c. 1900   1,716/2,145
$4,605   £3,220

ALLEN, SAMUEL (ascribed to) [C5/188] Gold Violin
Bow (Kenneth Warren & Son Ltd., Chicago, October
27, 1977)   3,000/4,000
$7,050   £4,583

BAUSCH [B9/73A] Fine Gold Violin Bow   876/1,460
$1,175   £805

BAUSCH (workshop of) [Sk5/372] Silver Violin Bow
                                   400/600
$230   £150

BAZIN [28,247/16] Silver Violin Bow
                                   1,200/1,800 NS

BAZIN (workshop of) [2029/186] French Nickel
Violin Bow   400/600
$633   £443

BAZIN (workshop of) [7503/68] Silver Violin Bow:
Mirecourt, c. 1930   2,000/2,500 NS

BAZIN, CHARLES [Sk11/148] French Silver Violin
Bow   2,000/2,400
$2,300   £1,610

BAZIN, CHARLES [Sk11/184] Silver Violin Bow
                                   800/1,200
$1,150   £805

BAZIN, CHARLES (workshop of) [C11/160] Nickel
Violin Bow   1,001/1,287 NS

BAZIN, CHARLES (workshop of) [Sk5/146] Silver
Violin Bow   1,800/2,400
$2,070   £1,346

BAZIN, CHARLES (II) [S1114/114] Silver Violin
Bow: Mirecourt, mid 20th C.   572/858 NS

BAZIN, CHARLES ALFRED [C11/78] Silver and
Ivory Violin Bow   1,430/2,145 NS

BAZIN, CHARLES ALFRED [S7/108] Silver Violin
Bow: Mirecourt, c. 1950   906/1,208
$1,540   £1,020

BAZIN, CHARLES NICHOLAS [C5/55] Good Silver
and Tortoiseshell Violin Bow   2,200/2,400
$2,820   £1,833

BAZIN, CHARLES NICHOLAS [P9/142] Nickel
Violin Bow: c. 1880 (J.F. Raffin, Paris, November 30,
1999)   846/987
$1,946   £1,380

BAZIN, CHARLES NICHOLAS (workshop of)
[C5/226] Silver Violin Bow with later adjuster
                                   600/800
$2,233   £1,451

BAZIN, LOUIS [C3/74] Nickel Violin Bow without
hair and wrap   942/1,256
$722   £460

BAZIN, LOUIS [C5/204] Silver Violin Bow (Jean-
François Raffin, Paris, December 11, 1992)
                                   2,500/3,500
$3,525   £2,291

BAZIN, LOUIS [C3/126] Gold Violin Bow with later
frog, without hair and wrap   1,570/1,884 NS

BAZIN, LOUIS [P3/153] Nickel Violin Bow with full
hair: c. 1940 (Jean-François Raffin, August 3, 1998)
                                   1,422/1,896
$1,454   £920

BAZIN, LOUIS [Sk5/61] Silver Violin Bow
                                   3,000/5,000
$3,220   £2,093

BAZIN, LOUIS [Sk5/153] Silver Violin Bow
                                   2,000/2,400
$2,185   £1,420

BAZIN, LOUIS [Sk5/173] Silver Violin Bow
1,800/2,000
$2,875   £1,869

BAZIN, LOUIS (II) [S1114/93] Silver Violin Bow:
Mirecourt, mid 20th C.   1,001/1,430 NS

BAZIN FAMILY (MEMBER OF) [S7/104] Silver
Violin Bow: Mirecourt, c. 1920   1,057/1,510 NS

BERNARDEL, LEON [S3/151] Silver Violin Bow:
Paris, c. 1920   942/1,256
$1,353   £862

BETTS, JOHN (ascribed to) [P11/176] Elegant Old
English Violin Bow with full hair: London, c. 1800
2,860/3,575 NS

BISHOP, EDGAR [B5/78] Fine Silver Violin Bow
1,800/2,250
$2,070   £1,380

BLONDELET, H. EMILE [S1114/87] Silver Violin
Bow: probably Mirecourt, early 20th C.   572/858 NS

BRYANT, P.W. [P11/146] Good Silver Violin Bow
with full hair: c. 1940   1,430/2,145
$1,316   £920

BULTITUDE, ARTHUR RICHARD [B7/19] Gold
and Tortoiseshell Violin Bow w/double bow case:
1953   1,800/2,250
$2,933   £1,955

BULTITUDE, ARTHUR RICHARD [S7/98] Chased
Gold and Tortoiseshell Violin Bow: Hawkhurst, 1968
2,265/3,020
$3,624   £2,400

BULTITUDE, ARTHUR RICHARD [S10/50] Gold
Violin Bow: Hawkhurst, c. 1975   2,000/3,000 NS

BUTHOD, CHARLES [B9/89] Silver Violin Bow
876/1,460 NS

CARESSA & FRANCAIS [S3/169] Silver Violin Bow:
Paris, c. 1925   1,256/1,884
$2,167   £1,380

CHANOT, G.A. [B9/81] Good Silver Violin Bow
1,168/1,752 NS

COLAS, PROSPER [C5/51] Silver Violin Bow with
tinsel wrap   1,400/1,600
$1,880   £1,222

COLAS, PROSPER [S7/260] Nickel Violin Bow:
Paris, c. 1910   604/906
$1,631   £1,080

COLAS, PROSPER [S1114/217] Silver Violin Bow:
Paris, c. 1900 (William Lewis, Chicago, December 29,
1964)   2,574/3,575
$3,089   £2,160

COLLIN-MEZIN, CH.J.B. (II) [S7/240] Silver and
Ivory Violin Bow: Mirecourt, c. 1900   906/1,208 NS

CUNIOT-HURY [P9/132] Silver Violin Bow lacking
hair: c. 1900 (Jean-François Raffin, Paris, October
19, 1999)   987/1,128
$1,135   £805

CUNIOT-HURY, EUGENE [S7/117] Silver Violin
Bow: Mirecourt, c. 1900   755/1,057 NS

CUNIOT-HURY, EUGENE [S7/233] Silver Violin
Bow: Paris, c. 1900   755/1,057 NS

CUNIOT-HURY, EUGENE [S1114/74] Silver Violin
Bow: Mirecourt, c. 1900   858/1,144
$1,630   £1,140

DODD [B11/12] Silver Violin Bow with repairs to the
stick near the button   858/1,430
$822   £575

DODD [C3/73] English Silver Violin Bow
785/1,099 NS

DODD (attributed to) [P3/166] Silver Violin Bow
1,264/1,422
$2,362   £1,495

DODD, JAMES [C5/190] Gold Violin Bow (Kenneth
Warren & Son, Ltd., Chicago, January 11, 1979)
4,000/6,000
$6,463   £4,201

DODD, JAMES [Sk5/73] Silver Violin Bow with later
ivory frog   600/800
$863   £561

DODD, JOHN [C11/62] Silver Violin Bow (Edward
Withers, Ltd., London, March 20, 1996) 2,145/3,575
$3,697   £2,585

DODD, JOHN [C11/77] English Silver Violin Bow
2,145/2,860 NS

DODD, JOHN [S10/93] Silver and Ivory Violin Bow:
Kew, early 19th C. (Kagan & Gaines Co., Chicago,
June 6, 1963)   2,500/3,500
$3,300   £2,277

DODD, JOHN [S10/99] Silver Violin Bow: Kew,
early 19th C.   2,000/2,500 NS

DODD, JOHN [S7/118] Ebony Violin Bow with
repaired stick: London, early 19th C.   755/1,057
$725   £480

DODD, JOHN KEW [Sk5/70] Gold Violin Bow without hair   1,000/1,200
$2,645   £1,719

DODD, THOMAS [S10/102] Silver Violin Bow:
London, c. 1810–20   2,000/3,000
$2,400   £1,656

DODD FAMILY (MEMBER OF) [C5/198] Silver
Violin Bow   1,200/1,400
$1,998   £1,299

DOLLING, KURT [C3/128] German Violin Bow
471/785 NS

DOLLING, KURT [S7/245] Silver Violin Bow:
Erlbach, mid 20th C.   604/906 NS

DOLLING, HEINZ [S1114/71] Silver and
Tortoiseshell Violin Bow: Wertnitzgrün, mid 20th C.
715/1,001 NS

DOLLING, HEINZ [Sk11/109] Silver Violin Bow
500/700
$748   £523

DUCHAINE, NICHOLAS [B9/92] French Violin Bow 730/1,460 NS

DUCHENE, NICOLAS [B11/13] Violin Bow with damage to stick (Etienne Vatelot) 1,430/2,145
$1,480 £1,035

DUPREE, EMILE [B9/100] Silver Violin Bow 584/876 NS

ENEL, CHARLES [S7/227] Silver Violin Bow: Paris, second quarter 20th C. 1,510/2,265
$1,631 £1,080

ENEL, CHARLES [S1114/116] Silver Violin Bow 1,144/1,716
$1,287 £900

EURY, FRANCOIS [Sk11/155] French Silver Violin Bow (Jean-Christophe Graff, Strasbourg, April 22, 1977) 6,000/8,000 NS

EURY, NICOLAS [C5/52] Silver Violin Bow (Etienne Vatelot, Paris, September 11, 1995)10,000/15,000 NS

EURY, NICOLAS [C11/53] Silver Violin Bow (Etienne Vatelot, Paris, September 11, 1995) 6,435/9,295 NS

FETIQUE, JULES [B11/8] Silver Violin Bow (Jean-François Raffin) 5,720/8,580
$6,249 £4,370

FETIQUE, JULES [C3/69] Good Silver Violin Bow (Bernard Millant, Paris, March 7, 1999) 2,826/3,454
$5,778 £3,680

FETIQUE, MARCEL [S3/100] Silver and Ivory Violin Bow: Paris, c. 1930 5,495/7,065
$7,583 £4,830

FETIQUE, MARCEL [S1114/203] Silver Violin Bow: Paris, mid 20th C. 2,145/2,860
$3,775 £2,640

FETIQUE, VICTOR [C3/122] Good Silver Violin Bow 2,512/2,826
$3,611 £2,300

FETIQUE, VICTOR [C3/68] Silver Violin Bow without hair and wrap 3,140/3,925
$6,500 £4,140

FETIQUE, VICTOR [C5/189] Silver Violin Bow 4,500/6,500
$5,288 £3,437

FETIQUE, VICTOR [C11/65] Fine Silver Violin Bow (Jean-François Raffin, Paris, June 5, 2000) 3,575/4,290
$4,369 £3,055

FETIQUE, VICTOR [P11/142] Good Silver Violin Bow with full hair: Paris 1,430/2,145
$3,618 £2,530

FETIQUE, VICTOR [S7/231] Gold Violin Bow: Paris, c. 1920 7,550/10,570
$11,778 £7,800

FETIQUE, VICTOR [S7/238] Nickel Violin Bow with probably later frog and adjuster: Paris, c. 1920 1,510/2,265
$1,631 £1,080

FETIQUE, VICTOR [S7/74] Silver Violin Bow: Paris, c. 1920 3,020/4,530 NS

FETIQUE, VICTOR [S1114/77] Gold Violin Bow: Paris, c. 1920 5,720/8,580
$6,521 £4,560

FETIQUE, VICTOR [S1114/84] Silver Violin Bow: Paris, c. 1920 2,574/3,575 NS

FETIQUE, VICTOR [Sk5/64] Silver Violin Bow (Jean-François Raffin, Paris, April 6, 1995) 4,000/7,000
$4,600 £2,990

FETIQUE, VICTOR [Sk11/189] French Silver Violin Bow with head graft 600/800
$374 £262

FETIQUE, VICTOR (ascribed to) [S1114/94] Silver Violin Bow: Paris, early 20th C. (Jean-François Raffin, Paris, February 8, 2000) 2,145/3,575
$2,574 £1,800

FINKEL [B9/98] Silver Violin Bow 1,168/1,752
$1,259 £863

FINKEL (workshop of) [C5/207] Silver Violin Bow 600/800
$705 £458

FINKEL (workshop of) [C5/214] Silver Violin Bow 600/800
$823 £535

FINKEL, SIEGFRIED [S3/164] Silver Violin Bow: Brienz, mid 20th C. 1,099/1,570 NS

FINKEL, SIEGFRIED [S1114/184] Silver Violin Bow: Brienz, mid 20th C. 715/1,001
$772 £540

FRITSCH, JEAN [S7/121] Silver Violin Bow: Paris, c. 1940 755/1,057 NS

GAND, CHARLES NICOLAS EUGENE [S3/87] Silver Violin Bow: Paris, late 19th C. 942/1,256
$2,528 £1,610

GAULARD [B7/32] Bone Violin Bow 3,750/4,500 NS

GAULARD [Bf3/6218] Rare Ivory Violin Bow with later ivory adjuster (Harry Duffy, February 9, 1991) 2,000/3,000
$2,875 £1,840

GAUTIE, P. & SON [C3/77] Silver Violin Bow without hair, with original tinsel wrap (Jean-François Raffin, Paris, June 7, 1999) 3,454/4,082
$4,694 £2,990

GEROME, ROGER [S7/257] Silver Violin Bow: mid 20th C. 755/1,057 NS

GEROME, ROGER [S7/259] Silver and Tortoiseshell Violin Bow: mid 20th C. 1,057/1,510
$1,178 £780

GEROME, ROGER [S1114/92] Gold Violin Bow 1,001/1,430
$1,287 £900

GRAND ADAM [Sk5/59] Fine French Silver Violin Bow: c. 1850 (Bernard Millant, Paris, March 12, 1996) 18,000/20,000 NS

GRUNKE, RICHARD [Sk11/86] Silver Violin Bow
800/1,200
$1,150   £805

GRUNKE, RICHARD [Sk5/147] Gold Violin Bow
1,000/2,000
$2,185   £1,420

GRUNKE, RICHARD [Sk11/198] Silver Violin Bow
600/800
$1,150   £805

HART & SON [S3/75] Gold and Tortoiseshell Violin
Bow: London, c. 1910   2,198/2,826
$2,347   £1,495

HEL (workshop of) [S10/57] Silver Violin Bow: Lille,
late 19th C.   1,000/1,500
$1,680   £1,159

HERMANN, A. [B9/113] Silver Violin Bow lacking
hair   292/438
$269   £184

HILL, W.E. & SONS [Sk5/60] Silver Violin Bow
1,800/2,400
$2,300   £1,495

HILL, W.E. & SONS [Sk5/68] Silver Violin Bow
1,600/1,800
$2,185   £1,420

HILL, W.E. & SONS [Sk11/85] Silver Violin Bow:
c. 1944   1,000/1,200
$2,185   £1,530

HILL, W.E. & SONS [Sk11/91] Gold Violin Bow
with loss to adjuster and pearl slide, some repair
500/700
$1,035   £725

HILL, W.E. & SONS [Sk11/113] Silver Violin Bow
with partial hair and grip   1,000/1,500 NS

HILL, W.E. & SONS [Sk11/151] Silver Violin Bow
1,000/1,500
$2,300   £1,610

HILL, W.E. & SONS [Sk11/190] Silver Violin Bow
with head spline   600/800
$805   £564

HILL, W.E. & SONS [B7/17] Silver Violin Bow
1,800/2,250 NS

HILL, W.E. & SONS [B7/22] Silver Violin Bow
2,250/3,000 NS

HILL, W.E. & SONS [B7/31] Silver Violin Bow
1,500/2,250
$1,725   £1,150

HILL, W.E. & SONS [B9/111] Good Silver Violin
Bow   1,168/1,752
$1,679   £1,150

HILL, W.E. & SONS [B11/9] Silver and Tortoiseshell
Violin Bow with pinned head   1,144/1,716 NS

HILL, W.E. & SONS [B11/17] Silver Violin Bow
1,144/1,716 NS

HILL, W.E. & SONS [B11/24] Silver Violin Bow
1,430/2,145 NS

HILL, W.E. & SONS [B11/32] Gold and Tortoiseshell
Violin Bow   2,860/5,720
$3,618   £2,530

HILL, W.E. & SONS [B11/34] Silver Violin Bow
858/1,430
$1,398   £978

HILL, W.E. & SONS [B11/46] Silver Violin Bow
1,430/2,145 NS

HILL, W.E. & SONS [B11/48] Silver Violin Bow
1,430/2,145 NS

HILL, W.E. & SONS [B11/52] Silver Violin Bow
1,430/2,145 NS

HILL, W.E. & SONS [B11/57] Silver Violin Bow
1,430/2,145
$1,973   £1,380

HILL, W.E. & SONS [C3/49] Good Silver Violin Bow
partially haired without wrap   2,355/3,140
$4,333   £2,760

HILL, W.E. & SONS [C3/63] Silver Violin Bow
1,256/1,884
$2,889   £1,840

HILL, W.E. & SONS [C3/70] Gold Violin Bow
2,355/3,140
$7,222   £4,600

HILL, W.E. & SONS [C5/58] Silver and Tortoiseshell
Violin Bow   2,000/3,000
$4,113   £2,673

HILL, W.E. & SONS [C11/44] Tortoiseshell Violin
Bow   2,145/2,860 NS

HILL, W.E. & SONS [C11/56] Gold and Tortoiseshell Violin Bow   2,860/4,290
$6,721   £4,700

HILL, W.E. & SONS [C11/66] Silver Violin Bow with
original tinsel wrap and without hair   858/1,144
$1,427   £998

HILL, W.E. & SONS [C11/73] Gold and Ivory Violin
Bow   5,720/8,580
$10,082   £7,050

HILL, W.E. & SONS [P2/92] Silver Violin Bow with
almost full hair: London   1,590/2,385
$3,840   £2,415

HILL, W.E. & SONS [P2/101] Silver Violin Bow:
London   1,272/1,431
$2,286   £1,438

HILL, W.E. & SONS [P2/121] Good Silver Violin
Bow with full hair: London   954/1,113
$1,554   £978

HILL, W.E. & SONS [P2/142] Gold Violin Bow with
full hair, w/box: London   1,272/1,431
$3,108   £1,955

HILL, W.E. & SONS [P3/142] Silver Violin Bow with
full hair: London   1,264/1,422
$2,726   £1,725

HILL, W.E. & SONS [P3/145] Silver Violin Bow to
be rehaired: London   1,580/2,370
$2,544   £1,610

HILL, W.E. & SONS [P3/171] Silver Violin Bow with
full hair: London   948/1,106
$2,544   £1,610

HILL, W.E. & SONS [P6/192] Good Silver Violin
Bow: London   1,812/2,265
$2,431   £1,610

HILL, W.E. & SONS [P6/193] Good Silver Violin
Bow: London   1,208/1,510
$1,737   £1,150

HILL, W.E. & SONS [P6/207] Silver Violin Bow
without hair: London   1,057/1,208
$1,997   £1,323

HILL, W.E. & SONS [P9/125] Silver Violin Bow:
London   127/1,410 NS

HILL, W.E. & SONS [P11/154] Good Silver Violin
Bow with full hair: London   1,716/2,145
$2,302   £1,610

HILL, W.E. & SONS [P11/156] Good Silver Violin
Bow with full hair: London   2,145/2,860
$3,453   £2,415

HILL, W.E. & SONS [P11/157] Good Silver Violin
Bow without hair: London   1,144/1,287
$1,809   £1,265

HILL, W.E. & SONS [P11/160] Good Silver Violin
Bow with some hair: London   1,001/1,144
$2,796   £1,955

HILL, W.E. & SONS [P11/162] Good Silver Violin
Bow needing rehairing: London   2,145/2,574
$3,125   £2,185

HILL, W.E. & SONS [P11/163] Silver Violin Bow
with full hair: London   930/1,001
$1,316   £920

HILL, W.E. & SONS [P11/165] Silver Violin Bow
requiring rehairing: London   715/858
$1,316   £920

HILL, W.E. & SONS [P11/168] Silver Violin Bow
with full hair: London   1,001/1,287
$1,809   £1,265

HILL, W.E. & SONS [P11/169] Silver Violin Bow
requiring rehairing: London   858/1,001
$822   £575

HILL, W.E. & SONS [P11/179] Good Silver Violin
Bow with full hair: London   2,145/2,860
$2,467   £1,725

HILL, W.E. & SONS [P11/192] Gold Violin Bow
with full hair: London   1,716/2,145
$4,111   £2,875

HILL, W.E. & SONS [P11/196] Silver Violin Bow
with full hair: London   858/1,001
$987   £690

HILL, W.E. & SONS [P11/197] Silver Violin Bow
with some use and wear: London   1,001/1,144
$1,480   £1,035

HILL, W.E. & SONS [P11/198] Good Silver Violin
Bow with full hair: London   1,716/2,145
$3,453   £2,415

HILL, W.E. & SONS [P11/206] Good Silver Violin
Bow with full hair: London   1,001/1,144
$2,302   £1,610

HILL, W.E. & SONS [P11/217] Good gold Violin
Bow with full hair: London   2,860/3,575
$3,289   £2,300

HILL, W.E. & SONS [S3/79] Silver Violin Bow:
London, 1927   1,570/2,198
$1,986   £1,265

HILL, W.E. & SONS [S3/95] Gold and Tortoiseshell
"Fleur-de-Lys" Violin Bow: London, 1957
                3,140/4,710 NS

HILL, W.E. & SONS [S3/185] Gold and Tortoiseshell
"Fleur-de-Lys" Violin Bow: London, c. 1915
                3,925/5,495
$5,778   £3,680

HILL, W.E. & SONS [S7/99] Gold Violin Bow:
London, mid 20th C.   2,114/2,718
$3,443   £2,280

HILL, W.E. & SONS [S7/124] Silver Violin Bow with
minor damage to head: London, 1950   1,208/1,812
$2,174   £1,440

HILL, W.E. & SONS [S10/63] Silver and Tortoiseshell "Fleur-de-Lys" Violin Bow w/bow box: London,
1959   3,000/4,000
$3,600   £2,484

HILL, W.E. & SONS [S10/72] Silver and Tortoiseshell Violin Bow: London, 1934   500/700
$2,700   £1,863

HILL, W.E. & SONS [S10/74] Gold and Tortoiseshell
"Fleur-de-Lys" Violin Bow w/bow box: London,
1969   3,000/5,000
$6,000   £4,140

HILL, W.E. & SONS [S10/87] Silver and Tortoiseshell Violin Bow: London, c. 1920   3,000/5,000
$3,600   £2,484

HILL, W.E. & SONS [S10/101] Silver Violin Bow:
London, 1934   2,000/2,500 NS

HILL, W.E. & SONS [S10/104] Silver and Tortoiseshell Violin Bow: London, c. 1920 (Wm. Lewis &
Son, Chicago, December 3, 1965)   3,000/4,000
$5,700   £3,933

HILL, W.E. & SONS [S1114/68] Gold Violin Bow:
London, 1920   2,145/2,860
$2,917   £2,040

HILL, W.E. & SONS [S1114/78] Gold and Tortoiseshell "Fleur-de-Lys" Violin Bow: London, 1964
                3,575/4,290
$5,834   £4,080

HILL, W.E. & SONS [S1114/95] Silver and Tortoiseshell Violin Bow: London, c. 1940   2,145/2,860
$3,775   £2,640

HILL, W.E. & SONS [S1114/100] Silver Violin Bow: London, 1927   1,430/2,145
$1,544   £1,080

HILL, W.E. & SONS [S1114/105] Chased Silver and Tortoiseshell "Silver Jubilee" Violin Bow w/case: London, 1977   2,145/2,860
$3,260   £2,280

HILL, W.E. & SONS [S1114/180] Gold Violin Bow: London, c. 1910   858/1,144 NS

HILL, W.E. & SONS [S1114/193] Chased Gold Violin Bow: London, c. 1895   3,575/5,005 NS

HILL, W.E. & SONS [S1114/201] Gold and Tortoiseshell "Fleur-de-Lys" Violin Bow: London, 1934   3,575/5,005
$4,462   £3,120

HILL, W.E. & SONS [S1114/213] Silver Violin Bow: London, 1928   572/858
$1,630   £1,140

HOYER, C.A. [S7/254] Silver Violin Bow: Markneukirchen   604/906 NS

HOYER, OTTO [C5/199] Silver Violin Bow 700/900
$940   £611

HOYER, OTTO [C5/221] Silver Violin Bow without hair   400/600
$646   £420

HOYER, OTTO [C11/128] Silver Violin Bow   715/858
$1,008   £705

HOYER, OTTO [Sk11/120] Silver Violin Bow with repair   300/500
$173   £121

HOYER, OTTO A. [B9/107] Silver Violin Bow   730/1,022 NS

HOYER, OTTO A. [S10/49] Gold Violin Bow: Markneukirchen, mid 20th C.   1,000/1,500
$1,200   £828

HOYER, OTTO A. [S3/76] Gold "Picture" Violin Bow: Markneukirchen, 1928   942/1,256
$2,889   £1,840

HOYER, OTTO A. [Sk5/107] Silver Violin Bow   600/800
$1,265   £822

HOYER, OTTO A. [Sk11/210] Silver Violin Bow   600/800
$575   £403

HURY, CUNIOT [B2/52] Nickel Violin Bow 480/800
$773   £483

HUSSON, CHARLES [C3/55] Silver Violin Bow   1,570/2,355
$1,986   £1,265

JOMBAR, P. [B9/104] Silver Violin Bow   730/1,022
$806   £552

JOMBAR, PAUL [B11/23] Nickel Violin Bow: Paris   858/1,430
$1,562   £1,093

JOMBAR, PAUL [C3/120] Silver Violin Bow without hair or wrap   1,256/1,884
$2,347   £1,495

JOMBAR, PAUL [S7/81] Silver Violin Bow: Paris, early 20th C.   1,510/2,265
$1,721   £1,140

KITTEL, NICOLAUS (ascribed to) [S10/75] Gold and Tortoiseshell Violin Bow: St. Petersberg, mid 19th C. (Wm. Lewis & Son, Chicago, December 4, 1968)   15,000/25,000 NS

KNOPF, CHRISTIAN WILHELM [C5/61] Fine German Violin Bow: c. 1820   3,200/3,800
$6,463   £4,201

KNOPF, H.R. [B9/86] Fine Silver Violin Bow   1,460/2,190 NS

LABERTE [P2/140] Nickel Violin Bow lacking hair (Jean-François Raffin, Paris, June 7, 1999)   477/557
$549   £345

LABERTE (attributed to) [C3/58] Nickel Violin Bow without hair (Jean-François Raffin, Paris, June 11, 1998)   471/628 NS

LABERTE, MARC [P6/228] Silver Violin Bow   906/1,057 NS

LABERTE, MARC [C3/57] Silver Violin Bow (Jean-François Raffin, Paris, December 11, 1998)   1,256/1,884
$2,528   £1,610

LABERTE, MARC [Sk5/154] Silver Violin Bow (Jean François Raffin, Paris, August 3, 1998) 1,200/1,400
$1,265   £822

LAFLEUR, JOSEPH RENE (attributed to) [C5/59] Gold Violin Bow (Lyon & Healy, Chicago, August 8, 1950)   6,000/8,000 NS

LAMY, A. [C3/54] Silver Violin Bow without hair, with original tinsel wrap (Jean-François Raffin, Paris, December 11, 1998)   3,140/4,710
$5,778   £3,680

LAMY, A. [P11/171] Good Silver Violin Bow without hair: Paris   4,290/5,005 NS

LAMY, A. [P11/178] Good Silver Violin Bow with full hair: Paris (Etienne Vatelot, Paris, June 14, 1996)   5,005/5,720

LAMY, A. [P11/216] Silver Violin Bow with full hair: Paris   4,290/5,005
$4,934   £3,450

LAMY, A. (ascribed to) [C11/70] Nickel Violin Bow (Jean-François Raffin, Paris, June 6, 2000)   1,144/1,716
$1,175   £822

LAMY, A.J. [C11/75] Nickel Violin Bow unhaired with pearl slide missing from ebony frog (Jean-François Raffin, Paris, June 5, 2000) 2,574/3,146 NS

LAMY, ALFRED [B11/11] Silver Violin Bow with worn stamp (Jean-François Raffin)   4,290/5,720
$6,907   £4,830

LAMY, ALFRED [Bf3/6217] Good Silver Violin Bow
with later ebony adjuster (Kenneth Warren & Son,
August 29, 1998) 4,000/6,000
4,025 £2,576

LAMY, ALFRED [C5/202] Silver Violin Bow
2,000/3,000
$5,875 £3,819

LAMY, ALFRED JOSEPH [S3/89] Silver Violin Bow:
Paris, c. 1890 4,710/6,280
$9,389 £5,980

LAMY, ALFRED JOSEPH [S3/161] Silver Violin
Bow: Paris, c. 1890 (Wm. Lewis & Son, Chicago,
November 18, 1959) 6,280/9,420
$13,541 £8,625

LAMY, ALFRED JOSEPH [S7/241] Silver Violin
Bow: Paris, c. 1900 6,040/9,060 NS

LAMY, ALFRED JOSEPH [Sk5/65] Silver Violin Bow
with possibly later frog 4,500/5,500 NS

LAMY, HIPPOLYTE CAMILLE [P9/114] Silver
Violin Bow lacking hair: Paris, c. 1920 (Jean-François
Raffin, Paris, May 16, 2000) 4,935/5,640 NS

LAMY, HIPPOLYTE CAMILLE [P11/180] Silver
Violin Bow without hair: Paris, c. 1920 (Jean-François Raffin, Paris, May 16, 2000) 4,290/5,005 NS

LAMY, JULES [C3/52] Good Silver Violin Bow
2,512/2,826
$3,069 £1,955

LANDON, CHRISTOPHE [C5/205] Gold and
Tortoiseshell Violin Bow 1,800/2,200
$3,525 £2,291

LAPIERRE [B11/6] Gold Violin Bow 1,001/1,573
$1,151 £805

LAPIERRE, MARCEL [Sk5/78] Silver Violin Bow
1,000/1,400
$1,495 £972

LAPIERRE, MARCEL [C5/195] Silver Violin Bow
1,400/1,600
$1,763 £1,146

LEE, JOHN NORWOOD [Bf3/6210] Silver Violin
Bow: Chicago, c. 1990 1,200/1,800
$978 £626

LEE, JOHN NORWOOD [S10/106] Gold Violin
Bow with inlaid yin-yang symbols: Chicago, late
20th C. 4,500/6,000 NS

LOTTE, FRANCOIS [C5/210] Silver Violin Bow
1,000/1,500
$1,116 £725

LOTTE, ROGER-FRANCOIS [P2/99] Silver Violin
Bow with full hair (Jean-François Raffin, Paris, June
14, 1998) 1,272/1,431
$1,463 £920

LOTTE, ROGER-FRANCOIS [P2/119] Nickel Violin
Bow with full hair (Jean-François Raffin, Paris, June
7, 1999) 795/954 NS

LUPOT, F. (attributed to) [B7/25] Fine Silver Violin
Bow with later button 4,500/7,500 NS

LUPOT, FRANCOIS [C5/185] Silver Violin Bow
(Phillipe Dupuy, Paris, September 19, 1989)
8,000/10,000 NS

LUPOT, FRANCOIS [C11/126] Good Silver Violin
Bow: c. 1825 (Jean-François Raffin, Paris, March 26,
2000) 4,290/5,720 NS

LUPOT, FRANCOIS [C11/155] Silver Violin Bow
(Phillip Dupuy, Paris, September 19, 1989)
5,720/8,580 NS

LUPOT, FRANCOIS (II) [S3/94] Silver Violin Bow
without hair: Paris, c. 1830 3,925/5,495
$10,833 £6,900

MACKENZIE, D.C. [C5/218] Silver Violin Bow
800/1,200
$705 £458

MACKENZIE, D.C. [C5/219] Silver Violin Bow
800/1,200
$940 £611

MAIRE, NICOLAS [S1114/91] Silver Violin Bow:
Paris, mid 19th C. 8,580/11,440 NS

MAIRE, NICOLAS (attributed to) [C5/113] Fine
Silver Violin Bow 14,000/16,000 NS

MALINE (attributed to) [P11/212] Good French
Silver Violin Bow with full hair 1,716/2,145
$3,947 £2,760

MALINE, GUILLAUME [S7/221] Silver Violin Bow:
Paris, mid 19th C. 3,775/5,285 NS

MALINE, GUILLAUME [S7/88] Silver Violin Bow
with possibly damaged stick: Paris, c. 1840
4,530/7,550 NS

MARCOLTE [B9/116] Silver Violin Bow (Jean-
François Raffin) 657/803 NS

MARISSAL, OLIVIER [S1114/178] Silver Violin
Bow: Lille, 20th C. 572/858
$858 £600

MARTIN, J. [C3/75] Nickel Violin Bow without hair,
wrap, or ivory tip 628/942
$758 £483

MARTIN, JEAN JOSEPH [S3/144] Nickel Converted
"Self-Rehairing" Violin Bow with later ebony frog:
Paris, late 19th C. 1,570/2,355
$2,167 £1,380

MATTHEWS, PHILIP [S3/162] Silver Violin Bow:
Kew, late 20th C. 942/1,256 NS

MATTHEWS, PHILIP [S3/182] Silver Violin Bow:
Kew, late 20th C. 707/1,021 NS

MILLANT, ROGER & MAX [S1114/65] Silver
Violin Bow: Paris 1,144/1,716
$1,373 £960

MOINEL & CHERPITEL [S3/142] Silver Violin
Bow: Paris, early 20th C. 628/942
$2,167 £1,380

MORIZOT, L. [B7/35] Silver Violin Bow
2,250/3,750 NS

MORIZOT, L. [B11/16] Silver Violin Bow 715/1,001
$740 £518

MORIZOT, L. [P11/208] French Silver Violin Bow
with full hair 1,144/1,287
$1,579 £1,104

MORIZOT, L. [P11/214] Good Gold Violin Bow
with almost full hair 2,860/3,575
$3,947 £2,760

MORIZOT, LOUIS [B7/11] Silver Violin Bow
1,500/2,250
$1,380 £920

MORIZOT, LOUIS [C11/58] Silver Violin Bow
(Jean-François Raffin, Paris, June 6, 2000)
1,430/2,145
$1,680 £1,175

MORIZOT, LOUIS [S7/261] Silver Violin Bow:
Mirecourt, c. 1930 1,510/2,265
$1,812 £1,200

MORIZOT, LOUIS [S10/88] Gold and Tortoiseshell
Violin Bow: Mirecourt, c. 1930 2,500/3,500
$5,700 £3,933

MORIZOT, LOUIS [Sk5/177] Silver Violin Bow:
c. 1925 (Jean-François Raffin, Paris, June 24, 1999)
3,500/5,000
$4,025 £2,616

MORIZOT, LOUIS [Sk5/62] Silver Violin Bow
2,000/2,500 NS

MORIZOT, LOUIS [Sk5/66] Silver Violin Bow
3,000/4,000 NS

MORIZOT, LOUIS (II) [S1114/69] Silver Violin Bow:
Mirecourt, 20th C. 1,001/1,430
$1,888 £1,320

MORIZOT, LOUIS (II) [S1114/170] Silver Violin
Bow: Mirecourt, mid 20th C. 858/1,144
$944 £660

MORIZOT (FRERES), LOUIS [P2/129] Nickel
Violin Bow with full hair (Jean-François Raffin, Paris,
June 14, 1998) 636/716
$731 £460

MORIZOT (FRERES), LOUIS [C11/147] Silver
Violin Bow (Jean-François Raffin, Paris, June 6,
2000) 2,145/2,860 NS

MORIZOT (FRERES), LOUIS [C11/54] Silver Violin
Bow (Jean François Raffin, Paris, June 5, 2000)
1,430/1,716 NS

MORIZOT FAMILY [C11/57] Silver Violin Bow
1,144/1,430 NS

MORTH [B7/29] Gold Violin Bow 1,500/2,250 NS

NAVEA-VERA, DANIEL [Bf3/6212] Fine Gold and
Ivory Violin Bow 1,500/2,250
$1,725 £1,104

NEUDORFER, RUDOLPH [S1114/86] Gold and
Blonde Tortoiseshell Violin Bow after Peccatte
1,430/2,145 NS

NEUDORFER, RUDOLPH [S1114/97] Silver Violin
Bow: mid 20th C. 715/1,001 NS

NEUDORFER, RUDOLPH [S1114/202] Gold Violin
Bow after Peccatte 1,144/1,430
$2,746 £1,920

NORRIS & BARNES [S7/263] Transitional Ivory
Violin Bow: London, c. 1770 755/1,057
$1,359 £900

NURNBERGER (workshop of) [Sk11/111] Gold
Violin Bow 600/800
$920 £644

NURNBERGER (workshop of) [Sk11/220] Silver
Violin Bow with repair 200/400
$144 £101

NURNBERGER, ALBERT [B7/4] Gold Violin Bow
2,250/3,000
$2,933 £1,955

NURNBERGER, ALBERT [B7/24] Silver Violin Bow
1,200/1,800
$1,380 £920

NURNBERGER, ALBERT [Bf3/6214A] Silver Violin
Bow 800/1,200
$1,840 £1,178

NURNBERGER, ALBERT [P11/108] Good Silver
Violin Bow with full hair 1,430/2,145
$1,480 £1,035

NURNBERGER, ALBERT [C5/50] Silver Violin Bow
without hair 800/1,200
$1,645 £1,069

NURNBERGER, ALBERT [C3/61] Silver Violin Bow
942/1,256
$903 £575

NURNBERGER, ALBERT [C5/213] Silver Violin
Bow 600/800
$2,585 £1,680

NURNBERGER, ALBERT [C11/74] Silver Violin
Bow 715/1,001
$924 £646

NURNBERGER, ALBERT [C11/131] Silver Violin
Bow 501/644
$1,344 £940

NURNBERGER, ALBERT [Sk5/101] Silver Violin
Bow 2,800/3,200 NS

NURNBERGER, ALBERT [Sk11/101] Silver Violin
Bow 600/800
$1,093 £765

NURNBERGER, ALBERT (workshop of) [Sk11/204]
Silver Violin Bow 600/800
$403 £282

NURNBERGER, FRANZ ALBERT (II) [S10/62]
Silver Violin Bow: Markneukirchen, c. 1895
600/1,000
$1,440 £994

NURNBERGER, KARL ALBERT [S7/80] Silver
Violin Bow: Markneukirchen, c. 1950 906/1,208
$1,087 £720

NURNBERGER, KARL ALBERT [S7/217] Silver Violin Bow: Markneukirchen 1,208/1,812 $1,450 £960

NURNBERGER, KARL ALBERT [S7/252] Silver Violin Bow: Markneukirchen, c. 1950 1,208/1,812 $1,450 £960

NURNBERGER, KARL ALBERT [S1114/73] Silver Violin Bow: Markneukirchen, mid 20th C. 1,144/1,716 $2,574 £1,800

OUCHARD, E. [B7/33] Silver Violin Bow without hair 3,000/4,500 NS

OUCHARD, EMILE [B7/9] Nickel Violin Bow 900/1,200 NS

OUCHARD, EMILE [B7/12] Silver Violin Bow 1,500/2,250 NS

OUCHARD, EMILE [B11/18] Nickel Violin Bow 572/858 $904 £633

OUCHARD, EMILE [B11/21] Silver Violin Bow 858/1,144 $987 £690

OUCHARD, EMILE [C3/48] Silver Violin Bow without hair 3,140/3,925 NS

OUCHARD, EMILE [C3/64] Silver Violin Bow 2,198/2,512 NS

OUCHARD, EMILE A. [B11/5] Silver and Ivory Violin Bow 4,290/6,435 NS

OUCHARD, EMILE A. [S3/157] Silver and Ivory Violin Bow: Paris, c. 1940 4,710/6,280 NS

OUCHARD, EMILE A. [S1114/76] Silver Violin Bow: Paris, c. 1940 (Etienne Vatelot, Paris, March 8, 1989) 2,860/4,290 $5,491 £3,840

OUCHARD, EMILE FRANCOIS [S3/148] Silver Violin Bow: Mirecourt, c. 1940 (Jean-François Raffin, Paris, October 10, 1998) 942/1,256 $2,708 £1,725

OUCHARD, EMILE FRANCOIS [S7/262] Silver Violin Bow: Mirecourt, c. 1930 2,265/3,020 $2,718 £1,800

OUCHARD, EMILE FRANCOIS [S1114/214] Silver Violin Bow: Mirecourt, early 20th C. 1,716/2,288 $1,888 £1,320

OUCHARD, EMILE FRANCOIS [S1114/66] Silver Violin Bow: Mirecourt, early 20th C. (Etienne Vatelot, Paris, November 4, 1997) 2,145/2,860 $4,462 £3,120

PAESOLD, RODERICH [S7/224] Silver Violin Bow: Bad Brambach, mid 20th C. 604/906 NS

PAJEOT, E. [B7/18] Silver Violin Bow (J. Roda, 1966) 3,000/4,500 $4,830 £3,220

PAJEOT, ETIENNE [C5/77] Silver Violin Bow (Bein & Fushi, Chicago, January 8, 1997) 18,000/22,000 $18,800 £12,220

PAJEOT, ETIENNE [S10/92] Silver and Ivory Violin Bow: Paris, c. 1830 8,000/12,000 $19,150 £13,213

PAJEOT, ETIENNE [S1114/219] Silver Violin Bow: Paris, c. 1840 10,010/14,300 $10,296 £7,200

PAJEOT-MAIRE [S1114/179] Nickel Violin Bow: Paris, mid 19th C. (Bernard Millant, Paris, March 26, 1999) 2,860/4,290 $4,462 £3,120

PAJEOT FAMILY, MEMBER OF [C11/68] Good French Silver Violin or Viola Bow 3,575/5,005 NS

PANORMO [B9/95] Silver Violin Bow 876/1,460 NS

PANORMO, LOUIS [Sk5/83] Silver Violin Bow 2,500/4,000 NS

PANORMO, LOUIS [P11/183] English Silver Violin Bow with stick lengthened by a few millimeters 2,145/2,574 NS

PECCATTE, CHARLES [B7/20] Silver Violin Bow 4,500/7,500 $4,313 £2,875

PECCATTE, CHARLES [C5/78] Good Silver Violin Bow 6,000/8,000 $8,813 £5,728

PECCATTE, DOMINIQUE [S3/98] Silver Violin Bow: Paris, c. 1850 (Benjamin Koodlach, Port Hueneme, November 20, 1973) 23,550/31,400 $41,527 £26,450

PECCATTE, DOMINIQUE [S10/65] Gold and Tortoiseshell Violin Bow: Paris, mid 19th C. (Wm. Lewis & Son, Chicago, August 28, 1969) 40,000/60,000 $41,000 £28,290

PECCATTE, DOMINIQUE [Sk5/119] Fine French Silver Violin Bow (Wm. Lewis & Son, Chicago, September 6, 1956) 24,000/28,000 $23,000 £14,950

PECCATTE FAMILY (MEMBER OF) [C5/75] Silver Violin Bow 8,000/12,000 NS

PECCATTE FAMILY (MEMBER OF) [S3/86] Silver Violin Bow with possibly later ebony frog: Paris, c. 1850 9,420/12,560 $21,666 £13,800

PECCATTE FAMILY (MEMBER OF) [C11/45] Good Silver Violin Bow 14,300/21,450 NS

PENZEL, E. [C11/261] Silver Violin Bow 286/358 $436 £305

PENZEL, GERHARD [Sk5/166] Silver Violin Bow 600/800 $518 £336

PENZEL, K. GERHARD [S7/97] Gold and Tortoiseshell Violin Bow: Germany, mid 20th C. 604/906 $870 £576

PERSOIS [S3/97] Silver Violin Bow: Paris, c. 1840
15,700/23,550 $34,305   £21,850

PERSOIS, JEAN (attributed to) [S1114/89] Silver
Violin Bow: Paris, mid 19th C.   4,290/7,150
$4,805   £3,360

PFRETZSCHNER [B9/97] Nickel Violin Bow
730/1,022
$756   £518

PFRETZSCHNER [B9/106] Silver Violin Bow
438/730
$470   £322

PFRETZSCHNER (workshop of) [Sk11/96] Gold
Violin Bow   1,000/2,000
$1,150   £805

PFRETZSCHNER, E.R. [Sk5/148] Gold Violin Bow
800/1,200
$1,035   £673

PFRETZSCHNER, H.R. [B2/40] Silver Violin Bow
800/1,120
$846   £529

PFRETZSCHNER, H.R. [B7/15] Silver Violin Bow
900/1,500
$1,035   £690

PFRETZSCHNER, H.R. [C5/208] Silver and
Tortoiseshell Violin Bow without hair   800/1,200
$2,350   £1,528

PFRETZSCHNER, H.R. [S3/88] Silver Violin Bow:
Markneukirchen, c. 1960   942/1,256 NS

PFRETZSCHNER, H.R. [S7/77] Silver Violin Bow:
Markneukirchen, 20th C.   755/1,057
$815   £540

PFRETZSCHNER, H.R. [S7/92] Nickel Violin Bow
w/3 bows: Markneukirchen, 20th C.   1,208/1,812 NS

PFRETZSCHNER, H.R. [S7/112] Silver Violin Bow
w/viola bow: Markneukirchen, mid 20th C.
1,057/1,510
$1,450   £960

PFRETZSCHNER, H.R. [S1114/106] Nickel Violin
Bow with 3 nickel bows   572/858
$601   £420

PFRETZSCHNER, H.R. [Sk11/185] Silver Violin
Bow with repair   300/500
$259   £181

PFRETZSCHNER, L. [B7/23] Silver Violin Bow
900/1,200
$1,208   £805

PFRETZSCHNER, W. [B2/49] Silver Violin Bow with
later nickel button   400/560
$442   £276

PFRETZSCHNER, WILHELM AUGUST [S3/168]
Silver Violin Bow: Markneukirchen, c. 1920   628/942
$1,353   £862

PILLOT [B2/41] Silver Violin Bow without hair
640/960
$736   £460

POIRSON [B7/10] Silver Violin Bow without hair
1,500/2,250 NS

POIRSON, JUSTIN [Bf3/6211] Silver Violin Bow
(Emilio Slaviero, November 10, 1993)   2,000/3,000
$2,588   £1,656

POIRSON, JUSTIN [S3/179] Silver Violin Bow: Paris,
c. 1900   1,256/1,884
$3,430   £2,185

PRAGER, GUSTAV [C11/129] Silver Violin Bow
286/429
$588   £411

PRAGER, GUSTAV [C11/275] Silver Violin Bow partially haired with original tinsel wrap   286/429
$538   £376

PRELL, HERMAN WILHELM [B7/13] Nickel Violin
Bow without hair   450/750
$380   £253

RAU [B9/108] Nickel Violin Bow   292/438 NS

RAU, AUGUST [C5/60] Gold and Tortoiseshell
Violin Bow without hair   1,000/1,500
$2,233   £1,451

RAU, AUGUST [C11/263] Silver Violin Bow
572/715 NS

RAU, AUGUST [S7/82] Nickel Violin Bow with later
adjuster, damaged stick, w/bow: Markneukirchen,
early 20th C.   604/906 NS

RAU, AUGUST [S7/251] Silver Violin Bow:
Markneukirchen   755/1,057 NS

RETFORD, WILLIAM [C11/150] Silver Violin Bow
1,716/2,002 NS

RICHAUME [B11/19] Silver Violin Bow
1,716/2,145 NS

ROTH, ERNST HEINRICH [Sk11/222] Silver Violin
Bow   300/400
$201   £141

SARTORY, E. [B7/37] Silver Violin Bow: Paris, 1920
6,000/9,000
$6,210   £4,140

SARTORY, E. [B11/31] Very Fine Silver Violin Bow:
Paris, c. 1900   8,580/14,300
$10,689   £7,475

SARTORY, E. [P2/106] Silver Violin Bow with full
hair: Paris   1,272/1,431
$9,143   £5,750

SARTORY, E. [P6/198] Silver Violin Bow: Paris
(Heinrich Bose, December 10, 1962)   7,550/9,060 NS

SARTORY, E. [P11/147] Silver Violin Bow without
lapping: Paris   4,290/5,005
$10,196   £7,130

SARTORY, E. [P11/173] Good Silver Violin Bow
with full hair: Paris   6,435/7,150
$10,689   £7,475

SARTORY, E. [P11/215] Good Silver Violin Bow
with full hair: Paris   5,720/7,150
$7,565   £5,290

SARTORY, EUGENE [Bf3/6216] Fine Silver Violin Bow   7,000/10,000
$6,325   £4,048

SARTORY, EUGENE [C3/46] Violin Bow with partial hair and original tinsel wrap   5,495/7,065
$12,639   £8,050

SARTORY, EUGENE [C11/43] Silver Violin Bow   6,864/7,436
$7,729   £5,405

SARTORY, EUGENE [C11/71] Silver Violin Bow   5,720/7,150
$6,721   £4,700

SARTORY, EUGENE [S3/80] Silver Violin Bow: Paris, c. 1895   3,140/4,710
$6,319   £4,025

SARTORY, EUGENE [S3/83] Silver Violin Bow with possibly later adjuster: Paris, c. 1910   6,280/9,420
$6,861   £4,370

SARTORY, EUGENE [S3/84] Silver Violin Bow: Paris, c. 1920   7,850/10,990
$11,736   £7,475

SARTORY, EUGENE [S3/143] Silver Violin Bow without hair and with original lapping: Paris, c. 1905   6,280/9,420
$9,930   £6,325

SARTORY, EUGENE [S3/160] Silver Violin Bow: Paris, c. 1930 (Wm. Lewis & Son, Lincolnwood, July 19, 1962)   9,420/12,560
$11,736   £7,475

SARTORY, EUGENE [S3/170] Silver Violin Bow: Paris, c. 1920 (Wm. Lewis & Son, Chicago, April 16, 1962)   9,420/12,560
$11,736   £7,475

SARTORY, EUGENE [S3/172] Silver Violin Bow: Paris, c. 1930   5,966/7,065
$9,028   £5,750

SARTORY, EUGENE [S3/183] Silver Violin Bow: Paris, c. 1900   7,850/10,990 NS

SARTORY, EUGENE [S3/186] Silver Violin Bow: Paris, c. 1895   7,850/10,990 NS

SARTORY, EUGENE [S7/91] Silver Violin Bow: Paris, c. 1910   5,738/6,795
$6,886   £4,560

SARTORY, EUGENE [S7/242] Silver Violin Bow: Paris, c. 1910   4,530/6,040
$8,154   £5,400

SARTORY, EUGENE [S10/60] Silver Violin Bow: Paris, c. 1920   7,000/10,000
$8,400   £5,796

SARTORY, EUGENE [S10/94] Silver Violin Bow: Paris, c. 1910   7,000/10,000
$8,400   £5,796

SARTORY, EUGENE [S1114/63] Silver Violin Bow: Paris, c. 1900 (Jean-François Raffin, Paris, December 4, 1999)   5,720/8,580
$11,154   £7,800

SARTORY, EUGENE [S1114/75] Silver Violin Bow: Paris, c. 1900 (Bernard Millant, Paris, June 29, 1994)   7,150/10,010
$15,444   £10,800

SARTORY, EUGENE [S1114/83] Silver Violin Bow: Paris, c. 1910   1,716/2,288 NS

SARTORY, EUGENE [S1114/88] Silver Violin Bow: Paris, c. 1920   5,720/8,580
$7,722   £5,400

SARTORY, EUGENE [S1114/168] Silver Violin Bow: Paris, c. 1905   5,005/7,150
$5,148   £3,600

SARTORY, EUGENE [S1114/191] Gold and Tortoiseshell Violin Bow: Paris, c. 1930   11,440/17,160 NS

SARTORY, EUGENE [Sk5/67] Silver Violin Bow   9,000/11,000
$10,350   £6,728

SARTORY, EUGENE [Sk5/88] Silver Violin Bow   6,500/8,500 NS

SARTORY, EUGENE [Sk5/92] Fine Gold Violin Bow   12,000/14,000
$19,550   £12,708

SARTORY, EUGENE [Sk5/98] Silver Violin Bow with later head   600/800
$863   £561

SARTORY, EUGENE [Sk5/105] Silver Violin Bow   4,000/6,000
$4,715   £3,065

SARTORY, EUGENE [Sk5/149] Silver Violin Bow: c. 1910   11,000/12,000 NS

SARTORY, EUGENE [Sk5/172] Silver Violin Bow   6,000/8,000
$8,050   £5,233

SARTORY, EUGENE [Sk11/87] French Silver Violin Bow   6,000/8,000
$6,900   £4,830

SARTORY, EUGENE [Sk11/97] French Silver Violin Bow without hair   9,000/11,000
$10,350   £7,245

SARTORY, EUGENE [Sk11/100] French Silver Violin Bow   10,000/12,000
$12,075   £8,453

SARTORY, EUGENE [Sk11/144] Silver Violin Bow: c. 1930   8,000/10,000
$6,900   £4,830

SCHINDLER, GUSTAV [Sk11/181] Silver Violin Bow   800/1,200
$863   £604

SCHUSTER, ADOLF [C11/55] Silver Violin Bow   644/787
$924   £646

SCHUSTER, ADOLF [C11/127] Silver Violin Bow   572/715
$839   £587

SCHUSTER, ADOLF C. [C11/67] Gold Violin Bow
1,430/2,145
$1,848   £1,292

SCHUSTER, ALBERT [Sk5/89] Silver Violin Bow
with partial hair   200/300
$489   £318

SCHUSTER, GOTHARD [C11/130] Silver Violin
Bow   1,001/1,287 NS

SCHUSTER, M.K. [Sk11/108] Silver Violin Bow
without hair   300/500 NS

SCHUSTER, W.R. [B7/27] Silver Violin Bow 450/750
$431   £288

SEIFERT, LOTHAR [S3/93] Gold and Ivory Violin
Bow   1,570/2,355
$1,625   £1,035

SEIFERT, LOTHAR [S7/113] Silver and Ivory Violin
Bow: Bubenreuth, mid 20th C.   604/906
$725   £480

SERDET, PAUL [S7/122] Silver Violin Bow: Paris,
c. 1920   1,510/2,265
$1,631   £1,080

SIMON, PAUL [B11/38] Very Fine Silver Violin Bow:
Paris, c. 1850   8,580/11,440
$13,978   £9,775

SIMON, PAUL [S3/159] Silver Violin Bow with damaged head: Paris, c. 1865 (Wm. Lewis & Son,
Chicago, December 3, 1965)   4,710/6,280
$5,055   £3,220

SIMON, PIERRE [S7/230] Gold and Tortoiseshell
Violin Bow: Paris, c. 1860   6,040/9,060
$23,330   £15,450

SIMON, PIERRE [S10/64] Gold and Tortoiseshell
Violin Bow: Paris, c. 1845 (Wm. Lewis & Son,
Chicago, May 3, 1967)   12,000/16,000
$38,125   £26,306

SIMON, PIERRE [S10/77] Gold and Tortoiseshell
Violin Bow with possibly later adjuster: Paris, c. 1845
(Wm. Lewis & Son, Chicago, February 25, 1963)
12,000/16,000
$13,200   £9,108

SIMON, PIERRE [S10/105] Silver and Tortoiseshell
Violin Bow: Paris, c. 1860 (Wm. Lewis & Son,
Chicago, June 19, 1960)   10,000/15,000
$15,600   £10,764

THIBOUVILLE-LAMY, J. [B7/6] Silver Violin Bow
w/double bow case   1,050/1,500 NS

THIBOUVILLE-LAMY, J. [Sk11/94] French Silver
Violin Bow with baleen wrap (Jean-François Raffin,
Paris, April 12, 2000)   800/1,200
$633   £443

THOMA, A. [B9/85] Nickel Violin Bow   117/175
$151   £104

THOMA, ARTHUR [S7/128] Gold Violin Bow
w/bow: Brambach, c. 1940   755/1,057 NS

THOMASSIN, C. [B7/28] Silver Violin Bow
3,000/4,500
$3,105   £2,070

THOMASSIN, C. [C11/64] Silver Violin Bow
1,716/2,288
$2,016   £1,410

THOMASSIN, C. [P11/159] Good Silver Violin Bow
with full hair: Paris   1,716/2,145 NS

THOMASSIN, C. [P11/166] Good Silver Violin Bow
without hair: Paris   1,144/1,287
$1,069   £748

THOMASSIN, C. [P11/188] Silver Violin Bow with
full hair   1,430/1,716 NS

THOMASSIN, C. [P11/228] Useful Nickel Violin
Bow with almost full hair: Paris   572/715
$411   £288

THOMASSIN, CLAUDE [B9/101A] Fine Silver
Violin Bow   2,920/4,380
$2,519   £1,725

THOMASSIN, CLAUDE [C3/119] Silver Violin Bow
without hair and with tinsel wrap   1,884/2,512
$3,972   £2,530

THOMASSIN, CLAUDE [C3/123] Violin Bow
2,355/3,140 NS

THOMASSIN, CLAUDE [S7/95] Nickel Violin Bow:
Paris, c. 1920   906/1,208
$997   £660

THOMASSIN, CLAUDE [Sk11/92] French Silver
Violin Bow   4,000/6,000
$3,335   £2,335

THOMASSIN, CLAUDE (workshop of) [C5/56]
Nickel Silver Violin Bow   1,400/1,600 NS

TUBBS, EDWARD [Bf3/6213] Rare Silver and Horn
Violin Bow   2,000/3,000
$1,725   £1,104

TUBBS, JAMES [B11/14] Silver Violin Bow
2,860/3,575 NS

TUBBS, JAMES [B11/15] Silver Violin Bow
2,574/3,146 NS

TUBBS, JAMES [B11/22] Silver Violin Bow
2,574/3,575 NS

TUBBS, JAMES [B11/30] Gold Violin Bow
5,720/8,580
$5,756   £4,025

TUBBS, JAMES [B11/44] Silver Violin Bow
2,860/4,290 NS

TUBBS, JAMES [B11/50] Silver Violin Bow
3,575/5,005
$3,947   £2,760

TUBBS, JAMES [C3/47] Good English Violin Bow
3,140/4,710 NS

TUBBS, JAMES [C5/63] Silver Violin Bow
3,000/5,000
$4,113   £2,673

TUBBS, JAMES [C5/187] Silver Violin Bow
5,500/7,500
$7,050 £4,583

TUBBS, JAMES [C5/194] Silver Violin Bow
3,500/5,000
$7,050 £4,583

TUBBS, JAMES [C11/48] Fine Gold Violin Bow
8,580/10,010 NS

TUBBS, JAMES [P6/203] Silver Violin Bow
3,020/4,530
$3,473 £2,300

TUBBS, JAMES [P6/245] Violin Bow 604/755
$729 £483

TUBBS, JAMES [P11/143] Good Silver Violin Bow
with full hair: London 2,145/2,860
$2,631 £1,840

TUBBS, JAMES [P11/151] Good Silver Violin Bow
with some hair 2,145/2,860
$3,453 £2,415

TUBBS, JAMES [P11/152] Elegant Shorter Violin
Bow measuring 27 1/4 inches excluding button:
London 1,144/1,287 NS

TUBBS, JAMES [P11/170] Silver Violin Bow with full
hair: London 1,144/1,287
$2,467 £1,725

TUBBS, JAMES [P11/187] Good Silver Violin Bow
with full hair 1,716/2,145
$3,947 £2,760

TUBBS, JAMES [P11/193] Gold Violin Bow with full
hair: London 3,146/4,004 NS

TUBBS, JAMES [P11/195] Silver Violin Bow with full
hair 2,145/2,860
$2,960 £2,070

TUBBS, JAMES [P11/218] Silver Violin Bow with
later frog 1,144/1,430
$987 £690

TUBBS, JAMES [S3/96] Chased Gold Violin Bow:
London, c. 1890 (Wm. Lewis & Son, Lincolnwood,
March 31, 1970) 10,990/15,700 NS

TUBBS, JAMES [S3/173] Chased Gold and Tortoiseshell Violin Bow: London, c. 1875 9,420/12,560 NS

TUBBS, JAMES [S3/184] Silver Violin Bow: London,
c. 1900 3,140/4,710
$6,861 £4,370

TUBBS, JAMES [S7/70] Silver Violin Bow: London,
c. 1900 2,265/3,020
$2,537 £1,680

TUBBS, JAMES [S7/84] Gold Violin Bow: London,
c. 1880 4,530/7,550
$5,074 £3,360

TUBBS, JAMES [S10/66] Chased Gold Presentation
Violin Bow: London, c. 1885 (Rudoph Wurlitzer Co.,
New York, June 19, 1928) 15,000/20,000
$18,000 £12,420

TUBBS, JAMES [S1114/98] Silver Violin Bow:
London, c. 1910 2,860/4,290
$4,118 £2,880

TUBBS, JAMES [S1114/190] Silver Violin Bow:
London, c. 1910 (Wm. Lewis & Sons, Lincolnwood,
November 5, 1964) 2,860/4,290
$3,432 £2,400

TUBBS, JAMES [S1114/192] Chased gold and tortoiseshell Violin Bow: London, c. 1875 (Roland
Baumgartner, Basel, May 20, 1994) 5,720/8,580 NS

TUBBS, JAMES [S1114/194] Chased Gold Violin
Bow: London, c. 1890 (Wm. Lewis & Son,
Lincolnwood, March 31, 1970) 7,150/10,010 NS

TUBBS, JAMES [Sk5/176] Silver Violin Bow
3,000/4,000
$3,335 £2,168

TUBBS, JAMES [Sk11/106] Gold Violin Bow
6,000/8,000 NS

TUBBS, JAMES (attributed to) [P6/191] Silver Violin
Bow 1,208/1,359
$1,302 £863

TUBBS, WILLIAM [P11/235] Silver Violin Bow with
damaged frog and without hair: c. 1850 572/715
$1,579 £1,104

TUBBS, WILLIAM (attributed to) [P2/96] Silver
Violin Bow requiring rehairing 1,908/2,385
$2,926 £1,840

VAN DER MEER, KAREL [S1114/64] Silver Violin
Bow: Amsterdam, c. 1900 858/1,144
$1,459 £1,020

VIGNERON, A. [B7/5] Silver Violin Bow without
hair 2,700/3,750
$2,415 £1,610

VIGNERON, A. [C3/51] Silver Violin Bow with original tinsel wrap 3,140/3,925 NS

VIGNERON, A. [P11/155] Good Silver Violin Bow
with full hair: Paris 2,145/2,860
$5,262 £3,680

VIGNERON, A. [P11/213] Good Silver Violin Bow
with almost full hair: Paris 3,575/4,290
$4,934 £3,450

VIGNERON, ANDRE [S7/111] Silver Violin Bow
with later adjuster: Paris, c. 1910 1,510/2,114
$3,986 £2,640

VIGNERON, ANDRE [S10/47] Silver Violin Bow:
Paris, early 20th C. 2,500/3,500
$6,000 £4,140

VIGNERON, ANDRE [S10/96] Silver Violin Bow:
Paris, c. 1910 (Richard Oppelt, New York, July 1,
1986) 4,000/6,000
$5,700 £3,933

VIGNERON, JOSEPH ARTHUR [S7/123] Silver
Violin Bow with later frog and adjuster, minor damage to head: Paris, c. 1890 1,208/1,812
$1,359 £900

VIGNERON, JOSEPH ARTHUR [S7/253] Silver
Violin Bow: Paris, c. 1890   2,718/3,775
$4,711   £3,120

VOIRIN, F.N. [C3/50] Good French Violin Bow
(Jacques Français, New York)   5,495/7,065
$7,222   £4,600

VOIRIN, F.N. [C3/65] Silver Violin Bow
                                   2,826/3,454 NS

VOIRIN, F.N. [C5/203] Silver Violin Bow with later
adjuster   4,000/6,000
$5,288   £3,437

VOIRIN, F.N. [P11/175] Good Silver Violin Bow
with full hair: Paris   4,290/5,720 NS

VOIRIN, FRANCOIS NICOLAS [Bf3/6219] Fine
Silver Violin Bow   3,000/5,000
$3,450   £2,208

VOIRIN, FRANCOIS NICOLAS [P3/136] Good
Gold Violin Bow with full hair: Paris, c. 1880 (Bernard Millant, Paris, June 16, 1999)   7,900/9,480 NS

VOIRIN, FRANCOIS NICOLAS [P6/194] Good
Gold Violin Bow with later adjuster: Paris, c. 1880
(Bernard Millant, Paris, June 16, 1999)
                                   6,040/7,550 NS

VOIRIN, FRANCOIS NICOLAS [S3/85] Silver
Violin Bow: Paris, c. 1870   3,925/5,495 NS

VOIRIN, FRANCOIS NICOLAS [S3/102] Silver
Violin Bow: Paris, c. 1860 (J. & A. Beare, London,
July 15, 1952)   2,355/3,140 NS

VOIRIN, FRANCOIS NICOLAS [S3/166] Silver
Violin Bow: Paris, c. 1870   1,884/2,512
$3,250   £2,070

VOIRIN, FRANCOIS NICOLAS [S3/171] Silver
Violin Bow: Paris, c. 1875 (Benjamin Koodlach, Port
Hueneme, October 12, 1971)   6,280/9,420
$6,319   £4,025

VOIRIN, FRANCOIS NICOLAS [S7/90] Silver
Violin Bow with minor damage to handle: Paris,
c. 1870   4,530/7,550 NS

VOIRIN, FRANCOIS NICOLAS [S7/250] Silver
Violin Bow: Paris, c. 1870   2,718/3,775 NS

VOIRIN, FRANCOIS NICOLAS [S10/51] Silver
Violin Bow: Paris, c. 1870   1,200/1,600
$1,440   £994

VOIRIN, FRANCOIS NICOLAS [S10/76] Gold and
Tortoiseshell Violin Bow: Paris, c. 1880 (Wm.
Moennig & Son, Philadelphia, June 7, 1976)
                                   10,000/15,000
$12,000   £8,280

VOIRIN, FRANCOIS NICOLAS [S1114/57] Silver
Violin Bow: Paris, c. 1870   3,575/5,005
$7,722   £5,400

VOIRIN, FRANCOIS NICOLAS [S1114/101] Silver
Violin Bow: France, c. 1870   2,145/2,860 NS

VOIRIN, FRANCOIS NICOLAS [S1114/167] Silver
Violin Bow: Paris, c. 1870   2,574/3,575 NS

VOIRIN, FRANCOIS NICOLAS [S1114/209] Silver
Violin Bow: Paris, c. 1875   2,145/2,860 NS

VOIRIN, FRANCOIS NICOLAS [S1114/218] Silver
Violin Bow: Paris, c. 1870 (Wm. Lewis & Son,
Lincolnwood, July 19, 1962)   5,720/8,580
$12,870   £9,000

VOIRIN, FRANCOIS NICOLAS [Sk5/178] Silver
Violin Bow (William Salchow, New York, September
28, 1999)   5,000/7,000 NS

VOIRIN, FRANCOIS NICOLAS [Sk11/146] French
Silver Violin Bow (William Salchow, New York,
January 10, 1992)   1,500/2,500
$4,370   £3,059

VUILLAUME [B9/76] Nickel Violin Bow   146/219
$168   £115

VUILLAUME, JEAN BAPTISTE [B9/119] Good
Silver Violin Bow: c. 1860   2,190/2,920
$4,030   £2,760

VUILLAUME, JEAN BAPTISTE [C3/62] Silver Violin
Bow   3,140/3,925
$9,930   £6,325

VUILLAUME, JEAN BAPTISTE [Sk11/134] French
Silver Violin Bow   6,000/8,000
$5,750   £4,025

VUILLAUME, JEAN BAPTISTE [Sk11/147] French
Nickel Violin Bow converted from self-rehairing style
                                   2,000/3,000 NS

VUILLAUME, JEAN BAPTISTE (attributed to)
[P11/184] French Silver Violin Bow with full hair:
Paris, c. 1860   2,145/2,860 NS

VUILLAUME, NICOLAS (workshop of) [S3/165]
Silver Violin Bow: Mirecourt, second half 19th C.
                                   1,099/1,570
$1,264   £805

WATSON, WILLIAM [S7/65] Gold and Tortoiseshell
Violin Bow: London, c. 1965   2,265/3,020
$2,174   £1,440

WATSON, WILLIAM [S10/46] Gold Violin Bow:
London, second half 20th C.   1,500/2,000
$1,800   £1,242

WATSON, WILLIAM [S10/91] Gold and Tortoiseshell Violin Bow: London, late 20th C.   2,000/2,500
$3,000   £2,070

WEICHOLD, R. [C5/215] Silver Violin Bow 600/800
$2,585   £1,680

WEICHOLD, RICHARD [Sk5/76] Silver Violin Bow
                                   600/800
$863   £561

WEICHOLD, RICHARD [Sk5/151] Gold Violin Bow
                                   1,000/1,200
$978   £635

WERNER, EMIL [C3/129] German Silver Violin
Bow   471/785
$542   £345

WILSON, GARNER [S1114/110] Gold Violin Bow:
Bury, 1980   1,001/1,430
$1,287   £900

WINKLER, F. [B9/96] Nickel Violin Bow   584/876
$588   £403

WUNDERLICH [B9/112] Nickel Violin Bow 292/584
$302   £207

WUNDERLICH, FRIEDRICH [B5/81] Silver Violin
Bow   750/1,050 NS

WUNDERLICH, FRIEDRICH [B9/79] Silver Violin
Bow   365/511
$403   £276

ZAPF, H. WALTER [B9/80] Nickel Violin Bow
                                                 365/511 NS

ZAPF, H. WALTER [B5/83] Nickel Violin Bow
                                                 750/1,050 NS

VIOLONCELLO

AINE, DIDIER NICOLAS [S1114/122] Violoncello
w/case: Mirecourt, c. 1830   10,010/14,300 NS

ALBANI, MICHAEL [B11/74] Rare Violoncello with
lion's-head finial: Graz, 1723   11,440/17,160 NS

BAILLY, PAUL [B7/61] Violoncello: Mirecourt, 1883
                                   15,000/22,500 NS

BAILLY, PAUL [B11/86] Violoncello: Mirecourt,
1883   10,010/14,300 NS

BANKS, BENJAMIN [P6/262] Fine and Rare English
Violoncello with some restorations, w/case, bow:
Salisbury, 1779   45,300/52,850 NS

BARRETT, JOHN [B11/77] Good English
Violoncello: London   17,160/21,450 NS

BERNARDEL, LEON [Sk5/29] French Violoncello
w/case: Paris, 1918   14,000/16,000
$11,500   £7,475

BERNARDEL, LEON (workshop of) [S3/125]
Violoncello: Paris, c. 1935   3,140/4,710
$4,694   £2,990

BETTS [B11/73] Very Fine English Violoncello:
London, c. 1810   21,450/28,600 NS

BETTS (ascribed to) [P11/270] English Violoncello
with restorations, w/cover: c. 1790   1,001/1,144
$5,262   £3,680

BLONDELET, H. EMILE [S7/203] Violoncello
w/cover: Paris, 1924   6,040/9,060 NS

BLONDELET, H. EMILE [Sk5/26] French
Violoncello w/case: Mirecourt, 1912   6,000/8,000
$10,925   £7,101

BOURLIER, NICOLAS [S1114/119] Violoncello:
Mirecourt, mid 19th C.   4,290/7,150
$10,296   £7,200

CASINI, ANTONIO [C5/111] Italian Violoncello
w/case: Modena, 17th C. (Jacques Français, New
York)   140,000/190,000 NS

CASINI, SERAFINO [Sk11/55] Italian Violoncello
w/case: Florence, 1932 (Bein & Fushi, Chicago,
January 16, 1998)   18,000/25,000 NS

CATENI, PIETRO [S3/136] Violoncello w/case, bow:
Livorno, c. 1800 (Dario D'Attili, New Jersey,
November 16, 1994)   39,250/54,950 NS

CAVANI, GIOVANNI [Sk11/58] Good Italian
Violoncello w/case: Spilamberto, c. 1935
                                       16,000/18,000
$26,450   £18,515

CHANOT, FRANCOIS [P11/20] Rare Violoncello in
good condition, w/cover: 1818   2,145/3,575
$4,276   £2,990

COINUS, ANDRE [B7/69] French Violoncello:
Mirecourt, 1929   4,500/7,500 NS

COINUS, ANDRE [B11/90] French Violoncello:
Mirecourt, 1929   2,860/4,290
$2,960   £2,070

CRASKE, GEORGE [B7/71] Fine English Violoncello
                                       15,000/22,500
$20,700   £13,800

CUTHBERT, ROBERT [P3/187] English Violoncello
in immediate playing condition, w/case: c. 1700 (D.R.
Hill & Son, Great Missenden, February 2, 2000)
                                       6,320/7,900
$11,811   £7,475

CUYPERS, JOHANNES [P3/189] Rare Violoncello
with restorable blemishes   22,120/25,280 NS

CUYPERS, JOHANNES [P11/254] Rare Violoncello
with restorable blemishes   8,580/10,010
$9,538   £6,670

DEARLOVE [P6/272] Violoncello with some restorable blemishes: Leeds, c. 1850   1,510/2,265
$4,862   £3,220

DECONET, MICHAEL [B11/93] Highly Important
Violoncello traced back to 1809: Venice, 1769 (J. &
A. Beare)   NS

DE MARCH, CARLO [S3/127] Violoncello w/case:
Venice, 1956 (maker's, Venice, March 9, 1957)
                                       18,840/25,120
$23,472   £14,950

DIEUDONNE, A. (attributed to) [P3/192] Good
Mirecourt Violoncello with minor table restorations:
c. 1950   3,950/4,740 NS

DIEUDONNE, A. (attributed to) [P6/281] Good
Mirecourt Violoncello with minor table restorations:
c. 1950   2,718/3,322
$3,820   £2,530

DOLLING, HERMANN (JR.) [P11/250] Good
German Violoncello with minor restorable blemishes:
c. 1900   2,860/3,575
$3,289   £2,300

FICKER, GUSTAVE AUGUST [S10/134] Violoncello:
Germany, 1976   1,000/1,500
$1,200   £828

FIORI BROTHERS [B11/98] Italian Violoncello:
Modena, 1817   14,300/21,450 NS

FIORINI, PAOLO [S1114/118] Violoncello:
Mirecourt, 1937   3,575/5,005
$9,438   £6,600

FORSTER, WILLIAM [B11/81] Fine English
Violoncello: London, c. 1790   20,020/25,740 NS

FORSTER, WILLIAM [P11/240] Good English
Violoncello with minor restored blemishes, w/case:
London, 1795 (W.E. Hill & Sons, Havenfields, June
27, 1978)   17,160/21,450
$16,445   £11,500

FURBER, JOHN [S7/202] Violoncello w/cover:
London, 1813   4,530/7,550
$4,530   £3,000

GAGLIANO, JOSEPH [Sk5/28] Fine Neapolitan
Violoncello w/case: Naples, 1772 (Etienne Vatelot,
Paris, May 16, 1962)   185,000/225,000 NS

GAILLARD-LAJOUS, JULES [P6/289] Good French
Violoncello with some restored table blemishes:
Mirecourt, c. 1870 (Jean-Jacques Rampal, Paris, June
25, 1999)   10,570/12,080
$19,102   £12,650

GIBERTINI, ANTONIO [C5/137] Italian Violoncello
w/case: Genoa, 1850   25,000/35,000 NS

GRANCINO, GIOVANNI [B7/90] Very Fine and
Important Italian Violoncello: Milan, 1695 (W.E. Hill
& Son, London, May 23, 1957) 225,000/300,000 NS

GRANCINO, GIOVANNI [B11/100] "Ex-Lutyens"
Violoncello: Milan, 1695 (W.E. Hill & Son, London,
May 23, 1957)   NS

GROSSMANN, MAX [P6/268] Good German
Violoncello with old restored blemishes, w/cover:
Berlin, 1910   3,775/4,530
$4,341   £2,875

GUERRA, ALBERTO [C5/132] Good Modern Italian
Violoncello w/case: Modena, 1965 (Igor Moroder,
Verona, June 1995)   15,000/20,000 NS

GUERSAN, LOUIS (attributed to) [P11/268]
Attractive French Violoncello with restorations:
c. 1760   1,001/1,144
$4,276   £2,990

HAMMIG, WIHELM HERMAN [S7/193] Violoncello w/bow, cover: Leipzig, 1905   6,040/9,060
$10,872   £7,200

HARDIE, MATTHEW [P3/188] Fine and Handsome
and Rare Scottish Violoncello in good condition,
w/case, bow: Edinburgh, 1818   15,800/18,960
$18,170   £11,500

HARRIS, CHARLES (attributed to) [P11/244]
English Violoncello with signs of much use, w/cover:
c. 1790   4,290/5,720
$9,209   £6,440

HEINICKE, MATHIAS [P9/161] Good Violoncello in
immediate playing condition, w/cover: 1924
                                     6,345/7,755
$6,486   £4,600

HILL, HENRY LOCKEY [Sk5/32] English
Violoncello w/case: London, c. 1820 (Rembert
Wurlitzer, November 13, 1952)   20,000/25,000 NS

HILL, LOCKEY [B7/66] English Violoncello: c. 1780
                                     7,500/10,500 NS

HILL, LOCKEY [B11/99] English Violoncello:
London, c. 1780   5,720/8,580 NS

HILL, W.E. & SONS [P11/241] Good Violoncello in
good condition, w/case: London   7,150/8,580
$7,894   £5,520

HORNUNG, PASQUALE [Bf3/6226] Modern Italian
Violoncello: Cremona, 1989 (maker's, 1989)
                                     6,000/10,000
$4,600   £2,944

HULL, ROBERT [C11/95] Contemporary English
Violoncello w/case, bow: 1978   3,575/4,290 NS

JACQUEMIN, RENE [C3/85] French Violoncello
                                     3,140/4,710
$6,139   £3,910

JAY, HENRY (attributed to) [P3/185] English
Violoncello with restorable blemishes: London,
c. 1780   4,740/5,530
$7,268   £4,600

JOHNSON, JOHN [Sk5/27] English Violoncello
w/case: London, 1753   3,000/5,000
$10,350   £6,728

KENNEDY, THOMAS [P11/238] Good English
Violoncello with some old restorations, w/case:
London, 1847   17,160/22,880
$19,734   £13,800

KENNEDY, THOMAS [P11/239] Fine and
Handsome English Violoncello with restored table
blemishes, w/case, 2 bows: London   17,160/21,450
$19,734   £13,800

KLOTZ, JOSEPH [C11/92] Good Child's Violoncello
w/soft case: c. 1794   5,720/7,150 NS

KONYA (workshop of) [C5/136] Contemporary
Violoncello w/case (Lajos Konya, Hungary, 1993)
                                     3,000/4,000 NS

LABERTE [P2/172] Mirecourt Violoncello in immediate playing condition, w/case, bow: c. 1900
                                     4,452/5,088
$7,497   £4,715

LABERTE-HUMBERT BROS. [B7/88] Violoncello:
Mirecourt, 1933   3,000/4,500
$2,415   £1,610

LECHI, ANTONIO [P3/197] Good Violoncello with
minor restorable table blemishes   3,160/4,740
$3,634   £2,300

LECHI, ANTONIO (attributed to) [B7/67]
Interesting Violoncello   9,000/12,000
$6,900   £4,600

MARCHETTI, ENRICO [C11/84] Fine Modern
Italian Violoncello w/case: Turin, 1912
                                     50,050/64,350
$75,611   £52,875

MARSIGLIESE, BIAGIO [Bf3/6223] Good Modern
Italian Violoncello: Rome, 1957   10,000/15,000
$6,900   £4,416

MELLEGARI, ENRICO [B7/80] Very Fine and Rare
Italian Violoncello: Turin, 1880 (W.E. Hill & Sons,
London, October 24, 1941)   30,000/45,000
$31,050   £20,700

MENNESSON, EMILE [B7/86] French Violoncello:
Reims, 1906   10,500/15,000 NS

MENNESSON, EMILE [B11/87] French Violoncello:
Reims, 1906   7,150/10,010 NS

MILLANT, ROGER & MAX [S3/132] Violoncello
w/case: Paris, 1951 (Hug & Co., Zurich, January 21,
1978)   14,130/18,840 NS

MILLANT, ROGER & MAX [S1114/138]
Violoncello w/case: Paris, 1951 (Hug & Co., Zurich,
January 21, 1978)   10,010/12,870

$15,444   £10,800

MORRISON, JOHN [C5/134] English Violoncello
w/case: London, c. 1795   30,000/40,000 NS

NEUNER & HORNSTEINER [B11/84] Violoncello
                2,860/4,290
$2,960   £2,070

NEUNER & HORNSTEINER [P6/280] Mittenwald
Violoncello with minor restorable blemishes: c. 1880
                2,265/3,020
$32,994   £21,850

NEUNER & HORNSTEINER [P11/251] Good
Violoncello in good condition, w/case, 2 bows:
Mittenwald, c. 1890   3,575/4,290
$5,262   £3,680

NEUNER, MATHIAS [B9/136] Violoncello
                2,920/5,840
$4,030   £2,760

NIX, CHARLES WILLIAM [P2/83] Viola or Small-
Size Violoncello in immediate playing condition,
w/case, bow: Worth, Sussex, 1928   636/795
$439   £276

NORMAN, BARAK AND NATHANIEL CROSS
[C3/118] English Violoncello w/case   12,560/18,840
$14,444   £9,200

NORRIS, ROB [B9/131] Violoncello   730/1,022
$756   £518

NOVELLI, NATALE [Bf3/6225] Good Modern
Italian Violoncello in near perfect condition: Milan,
1954 (Alfredo Primavera, Cremona, June 30, 1989)
                9,000/14,000
$9,200   £5,888

PAESOLD, R. [P9/184] Violoncello in immediate
playing condition, w/violoncello: 1992   705/846
$1,297   £920

PEDRAZZINI, GIUSEPPE [S3/135] Violoncello
w/case: Milan, 1934   50,240/59,660 NS

PELLIZON, GIOVANNI [Sk5/30] Italian Violoncello
w/case: Gorizia, c. 1800 (Kenneth Warren & Son,
Chicago, May 27, 1999)   25,000/35,000 NS

PETERNELLA, JAGO [Sk5/31] Italian Violoncello
w/case: 1933   32,000/40,000 NS

PEVERE, ERNESTO [C5/131] Good Italian
Violoncello for Iginio Siega, w/case: Ferrara, 1929
                30,000/40,000
$30,550   £19,858

PFAB, FRIEDRICH AUGUST [S1114/121]
Violoncello: Hamburg, 1870   2,574/3,575
$9,438   £6,600

PILLEMENT (workshop of) [S10/135] Violoncello:
France, mid 19th C.   5,000/7,000
$6,000   £4,140

PILLEMENT, FRANCOIS [P3/190] French
Violoncello in immediate playing condition: Paris,
c. 1790   4,740/6,320 NS

PILLEMENT, FRANCOIS [P6/282] French
Violoncello in immediate playing condition: Paris,
c. 1790   3,775/4,530
$4,862   £3,220

PIROT, CLAUDE [Sk5/36] French Violoncello
w/case: Paris, 1820 (Horacio Piniero, New York, June
10, 1990)   35,000/40,000 NS

PIROT, CLAUDE [Sk11/47] French Violoncello
w/case: Paris, 1820 (Horacio Piniero, New York, June
10, 1990)   28,000/32,000
$21,850   £15,295

RAYMAN, JACOB [C11/83] Rare and Early English
Violoncello: London, c. 1655   7,150/10,010
$36,966   £25,850

RICHARDSON, ARTHUR [P6/275] Fine and Rare
Violoncello in immediate playing condition, w/cover:
Crediton, 1919   7,550/9,060
$13,892   £9,200

ROBB, THOMAS [B5/196] Violin.   600/900 NS

ROCCA, ENRICO [S7/200] Violoncello w/case:
Genoa, 1912 (Etienne Vatelot, Paris, February 11,
1970)   45,300/60,400
$73,688   £48,800

ROCCA, GIUSEPPE (ascribed to) [S3/128]
Violoncello w/case: Turin, late 19th C. (Kenneth
Warren & Son, Chicago, April 12, 1977)
                62,800/94,200
$98,596   £62,800

ROSADONI, GIOVANNI [C5/127] Modern Italian
Violoncello w/case: Como, 1972   7,500/9,500
$8,813   £5,728

ROUDHLOF, F. & MAUCHAND [P6/284] Good
French Violoncello with some restorations: c. 1830
                3,020/3,775 NS

ROUDHLOF, F. & MAUCHAND [P9/170] Good
French Violoncello with some restorations: c. 1830
                2,115/2,538
$2,594   £1,840

ROUDHLOFF, FRANCOIS [P3/194] Good French
Violoncello with some restorations: c. 1830
                3,950/4,740 NS

SANNINO, VINCENZO [S1114/134] Violoncello
w/case: Rome, c. 1930   57,200/85,800 NS

SCHUSTER, JOSEF (workshop of) [C5/128] German
Violoncello   3,000/4,000
$3,290   £2,139

SILVESTRE & MAUCOTEL [C3/86] Good French
Violoncello w/case: Paris, 1909   15,700/18,840
$15,347   £9,775

SMITH, THOMAS [P3/184] Fine and Handsome
English Violoncello in immediate playing condition,
w/case: London, 1773 (Hart & Son, London, July 25,
1928)   12,640/14,220
$27,255   £17,250

STAINER, JACOB (attributed to) [Bf3/6224]
Bohemian Violoncello: c. 1770   10,000/15,000
$6,900   £4,416

STAUDINGER, MATHAUS WENCESLAUS
[S3/126] Violoncello w/case, bow: Würzburg, 1779
                               5,495/7,850
$10,833   £6,900

STORIONI, LORENZO (attributed to) [C11/79]
Rare Cremonese Violoncello with possibly later scroll,
w/case: Cremona, c. 1778 (William Lewis and Son,
Chicago, December 16, 1948)   100,100/143,000
$115,473   £80,750

TECCHLER, DAVID [C5/112] Fine Italian
Violoncello: Rome, 1698 (Jacques Français, New
York, March 19, 1998)   250,000/350,000 NS

THIBOUT, JACQUES PIERRE [B11/85] Very Fine
French Violoncello: Paris, 1855 (J. & A. Beare)
                               57,200/85,800 NS

THIBOUVILLE-LAMY, J. [P6/278] Violoncello with
minor restorable blemishes, w/cover, bow: c. 1900
                               1,510/2,265
$2,084   £1,380

THIBOUVILLE-LAMY, J. [P9/164] Good Mirecourt
Violoncello w/cover, bow: c. 1900   3,525/4,230
$6,486   £4,600

THIBOUVILLE-LAMY, JEROME [S7/199]
Violoncello: Mirecourt, late 19th C.   4,530/6,040
$9,966   £6,600

VAN VESSEM, JAN [B11/75] Violoncello: 1950
                               2,145/2,860
$3,125   £2,185

VUILLAUME, JEAN BAPTISTE [P11/253] Violoncello with restorations, w/case: Paris, c. 1855 (W.E.
Hill & Sons, London, June 1933) 42,900/50,050 NS

VUILLAUME, JEAN BAPTISTE [S1114/124]
Violoncello w/case: Paris, 1847 (W.E. Hill & Sons,
London, August 28, 1918)   85,800/114,400
$130,845   £91,500

WATSON, JOHN [P11/267] Violoncello: Edinburgh,
1865   1,001/1,287
$2,138   £1,495

WILFER, ALBIN [B11/96] Fine German Violoncello:
Leipzig, 1913   5,720/8,580
$9,867   £6,900

WILLIS, ALAN [Sk11/49] Contemporary American
Violoncello w/case: Middlebury, Connecticut, 1983
                               6,000/10,000
$3,450   £2,415

WINTERLING, GEORG [S1114/126] Violoncello
w/case: Hamburg, 1907   14,300/21,450
$16,302   £11,400

WITHERS, EDWARD [P6/274] Fine and Handsome
Violoncello with minor restorable blemishes, w/cover:
London, c. 1840   10,570/12,080
$19,102   £12,650

WOLDRING, HENDRIK [C3/89] Good
Contemporary Violoncello in Baroque setup:
Garsthuizen, 1984   3,925/5,495
$3,972   £2,530

VIOLONCELLO BOW

BAZIN [B5/93] Silver Violoncello Bow
                               1,200/1,800 NS

BAZIN [S7/247] Silver Violoncello Bow with damaged handle: Mirecourt, c. 1930   604/906
$2,174   £1,440

BAZIN, CHARLES [Sk5/158] Silver Violoncello Bow
without hair   1,500/2,500
$2,070   £1,346

BAZIN, CHARLES NICHOLAS [C5/115] Silver
Violoncello Bow with later frog   3,000/4,000 NS

BAZIN, LOUIS [C3/133] Nickel Violoncello Bow
without hair, missing one eye (Jean-François Raffin,
Paris, June 7, 1999)   942/1,256
$1,083   £690

BAZIN, LOUIS [Sk5/162] Silver Violoncello Bow
with later frog and adjuster   2,500/3,500 NS

BELLIS, ANDREW [B9/125] Violoncello Bow
                               584/876 NS

BERNARDEL, LEON [S7/110] Silver Violoncello
Bow: Mirecourt or Paris, c. 1925 1,208/1,812 NS

BOUMAN, WILLIAM [S10/100] Ivory Baroque-Style
Violoncello Bow: The Hague, late 20th C.
                               1,000/1,500
$720   £497

BRISTOW, STEPHEN [S3/92] Silver Violoncello
Bow: London, 1982   1,884/2,512 NS

BULTITUDE, ARTHUR RICHARD [S7/216] Gold
and Tortoiseshell Violoncello Bow w/bow box:
Hawkhurst, 1966   2,114/2,718
$3,080   £2,040

BULTITUDE, ARTHUR RICHARD [S1114/109]
Gold Violoncello Bow: Hawkhurst, 1980 1,716/2,288
$1,888   £1,320

BULTITUDE, ARTHUR RICHARD [Sk11/114]
Silver Violoncello Bow   1,000/1,500
$1,035   £725

BUTHOD, CHARLES [B11/61] Silver Violoncello
Bow   858/1,430
$822   £575

CLUTTERBUCK, J. [P9/128] Gold Violoncello Bow
1,128/1,269
$1,216   £863

CLUTTERBUCK, JOHN [S10/97] Ivory Baroque-
Style Violoncello Bow: late 20th C.   800/1,200 NS

CONIA, STEFANO [Bf3/6215] Silver Violoncello
Bow   1,200/1,800 NS

CUNIOT-HURY [C11/119] Nickel Violoncello Bow
(Jean-François Raffin, Paris, June 6, 2000)
2,145/3,575 N/S

DABER, J.F. [Sk5/110] French Silver Violoncello
Bow: Lyon   1,200/1,500
$1,495   £972

DODD, J. [B7/58] Silver and Ivory Violoncello Bow
1,800/2,250 NS

DODD, JOHN [Sk11/119] Silver Violoncello Bow
3,500/4,000
$2,760   £1,932

DODD, JOHN KEW [Sk5/160] Silver Violoncello
Bow   4,500/6,000 NS

DODD, JOHN KEW [Sk5/174] Silver Violoncello
Bow (William Salchow, New York, April 1, 2000)
4,000/6,000 NS

EURY, NICOLAS [Bf3/6220] Fine Silver Violoncello
Bow (Paul Siefried, February 9, 1996)
8,000/10,000 NS

FETIQUE, MARCEL [B11/47] Silver Violoncello
Bow   2,145/2,860 NS

FETIQUE, VICTOR [C5/117] Silver Violoncello Bow
5,000/6,000 NS

FETIQUE, VICTOR [P11/194] Silver Violoncello
Bow with full hair: c. 1930 (Jean-François Raffin,
Paris, May 26, 2000)   1,716/2,145
$1,973   £1,380

FETIQUE, VICTOR [S3/104] Silver Violoncello Bow:
Paris, c. 1920   1,884/2,512
$3,069   £1,955

FETIQUE, VICTOR [S7/258] Silver Violoncello Bow:
Paris, c. 1920   3,020/4,530
$3,262   £2,160

FINKEL, JOHANNES S. [S1114/228] Nickel
Violoncello Bow w/silver violincello bow: late 20th C.
715/1,001 NS

GILLET, LOUIS [C5/119] Silver Violoncello Bow
with later frog and adjuster   1,500/2,000
$1,880   £1,222

GILLET, LOUIS [C5/121] Silver Violoncello Bow
(Kenneth Warren and Son, Ltd., Chicago, April 27,
1981)   1,500/2,000
$1,880   £1,222

HART & SON [P6/222] Silver Violoncello Bow:
London   755/906 NS

HEL, PIERRE JEAN HENRI [S3/101] Silver
Violoncello Bow: Lille, first quarter 20th C.
2,355/3,925
$2,889   £1,840

HENRY, EUGENE [S3/77] Silver Violoncello Bow:
Paris, c. 1880   1,256/1,884 NS

HENRY, J.V. [Sk5/116] Fine French Silver Violoncello
Bow   8,000/10,000 NS

HENRY, JOSEPH [P6/199] Good Silver Violoncello
Bow: Paris, c. 1860   6,040/7,550
$21,706   £14,375

HENRY, JOSEPH (attributed to) [S3/81] Silver
Violoncello Bow: Paris, mid 19th C.   4,710/7,850
$5,055   £3,220

HILL, W.E. & SONS [B7/52] Silver Violoncello Bow
without hair   1,800/2,250
$1,725   £1,150

HILL, W.E. & SONS [B7/59] Gold and Tortoiseshell
Violoncello Bow   3,000/4,500 NS

HILL, W.E. & SONS [B11/45] Silver Violoncello Bow
2,145/2,860
$1,069   £748

HILL, W.E. & SONS [B11/60] Silver Violoncello Bow
2,288/2,860
$3,947   £2,760

HILL, W.E. & SONS [B11/64] Silver Violoncello Bow
2,860/3,575 NS

HILL, W.E. & SONS [B11/66] Silver Violoncello Bow
1,859/2,145
$1,398   £978

HILL, W.E. & SONS [B11/69] Silver Violoncello Bow
2,145/3,575
$1,973   £1,380

HILL, W.E. & SONS [C11/121] Silver Violoncello
Bow   429/715
$1,008   £705

HILL, W.E. & SONS [P2/122] Silver Violoncello Bow
with full hair: London   477/636
$1,317   £828

HILL, W.E. & SONS [P6/185] Good Silver
Violoncello Bow: London   1,510/2,265
$1,737   £1,150

HILL, W.E. & SONS [P6/197] Silver Violoncello
Bow: London   1,359/1,510 NS

HILL, W.E. & SONS [P6/200] Silver Violoncello
Bow: London   906/1,057
$1,910   £1,265

HILL, W.E. & SONS [P6/202] Good Silver
Violoncello Bow: London   1,510/1,812
$2,518   £1,668

HILL, W.E. & SONS [S3/78] Silver Violoncello Bow
without hair: London, c. 1940   1,884/2,512
$2,889   £1,840

HILL, W.E. & SONS [S7/69] Silver Violoncello Bow: London, c. 1940   1,510/2,265
$1,631   £1,080

HILL, W.E. & SONS [S10/53] Chased Gold and Tortoiseshell "Fleur-de-Lys" Violoncello Bow: London, 1960 (Wm. Lewis & Son, Chicago, October 22, 1962)   6,000/9,000
$7,800   £5,382

HILL, W.E. & SONS [S10/54] Gold and Tortoiseshell "Fleur-de-Lys" Violoncello Bow: London, 1931 (Wm. Lewis & Son, Chicago, December 3, 1965)
          6,000/8,000
$8,400   £5,796

HILL, W.E. & SONS [Sk5/115] Silver Violoncello Bow   1,800/2,200
$1,955   £1,271

HILL, W.E. & SONS [Sk11/117] Gold Violoncello Bow   3,500/4,000
$3,680   £2,576

HILL, W.E. & SONS (attributed to) [C3/131] Gold Violoncello Bow   2,198/2,512
$2,347   £1,495

JOMBAR, PAUL [B7/54] Silver Violoncello Bow without hair   1,500/2,250 NS

KNOPF, CHRISTIAN WILHELM [C11/112] Silver Violoncello Bow   1,430/2,145
$2,016   £1,410

KOVANDA, FRANK [Sk11/116] Silver Violoncello Bow   1,000/1,200
$667   £467

KUDANOWSKI [P3/159] Good Silver Violoncello Bow   1,106/1,264 NS

KUDANOWSKI [P6/224] Good Silver Violoncello Bow   755/906 NS

KUDANOWSKI [P9/154] Good Silver Violoncello Bow   564/635
$519   £368

LAMY, A. [C5/118] Silver Violoncello Bow with later frog   3,000/4,000
$3,290   £2,139

LAMY, ALFRED [B7/39] Silver Violoncello Bow   9,000/12,000 NS

LAMY, ALFRED JOSEPH [B11/54] Silver Violoncello Bow   5,720/8,580 NS

LAMY, ALFRED JOSEPH [S3/109] Silver Violoncello Bow: Paris, c. 1910 (Bernard Millant, Paris, December 5, 1998)   6,280/9,420
$7,222   £4,600

LAMY, ALFRED JOSEPH [S1114/104] Silver Violoncello Bow: Paris, c. 1910   2,574/3,575
$2,574   £1,800

LAMY, ALFRED JOSEPH [Sk5/159] Silver Violoncello Bow with possibly later adjuster
          6,000/8,000 NS

LANGONET, EUGENE [S3/103] Silver Violoncello Bow: Nantes, first half 20th C.   628/942
$542   £345

LAPIERRE, MARCEL [C5/125] Silver Violoncello Bow with later adjuster   1,500/2,000 NS

LOTTE, ROGER-FRANCOIS [S1114/226] Silver Violoncello Bow: Mirecourt, mid 20th C. 1,144/1,716
$1,373   £960

LUPOT, FRANCOIS (II) (ascribed to) [S10/70] Silver Violoncello Bow: first half 19th C. (Joseph Chanot, London, July 5, 1929)   1,200/1,500
$1,800   £1,242

MAIRE, NICOLAS [S3/108] Violoncello Bow with repaired head: Paris, c. 1860   7,065/8,635
$7,222   £4,600

MAIRE, NICOLAS [Sk5/117] Silver Violoncello Bow with later frog   4,000/6,000
$3,680   £2,392

MALINE, GUILLAUME [B7/38] Fine Silver French Violoncello Bow: c. 1850   6,000/9,000 NS

MALINE, GUILLAUME [B11/62] Silver French Violoncello Bow: Paris, c. 1850   4,290/7,150 NS

METTAL, WALTER [S1114/220] Silver Violoncello Bow w/violincello bow: late 20th C.   715/1,001 NS

METTAL, WALTER [S1114/234] Gold Violoncello Bow   715/1,001
$1,459   £1,020

MORIZOT, LOUIS [B7/51] Silver Violoncello Bow (Jean-François Raffin, Paris, 1999)   1,500/2,250 NS

MORIZOT, LOUIS [S7/239] Silver Violoncello Bow with possibly later frog and adjuster: Mirecourt, c. 1930   1,510/2,265 NS

MORIZOT FRERES [C11/115] Silver Violoncello Bow (Jean-François Raffin, Paris, September 8, 1998)
          2,002/2,288
$2,352   £1,645

MORIZOT FRERES [S1114/174] Silver Violoncello Bow: Mirecourt, c. 1950 (Jean-François Raffin, Paris, January 26, 1999)   1,430/2,145 NS

MORIZOT (FRERES), LOUIS [C3/132] Silver and Ivory Violoncello Bow (Jean-François Raffin, Paris, June 14, 1998)   2,512/2,826 NS

NAVEA-VERA, DANIEL [Bf3/6221] Fine Gold and Tortoiseshell Violoncello Bow   2,000/3,000
$2,070   £1,325

NEUDORFER, RUDOLPH [S1114/230] Nickel Violoncello Bow   572/858 NS

NURNBERGER, A. [B9/124] Silver Violoncello Bow   438/730
$638   £437

NURNBERGER, ALBERT [B7/21] Silver Violoncello Bow   3,000/4,500 NS

NURNBERGER, ALBERT [B7/40] Silver German Violoncello Bow   1,500/2,250
$1,725   £1,150

NURNBERGER, ALBERT [B7/60] Silver Violoncello Bow 1,800/2,250 $2,070 £1,380

NURNBERGER, ALBERT [C5/120] Silver Violoncello Bow 1,400/1,800 NS

OUCHARD, EMILE [C11/122] French Silver Violoncello Bow 1,716/2,002 $2,520 £1,762

OUCHARD, EMILE A. [B11/59] Silver Violoncello Bow 2,860/3,575 $5,262 £3,680

OUCHARD, EMILE FRANCOIS [S3/99] Silver Violoncello Bow: Mirecourt, first half 20th C. 1,884/2,512 $2,708 £1,725

PANORMO (attributed to) [P2/135] Interesting English Violoncello Bow w/bow 636/795 $3,108 £1,955

PECCATTE, DOMINIQUE [Sk5/171] Fine French Silver Violoncello Bow with later frog and adjuster, without hair (William Salchow, New York, April 1, 2000) 10,000/12,000 NS

PECCATTE, FRANCOIS [C11/116] Nickel Violoncello Bow (Jean-François Raffin, Paris, March 24, 2000) 4,290/5,720 $4,705 £3,290

PECCATTE, FRANCOIS [S3/107] Silver Violoncello Bow: Paris, c. 1850 12,560/18,840 $14,444 £9,200

PFRETZSCHNER, H.R. [B11/67] Silver Violoncello Bow 1,430/2,145 $1,645 £1,150

PFRETZSCHNER, H.R. [S3/152] Silver Violoncello Bow with small repair near the lapping: Markneukirchen, early 20th C. 1,099/1,413 $1,083 £690

PFRETZSCHNER, H.R. [S7/96] Silver Violoncello Bow: Markneukirchen, 20th C. 906/1,208 NS

PFRETZSCHNER, H.R. [C11/125] Silver Violoncello Bow 1,144/1,716 $1,427 £998

PFRETZSCHNER, H.R. (workshop of) [Sk5/113] Silver Violoncello Bow 1,000/1,400 $920 £598

PFRETZSCHNER, HERMANN RICHARD [S3/150] Silver Violoncello Bow: Markneukirchen, c. 1920 (Heiko Wunderlich, Bad Brambach, May 28, 1999) 1,256/1,884 $1,986 £1,265

POIRSON, JUSTIN [S1114/195] Silver Violoncello Bow: Paris, c. 1900 1,716/2,288 NS

SARTORY, EUGENE [B7/48] Silver Violoncello Bow: Paris, c. 1915 7,500/10,500 NS

SARTORY, EUGENE [B7/49] Silver Violoncello Bow 6,000/9,000 NS

SARTORY, EUGENE [B7/50] Fine Silver French Violoncello Bow: Paris, c. 1895 6,000/9,000 NS

SARTORY, EUGENE [B11/43] Silver Violoncello Bow: Paris, c. 1915 7,150/10,010 $7,400 £5,175

SARTORY, EUGENE [B11/58] Silver Violoncello Bow: Paris, c. 1895 4,290/7,150 $6,249 £4,370

SARTORY, EUGENE [Bf3/6222] Good Silver Violoncello Bow 13,000/18,000 NS

SARTORY, EUGENE [C11/110] Silver Violoncello Bow without hair 6,435/9,295 $6,721 £4,700

SARTORY, EUGENE [S3/110] Silver Violoncello Bow: Paris, c. 1920 (Wm. Lewis & Son, Chicago, April 16, 1962) 12,560/18,840 $18,958 £12,075

SARTORY, EUGENE [Sk5/108] Silver Violoncello Bow 12,000/14,000 $10,925 £7,101

SARTORY, EUGENE [Sk5/157] Silver Violoncello Bow 10,000/12,000 NS

SARTORY, EUGENE [Sk11/123] Silver Violoncello Bow 5,000/7,000 NS

SCHUSTER, ADOLF [B9/128] Good Silver Violoncello Bow 730/1,022 NS

SCHUSTER, ADOLF C. [B7/55] Silver Violoncello Bow 1,200/1,800 $1,294 £863

SCHUSTER, ADOLF C. [B7/56] Silver Violoncello Bow 1,200/1,800 NS

SCHUSTER, ADOLPH CURT [B11/41] Silver Violoncello Bow 715/1,001 $1,233 £863

SCHUSTER, ALBERT [Sk5/109] Silver Violoncello Bow 800/1,000 $1,150 £748

SEIFERT (workshop of) [Sk11/126] Silver Violoncello Bow 400/600 $431 £302

SIMON, PAUL (attributed to) [S3/145] Silver Violoncello Bow 1,884/2,512 NS

SIMON, PIERRE [S7/116] Silver Violoncello Bow: Paris, c. 1860 6,040/9,060 $6,342 £4,200

SIMON, PIERRE [S1114/60] Silver Violoncello Bow: Paris, c. 1860 5,720/8,580 $6,006 £4,200

STEINEL, G. RUDI [Sk11/212] Silver Violoncello Bow 400/600 $374 £262

THIBOUVILLE-LAMY, JEROME [C3/135] Violoncello Bow with later adjuster 942/1,256 $1,264 £805

THIBOUVILLE-LAMY, JEROME [S7/79] Silver
Violoncello Bow: Mirecourt, c. 1900 1,510/2,265 NS

THOMACHOT, S. [C11/111] Gold Violoncello Bow
1,716/2,002
$3,697   £2,585

THOMASSIN, CLAUDE [Sk11/122] French Silver
Violoncello Bow missing ivory tip   1,600/1,800
$2,185   £1,530

TUBBS, JAMES [P11/153] Interesting Silver
Violoncello Bow with nearly full hair   2,145/2,860
$6,578   £4,600

TUBBS, JAMES [S10/55] Gold and Tortoiseshell
Violoncello Bow: London, c. 1870 (Wm. Lewis &
Son, Chicago, April 16, 1962)   4,000/6,000
$7,500   £5,175

TUBBS, THOMAS [C5/123] Silver Violoncello Bow
with later frog and button   1,200/1,400
$1,175   £764

VAN DER MEER, KAREL [S7/120] Silver Violoncello Bow: Amsterdam, c. 1910   1,812/2,416 NS

VAN DER MEER, KAREL [S1114/82] Silver Violoncello Bow: Netherlands, early 20th C.   858/1,144 NS

VIGNERON, A. [B11/68] Silver Violoncello Bow
715/1,001
$3,125   £2,185

VIGNERON, JOSEPH ARTHUR [S1114/205] Silver
Violoncello Bow: Paris, c. 1890   3,575/5,005
$6,864   £4,800

VOIRIN, F.N. [B11/39] Fine Silver Violoncello Bow
with no hair; cloth lapping   4,290/5,720 NS

VOIRIN, F.N. [P3/155] Silver Violoncello Bow with
full hair: Paris   1,264/1,422
$1,454   £920

VOIRIN, F.N. [C11/114] Silver Violoncello Bow
(Jean-François Raffin, Paris, March 22, 2000)
4,290/5,720
$6,721   £4,700

VOIRIN, FRANCOIS NICOLAS [B7/57] Silver
Violoncello Bow with repaired stick   2,250/3,000 NS

VOIRIN, FRANCOIS NICOLAS [S3/156] Silver
Violoncello Bow: Paris, c. 1875   1,570/2,355
$1,625   £1,035

VOIRIN, FRANCOIS NICOLAS [S7/83] Silver
Violoncello Bow with later frog and adjuster: Paris,
c. 1870   3,020/4,530 NS

VOIRIN, FRANCOIS NICOLAS [S7/115] Silver
Violoncello Bow: Paris, c. 1870   4,530/6,040
$4,530   £3,000

VOIRIN, FRANCOIS NICOLAS [S1114/206] Silver
Violoncello Bow: Paris, c. 1870 (Wm. Lewis & Son,
Chicago, January 26, 1966)   8,580/11,440 NS

VOIRIN, FRANCOIS NICOLAS [Sk5/142] Silver
Violoncello Bow   8,000/10,000 NS

VUILLAUME, JEAN BAPTISTE [Sk5/87] Silver
Violoncello Bow (Rembert Wurlitzer, New York,
February 8, 1957)   4,500/6,000
$6,038   £3,924

VUILLAUME, JEAN BAPTISTE [S7/114] Silver
Converted Self-Rehairing Violoncello Bow w/bow
box: Paris, c. 1850   4,530/7,550
$12,684   £8,400

WILSON, GARNER [P2/112] Good Silver
Violoncello Bow with full hair   795/954
$1,189   £748

WINKLER, FRANZ [Sk11/127] Silver Violoncello
Bow   600/800
$633   £443

WITHERS, GEORGE [S1114/225] Silver Violoncello
Bow: London, early 20th C.   572/858 NS

Five-Year Summary

sales by
item and
maker

HOW TO READ THE SUMMARY
BY ITEM AND MAKER

Beginning on the next page, you will find the five-year Summary by Item and Maker, with monetary values expressed in dollars and pounds sterling. This section summarizes the more detailed data found in the first part of the guide (the Item-by-Item Listings) and combines it with auction information from the preceding four years. Hence you will find a brief overview of the items offered from 1996 through 2000, arranged alphabetically by item—viola, violin, violoncello, etc.—and, within each item category, by maker. Items that have been offered as being "attributed to" or "ascribed to" a particular maker are shown separately from those identified as "by" that maker. (You may find inconsistencies in the way names have been given—a first initial in one case, a full name in the next. These problems have been raised and discussed in the Introduction.)

In the second column, you will find a numeric count of the items by that maker that were offered at auction during the 1996–2000 period. To the immediate right is the count of those items that were actually sold. If none sold, you will see a zero here. (If you are looking for information on a particular maker and cannot find the name, it is because no items by that maker were offered at auction during this period.)

In the next three columns are monetary values. First is the lowest sale price of an item by that maker, then the highest, and finally the average. If only one item was sold, you will find the same number in all three columns. Please use extreme caution in assessing these monetary values. From a purely statistical point of view, they are almost completely unreliable. Nonetheless, they can be construed, within narrow limits, as reflective of the current market. This is also a good place to repeat what was said earlier: this guide does not reflect upon the playing qualities or the physical condition of the items offered at auction. The only way to assess these factors is through personal experience.

Maker	Items		Selling Prices		
	Bid	Sold	Low	High	Avg

ACCORDION

BUSSON	1	1	$405 £253	$405 £253	$405 £253
CASALI	1	0			
SCANDALLI	2	0			
SOPRANI, PAOLO	2	1	$225 £138	$225 £138	$225 £138
TANZBAR	1	1	$1,955 £1,232	$1,955 £1,232	$1,955 £1,232

ÆOLA

| WHEATSTONE & CO., C. | 4 | 4 | $1,061 £690 | $2,252 £1,380 | $1,704 £1,043 |

ÆOLIAN HARP

| PROWSE & CO., KEITH | 1 | 1 | $648 £456 | $648 £456 | $648 £456 |

ARPANETTA

| KARP, JOHANN | 1 | 1 | $11,836 £7,130 | $11,836 £7,130 | $11,836 £7,130 |

BAGPIPES

COULLIE, THOMAS	1	1	$2,720 £1,610	$2,720 £1,610	$2,720 £1,610
HEDWORTH, WILLIAM	1	1	$2,332 £1,380	$2,332 £1,380	$2,332 £1,380
HENDERSON, PETER	1	1	$4,260 £3,000	$4,260 £3,000	$4,260 £3,000
LAWRIE, R.G.	1	1	$778 £483	$778 £483	$778 £483
REID, ROBERT	4	3	$1,149 £713	$5,440 £3,220	$3,233 £1,924
ROBERTSON	1	1	$6,765 £4,025	$6,765 £4,025	$6,765 £4,025

BANDURRIA

| ANDRADE, JOAO MIGUEL | 1 | 1 | $324 £195 | $324 £195 | $324 £195 |

BANJEAURINE

| HAYNES CO., JOHN C. | 1 | 0 | | | |

BANJELE

| SMECK, ROY | 1 | 1 | $75 £46 | $75 £46 | $75 £46 |

BANJO

| ABBOTT, J. | 2 | 1 | $164 £98 | $164 £98 | $164 £98 |

Banjo

Maker	Items		Selling Prices		
	Bid	Sold	Low	High	Avg
BACON & DAY	5	4	$144	$1,455	$687
			£86	£902	£419
BACON BANJO CO.	1	1	$431	$431	$431
			£262	£262	£262
BARNES & MULLINS	1	1	$217	$217	$217
			£132	£132	£132
CHAMBERLAIN, J.	1	1	$501	$501	$501
			£299	£299	£299
CONTESSA	1	0			
DALLAS, D.E.	1	1	$212	$212	$212
			£138	£138	£138
DALLAS, J.E.	1	1	$348	$348	$348
			£230	£230	£230
DANIELS, J.	1	1	$159	$159	$159
			£104	£104	£104
DOBSON CO.	1	1	$231	$231	$231
			£143	£143	£143
DOBSON, E.C.	1	1	$150	$150	$150
			£98	£98	£98
DOBSON, E.D.W.G.	1	1	$345	$345	$345
			£207	£207	£207
DOBSON, GEORGE	1	1	$230	$230	$230
			£138	£138	£138
DORE BROS.	1	0			
EPIPHONE	1	1	$690	$690	$690
			£414	£414	£414
ESSEX, CLIFFORD	7	5	$373	$1,121	$594
			£230	£748	£384
FAIRBANKS & COLE	1	1	$374	$374	$374
			£224	£224	£224
FAIRBANKS CO., A.C.	2	1	$3,163	$3,163	$3,163
			£1,898	£1,898	£1,898
GIBSON CO.	2	2	$2,070	$4,893	$3,482
			£1,257	£3,034	£2,145
GRAY	1	1	$500	$500	$500
			£334	£334	£334
GRETSCH	1	0			
GREY & SONS, JOHN	3	2	$52	$604	$328
			£35	£368	£201
HANDEL, J.T.C.	1	1	$141	$141	$141
			£92	£92	£92
HAYNES CO., JOHN C.	2	1	$150	$150	$150
			£90	£90	£90
HUNT, H.H.	1	1	$104	$104	$104
			£63	£63	£63
JEDSON	2	2	$338	$380	$359
			£207	£230	£219
LANGE, WILLIAM L.	4	4	$201	$1,725	$733
			£122	£1,047	£451
LOCKE, G.S.	1	1	$316	$316	$316
			£190	£190	£190
LUDWIG	3	2	$460	$748	$604
			£272	£442	£357
LYON & HEALY	1	1	$132	$132	$132
			£81	£81	£81

Selling Prices Maker	Items Bid	Sold	Low	High	Avg
MANSFIELD, E.B.	1	1	$518 £311	$518 £311	$518 £311
MORRISON, JAMES A.	1	1	$460 £276	$460 £276	$460 £276
SCHALL, J.B.	1	1	$100 £81	$100 £81	$100 £81
SHELTONE	1	1	$112 £69	$112 £69	$112 £69
SLINGERLAND (attributed to)	1	0			
STEWART, S.S.	5	3	$271 £161	$611 £397	$459 £293
STROMBERG, CHARLES & ELMER	1	1	$403 £282	$403 £282	$403 £282
TEMLETT, W.	2	2	$223 £144	$637 £414	$430 £279
THOMPSON & ODELL	2	2	$201 £121	$230 £140	$216 £130
TURNER, JOHN ALVEY	2	2	$209 £127	$290 £173	$249 £150
TURNER, WILLIAM	1	0			
VEGA COMPANY	16	12	$201 £122	$4,600 £3,220	$1,250 £736
WARD & SON	1	1	$168 £109	$168 £109	$168 £109
WASHBURN	1	1	$380 £253	$380 £253	$380 £253
WEAVER	1	1	$196 £115	$196 £115	$196 £115
WELTTON	1	1	$132 £81	$132 £81	$132 £81
WEYMANN CO.	2	2	$173 £112	$529 £328	$351 £220
WILKES, F.C.	1	1	$180 £115	$180 £115	$180 £115
WINDER, J.G.	1	1	$262 £161	$262 £161	$262 £161
WINDSOR	1	1	$1,880 £1,150	$1,880 £1,150	$1,880 £1,150
WINDSOR, A.O.	1	1	$85 £52	$85 £52	$85 £52

BANJO-GUITAR

VEGA COMPANY	1	1	$1,035 £612	$1,035 £612	$1,035 £612

BANJOLELE

DALLAS, J.E.	1	1	$151 £92	$151 £92	$151 £92
FORMBY, GEORGE	1	1	$289 £172	$289 £172	$289 £172
STEWART, S.S.	1	1	$144 £93	$144 £93	$144 £93

| Maker | Items | | Selling Prices | | |
	Bid	Sold	Low	High	Avg
BANJO-MANDOLIN					
RELIANCE	1	1	$94	$94	$94
			£58	£58	£58
TIERI	1	1	$86	$86	$86
			£51	£51	£51
BARITONE					
BUNDY	1	1	$184	$184	$184
			£112	£112	£112
LYON & HEALY	1	0			
MARCEAU & CO.	1	0			
SAPORETTI & CAPPARELI	1	0			
BASS GUITAR					
FENDER	3	2	$525	$972	$748
			£322	£575	£449
GIBSON CO.	1	1	$806	$806	$806
			£495	£495	£495
GOODFELLOW CO.	1	0			
HOFNER	3	2	$18	$70	$44
			£12	£46	£29
HOFNER, KARL	2	1	$700	$700	$700
			£414	£414	£414
JOURDAN	1	0			
BASSET HORN					
ALBERT, E.	1	1	$943	$943	$943
			£575	£575	£575
BASSOON					
ADLER & CO., OSCAR	1	1	$2,051	$2,051	$2,051
			£1,265	£1,265	£1,265
BESSON & CO.	1	1	$288	$288	$288
			£173	£173	£173
BILTON	3	1	$773	$773	$773
			£483	£483	£483
BILTON, R.	1	0			
BIZEY, CHARLES	1	0			
BOOSEY & CO.	1	0			
BUCHNER, F.	1	1	$3,259	$3,259	$3,259
			£1,955	£1,955	£1,955
BUFFET	1	0			
BUFFET, CRAMPON & CO.	2	2	$262	$463	$363
			£161	£288	£224
CABART	1	1	$425	$425	$425
			£253	£253	£253
CUVILLIER (ascribed to)	1	1	$271	$271	$271
			£161	£161	£161
DE LUIGI, GIACOMO	1	1	$1,527	$1,527	$1,527
			£920	£920	£920

Maker	Items		Selling Prices		
	Bid	Sold	Low	High	Avg
DUPRE, PAUL	1	1	$633	$633	$633
			£386	£386	£386
FELCHLIN, JOSEF KARL	1	1	$993	$993	$993
			£598	£598	£598
GALANDER	1	0			
HASENEIER, H.F.	1	1	$1,121	$1,121	$1,121
			£690	£690	£690
HAWKES & SON	1	1	$168	$168	$168
			£104	£104	£104
HECKEL	5	4	$1,845	$14,098	$6,425
			£1,092	£8,625	£3,924
HIRSBRUNNER FAMILY (MEMBER OF)	2	2	$1,622	$3,054	$2,338
			£977	£1,840	£1,409
HOLLER	1	1	$1,196	$1,196	$1,196
			£782	£782	£782
HOWARTH	1	1	$403	$403	$403
			£276	£276	£276
KOHLERT & SONS	1	1	$672	$672	$672
			£437	£437	£437
KOHLERT'S SOHNE, V.	1	1	$382	$382	$382
			£230	£230	£230
LAFLEUR, J.R. & SON	1	1	$471	$471	$471
			£291	£291	£291
LINTON MANUFACTURING CO.	1	1	$147	$147	$147
			£96	£96	£96
LUDWIG, FRANZ	1	1	$1,527	$1,527	$1,527
			£920	£920	£920
MAHILLON, C.	2	1	$201	$201	$201
			£138	£138	£138
METZLER & CO., G.	1	0			
MILHOUSE, WILLIAM	7	3	$751	$1,749	$1,406
			£460	£1,035	£843
MILHOUSE, WILLIAM & W. WHEATCROFT	1	0			
PARKER, JOHN	1	1	$725	$725	$725
			£437	£437	£437
RUDALL, CARTE & CO.	1	0			
SAVARY	1	0			
SAVARY, J.N. (JEUNE)	2	1	$789	$789	$789
			£483	£483	£483
SAVARY, JEAN NICHOLAS	1	0			
SCHREIBER	4	4	$1,266	$1,671	$1,469
			£828	£1,093	£960
SCHREIBER & SOHN	1	1	$604	$604	$604
			£414	£414	£414
SCHREIBER & SOHNE, W.	1	1	$863	$863	$863
			£526	£526	£526
TRIEBERT	1	1	$1,055	$1,055	$1,055
			£690	£690	£690
TRIEBERT & SONS, GUILLAUME	2	2	$458	$1,689	$1,074
			£276	£1,035	£656
WOOD & IVY	2	0			

Maker	Items		Selling Prices		
	Bid	Sold	Low	High	Avg

BUGLE

Maker	Bid	Sold	Low	High	Avg
BESSON, FONTAINE	1	0			
CLEMENTI & CO.	1	1	$4,025 £2,415	$4,025 £2,415	$4,025 £2,415
COUESNON & CO.	1	0			
CURTIS & SON, RICHARD	1	0			
FIRTH, HALL & POND	1	1	$3,163 £1,898	$3,163 £1,898	$3,163 £1,898
LOGIER, JOHN BERNHARD	1	1	$3,163 £1,898	$3,163 £1,898	$3,163 £1,898
MILLENS, J.	1	0			
SAURLE, MICHAEL	2	1	$2,619 £1,587	$2,619 £1,587	$2,619 £1,587
THIBOUVILLE-LAMY, J.	1	0			
WHITE & CO., H.N.	1	0			

BUGLET

Maker	Bid	Sold	Low	High	Avg
KEAT & SONS, H.	1	0			

CAVAQUINHO

Maker	Bid	Sold	Low	High	Avg
D'ATHOUGUIA, RUFINO FELIX	1	1	$1,028 £635	$1,028 £635	$1,028 £635

CHAMBER BASS

Maker	Bid	Sold	Low	High	Avg
DOLLING, HERMANN (JR.)	1	1	$5,257 £3,105	$5,257 £3,105	$5,257 £3,105
GILKES, SAMUEL	1	0			
HILL, JOSEPH (ascribed to)	1	0			
PALLOTTA, PIETRO (attributed to)	1	0			
POLLMAN	1	1	$7,123 £4,370	$7,123 £4,370	$7,123 £4,370

CITTERN

Maker	Bid	Sold	Low	High	Avg
BRODERIP & WILKINSON	1	1	$730 £437	$730 £437	$730 £437
LIESSEM, R.	1	1	$867 £518	$867 £518	$867 £518
RUTHERFORD	1	1	$1,252 £748	$1,252 £748	$1,252 £748

CLARINET

Maker	Bid	Sold	Low	High	Avg
ALBERT, E.	2	2	$415 £253	$981 £598	$698 £426
ALBERT, EUGENE A.	1	1	$764 £460	$764 £460	$764 £460
AMMANN, ULRICH	2	1	$6,491 £3,910	$6,491 £3,910	$6,491 £3,910
ASTOR & CO.	1	0			
BASSI, LUCIAN	1	1	$147 £92	$147 £92	$147 £92

	Items		Selling Prices		
Maker	Bid	Sold	Low	High	Avg
BAUMANN	1	1	$1,680 £1,012	$1,680 £1,012	$1,680 £1,012
BERNAREGGI	1	1	$374 £228	$374 £228	$374 £228
BESSON	2	2	$76 £52	$121 £81	$98 £66
BETTONEY, H.	1	1	$259 £161	$259 £161	$259 £161
BILTON	3	3	$460 £276	$1,725 £1,035	$882 £537
BILTON, RICHARD	2	2	$638 £391	$763 £462	$700 £427
BILTON, RICHARD (workshop of)	1	0			
BOOSEY & CO.	5	2	$94 £58	$321 £196	$207 £127
BOOSEY & HAWKES	21	17	$74 £46	$915 £598	$395 £256
BRAUN	1	1	$587 £345	$587 £345	$587 £345
BRONSEL, T.	1	1	$201 £127	$201 £127	$201 £127
BUESCHER	3	3	$77 £46	$230 £140	$154 £97
BUFFET, CRAMPON & CO.	2	1	$1,055 £632	$1,055 £632	$1,055 £632
CHIBONVILLE FRERES	1	1	$575 £374	$575 £374	$575 £374
CHRISTIANI	1	1	$576 £345	$576 £345	$576 £345
CLEMENT & CO.	1	1	$905 £552	$905 £552	$905 £552
CLEMENTI & CO.	2	1	$348 £230	$348 £230	$348 £230
CONN, USA	1	1	$278 £173	$278 £173	$278 £173
COWLAN, MICHAEL	1	1	$221 £138	$221 £138	$221 £138
CRAMPON & CO.	1	1	$242 £150	$242 £150	$242 £150
D'ALMAINE & CO.	2	2	$276 £184	$699 £414	$488 £299
DAVIS	1	1	$52 £35	$52 £35	$52 £35
DISTIN, HENRY	1	1	$133 £80	$133 £80	$133 £80
DISTIN & CO.	1	1	$800 £529	$800 £529	$800 £529
DUVAL, RENE	1	0			
ELKHART	1	1	$132 £81	$132 £81	$132 £81
FINGERHUTH, CHRISTIAN	1	1	$1,240 £747	$1,240 £747	$1,240 £747
FLEISCHMANN, ANTON	1	1	$331 £206	$331 £206	$331 £206

Maker	Items Bid	Sold	Selling Prices Low	High	Avg
GEROCK & WOLF	1	1	$460 £281	$460 £281	$460 £281
GILMER & CO.	1	1	$131 £81	$131 £81	$131 £81
GOODLAD & CO.	1	1	$283 £173	$283 £173	$283 £173
GOULDING	1	1	$846 £518	$846 £518	$846 £518
GOULDING & CO.	2	2	$383 £230	$730 £437	$557 £334
GRAFTON	1	1	$502 £299	$502 £299	$502 £299
GRANDJON, J.	1	1	$374 £243	$374 £243	$374 £243
HALL & SON, WILLIAM	1	1	$230 £140	$230 £140	$230 £140
HASENEIER, H.F.	1	1	$1,431 £862	$1,431 £862	$1,431 £862
HAWKES & SON	4	4	$94 £58	$391 £242	$247 £152
HAWKES & SONS	2	2	$104 £63	$528 £322	$316 £193
HEROUARD PERE ET FILS	1	0			
KEY	1	1	$943 £575	$943 £575	$943 £575
KLEMM & BRO.	1	1	$920 £552	$920 £552	$920 £552
KOHLER & SON	1	1	$1,336 £805	$1,336 £805	$1,336 £805
KOHLERT, VINCENZ FERARIUS	1	0			
KRUSPE, C.	2	1	$393 £238	$393 £238	$393 £238
LEBLANC	1	0			
LEBLANC, GEORGES	2	1	$2,290 £1,388	$2,290 £1,388	$2,290 £1,388
LEDUC	1	1	$58 £35	$58 £35	$58 £35
LOT, ISADORE	1	1	$397 £247	$397 £247	$397 £247
MARTIN BROS.	2	1	$575 £345	$575 £345	$575 £345
MEINEL, CLEMENS	1	1	$764 £460	$764 £460	$764 £460
METZLER & CO.	3	3	$247 £150	$496 £299	$388 £234
MEYER, KARL	1	1	$176 £104	$176 £104	$176 £104
MILHOUSE	1	1	$3,055 £1,852	$3,055 £1,852	$3,055 £1,852
MILLER, GEORGE	3	3	$469 £299	$2,673 £1,610	$1,319 £797
MOLLENHAUER, JOHANN ANDREAS	1	1	$438 £264	$438 £264	$438 £264
MONNIG GEBRUDER	1	1	$1,718 £1,035	$1,718 £1,035	$1,718 £1,035

	Items		Selling Prices		
Maker	Bid	Sold	Low	High	Avg
NICHOLSON, CHARLES	1	1	$151	$151	$151
			£92	£92	£92
NOBLET	3	1	$84	$84	$84
			£58	£58	£58
PAN-AMERICAN	1	0			
PASK, JOHN	1	1	$611	$611	$611
			£368	£368	£368
PEACHEY, G.	1	1	$385	$385	$385
			£230	£230	£230
POTTER, SAMUEL	1	1	$461	$461	$461
			£276	£276	£276
PRESTON, JOHN	1	0			
PURDAY	1	0			
RAMPONE, AGOSTINO	1	1	$1,336	$1,336	$1,336
			£805	£805	£805
REILLY, J.	1	1	$492	$492	$492
			£322	£322	£322
ROTTENBURGH, G.A.	1	1	$1,128	$1,128	$1,128
			£690	£690	£690
ROUSTAGNEQ	1	1	$1,718	$1,718	$1,718
			£1,035	£1,035	£1,035
RUDALL, CARTE & CO.	3	3	$104	$226	$160
			£69	£138	£100
SCHUSTER & CO., G.	1	1	$1,107	$1,107	$1,107
			£667	£667	£667
SELMER	4	4	$248	$525	$358
			£155	£322	£229
SELMER, HENRI	4	3	$168	$611	$347
			£104	£368	£211
SELMER BUNDY	2	1	$115	$115	$115
			£70	£70	£70
THIBOUVILLE	1	1	$230	$230	$230
			£140	£140	£140
THIBOUVILLE-LAMY, J.	3	3	$61	$316	$150
			£40	£193	£93
TRIEBERT	1	1	$180	$180	$180
			£115	£115	£115
UHLMANN, JOHANN TOBIAS	1	1	$1,431	$1,431	$1,431
			£862	£862	£862
WHITELY	1	1	$805	$805	$805
			£483	£483	£483
WINNEN, JEAN	1	1	$311	$311	$311
			£184	£184	£184
WOLF & CO., ROBERT	1	1	$181	$181	$181
			£115	£115	£115
WOOD, JAMES	1	1	$232	$232	$232
			£138	£138	£138
WOOD, JAMES & SON	1	1	$125	$125	$125
			£75	£75	£75
WOOD & IVY	3	2	$649	$1,380	$1,015
			£391	£828	£610
WREDE, H.	2	2	$319	$518	$418
			£196	£337	£266

Maker	Items		Selling Prices		
	Bid	Sold	Low	High	Avg

CLAVICHORD

GOFF, THOMAS	1	1	$1,704 £1,200	$1,704 £1,200	$1,704 £1,200
GOUGH, HUGH PERCIVAL HENRY	1	1	$1,222 £794	$1,222 £794	$1,222 £794
HERZ, ERIC	1	1	$2,185 £1,437	$2,185 £1,437	$2,185 £1,437
PALAZZI, NICOLA	1	1	$11,658 £6,900	$11,658 £6,900	$11,658 £6,900
SONDERMANN, MARCUS GABRIEL	1	1	$29,288 £20,625	$29,288 £20,625	$29,288 £20,625

CONCERTINA

BOSTOCK	1	1	$2,513 £1,495	$2,513 £1,495	$2,513 £1,495
CASE, GEORGE	3	3	$160 £98	$695 £437	$466 £286
CHIDLEY, ROCK	6	2	$380 £230	$873 £529	$626 £380
CRABB, HENRY	2	2	$807 £483	$2,905 £1,783	$1,856 £1,133
EBBLEWHITE	1	0			
JEFFRIES	7	7	$1,055 £632	$4,481 £2,910	$3,425 £2,165
JEFFRIES, C.	1	1	$2,184 £1,527	$2,184 £1,527	$2,184 £1,527
JEFFRIES, CHARLES	12	12	$2,120 £1,380	$4,660 £2,875	$3,639 £2,244
JEFFRIES BROS.	1	0			
JONES	1	1	$1,710 £1,093	$1,710 £1,093	$1,710 £1,093
JONES, C.	1	1	$173 £115	$173 £115	$173 £115
JONES, GEORGE	3	2	$1,220 £748	$1,783 £1,093	$1,501 £920
JONES, WILLIAM H.	1	1	$1,215 £748	$1,215 £748	$1,215 £748
LACHENAL	43	33	$59 £35	$1,482 £978	$504 £317
LACHENAL, LOUIS	4	2	$261 £161	$321 £207	$291 £184
LACHENAL & CO.	24	19	$93 £58	$1,704 £1,200	$815 £516
METZLER & CO.	1	1	$80 £52	$80 £52	$80 £52
PARISH, THOMAS	1	1	$261 £173	$261 £173	$261 £173
PEAKE, J.	2	1	$151 £98	$151 £98	$151 £98
PROWSE & CO., KEITH	1	1	$345 £230	$345 £230	$345 £230
VICKERS	1	1	$508 £299	$508 £299	$508 £299

Maker	Items Bid	Sold	Low	Selling Prices High	Avg
WHEATSTONE, C.	31	23	$145 £86	$2,846 £1,725	$721 £445
WHEATSTONE, C. (attributed to)	2	1	$783 £483	$783 £483	$783 £483
WHEATSTONE, CHARLES	1	1	$698 £423	$698 £423	$698 £423
WHEATSTONE & CO., C.	25	20	$466 £288	$4,963 £2,990	$1,396 £865
WOODWARD	1	1	$72 £46	$72 £46	$72 £46

CONTRABASSOON

Maker	Bid	Sold	Low	High	Avg
HECKEL	3	0			
MONNIG, FRITZ	1	1	$5,263 £3,220	$5,263 £3,220	$5,263 £3,220

CORNET

Maker	Bid	Sold	Low	High	Avg
ANTON (SR.), EBERHARD	1	0			
BESSON	2	2	$123 £81	$1,049 £632	$586 £356
BESSON & CO.	4	4	$98 £60	$466 £276	$268 £162
BOOSEY & CO.	4	2	$85 £52	$805 £483	$445 £267
BOOSEY & HAWKES	2	2	$97 £63	$457 £299	$277 £181
BOSTON MUSICAL INSTRUMENT MANUFACTURER	1	1	$288 £175	$288 £175	$288 £175
CONN, C.G.	1	1	$748 £449	$748 £449	$748 £449
CONN, USA	1	1	$690 £414	$690 £414	$690 £414
CORTON	2	0			
COURTOIS, ANTOINE	1	1	$202 £141	$202 £141	$202 £141
COURTURIER, ERNST ALBERT	1	1	$463 £288	$463 £288	$463 £288
DISTIN, HENRY	2	2	$805 £526	$863 £530	$834 £528
DUPONT, M.	1	1	$92 £56	$92 £56	$92 £56
GLASS	1	1	$283 £173	$283 £173	$283 £173
GLASSL, EGIDIUS	1	1	$802 £483	$802 £483	$802 £483
GRAVES, J.G.	1	1	$113 £69	$113 £69	$113 £69
HAWKES & SON	1	1	$256 £161	$256 £161	$256 £161
HILLYARD, W.	2	1	$405 £288	$405 £288	$405 £288

Maker	Items		Selling Prices		
	Bid	Sold	Low	High	Avg
HULLER, EMMANUEL	1	1	$1,145 £690	$1,145 £690	$1,145 £690
KOHLER	2	2	$1,789 £1,127	$2,738 £1,725	$2,263 £1,426
LAFLEUR, J.R. & SON	3	0			
LYON & HEALY	1	1	$916 £552	$916 £552	$916 £552
MARCEAU & CO.	1	0			
MORITZ, C.W.	1	0			
OLDS & SON	1	1	$690 £414	$690 £414	$690 £414
PACE & SON, CHARLES	1	1	$477 £336	$477 £336	$477 £336
SCHUSTER & CO., G.	1	1	$690 £414	$690 £414	$690 £414
STAR	1	1	$1,265 £764	$1,265 £764	$1,265 £764
THIBOUVILLE-LAMY, J.	2	1	$150 £92	$150 £92	$150 £92
WHITE & CO., H.N.	1	1	$115 £76	$115 £76	$115 £76
WOODS & CO.	2	1	$77 £46	$77 £46	$77 £46
WURLITZER CO., RUDOLPH	1	1	$144 £86	$144 £86	$144 £86

CORNOPEAN

Maker	Items		Selling Prices		
KOHLER, JOHN	1	1	$6,217 £3,680	$6,217 £3,680	$6,217 £3,680

CRUMHORN

Maker	Items		Selling Prices		
GUNTHER	1	0			

CYMBALUM

Maker	Items		Selling Prices		
SCHUNDA, JOSEF V.	2	0			

DOUBLE BASS

Maker	Items		Selling Prices		
BERGONZI, NICOLO	1	1	$124,369 £76,300	$124,369 £76,300	$124,369 £76,300
CUNE, RENE	1	1	$4,520 £2,990	$4,520 £2,990	$4,520 £2,990
DERAZEY, JUSTIN	1	1	$13,530 £8,050	$13,530 £8,050	$13,530 £8,050
FENDT, BERNARD SIMON	1	1	$36,708 £21,850	$36,708 £21,850	$36,708 £21,850
FRAMUS	1	1	$2,185 £1,420	$2,185 £1,420	$2,185 £1,420
GARIMBERTI, FERDINANDO	1	1	$17,621 £11,500	$17,621 £11,500	$17,621 £11,500
GILKES, WILLIAM	1	0			
HAMMIG, JOHANN CHRISTIAN	1	0			

Maker	Items Bid	Sold	Low	Selling Prices High	Avg
MONTAGNANA, DOMENICO	1	1	$251,910 £155,500	$251,910 £155,500	$251,910 £155,500
PILLEMENT, FRANCOIS	2	1	$12,617 £7,935	$12,617 £7,935	$12,617 £7,935
POLLMAN	2	2	$4,420 £2,875	$8,746 £5,175	$6,583 £4,025
PRENTICE, RONALD	3	2	$6,521 £4,025	$7,499 £4,629	$7,010 £4,327
PRESCOTT, ABRAHAM	1	1	$8,050 £5,635	$8,050 £5,635	$8,050 £5,635
STANLEY, ROBERT	1	0			
VILLA, LUIGI	3	3	$5,377 £3,220	$9,218 £5,520	$6,786 £4,063
WILFER, E. (ascribed to)	1	1	$2,062 £1,265	$2,062 £1,265	$2,062 £1,265

DOUBLE BASS BOW

Maker	Items Bid	Sold	Low	Selling Prices High	Avg
BAILEY, G.E.	1	1	$1,019 £633	$1,019 £633	$1,019 £633
BRYANT, P.W.	2	2	$1,216 £863	$2,251 £1,389	$1,733 £1,126
BRYANT, PERCIVAL WILFRED	4	4	$1,944 £1,207	$2,437 £1,495	$2,073 £1,308
FETIQUE, VICTOR	4	3	$2,347 £1,495	$5,991 £3,910	$4,342 £2,760
HILL, W.E. & SONS	1	1	$387 £230	$387 £230	$387 £230
LA MAY	1	0			
LAPIERRE	2	0			
LAPIERRE, MARCEL	2	2	$1,687 £1,035	$2,875 £1,745	$2,281 £1,390
LEE, JOHN NORWOOD	1	0			
LOTTE, FRANCOIS	1	1	$1,018 £661	$1,018 £661	$1,018 £661
MORIZOT, L.	2	2	$1,316 £920	$1,986 £1,265	$1,651 £1,093
MORIZOT, LOUIS	1	1	$1,840 £1,137	$1,840 £1,137	$1,840 £1,137
MORIZOT, LOUIS (II)	1	1	$1,828 £1,092	$1,828 £1,092	$1,828 £1,092
NURNBERGER (workshop of)	1	1	$1,380 £966	$1,380 £966	$1,380 £966
NURNBERGER, KARL ALBERT	1	0			
PECATTE, CHARLES	1	0			
PFRETZSCHNER, H.R.	4	2	$778 £506	$1,453 £897	$1,116 £702
RAU, AUGUST	1	1	$1,344 £805	$1,344 £805	$1,344 £805
THIBOUVILLE-LAMY, J.	1	1	$2,571 £1,587	$2,571 £1,587	$2,571 £1,587
THOMASSIN, CLAUDE	1	1	$792 £517	$792 £517	$792 £517

| Maker | Items | | Selling Prices | | |
	Bid	Sold	Low	High	Avg
TUBBS, JAMES	2	1	$1,317 £828	$1,317 £828	$1,317 £828
ULLMANN, GIORGIO	1	1	$881 £575	$881 £575	$881 £575
VICKERS, J.E.	2	1	$345 £207	$345 £207	$345 £207
WANKA, HERBERT	1	1	$1,139 £690	$1,139 £690	$1,139 £690
WERNER, ERICH	1	1	$528 £322	$528 £322	$528 £322
WINKLER, F.	1	1	$345 £224	$345 £224	$345 £224

DULCIMER

EBBLEWHITE	1	0			

EDEOPHONE

LACHENAL & CO.	5	4	$782 £471	$2,400 £1,455	$1,537 £927

ENGLISH HORN

ALBERT, JACQUES	1	1	$820 £506	$820 £506	$820 £506
BOOSEY & HAWKES	1	1	$739 £483	$739 £483	$739 £483
CABART	1	1	$1,007 £690	$1,007 £690	$1,007 £690
FORNARI, ANDREAS	2	0			
HOWARD	1	1	$1,091 £713	$1,091 £713	$1,091 £713
LOREE, F.	1	1	$993 £598	$993 £598	$993 £598
LOUIS	2	2	$1,091 £713	$1,196 £782	$1,143 £748
TRIEBERT & SONS, GUILLAUME	3	3	$3,054 £1,840	$9,759 £5,980	$6,774 £4,140
ZIEGLER, I.	1	1	$3,818 £2,300	$3,818 £2,300	$3,818 £2,300

EPINETTE DES

LAMBERT, A.	1	1	$476 £287	$476 £287	$476 £287

EUPHONIUM

BESSON	1	1	$457 £299	$457 £299	$457 £299
BOOSEY & HAWKES	2	2	$457 £299	$563 £368	$510 £334

FIFE

CAHUSAC	1	1	$483 £322	$483 £322	$483 £322

Maker	Items		Selling Prices		
	Bid	Sold	Low	High	Avg
GEROCK, CHRISTOPHER	1	0			
HAWKES & SON	1	0			
HOLLINGS, WILLIAM	1	0			
MILHOUSE, WILLIAM	1	1	$191 £115	$191 £115	$191 £115
SIMPSON	1	1	$142 £86	$142 £86	$142 £86
WOLF & FIGG	1	1	$113 £75	$113 £75	$113 £75

FLAGEOLET

Maker	Bid	Sold	Low	High	Avg
BAINBRIDGE	1	1	$414 £276	$414 £276	$414 £276
BAINBRIDGE, WILLIAM	4	4	$243 £161	$1,262 £747	$796 £480
BAINBRIDGE & WOOD	5	5	$529 £345	$3,627 £2,185	$1,428 £880
BUHNER & KELLER	1	1	$955 £575	$955 £575	$955 £575
BUTHOD & THIBOUVILLE	1	1	$938 £575	$938 £575	$938 £575
CARD, W.	1	1	$289 £172	$289 £172	$289 £172
GARRETT, R.	1	1	$217 £138	$217 £138	$217 £138
HASTRICK	1	0			
LAMBERT, JEAN NICOLAS	1	1	$955 £575	$955 £575	$955 £575
MARGUERITAT	1	1	$1,240 £747	$1,240 £747	$1,240 £747
PROWSE & CO., KEITH	1	1	$712 £437	$712 £437	$712 £437
SATZGER	1	0			
SIMPSON	1	1	$807 £564	$807 £564	$807 £564
SIMPSON, JOHN	3	2	$237 £150	$955 £575	$596 £362

FLAGEOLET-FLUTE

Maker	Bid	Sold	Low	High	Avg
BAINBRIDGE	1	1	$587 £391	$587 £391	$587 £391

FLUEGELHORN

Maker	Bid	Sold	Low	High	Avg
ANSINGH & CO., D.	1	0			

FLUGELHORN

Maker	Bid	Sold	Low	High	Avg
BESSON & CO.	1	1	$575 £345	$575 £345	$575 £345
LOW, JACOB	1	1	$1,909 £1,150	$1,909 £1,150	$1,909 £1,150
OTTO, FRANZ	1	1	$916 £552	$916 £552	$916 £552

Maker	Items		Selling Prices		
	Bid	Sold	Low	High	Avg
SCHUSTER & CO.	1	1	$633	$633	$633
			£380	£380	£380

FLUTE

Maker	Bid	Sold	Low	High	Avg
ALEXANDER GEBRUDER	1	1	$458	$458	$458
			£276	£276	£276
ARMSTRONG, W.T.	1	0			
ARMSTRONG CO.	1	1	$354	$354	$354
			£230	£230	£230
ASTOR & CO.	3	3	$575	$1,199	$846
			£374	£727	£520
ASTOR & CO., GEORGE	1	0			
BAINBRIDGE & WOOD	3	2	$224	$2,294	$1,259
			£138	£1,495	£817
BARLASSINA, GIUSEPPE	1	0			
BERCIOUX, EUGENE	1	1	$1,783	$1,783	$1,783
			£1,093	£1,093	£1,093
BEUKERS, WILLEM	1	0			
BEYER	1	1	$537	$537	$537
			£368	£368	£368
BILTON	2	1	$219	$219	$219
			£138	£138	£138
BILTON, RICHARD	3	2	$436	$763	$600
			£265	£462	£363
BLESSING	1	1	$209	$209	$209
			£138	£138	£138
BOEHM & MENDLER	1	1	$11,658	$11,658	$11,658
			£6,900	£6,900	£6,900
BOIE, FRIEDRICH	1	1	$1,314	$1,314	$1,314
			£805	£805	£805
BONN, G.W.	1	0			
BONNEVILLE	1	0			
BOOSEY & CO.	2	2	$515	$583	$549
			£322	£345	£334
BOOSEY & HAWKES	11	6	$74	$205	$152
			£46	£127	£94
BUFFET	4	3	$104	$309	$190
			£69	£184	£119
BUFFET, CRAMPON & CO.	1	0			
BUNDY	1	1	$147	$147	$147
			£92	£92	£92
BUTLER	1	1	$189	$189	$189
			£115	£115	£115
BUTLER, GEORGE	1	1	$103	$103	$103
			£63	£63	£63
BUTTON & CO.	1	1	$134	$134	$134
			£80	£80	£80
CABART	5	2	$103	$195	$149
			£63	£127	£95
CAHUSAC	4	2	$566	$1,128	$847
			£345	£690	£518
CAHUSAC, THOMAS	3	3	$120	$816	$486
			£75	£483	£301

ALFRED LAMY | Silver Violin Bow | Christie's, May 5, 2000, Lot 202

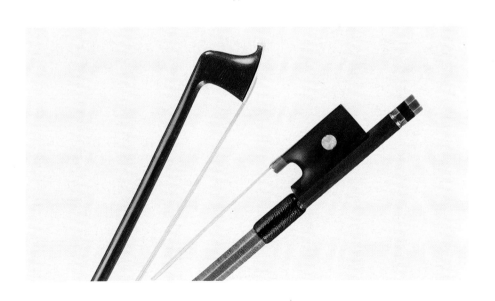

JEAN PERSOIS | Silver Violin Bow | Sotheby's, March 14, 2000, Lot 97

HENDRIK JACOBS | Fine Dutch Violin | Christie's, May 5, 2000, Lot 106

MARINO CAPICCHIONI | Good Modern Italian Viola: Rimini, 1965 | Christie's, May 5, 2000, Lot 140

CARLO TONINI | Violin: Venice, 1720 | Christie's, May 5, 2000, Lot 91

EDWARD WITHERS | Fine and Handsome Violoncello: London, c. 1840 | Phillips, June 2, 2000, Lot 274

MANUEL RAMIREZ | Fine and Handsome Spanish Viola: Madrid, 1910 | Phillips, March 13, 2000, Lot 62

MATTHEW HARDIE | Fine and Rare Scottish Violoncello: Edinburgh, 1818 | Phillips, March 13, 2000, Lot 188

GUISEPPE ROCCA | Violin: Turin, 1849 | Sotheby's, March 14, 2000, Lot 54

Maker	Items		Selling Prices		
	Bid	Sold	Low	High	Avg
CAHUSAC, THOMAS (SR.)	1	1	$1,199	$1,199	$1,199
			£727	£727	£727
CLEMENTI & CO.	7	4	$318	$1,964	$867
			£196	£1,190	£554
COLAS, PROSPER	1	0			
COLONIEU, MARIUS HENRY	3	1	$264	$264	$264
			£161	£161	£161
CONN, USA	1	1	$485	$485	$485
			£287	£287	£287
CORONET	1	0			
COUESNON	1	0			
CRONE, GOTTLEIB	1	0			
CRONE, JOHANN AUGUST	1	0			
CUVILLIER	1	1	$1,145	$1,145	$1,145
			£690	£690	£690
D'ALMAINE & CO.	3	2	$179	$873	$526
			£109	£529	£319
DAWKINS & CO., THOMAS	1	1	$1,108	$1,108	$1,108
			£780	£780	£780
DELUSSE, CHRISTOPHER	1	1	$4,771	$4,771	$4,771
			£3,360	£3,360	£3,360
DODD	1	1	$72	$72	$72
			£46	£46	£46
DOLLING FAMILY (MEMBER OF)	1	1	$840	$840	$840
			£506	£506	£506
DROUET	1	1	$2,113	$2,113	$2,113
			£1,265	£1,265	£1,265
DROUET, LOUIS	5	5	$622	$6,217	$2,753
			£368	£3,680	£1,640
DUBOIS & COUTURIER	2	1	$573	$573	$573
			£345	£345	£345
EISENBRANDT, HEINRICH CHRISTIAN	1	1	$6,325	$6,325	$6,325
			£4,111	£4,111	£4,111
ELKHART	4	0			
EMBACH, LUDWIG	1	1	$611	$611	$611
			£370	£370	£370
FIRTH & HALL	1	1	$265	$265	$265
			£165	£165	£165
FIRTH, HALL & POND	3	3	$230	$489	$357
			£138	£322	£230
FISCHER, CARL	1	1	$115	$115	$115
			£70	£70	£70
FLORIO, PIETRO GRASSI	1	1	$1,964	$1,964	$1,964
			£1,190	£1,190	£1,190
FRENCH, G.	1	1	$283	$283	$283
			£184	£184	£184
FREYER, JOHANN GOTTLIEB	2	2	$2,471	$13,632	$8,051
			£1,610	£9,600	£5,605
FREYER & MARTIN	2	0			
GARRETT	1	1	$230	$230	$230
			£138	£138	£138
GAUTROT (AINE)	2	1	$370	$370	$370
			£224	£224	£224

Maker	Items		Selling Prices		
	Bid	Sold	Low	High	Avg
GEHRING	1	1	$6,706	$6,706	$6,706
			£4,370	£4,370	£4,370
GEMEINHARDT	3	2	$212	$309	$260
			£126	£184	£155
GEROCK, CHRISTOPHER	4	1	$324	$324	$324
			£195	£195	£195
GLIER, JOHANN WILHELM	1	1	$1,909	$1,909	$1,909
			£1,150	£1,150	£1,150
GODEFROY, CLAIR	1	1	$3,478	$3,478	$3,478
			£2,070	£2,070	£2,070
GODEFROY, CLAIR (AINE)	5	3	$676	$2,291	$1,434
			£414	£1,380	£866
GOODLAD & CO.	1	1	$840	$840	$840
			£506	£506	£506
GOULDING & CO.	2	1	$291	$291	$291
			£172	£172	£172
GOULDING & D'ALMAINE	3	3	$135	$498	$298
			£81	£299	£197
GOULDING D'ALMAINE POTTER	2	2	$535	$955	$745
			£322	£575	£449
GRENSER, CARL AUGUSTIN (I)	1	0			
GRENSER, H. & WIESNER	1	0			
GRENSER, JOHANN HEINRICH	4	1	$8,861	$8,861	$8,861
			£6,240	£6,240	£6,240
GREVE, ANDREAS	1	0			
HALE, JOHN	1	0			
HALL, WILLIAM	1	1	$288	$288	$288
			£173	£173	£173
HALL & SON, WILLIAM	1	1	$397	$397	$397
			£247	£247	£247
HANN, RICHARD	1	0			
HAWKES & SON	2	1	$298	$298	$298
			£184	£184	£184
HAYNES & CO.	3	3	$1,265	$2,185	$1,648
			£782	£1,350	£1,019
HAYNES CO., WILLIAM S.	3	3	$863	$2,070	$1,514
			£567	£1,242	£956
HEROUARD FRERES	1	0			
HILL, HENRY	1	1	$488	$488	$488
			£299	£299	£299
HIRSCHSTEIN, MATHAUS	1	1	$1,704	$1,704	$1,704
			£1,200	£1,200	£1,200
HOPKINS, A.	1	1	$1,265	$1,265	$1,265
			£822	£822	£822
HUELLER, G.H.	1	1	$463	$463	$463
			£288	£288	£288
HUSSON & BUTHOD	1	1	$300	$300	$300
			£184	£184	£184
JACOBS, HENDRIK	1	1	$30,728	$30,728	$30,728
			£18,400	£18,400	£18,400
JAMES, TREVOR J.	5	1	$130	$130	$130
			£81	£81	£81
JULLIOT, DJALMA	2	0			

Maker	Items		Selling Prices		
	Bid	Sold	Low	High	Avg
KAUFFMANN, ANDREW	3	2	$1,193	$1,606	$1,399
			£840	£1,035	£938
KOCH, S.	2	2	$1,260	$4,009	$2,635
			£805	£2,415	£1,610
KOHLER, JOHN	1	0			
KUSDER, HENRY	1	1	$3,284	$3,284	$3,284
			£1,955	£1,955	£1,955
LANGLOIS, A.M.	1	1	$678	$678	$678
			£437	£437	£437
LAWSON	3	2	$699	$878	$789
			£414	£529	£472
LEBRET	1	1	$816	$816	$816
			£483	£483	£483
LEBRET, LOUIS LEON JOSEPH	1	1	$382	$382	$382
			£230	£230	£230
LEROUX (AINE)	2	1	$588	$588	$588
			£357	£357	£357
LOT, LOUIS	5	4	$967	$9,694	$4,048
			£575	£5,980	£2,516
LUVONI, UBALDO	1	1	$612	$612	$612
			£362	£362	£362
MAHILLON, C.	1	1	$535	$535	$535
			£322	£322	£322
MARTIN BROS.	2	1	$1,943	$1,943	$1,943
			£1,150	£1,150	£1,150
MATEKI	1	1	$2,452	$2,452	$2,452
			£1,495	£1,495	£1,495
MAYBRICK, WILLIAM	1	0			
METZLER	5	3	$128	$178	$152
			£78	£115	£97
METZLER, VALENTIN	3	1	$407	$407	$407
			£241	£241	£241
METZLER & CO.	2	2	$112	$432	$272
			£69	£265	£167
MILHOUSE, WILLIAM	1	1	$1,565	$1,565	$1,565
			£943	£943	£943
MILLIGAN	1	1	$400	$400	$400
			£241	£241	£241
MOLLENHAUER & SONS, J.	2	1	$261	$261	$261
			£161	£161	£161
MONZANI	5	2	$773	$895	$834
			£460	£552	£506
MONZANI, TEBALDO	2	1	$858	$858	$858
			£517	£517	£517
MONZANI & CO.	16	10	$285	$3,928	$1,434
			£184	£2,381	£899
NAUST	1	1	$26,098	$26,098	$26,098
			£16,100	£16,100	£16,100
NEDDERMANN, JOHANN ADOPH	2	1	$764	$764	$764
			£460	£460	£460
NEUZIL, JOHANN	1	0			
NICHOLSON, CHARLES	1	1	$1,933	$1,933	$1,933
			£1,150	£1,150	£1,150

Maker	Items Bid	Sold	Low	Selling Prices High	Avg
NOBLET BROS.	1	1	$763 £462	$763 £462	$763 £462
OPPENHEIM, H.	1	1	$802 £483	$802 £483	$802 £483
OTTEN, JOHN	2	2	$282 £173	$394 £242	$338 £207
OTTO, JOHANN GEORG	1	0			
PAN-AMERICAN	1	0			
PAXMAN BROS.	1	0			
PEARL	3	1	$470 £322	$470 £322	$470 £322
PFAFF, FRANZ	1	0			
PFAFF, JOHN	1	1	$331 £206	$331 £206	$331 £206
POND & CO., WM. A.	1	1	$518 £337	$518 £337	$518 £337
POTTER	6	3	$84 £58	$336 £219	$214 £138
POTTER, HENRY	1	1	$224 £138	$224 £138	$224 £138
POTTER, RICHARD	4	4	$1,124 £699	$3,353 £2,185	$2,058 £1,294
POTTER, WILLIAM HENRY	15	10	$102 £63	$894 £529	$552 £332
PROSER	3	2	$773 £460	$1,107 £667	$940 £564
PROWSE, THOMAS	5	5	$394 £241	$1,093 £656	$680 £407
PROWSE & CO., KEITH	1	1	$601 £368	$601 £368	$601 £368
PRUNIER	1	0			
RITTERSHAUSEN, E.	1	0			
ROESSLER, HEINZ	2	1	$469 £288	$469 £288	$469 £288
RUDALL, CARTE & CO.	44	27	$85 £52	$4,963 £2,990	$826 £504
RUDALL & ROSE	9	9	$442 £288	$4,880 £2,990	$1,841 £1,125
RUDALL, ROSE, CARTE & CO.	5	5	$331 £206	$3,491 £2,116	$1,616 £1,005
SCHAEFFER, EVETTE	1	1	$840 £506	$840 £506	$840 £506
SCHOTT, B. (FILS)	1	1	$573 £345	$573 £345	$573 £345
SCHUCHART	1	1	$1,352 £805	$1,352 £805	$1,352 £805
SCHUCHART, JOHN JUST	1	0			
SELMER	1	0			
SICCAMA, ABEL	6	3	$305 £184	$1,145 £690	$687 £415
SIMPSON	1	1	$4,235 £2,760	$4,235 £2,760	$4,235 £2,760
SIMPSON, JOHN	2	2	$350 £207	$1,199 £727	$774 £467

| Maker | Items | | Selling Prices | | |
	Bid	Sold	Low	High	Avg
STANESBY, THOMAS	1	1	$9,706 £6,325	$9,706 £6,325	$9,706 £6,325
STRASSER, MARIGAUX, LEMAIRE	1	1	$453 £276	$453 £276	$453 £276
SZEPESSY, BELA	1	1	$8,818 £5,290	$8,818 £5,290	$8,818 £5,290
THIBOUVILLE, MARTIN (L'AINE)	1	1	$764 £460	$764 £460	$764 £460
THORSEN, NIELS CHRISTENSEN	1	1	$960 £575	$960 £575	$960 £575
TULOU, JEAN-LOUIS	3	1	$756 £483	$756 £483	$756 £483
UEBEL	1	1	$189 £123	$189 £123	$189 £123
WALLIS, JOSEPH & SON	1	0			
WELSH, THOMAS	1	1	$526 £322	$526 £322	$526 £322
WHEATSTONE, C.	1	1	$237 £150	$237 £150	$237 £150
WHITAKER & CO.	1	0			
WILLIAMS, E.G.	1	1	$329 £195	$329 £195	$329 £195
WILLIS, JOHN	3	0			
WOOD, JAMES & SON	1	1	$1,049 £632	$1,049 £632	$1,049 £632
WOOD & IVY	3	1	$545 £330	$545 £330	$545 £330
WYLDE, HENRY	2	2	$535 £345	$2,332 £1,380	$1,433 £863
XAVER, FRANZ	1	1	$1,541 £920	$1,541 £920	$1,541 £920
XAVER, FRANZ (attributed to)	1	0			
YAMAHA	6	5	$121 £81	$1,075 £633	$518 £310

FLUTE/PICCOLO

Maker	Bid	Sold	Low	High	Avg
NICHOLSON	2	1	$224 £138	$224 £138	$224 £138

FRENCH HORN

Maker	Bid	Sold	Low	High	Avg
BOOSEY & HAWKES	2	1	$170 £104	$170 £104	$170 £104
DALLAS	1	0			
GREY & SONS, JOHN	1	1	$151 £104	$151 £104	$151 £104
KNOPF	2	0			
MAHILLON, C.	1	1	$496 £299	$496 £299	$496 £299
MILLEREAU	1	0			
PAXMAN	1	1	$449 £299	$449 £299	$449 £299
STOWASSER, ADOLF	1	0			

Maker	Items		Selling Prices		
	Bid	Sold	Low	High	Avg

GALOUBET

Maker	Bid	Sold	Low	High	Avg
LONG	1	1	$1,069 £644	$1,069 £644	$1,069 £644

GIRAFFENFLUGEL

Maker	Bid	Sold	Low	High	Avg
SCHEHL, KARL	1	0			

GLOCKENSPIEL

Maker	Bid	Sold	Low	High	Avg
PREMIER	1	1	$282 £173	$282 £173	$282 £173

GUITAR

Maker	Bid	Sold	Low	High	Avg
ABBOTT	1	1	$750 £460	$750 £460	$750 £460
ARAM, KEVIN	1	1	$3,749 £2,300	$3,749 £2,300	$3,749 £2,300
ARIA	1	1	$124 £81	$124 £81	$124 £81
AUBRY, JACQUES	1	0			
BARRY	1	1	$1,336 £805	$1,336 £805	$1,336 £805
BARTON, PETER	1	1	$2,392 £1,495	$2,392 £1,495	$2,392 £1,495
BAY STATE	1	1	$1,323 £823	$1,323 £823	$1,323 £823
BAZZOLO, THOMAS	1	0			
BELLIDO, JOSE LOPEZ	1	1	$863 £575	$863 £575	$863 £575
BERNABE, PAULINO	2	0			
BERTET, JOSEPH R. (attributed to)	2	1	$1,789 £1,084	$1,789 £1,084	$1,789 £1,084
BERWIND, J.	2	1	$1,380 £828	$1,380 £828	$1,380 £828
BOHLIN, GEORG	1	0			
BOOSEY & CO.	1	1	$1,456 £862	$1,456 £862	$1,456 £862
BORREGUERO, MODESTO	1	1	$1,320 £805	$1,320 £805	$1,320 £805
BOUCHET, ROBERT	3	3	$26,476 £17,193	$30,912 £18,400	$28,847 £17,614
BOULLANGIER, CHARLES (attributed to)	1	1	$280 £173	$280 £173	$280 £173
BOULLANGIER, G.	2	2	$168 £109	$1,508 £955	$838 £532
BURNS	2	1	$1,125 £690	$1,125 £690	$1,125 £690
CAMACHO, RODOLFO	1	0			
CAMACHO, VICENTE	1	0			
CARPIO, RICARDO SANCHIS	1	1	$754 £460	$754 £460	$754 £460
CHIQUITA	1	1	$1,125 £690	$1,125 £690	$1,125 £690

| Maker | Items | | Selling Prices | | |
	Bid	Sold	Low	High	Avg
COLUMBIAN	2	2	$131	$225	$178
			£81	£138	£109
CONDE, HERMANOS	2	0			
CONTRERAS, M.G.	1	1	$377	$377	$377
			£230	£230	£230
CONTRERAS, MANUEL	7	2	$1,304	$1,845	$1,575
			£805	£1,092	£949
D'ANGELICO	1	0			
D'ANGELICO, JOHN	6	3	$9,258	$25,300	$18,803
			£5,740	£17,710	£12,551
DANELECTRO	1	0			
DEL PILAR, GUILLERMO	1	0			
DOBRO	4	4	$463	$1,062	$640
			£287	£632	£392
DREAPER	2	1	$487	$487	$487
			£299	£299	£299
DUBOIS	1	1	$2,215	$2,215	$2,215
			£1,560	£1,560	£1,560
EPIPHONE	3	2	$546	$720	$633
			£328	£497	£412
ESPINOSA, JULIAN	1	1	$580	$580	$580
			£345	£345	£345
ESTRUCH, JUAN	1	0			
FABRICATORE, GENNARO	6	4	$712	$3,125	$1,446
			£437	£2,185	£949
FABRICATORE, GIOVANNI BATTISTA	2	1	$1,783	$1,783	$1,783
			£1,035	£1,035	£1,035
FAVILLA GUITARS	1	1	$165	$165	$165
			£102	£102	£102
FAVILLA, HERK (workshop of)	1	1	$288	$288	$288
			£175	£175	£175
FENDER	9	7	$289	$937	$623
			£172	£575	£380
FERNANDEZ, ARCANGEL	2	1	$5,377	$5,377	$5,377
			£3,220	£3,220	£3,220
FISCHER, CARL	2	1	$535	$535	$535
			£322	£322	£322
FLEESON, MARTIN	1	0			
FLETA, IGNACIO	3	1	$26,432	$26,432	$26,432
			£17,250	£17,250	£17,250
FLETA & SONS, IGNACIO	2	2	$19,090	$20,645	$19,867
			£11,500	£12,650	£12,075
FRIEDERICH, DANIEL	1	1	$7,637	$7,637	$7,637
			£4,629	£4,629	£4,629
FRITH, STEPHEN	1	0			
FUSSINGER, J.T.	1	1	$1,166	$1,166	$1,166
			£690	£690	£690
GALLINOTTI, PIETRO	1	0			
GARCIA, ENRIQUE	2	0			
GARCIA, JOAQUIN	1	0			
GIBSON, WILLIAM	1	1	$1,049	$1,049	$1,049
			£632	£632	£632
GIBSON CO.	40	32	$184	$14,950	$1,841
			£112	£10,465	£1,193

Maker	Items		Selling Prices		
	Bid	Sold	Low	High	Avg
GOUDOT	1	0			
GRETSCH	6	5	$1,455	$6,561	$4,190
			£902	£4,025	£2,572
GRIMSHAW, EMIL	1	1	$604	$604	$604
			£368	£368	£368
GRUMMIT	1	0			
GUADAGNINI, CARLO (ascribed to)	1	1	$1,190	$1,190	$1,190
			£738	£738	£738
GUADAGNINI, FRANCESCO (ascribed to)	1	1	$1,610	$1,610	$1,610
			£952	£952	£952
GUILD	1	0			
GUTIERREZ, MANUEL	1	1	$2,386	$2,386	$2,386
			£1,680	£1,680	£1,680
HAGSTROM	1	0			
HAMER	1	0			
HANDEL, J.T.C.	2	0			
HARMONY	1	1	$221	$221	$221
			£138	£138	£138
HASHIMOTO	1	1	$293	$293	$293
			£196	£196	£196
HAUSER, HERMANN	5	3	$13,122	$49,350	$29,441
			£8,050	£32,078	£18,977
HAUSER, HERMANN (II)	1	1	$21,146	$21,146	$21,146
			£13,800	£13,800	£13,800
HAYNES CO., JOHN C.	1	0			
HENSE, DIETER	1	1	$675	$675	$675
			£402	£402	£402
HERNANDEZ, MANUEL & VICTORIANO AGUADO	1	1	$18,354	$18,354	$18,354
			£10,925	£10,925	£10,925
HERNANDEZ, SANTOS	3	2	$1,762	$7,668	$4,715
			£1,150	£5,400	£3,275
HERNANDEZ, SOBRINOS SANTOS	1	0			
HOFNER	5	2	$44	$134	$89
			£29	£80	£54
HOFNER, KARL	2	2	$244	$412	$328
			£150	£253	£201
HOPF, DIETER	1	0			
HOWE, ELIAS	1	0			
HOWELL, T.	1	1	$2,037	$2,037	$2,037
			£1,323	£1,323	£1,323
HUSSON, BUTHOD & THIBOUVILLE	1	1	$619	$619	$619
			£403	£403	£403
IBANEZ	1	1	$428	$428	$428
			£276	£276	£276
JONES, A.H.	1	1	$382	$382	$382
			£253	£253	£253
JONES, EDWARD B.	1	0			
KIMBARA	1	1	$112	$112	$112
			£69	£69	£69
KRINER, SIMON	1	0			
LACOTE	4	3	$1,273	$4,088	$2,938
			£828	£2,588	£1,867

Maker	Items		Selling Prices		
	Bid	Sold	Low	High	Avg
LACOTE, RENE (attributed to)	1	0			
LARSON (workshop of)	1	0			
LARSON BROS.	2	1	$397	$397	$397
			£246	£246	£246
LEVIN GOLIATH	1	1	$412	$412	$412
			£253	£253	£253
LIESSEM, R.	1	0			
LION, ARTHUR	1	1	$374	$374	$374
			£228	£228	£228
LONGMAN & BRODERIP	3	2	$1,145	$5,727	$3,436
			£690	£3,450	£2,070
LUTZEMBERGER	1	0			
MAIRE, FRANCAIS	1	1	$1,360	$1,360	$1,360
			£805	£805	£805
MANN	1	0			
MANZANERO, FELIX	1	0			
MARCHAND	1	1	$713	$713	$713
			£437	£437	£437
MARTIN	2	2	$1,312	$5,637	$3,474
			£805	£3,680	£2,243
MARTIN, CHRISTIAN FREDERICK	3	2	$2,070	$2,622	$2,346
			£1,257	£1,552	£1,404
MARTIN, E.	1	0			
MARTIN & CO., C.F.	35	34	$345	$16,100	$3,089
			£204	£9,660	£1,895
MARZAL, JESUS	1	0			
MAST, BLAISE	2	1	$2,619	$2,619	$2,619
			£1,587	£1,587	£1,587
MAST, JOSEPH LAURENT	1	1	$1,360	$1,360	$1,360
			£805	£805	£805
MATHIEU, MARESCHAL	1	0			
MOITESSIER, LOUIS	1	0			
MONTRON (attributed to)	1	0			
MONZINO, ANTONIO	1	1	$690	$690	$690
			£414	£414	£414
MOSELEY, SEMI	1	1	$288	$288	$288
			£175	£175	£175
MUSSER, D.	1	1	$6,748	$6,748	$6,748
			£4,140	£4,140	£4,140
NADERMAN, JEAN-HENRI	1	0			
NATIONAL	13	10	$259	$3,968	$2,143
			£153	£2,460	£1,310
NATIONAL DOBRO CORP.	1	1	$1,265	$1,265	$1,265
			£886	£886	£886
PADILLA, JUAN ROMAIN	1	1	$103	$103	$103
			£63	£63	£63
PANORMO	2	2	$2,050	$7,079	$4,565
			£1,265	£4,370	£2,818
PANORMO, JOSEPH	1	0			
PANORMO, LOUIS	18	17	$828	$4,582	$2,219
			£495	£2,760	£1,387
PERFUMO, JUAN	1	1	$1,595	$1,595	$1,595
			£978	£978	£978

Maker	Items		Selling Prices		
	Bid	Sold	Low	High	Avg
PETERSEN, HAROLD	3	3	$264	$360	$323
			£172	£230	£203
PETITJEAN (L'AINE)	3	1	$1,417	$1,417	$1,417
			£859	£859	£859
PIRETTI, ENRICO	1	0			
PONS FAMILY (MEMBER OF)	1	1	$3,109	$3,109	$3,109
			£1,840	£1,840	£1,840
PRESTON, JOHN	2	1	$638	$638	$638
			£391	£391	£391
RAMIREZ	2	1	$1,217	$1,217	$1,217
			£805	£805	£805
RAMIREZ, JOSE	9	5	$881	$4,485	$2,485
			£575	£2,990	£1,564
RAMIREZ, JOSE (workshop of)	1	1	$1,840	$1,840	$1,840
			£1,117	£1,117	£1,117
RAMIREZ, JOSE (I)	1	0			
RAMIREZ, JOSE (III)	4	1	$2,999	$2,999	$2,999
			£1,840	£1,840	£1,840
RAMIREZ, MANUEL	3	1	$4,229	$4,229	$4,229
			£2,760	£2,760	£2,760
RAMIREZ, MANUEL (workshop of)	1	1	$9,200	$9,200	$9,200
			£6,440	£6,440	£6,440
RAUCHE, MICHAEL	1	0			
RAY, R.	1	1	$437	$437	$437
			£299	£299	£299
REGAL CO.	1	1	$259	$259	$259
			£158	£158	£158
RHOUDLOFF, H.	1	1	$1,527	$1,527	$1,527
			£920	£920	£920
RICKENBACKER	3	3	$150	$4,686	$1,824
			£90	£2,875	£1,119
RIDOUT, MAGGIE	1	1	$396	$396	$396
			£242	£242	£242
RODRIGUEZ (SR.), MANUEL	1	1	$2,263	$2,263	$2,263
			£1,380	£1,380	£1,380
RODRIGUEZ, MIGUEL	1	0			
ROMANILLOS, JOSE	2	1	$8,435	$8,435	$8,435
			£5,175	£5,175	£5,175
ROUDHLOFF, D. & A. (attributed to)	1	1	$1,519	$1,519	$1,519
			£897	£897	£897
RUBIO, DAVID	1	0			
SALOMON (attributed to)	1	0			
SCHERZER	1	0			
SANAVIA, LEONE	1	1	$489	$489	$489
			£342	£342	£342
SCHMIDT & MAUL	1	1	$748	$748	$748
			£442	£442	£442
SELMER, HENRI	1	1	$21,252	$21,252	$21,252
			£12,650	£12,650	£12,650
SEMPLE, TREVOR	1	0			
SILVERTONE	3	2	$104	$345	$224
			£63	£210	£137
SIMPLICIO, FRANCISCO	1	1	$4,639	$4,639	$4,639
			£2,760	£2,760	£2,760

Maker	Items Bid	Sold	Selling Prices Low	High	Avg
SMALLMAN, GREG	1	0			
SPAIN, ROY	1	0			
STAUFFER (attributed to)	1	0			
STAUFFER, ANTON	1	0			
STAUFFER, JOHANN GEORG	1	0			
STROMBERG, CHARLES & ELMER	3	1	$10,350 £6,122	$10,350 £6,122	$10,350 £6,122
STROMBERG, ELMER	1	1	$18,400 £11,040	$18,400 £11,040	$18,400 £11,040
THIBOUVILLE-LAMY, J.	1	1	$562 £345	$562 £345	$562 £345
THOMSON	1	1	$934 £575	$934 £575	$934 £575
VEGA COMPANY	3	3	$345 £207	$2,990 £1,794	$1,275 £765
VELASQUEZ, JOSE LUIS	1	1	$115 £70	$115 £70	$115 £70
VELASQUEZ, MANUEL	2	0			
VENTAPANE, PASQUALE	1	0			
VILLA, LUIGI	1	0			
VINACCIA, GAETANO	1	0			
VINACCIA, GENNARO & ACHILLE	2	1	$1,417 £859	$1,417 £859	$1,417 £859
VOX	1	1	$562 £345	$562 £345	$562 £345
WASHBURN	1	0			
WOODFIELD, PHILIP	1	0			
YAMAHA	1	1	$811 £483	$811 £483	$811 £483
ZEMAITIS, A.G. (TONY)	1	0			

GUITAR-HARP

LEVIEN, MORDAUNT	1	1	$485 £287	$485 £287	$485 £287

GUITAR-LUTE

HAUSER, HERMANN	1	1	$1,093 £656	$1,093 £656	$1,093 £656

GUITARRA

ANDRADE, JOAO MIGUEL	1	1	$182 £109	$182 £109	$182 £109

HARP

BANKS, BENJAMIN	1	1	$1,431 £862	$1,431 £862	$1,431 £862
BLAZDELL, A.	1	1	$2,142 £1,323	$2,142 £1,323	$2,142 £1,323
DELVEAU	1	1	$3,864 £2,300	$3,864 £2,300	$3,864 £2,300
EGAN, JOHN	1	0			

Maker	Bid	Sold	Low	High	Avg
				Selling Prices	
			Low	*High*	*Avg*
ERARD	1	1	$4,499 £2,760	$4,499 £2,760	$4,499 £2,760
ERARD, J.	1	1	$1,076 £644	$1,076 £644	$1,076 £644
ERARD, SEBASTIAN	14	14	$1,316 £920	$8,570 £5,290	$4,083 £2,514
ERARD, SEBASTIAN & PIERRE	11	11	$1,728 £1,035	$12,751 £7,590	$5,610 £3,466
ERARD & CIE.	2	1	$4,200 £2,530	$4,200 £2,530	$4,200 £2,530
ERAT, I. & I.	2	1	$3,003 £1,840	$3,003 £1,840	$3,003 £1,840
ERAT, J.	2	1	$1,969 £1,208	$1,969 £1,208	$1,969 £1,208
ERAT, J. & J.	1	1	$7,297 £5,175	$7,297 £5,175	$7,297 £5,175
HOLDERNESSE, CHARLES	2	2	$1,336 £805	$6,217 £3,680	$3,777 £2,243
LIGHT, EDWARD	4	3	$661 £437	$4,168 £2,760	$1,947 £1,273
MOFFAT, J.W.	1	0			
MORLEY, JOHN	2	0			
MUIR CO.	1	0			
MUIR WOOD & CO.	1	1	$2,820 £1,725	$2,820 £1,725	$2,820 £1,725
NADERMANN, HENRY	1	1	$9,603 £5,750	$9,603 £5,750	$9,603 £5,750
NADERMANN FAMILY (MEMBER OF)	1	0			
SEROUET, E.	1	1	$1,032 £633	$1,032 £633	$1,032 £633
STUMPFF, J.A.	1	1	$2,129 £1,323	$2,129 £1,323	$2,129 £1,323
STUMPFF, J.C.	1	0			
VENTURA, A.B. (attributed to)	1	1	$2,291 £1,380	$2,291 £1,380	$2,291 £1,380

HARP-LUTE

Maker	Bid	Sold	Low	High	Avg
BARRY	2	1	$655 £397	$655 £397	$655 £397
CLEMENTI & CO.	1	0			
LIGHT, EDWARD	1	1	$840 £506	$840 £506	$840 £506

HARPSICHORD

Maker	Bid	Sold	Low	High	Avg
BACKERS, AMERICUS	2	1	$67,565 £41,400	$67,565 £41,400	$67,565 £41,400
BRITSEN, JORIS	2	0			
DOWD, WILLIAM	1	1	$18,400 £11,110	$18,400 £11,110	$18,400 £11,110
FRY, E.V.	1	1	$3,672 £2,185	$3,672 £2,185	$3,672 £2,185
HERZ, ERIC	1	1	$2,300 £1,513	$2,300 £1,513	$2,300 £1,513

Maker	Items Bid	Sold	Selling Prices Low	High	Avg
KIRCKMAN, ABRAHAM & JOSEPH	1	1	$36,467 £24,150	$36,467 £24,150	$36,467 £24,150
KIRCKMAN, JACOB	1	0			
KIRCKMAN, JACOB & ABRAHAM	1	1	$173,512 £102,700	$173,512 £102,700	$173,512 £102,700
PLEYEL	1	1	$5,345 £3,220	$5,345 £3,220	$5,345 £3,220
SHUDI, BURKAT & JOHN BROADWOOD	2	2	$104,746 £63,100	$201,135 £121,900	$152,941 £92,500

HELICON

Maker	Bid	Sold	Low	High	Avg
DE CART FRERES, FERDINAND & LOUIS	3	2	$393 £238	$524 £317	$458 £278

HORN

Maker	Bid	Sold	Low	High	Avg
BESSON	3	2	$97 £63	$114 £75	$106 £69
BLIGHT, J.	1	0			
BOOSEY & CO.	1	1	$156 £92	$156 £92	$156 £92
BOOSEY & HAWKES	2	2	$211 £138	$457 £299	$334 £219
BOSTON MUSICAL INSTRUMENT MANUFACTURER	1	1	$259 £168	$259 £168	$259 £168
CERVENY & SOHNE, V.F.	1	1	$764 £460	$764 £460	$764 £460
GROSS & BRAMBACH	1	1	$1,813 £1,092	$1,813 £1,092	$1,813 £1,092
KNOPF	1	1	$324 £207	$324 £207	$324 £207
KOHLERT'S SOHNE, V.	1	1	$458 £276	$458 £276	$458 £276
LAPINI	1	1	$403 £242	$403 £242	$403 £242
MILLEREAU	1	1	$414 £251	$414 £251	$414 £251
MULLER, C.A.	1	1	$535 £322	$535 £322	$535 £322
PERCIVAL, THOMAS	1	1	$436 £265	$436 £265	$436 £265
POTTER, HENRY	1	0			
SCHOPPER, ROBERT	2	0			
WEBER, CARL AUGUST	1	1	$1,049 £632	$1,049 £632	$1,049 £632
ZEDLITZ, EDUARD	1	1	$764 £460	$764 £460	$764 £460

HURDY-GURDY

Maker	Bid	Sold	Low	High	Avg
COLSON, NICOLAS	1	1	$1,413 £920	$1,413 £920	$1,413 £920

Maker	Items Bid	Sold	Selling Prices Low	High	Avg

KIT

JAY, HENRY	1	0			
PERRY	1	1	$2,332 £1,380	$2,332 £1,380	$2,332 £1,380
PERRY, THOMAS	1	0			

LUTE

BARRY	1	0			
BAUER, MATTHAUS	1	1	$705 £483	$705 £483	$705 £483
CHALLEN, CHRISTOPHER	1	1	$3,036 £1,840	$3,036 £1,840	$3,036 £1,840
DOLMETSCH, ARNOLD	2	1	$1,267 £782	$1,267 £782	$1,267 £782
GOFF, THOMAS	1	1	$1,457 £863	$1,457 £863	$1,457 £863
GOLD, PERL	1	1	$566 £345	$566 £345	$566 £345
GORRETT, JOHN	1	1	$526 £322	$526 £322	$526 £322
GUGGENBERGER, ANTON	1	0			
HARWOOD, IAN	2	1	$660 £403	$660 £403	$660 £403
HARWOOD, JOHN	2	1	$186 £115	$186 £115	$186 £115
HAUSER, HERMANN	1	0			
HOLMES, HENRY H.	3	2	$264 £161	$348 £207	$306 £184
JAKOB, RICHARD	1	0			
JORDAN, HANS	1	0			
KAROUBI, J.	1	0			
SPRIGGS, G.W.	1	1	$528 £322	$528 £322	$528 £322
TIEFFENBRUCKER, WENDELIN ("VENERE")	1	0			
WHITEMAN, DAVID	1	1	$540 £345	$540 £345	$540 £345

MANDO-CELLO

GIBSON CO.	2	1	$1,380 £816	$1,380 £816	$1,380 £816

MANDOLA

GARGANO, FRANCESCO	1	1	$368 £218	$368 £218	$368 £218
HOWE CO., ELIAS	1	1	$316 £221	$316 £221	$316 £221

MANDOLIN

ABBOTT	1	1	$171 £109	$171 £109	$171 £109

Maker	Items		Selling Prices		
	Bid	Sold	Low	High	Avg
BOHMANN, JOSEPH	2	1	$115 £70	$115 £70	$115 £70
CALACE	2	2	$504 £345	$1,209 £828	$856 £587
CALACE, GIUSEPPE	2	2	$4,857 £2,875	$14,092 £9,200	$9,474 £6,038
CALACE, NICOLA & RAFFAELLE	1	1	$3,749 £2,640	$3,749 £2,640	$3,749 £2,640
CALACE, RAFFAELE	2	2	$1,534 £920	$2,619 £1,587	$2,076 £1,254
CALACE & FIGLIO, RAFFAELE	3	3	$1,008 £705	$3,378 £2,070	$2.338 £1.462
CAPONETTO, LUIGI	2	1	$168 £104	$168 £104	$168 £104
CAPPIELLO, V. & G.	3	1	$113 £69	$113 £69	$113 £69
CASELLA, M.	1	1	$782 £518	$782 £518	$782 £518
CECCHERINI, UMBERTO	3	3	$154 £92	$482 £288	$308 £188
CIANI, RAPHAEL	1	1	$363 £225	$363 £225	$363 £225
DALLAS, J.E.	1	1	$230 £150	$230 £150	$230 £150
DEL PERUGIA, FERNANDO	2	2	$452 £278	$1,212 £704	$832 £491
DE MEGLIO, GIOVANNI	6	6	$149 £92	$657 £403	$335 £207
DE MEGLIO & FIGLIO	2	2	$230 £138	$324 £207	$277 £173
DE MUREDA	1	1	$129 £86	$129 £86	$129 £86
EMBERGHER, LUIGI	3	3	$2,215 £1,560	$8,018 £4,830	$6,030 £3,717
ESSEX, CLIFFORD	2	2	$241 £150	$597 £368	$419 £259
FABRICATORE, GIOVANNI	1	1	$1,455 £905	$1,455 £905	$1,455 £905
FANGA, LUIGI	1	0			
FERRARI & CO	4	3	$321 £207	$433 £273	$368 £233
FILANO, DONATO	1	1	$2,897 £2,040	$2,897 £2,040	$2,897 £2,040
GAROZZO, C.	1	1	$1,217 £805	$1,217 £805	$1,217 £805
GIBSON CO.	26	25	$345 £204	$3,335 £2,001	$1,129 £708
GRIMALDI, EMILIO	1	1	$4,504 £2,760	$4,504 £2,760	$4,504 £2,760
HOWE, ELIAS	1	1	$518 £311	$518 £311	$518 £311
IBANEZ	1	1	$707 £460	$707 £460	$707 £460
KAY	1	1	$92 £56	$92 £56	$92 £56

Maker	Items		Selling Prices		
	Bid	Sold	Low	High	Avg
LYON & HEALY	1	1	$150 £91	$150 £91	$150 £91
MAGLIONI, GENNARO	1	1	$169 £104	$169 £104	$169 £104
MANFREDI, GIUSEPPE	2	1	$2,137 £1,265	$2,137 £1,265	$2,137 £1,265
MARTELLO, CARLOS	2	1	$400 £265	$400 £265	$400 £265
MARTIN & CO., C.F.	6	5	$288 £173	$403 £282	$345 £220
MEGLIO & FIGLIO	1	1	$445 £276	$445 £276	$445 £276
MOLINARI, GIUSEPPE	1	1	$5,255 £3,220	$5,255 £3,220	$5,255 £3,220
MONZINO, ANTONIO	1	1	$1,164 £713	$1,164 £713	$1,164 £713
NAPOLI, DOMENICO BANONI	1	1	$891 £575	$891 £575	$891 £575
PECORARO, P.	1	1	$675 £414	$675 £414	$675 £414
PERRETTI, FRANCESCO & SON	3	2	$243 £161	$371 £230	$307 £196
PRESBLER, GIUSEPPE	1	0			
PUGLISI, GIUSEPPE	3	2	$288 £175	$2,440 £1,495	$1,364 £835
RINALDI, CARLO	1	1	$419 £293	$419 £293	$419 £293
ROCCA, ENRICO	1	0			
SALVINO & CO., A.	1	1	$618 £368	$618 £368	$618 £368
SILVESTRI, CARMINE	1	1	$1,028 £635	$1,028 £635	$1,028 £635
STEWART, S.S.	1	1	$431 £259	$431 £259	$431 £259
TONELLI, PIETRO	3	2	$201 £138	$231 £138	$216 £138
VARANO, MICHELE	2	1	$446 £288	$446 £288	$446 £288
VATIANI, PAOLO	1	1	$74 £46	$74 £46	$74 £46
VEGA COMPANY	1	0			
VINACCIA, ANTONIO	2	2	$2,864 £1,725	$9,927 £5,980	$6,395 £3,853
VINACCIA, GENNARO	1	0			
VINACCIA, GENNARO & ACHILLE	1	1	$2,215 £1,560	$2,215 £1,560	$2,215 £1,560
VINACCIA, GIOVANNI	1	1	$9,165 £5,555	$9,165 £5,555	$9,165 £5,555
VINACCIA, GIUSEPPE	2	2	$789 £483	$1,484 £899	$1,137 £691
VINACCIA BROS.	1	1	$1,380 £863	$1,380 £863	$1,380 £863
WASHBURN	3	3	$132 £82	$316 £193	$199 £122

Maker	Items Bid	Sold	Low	Selling Prices High	Avg
MANDOLIN-LYRE					
CALACE, RAFFAELE	1	1	$463 £287	$463 £287	$463 £287
CALACE FRATELLI	1	1	$1,035 £621	$1,035 £621	$1,035 £621
MANDOLINO					
FONTANELLI, GIOVANNI GIUSEPPE	1	1	$2,496 £1,449	$2,496 £1,449	$2,496 £1,449
NONEMACHER, CRISTIANO	1	1	$6,872 £4,140	$6,872 £4,140	$6,872 £4,140
MARTINSHORN					
MARTIN, MAX BERNHARDT	1	0			
MELLOPHONE					
HOLTON & CO.	1	0			
PEPPER	1	0			
PEPPER, J.W.	1	0			
YORK	1	0			
MUSETTE					
MARTIN BROS.	1	1	$436 £265	$436 £265	$436 £265
NORMAPHON					
WUNDERLICH	1	1	$5,463 £3,278	$5,463 £3,278	$5,463 £3,278
OBOE					
ADLER, FREDERIC GUILLAUME	2	0			
ALBERT, J.	1	1	$97 £63	$97 £63	$97 £63
ANCIUTI, JOHANNES MARIA	1	0			
ASTOR & CO., GEORGE	3	2	$407 £241	$3,436 £2,070	$1,922 £1,156
BAUER, JEAN	1	0			
BOOSEY & HAWKES	3	3	$317 £207	$422 £276	$358 £234
BUFFET	2	2	$242 £150	$2,628 £1,610	$1,435 £880
BUFFET, CRAMPON & CO.	1	1	$490 £299	$490 £299	$490 £299
BUISSON, F.	3	1	$334 £207	$334 £207	$334 £207
BUTHOD & THIBOUVILLE	1	1	$943 £575	$943 £575	$943 £575
DELUSSE, CHRISTOPHER	2	2	$3,754 £2,300	$9,759 £5,980	$6,756 £4,140

Maker	Items		Selling Prices		
	Bid	Sold	Low	High	Avg
DUVAL, RENE	2	1	$151	$151	$151
			£104	£104	£104
ENGELHARD, JOHANN FRIEDRICH	1	0			
GAUTROT-MARQUET	1	1	$477	$477	$477
			£336	£336	£336
GEDNEY, CALEB	1	1	$3,529	$3,529	$3,529
			£2,300	£2,300	£2,300
GOLDE	1	1	$4,600	$4,600	$4,600
			£2,990	£2,990	£2,990
GOLDE, CARL	2	1	$6,606	$6,606	$6,606
			£3,910	£3,910	£3,910
GOULDING & CO.	1	1	$5,112	$5,112	$5,112
			£3,600	£3,600	£3,600
GRENSER, CARL AUGUSTIN (I)	1	1	$18,768	$18,768	$18,768
			£11,500	£11,500	£11,500
GRENSER, JOHANN HEINRICH	1	0			
GRUNDMANN, JAKOB FREDERICH	1	1	$28,471	$28,471	$28,471
			£20,050	£20,050	£20,050
GRUNDMANN & FLOT	1	1	$826	$826	$826
			£506	£506	£506
GUERINI	1	0			
GULIELMINETTI	1	1	$2,137	$2,137	$2,137
			£1,265	£1,265	£1,265
HAWKES & CO.	1	1	$93	$93	$93
			£58	£58	£58
HAWKES & SON	2	1	$132	$132	$132
			£86	£86	£86
HECKEL	1	1	$827	$827	$827
			£506	£506	£506
HOE, JOHANN WOLFGANG	1	1	$10,686	$10,686	$10,686
			£6,325	£6,325	£6,325
HORAK & SOHN, W.	1	1	$1,909	$1,909	$1,909
			£1,150	£1,150	£1,150
HOWARTH	1	1	$535	$535	$535
			£345	£345	£345
HOWARTH & CO.	1	1	$336	$336	$336
			£207	£207	£207
HULLER, G.H.	1	1	$382	$382	$382
			£230	£230	£230
KATTOFEN, AMMON	1	1	$382	$382	$382
			£230	£230	£230
KOHLERT & SONS	1	1	$150	$150	$150
			£92	£92	£92
KREUL, HANS	1	0			
KRUSPE, FRIEDRICH WILHELM	1	1	$2,137	$2,137	$2,137
			£1,265	£1,265	£1,265
LAFLEUR, J.R. & SON	1	1	$150	$150	$150
			£92	£92	£92
LOREE, F.	6	4	$705	$1,548	$1,233
			£483	£1,012	£782
LOREE, FRANCOIS	2	0			
LOUIS	1	0			
LUDWIG, FRANZ	2	2	$3,436	$4,582	$4,009
			£2,070	£2,760	£2,415

Maker	Items Bid	Sold	Selling Prices Low	High	Avg
LUDWIG & MARTINKA	2	2	$1,456 £862	$4,963 £2,990	$3,210 £1,926
MILHOUSE, RICHARD	1	1	$3,627 £2,185	$3,627 £2,185	$3,627 £2,185
MILHOUSE, WILLIAM	2	2	$818 £576	$3,710 £2,248	$2,264 £1,412
MOLLENHAUER, CONRAD	1	0			
MONNIG, OTTO	3	2	$764 £460	$802 £483	$783 £472
MONNIG GEBRUDER	4	1	$179 £109	$179 £109	$179 £109
MORTON, ALFRED	1	1	$155 £92	$155 £92	$155 £92
MORTON & SONS, A.	2	1	$180 £115	$180 £115	$180 £115
NOBLET	2	1	$289 £184	$289 £184	$289 £184
OMS	1	1	$8,160 £4,830	$8,160 £4,830	$8,160 £4,830
PANORMO, VINCENZO	1	0			
PARADIS	1	1	$86 £57	$86 £57	$86 £57
PINDER, HEINRICH FRANZ EDUARD	1	1	$916 £552	$916 £552	$916 £552
REICHENBACHER, ERNST	1	1	$1,943 £1,150	$1,943 £1,150	$1,943 £1,150
REIST, H.	1	1	$4,801 £2,910	$4,801 £2,910	$4,801 £2,910
RICHTERS, HENDRIK	1	1	$22,522 £13,800	$22,522 £13,800	$22,522 £13,800
ROESSLER, HEINZ	1	1	$432 £265	$432 £265	$432 £265
ROTTENBURGH, JOANNES HYACINTHUS (I)	1	1	$24,398 £14,950	$24,398 £14,950	$24,398 £14,950
RUDALL, CARTE & CO.	2	2	$132 £81	$334 £207	$233 £144
SATTLER, CARL WILHELM	1	1	$7,507 £4,600	$7,507 £4,600	$7,507 £4,600
SCHLEGEL, JEREMIAS	2	1	$1,240 £747	$1,240 £747	$1,240 £747
SCHUCK, M.	1	1	$575 £374	$575 £374	$575 £374
SELMER	1	1	$169 £104	$169 £104	$169 £104
SHARPE, JOHN	2	2	$622 £368	$1,527 £920	$1,074 £644
SIMPSON, JOHN	1	0			
STANESBY, THOMAS SR. & JR.	1	1	$11,261 £6,900	$11,261 £6,900	$11,261 £6,900
STARK	1	1	$196 £115	$196 £115	$196 £115
STEHLE	1	1	$1,049 £632	$1,049 £632	$1,049 £632

Maker	Items		Selling Prices		
	Bid	Sold	Low	High	Avg
TRIEBERT	1	0			
TRIEBERT & SONS, GUILLAUME	1	1	$1,622	$1,622	$1,622
			£977	£977	£977
UHLMANN, JOHANN TOBIAS	1	1	$2,291	$2,291	$2,291
			£1,380	£1,380	£1,380
WARD & SONS	1	1	$207	$207	$207
			£127	£127	£127
WEYGANDT, T.J.	1	1	$6,109	$6,109	$6,109
			£3,680	£3,680	£3,680

OBOE D'AMORE

Maker	Items		Selling Prices		
OBERLENDER, JOHANN WILHELM (I)	1	1	$54,553	$54,553	$54,553
			£33,063	£33,063	£33,063

OCTAVIN

Maker	Items		Selling Prices		
ADLER & CO., OSCAR	1	1	$1,852	$1,852	$1,852
			£1,152	£1,152	£1,152

OPHICLEIDE

Maker	Items		Selling Prices		
BONNEL	1	1	$2,064	$2,064	$2,064
			£1,265	£1,265	£1,265
HENRI	2	1	$1,309	$1,309	$1,309
			£794	£794	£794

ORGAN

Maker	Items		Selling Prices		
GREEN, SAMUEL	1	0			
PISTOR, EDWARD & JOHN	1	0			
SNETZLER, JOHN	1	1	$69,638	$69,638	$69,638
			£42,205	£42,205	£42,205
STUMPHLER, JOHANN STEPHAN (ascribed to)	1	0			

PHONO-FIDDLE

Maker	Items		Selling Prices		
EVANS & CO., GEORGE	1	1	$840	$840	$840
			£506	£506	£506
HOWSON, A.T.	5	4	$131	$447	$245
			£81	£276	£151
STROH, CHARLES	1	1	$687	$687	$687
			£414	£414	£414
STROVIOL	2	2	$180	$248	$214
			£115	£161	£138

PIANINO

Maker	Items		Selling Prices		
CHAPPELL	1	1	$13,600	$13,600	$13,600
			£8,050	£8,050	£8,050

PIANO

Maker	Items		Selling Prices		
BERNHARDT, P.	1	1	$6,756	$6,756	$6,756
			£4,140	£4,140	£4,140
BEYER, ADAM	2	2	$1,190	$2,619	$1,904
			£740	£1,587	£1,164

| Maker | Items | | Selling Prices | | |
	Bid	Sold	Low	High	Avg
BLUTHNER	1	1	$2,141 £1,380	$2,141 £1,380	$2,141 £1,380
BOSENDORFER	1	1	$387,500 £233,973	$387,500 £233,973	$387,500 £233,973
BROADWOOD, JOHN	1	0			
BROADWOOD, JOHN & SONS	3	2	$326 £198	$2,346 £1,438	$1,336 £818
CHALLEN & HOLLIS	2	0			
CLEMENTI, MUZIO	4	3	$464 £276	$1,835 £1,092	$1,123 £686
CLEMENTI & CO.	3	2	$1,874 £1,320	$2,837 £1,719	$2,356 £1,520
COLLARD & COLLARD	1	1	$2,291 £1,380	$2,291 £1,380	$2,291 £1,380
EDWARDS, WILLIAM	1	1	$3,003 £1,840	$3,003 £1,840	$3,003 £1,840
GANER, CHRISTOPHER	1	1	$916 £595	$916 £595	$916 £595
GANER, CHRISTOPHER (attributed to)	1	1	$188 £115	$188 £115	$188 £115
HAXBY, THOMAS	2	2	$1,240 £747	$2,854 £1,840	$2,047 £1,294
HEINTZMAN & CO.	1	1	$3,450 £2,174	$3,450 £2,174	$3,450 £2,174
KIRCKMAN, JACOB & ABRAHAM	2	0			
KLEIN, F.A.	2	0			
LONGMAN, JAMES	1	1	$1,641 £977	$1,641 £977	$1,641 £977
LONGMAN & CO.	2	1	$1,240 £747	$1,240 £747	$1,240 £747
LONGMAN & BRODERIP	10	9	$960 £575	$2,720 £1,800	$1,862 £1,139
LONGMAN, CLEMENTI & CO.	1	1	$1,408 £863	$1,408 £863	$1,408 £863
MORNINGTON, ROBERT	1	0			
PHILLIPS, W.	1	1	$1,222 £794	$1,222 £794	$1,222 £794
PLEYEL	1	0			
POHLMAN, JOHANNES	1	1	$1,689 £1,035	$1,689 £1,035	$1,689 £1,035
PRESTON, THOMAS	2	1	$1,145 £690	$1,145 £690	$1,145 £690
ROLFE, WILLIAM & SONS	1	0			
ROLOFF, H.	2	0			
SEEBURG	2	2	$1,725 £1,087	$2,530 £1,594	$2,128 £1,340
STEINWAY & SONS	1	0			
STEWART, NEIL & MALCOLM	1	1	$1,193 £840	$1,193 £840	$1,193 £840
STODART, M. & W.	1	1	$618 £368	$618 £368	$618 £368
STODART, WILLIAM & SON	1	1	$6,606 £3,910	$6,606 £3,910	$6,606 £3,910

Maker	Items		Selling Prices		
	Bid	Sold	Low	High	Avg
WACHTL, JOSEPH & JACOB BLEYER	2	1	$15,336 £10,800	$15,336 £10,800	$15,336 £10,800
WEBLEN, ALEXANDER	1	0			

PIANOFORTE

Maker	Bid	Sold	Low	High	Avg
BROADWOOD, JOHN	1	0			
BROADWOOD, JOHN & SONS	6	5	$1,909 £1,150	$27,201 £16,100	$14,717 £9,457
COLLARD & COLLARD	1	1	$3,245 £1,955	$3,245 £1,955	$3,245 £1,955
CRISI, VINCENZO	1	1	$9,759 £5,980	$9,759 £5,980	$9,759 £5,980
EHLERS, JOACHIM	1	0			
FIRTH & HALL	1	1	$920 £552	$920 £552	$920 £552
GRAF, CONRAD	2	2	$26,275 £16,100	$38,859 £23,000	$32,567 £19,550
HANCOCK, CRANG	1	1	$22,941 £14,950	$22,941 £14,950	$22,941 £14,950
HAWKINS, JOHN ISAAC	1	1	$34,362 £20,700	$34,362 £20,700	$34,362 £20,700
LONGMAN & BRODERIP	1	1	$17,830 £10,925	$17,830 £10,925	$17,830 £10,925
LONGMAN, CLEMENTI & CO.	1	0			
SCHANZ, JOHANN	1	1	$33,823 £20,499	$33,823 £20,499	$33,823 £20,499
STEIN, JOHANN ANDREAS	1	1	$76,872 £45,500	$76,872 £45,500	$76,872 £45,500
STEIN, MATTHAUS ANDREAS	1	1	$27,201 £16,100	$27,201 £16,100	$27,201 £16,100
STODART, M. & W.	2	1	$9,165 £5,555	$9,165 £5,555	$9,165 £5,555
TOMKISON, THOMAS	1	1	$1,687 £1,035	$1,687 £1,035	$1,687 £1,035

PICCOLO

Maker	Bid	Sold	Low	High	Avg
BESSON & CO.	1	1	$207 £127	$207 £127	$207 £127
BUTLER	1	1	$150 £92	$150 £92	$150 £92
D'ALMAINE & CO.	1	1	$511 £360	$511 £360	$511 £360
GAND, CHARLES	1	0			
GOULDING & CO.	1	1	$188 £115	$188 £115	$188 £115
HAWKES & SON	1	1	$158 £98	$158 £98	$158 £98
HAYNES & CO.	1	1	$748 £462	$748 £462	$748 £462
HAYNES CO., WILLIAM S.	1	1	$382 £230	$382 £230	$382 £230
KOHLER & SON	1	0			

Maker	Items Bid	Sold	Low	Selling Prices High	Avg
KRUSPE, C.	1	0			
LOT, LOUIS	7	2	$414 £253	$771 £476	$592 £365
MAHILLON & CO., C.	1	1	$86 £58	$86 £58	$86 £58
MONZANI	1	1	$714 £460	$714 £460	$714 £460
RITTERSHAUSEN, E.	1	1	$150 £98	$150 £98	$150 £98
RUDALL, CARTE & CO.	9	6	$94 £58	$317 £207	$184 £117
SELMER	1	0			
THIBOUVILLE-LAMY, J.	1	1	$56 £35	$56 £35	$56 £35
WALLIS, JOSEPH	2	1	$725 £437	$725 £437	$725 £437

POCHETTE

Maker	Bid	Sold	Low	High	Avg
AMAN, GEORG	2	1	$4,880 £2,990	$4,880 £2,990	$4,880 £2,990
BAADER, J. (workshop of)	1	1	$978 £593	$978 £593	$978 £593
BETTS, JOHN	1	1	$642 £380	$642 £380	$642 £380
BETTS, JOHN (attributed to)	1	0			
WORLE, MATHIAS	2	2	$4,888 £2,891	$9,919 £6,150	$7,403 £4,520

QUINTON

Maker	Bid	Sold	Low	High	Avg
GUERSAN, LOUIS	2	2	$4,663 £2,760	$4,673 £2,760	$4,668 £2,760

RACKET BASSOON

Maker	Bid	Sold	Low	High	Avg
BIZEY, CHARLES	1	0			

RAUSCHPFEIFE

Maker	Bid	Sold	Low	High	Avg
GUNTHER	1	0			

RECORDER

Maker	Bid	Sold	Low	High	Avg
ADLER, JOHANNES	1	1	$46 £30	$46 £30	$46 £30
AULOS	1	1	$35 £23	$35 £23	$35 £23
DENNER, JOHANN CHRISTOPH	1	0			
DOLMETSCH	2	1	$285 £196	$285 £196	$285 £196
EICHENTOPF, JOHANN HEINRICH	1	1	$20,645 £12,650	$20,645 £12,650	$20,645 £12,650
GOBLE, ROBERT	1	0			
HOHNER	1	1	$9 £6	$9 £6	$9 £6

Maker	Items		Selling Prices		
	Bid	Sold	Low	High	Avg
MOECK	1	1	$173	$173	$173
			£112	£112	£112
OBERLENDER, JOHANN WILHELM (I)	1	0			
RIPPERT, JEAN JACQUES	2	1	$17,181	$17,181	$17,181
			£10,350	£10,350	£10,350
STANESBY, THOMAS	2	1	$40,801	$40,801	$40,801
			£24,150	£24,150	£24,150
STANESBY, THOMAS JR.	1	1	$20,999	$20,999	$20,999
			£12,650	£12,650	£12,650
VON HUENE, FRIEDRICH	1	1	$1,610	$1,610	$1,610
			£966	£966	£966

ROTHPHONE

Maker	Items		Selling Prices		
BOTTALI, A.M.	1	1	$2,291	$2,291	$2,291
			£1,380	£1,380	£1,380
BOTTALI FRATELLI, A.M.	2	2	$3,054	$6,109	$4,582
			£1,840	£3,680	£2,760

SARRUSOPHONE

Maker	Items		Selling Prices		
CONN, C.G.	1	0			
ORSI, ROMEO	1	0			
RAMPONE	1	1	$5,345	$5,345	$5,345
			£3,220	£3,220	£3,220

SAW

Maker	Items		Selling Prices		
FELDMANN, C.	1	1	$56	$56	$56
			£34	£34	£34
SANDVICKENS, JERNVERKS A.B.	1	1	$133	$133	$133
			£80	£80	£80

SAXHORN

Maker	Items		Selling Prices		
KLEMM & BRO.	1	1	$3,163	$3,163	$3,163
			£1,898	£1,898	£1,898
ZOEBISCH & SONS, C.A.	1	1	$802	$802	$802
			£483	£483	£483

SAXOPHONE

Maker	Items		Selling Prices		
BOOSEY & HAWKES	1	0			
BUESCHER	15	12	$149	$1,260	$607
			£92	£805	£388
BUFFET, CRAMPON & CO.	3	1	$285	$285	$285
			£196	£196	£196
CABART	2	1	$338	$338	$338
			£207	£207	£207
COHN	2	2	$522	$695	$608
			£345	£460	£403
CONN, C.G.	16	12	$271	$981	$566
			£161	£598	£356
COUESNON	1	1	$616	$616	$616
			£403	£403	£403
COUESNON & CO.	1	1	$472	$472	$472
			£288	£288	£288

| Maker | Items | | Selling Prices | | |
	Bid	Sold	Low	High	Avg
DOLNET, HENRI	1	1	$252 £173	$252 £173	$252 £173
DORE	1	0			
DUBOIS, RAYMOND	1	1	$259 £161	$259 £161	$259 £161
FOOTE	1	1	$377 £230	$377 £230	$377 £230
GRAFTON	10	8	$1,165 £713	$2,141 £1,380	$1,582 £980
GRASS	1	1	$331 £207	$331 £207	$331 £207
HAWKES & SON	6	5	$130 £81	$447 £276	$279 £170
HULLER, G.H.	1	1	$916 £552	$916 £552	$916 £552
LECOMTE & CO., A.	1	1	$1,495 £972	$1,495 £972	$1,495 £972
OEHLER, OSKAR	2	0			
SAX, ADOLPHE	4	3	$940 £575	$2,252 £1,380	$1,388 £863
SELMER	12	10	$336 £219	$3,525 £2,291	$1,632 £1,044
SELMER, HENRI	2	2	$1,792 £1,093	$2,260 £1,495	$2,026 £1,294
SELMER BUNDY	1	1	$150 £91	$150 £91	$150 £91
SIOMA	2	0			
STRASSER MARIGAUX	1	1	$161 £98	$161 £98	$161 £98
STRASSER, MARIGAUX, LEMAIRE	1	1	$630 £403	$630 £403	$630 £403
THIBOUVILLE-LAMY, J.	5	3	$155 £92	$559 £345	$374 £230

SERPENT

Maker	Bid	Sold	Low	High	Avg
CRAMER, JOHN	1	0			
GOULDING & D'ALMAINE	1	1	$3,360 £2,318	$3,360 £2,318	$3,360 £2,318
JORDAN, JAMES	1	1	$3,749 £2,640	$3,749 £2,640	$3,749 £2,640
MONK, CHRISTOPHER	1	1	$1,009 £621	$1,009 £621	$1,009 £621
PRETTY, F. (attributed to)	1	1	$2,056 £1,265	$2,056 £1,265	$2,056 £1,265
PRETTY, ROBERT	1	1	$2,277 £1,380	$2,277 £1,380	$2,277 £1,380
WOLF & CO., ROBERT	1	1	$4,200 £2,530	$4,200 £2,530	$4,200 £2,530

SOUSAPHONE

Maker	Bid	Sold	Low	High	Avg
BESSON	1	1	$805 £491	$805 £491	$805 £491
DE PRINS GEBRUDER	2	1	$393 £238	$393 £238	$393 £238

Maker	Items		Selling Prices		
	Bid	Sold	Low	High	Avg

SPINET

Maker	Bid	Sold	Low	High	Avg
BARTON (ascribed to)	4	0			
BARTON, GEORGE	1	0			
HAXBY, THOMAS	1	1	$12,601 £8,812	$12,601 £8,812	$12,601 £8,812
HITCHCOCK, JOHN	1	1	$20,730 £12,564	$20,730 £12,564	$20,730 £12,564
SHEAN, CHRISTIAN	1	0			
SISON, BENJAMIN	1	0			
SMITH, WILLIAM	1	1	$17,395 £10,350	$17,395 £10,350	$17,395 £10,350
STEWART, N.	1	1	$9,894 £6,440	$9,894 £6,440	$9,894 £6,440
WEBER, FERDINAND	1	1	$23,315 £13,800	$23,315 £13,800	$23,315 £13,800

SUSAPHONE

Maker	Bid	Sold	Low	High	Avg
PAXMAN BROS.	1	0			

SYMPHONIUM

Maker	Bid	Sold	Low	High	Avg
WHEATSTONE, C.	1	1	$3,651 £2,415	$3,651 £2,415	$3,651 £2,415

TAROGATO

Maker	Bid	Sold	Low	High	Avg
MOGYOROSSY, G.Y.	2	1	$786 £476	$786 £476	$786 £476

TIMPANI

Maker	Bid	Sold	Low	High	Avg
HAWKES & SON	1	1	$505 £299	$505 £299	$505 £299
HIGHAM, JOSEPH	1	0			

TIPLE

Maker	Bid	Sold	Low	High	Avg
MARTIN & CO., C.F.	2	2	$259 £155	$431 £255	$345 £205

TROMBONE

Maker	Bid	Sold	Low	High	Avg
BESSON	3	3	$79 £52	$106 £69	$91 £59
BOOSEY & CO.	1	1	$403 £242	$403 £242	$403 £242
BOOSEY & HAWKES	4	4	$160 £98	$334 £219	$220 £142
BUNDY	1	1	$141 £86	$141 £86	$141 £86
BURGER, JULIUS MAX	1	1	$428 £258	$428 £258	$428 £258
COURTOIS, ANTOINE (FILS)	2	1	$485 £287	$485 £287	$485 £287
DE CART FRERES, FERDINAND & LOUIS	1	1	$840 £506	$840 £506	$840 £506

Maker	Items		Selling Prices		
	Bid	Sold	Low	High	Avg
FICKHERT, WILHELM	1	0			
HAWKES & SON	1	1	$84 £52	$84 £52	$84 £52
RIVIERE & HAWKES	1	0			
ROUSSEAU, A.F.	1	1	$611 £368	$611 £368	$611 £368
RUDALL, CARTE & CO.	1	1	$188 £115	$188 £115	$188 £115
SENECAUT, PIERRE	1	1	$878 £529	$878 £529	$878 £529
VAN ENGELEN, H.	1	0			
WHITE & CO., H.N.	1	0			
ZELENKA, ANTONIN	1	1	$420 £253	$420 £253	$420 £253

TROMPE DE CHASSE

Maker	Bid	Sold	Low	High	Avg
GAUTROT (AINE)	1	1	$916 £552	$916 £552	$916 £552
RAOUX, MARCEL-AUGUSTE	2	0			
SCHMIDT, JOHANN JACOB	1	0			

TRUMPET

Maker	Bid	Sold	Low	High	Avg
BESSON	2	2	$281 £184	$387 £253	$334 £219
BESSON, FONTAINE	1	1	$56 £35	$56 £35	$56 £35
BOOSEY & HAWKES	1	1	$62 £40	$62 £40	$62 £40
CALICCHIO, DOMINIC	1	1	$1,495 £897	$1,495 £897	$1,495 £897
CONN, C.G.	2	1	$489 £298	$489 £298	$489 £298
COUESNON	1	0			
COURTOIS, ANTOINE (FILS)	1	1	$3,749 £2,640	$3,749 £2,640	$3,749 £2,640
COURTURIER, ERNST ALBERT	2	1	$748 £449	$748 £449	$748 £449
DE CLERCQ, L.	1	1	$535 £322	$535 £322	$535 £322
JAY CO., H.B.	1	0			
MAINZ, ALEXANDER	2	1	$1,173 £690	$1,173 £690	$1,173 £690
MIRAFONE	1	0			
OTTO, FRANZ	1	1	$878 £529	$878 £529	$878 £529
VICKERS	2	1	$151 £104	$151 £104	$151 £104
WHITE & CO., H.N.	1	0			

TUBA

Maker	Bid	Sold	Low	High	Avg
BESSON & CO.	2	1	$188 £115	$188 £115	$188 £115

Maker	Items		Selling Prices		
	Bid	Sold	Low	High	Avg
BOOSEY & HAWKES	5	5	$158	$668	$429
			£104	£437	£281
HALARI	2	0			
SUDRE, FRANCOIS	2	0			

UKULELE

ALOHA	1	1	$288	$288	$288
			£175	£175	£175
KAMAKA	1	1	$92	$92	$92
			£55	£55	£55
KUMALAE	2	2	$150	$201	$175
			£91	£119	£105
MARTIN & CO., C.F.	7	7	$374	$1,587	$905
			£224	£984	£560

UNION PIPES

REID, ROBERT	1	1	$1,199	$1,199	$1,199
			£727	£727	£727
ROBERTSON, HUGH	1	1	$7,636	$7,636	$7,636
			£4,600	£4,600	£4,600

VIOL

BISIACH, LEANDRO	1	0			
CARLETTI, NATALE	2	2	$1,955	$2,645	$2,300
			£1,369	£1,719	£1,544
CASTAGNERI, ANDREA	1	1	$3,109	$3,109	$3,109
			£1,840	£1,840	£1,840
COLETTI, A.	2	1	$1,898	$1,898	$1,898
			£1,265	£1,265	£1,265
COULY, JEAN	2	1	$2,302	$2,302	$2,302
			£1,610	£1,610	£1,610
CROSS, H. CHARLES (attributed to)	1	1	$839	$839	$839
			£518	£518	£518
EBERLE, JOHANN ULRICH	1	1	$30,550	$30,550	$30,550
			£18,515	£18,515	£18,515
EBERLE, JOHANN ULRICH (attributed to)	1	0			
EBERLE, TOMASO	1	1	$7,188	$7,188	$7,188
			£4,384	£4,384	£4,384
GAGLIANO, FERDINAND	1	1	$10,322	$10,322	$10,322
			£6,325	£6,325	£6,325
GUGGENBERGER, ANTON	5	1	$1,737	$1,737	$1,737
			£1,150	£1,150	£1,150
JORDAN, HANS	1	1	$955	$955	$955
			£575	£575	£575
KESSLER, DIETRICH	1	1	$1,002	$1,002	$1,002
			£598	£598	£598
ROSE, ROGER	2	1	$2,300	$2,300	$2,300
			£1,380	£1,380	£1,380
ROTA, JOANNES (attributed to)	1	0			
ROY, KARL	1	0			
SEELOS, JOHANN	1	1	$36,271	$36,271	$36,271
			£21,850	£21,850	£21,850

| | *Items* | | | *Selling Prices* | |
Maker	Bid	Sold	Low	High	Avg
STIEBER, ERNST	3	2	$529 £328	$4,033 £2,820	$2,281 £1,579
TIELKE (workshop of)	1	1	$12,780 £9,000	$12,780 £9,000	$12,780 £9,000
UDALRICUS, JOHANNES (attributed to)	2	1	$822 £506	$822 £506	$822 £506
UEBEL, WOLFGANG	2	2	$1,043 £690	$1,495 £1,047	$1,269 £868

VIOL BOW

DOLMETSCH, ARNOLD	1	0			
TUBBS, JAMES (attributed to)	2	1	$809 £483	$809 £483	$809 £483

VIOLA

ACOULON, ALFRED	1	0			
ALBANELLI, FRANCO	2	0			
AMATI, DOM NICOLO	1	0			
ANTONIAZZI, ROMEO	3	1	$39,675 £24,599	$39,675 £24,599	$39,675 £24,599
ANTONIAZZI, ROMEO (workshop of)	1	0			
ARASSI, ENZO	1	1	$5,175 £3,141	$5,175 £3,141	$5,175 £3,141
ARCANGELI, ULDERICO	1	0			
AREZIO, CLAUDIO	2	1	$4,397 £2,875	$4,397 £2,875	$4,397 £2,875
ARTMANN, GEORG VALENTIN	1	0			
ASCHAUER, LEO	1	1	$2,356 £1,560	$2,356 £1,560	$2,356 £1,560
ASHFORD, LAWRENCE	1	0			
ASTORI, GIOVANNI	1	1	$2,587 £1,656	$2,587 £1,656	$2,587 £1,656
ATTERMATT, JAN	1	0			
AUDINOT, PIERRE M.	1	1	$7,314 £4,600	$7,314 £4,600	$7,314 £4,600
AVERNA, GESUALDO	1	0			
AYERS, PAUL	1	0			
BAILLY, PAUL	4	1	$5,427 £3,795	$5,427 £3,795	$5,427 £3,795
BANKS, BENJAMIN	1	1	$7,079 £4,370	$7,079 £4,370	$7,079 £4,370
BANKS, JAMES & HENRY	2	2	$10,689 £7,475	$13,041 £8,050	$11,865 £7,763
BANKS FAMILY (MEMBER OF)	2	0			
BARBIERI, BRUNO	6	1	$2,846 £1,725	$2,846 £1,725	$2,846 £1,725
BARBIERI, ENZO	1	0			
BARBIERI, PAOLO	1	0			
BARGELLI, G.	2	0			
BARKER, J.	1	1	$1,585 £1,035	$1,585 £1,035	$1,585 £1,035

Maker	Items Bid	Sold	Selling Prices Low	High	Avg
BARNABETTI, GERONIMO	1	1	$2,131 £1,323	$2,131 £1,323	$2,131 £1,323
BARZONI, FRANCOIS	4	4	$1,252 £828	$2,944 £1,852	$1,982 £1,262
BASTON, VICTOR	3	1	$466 £288	$466 £288	$466 £288
BATELLI, ALFIO	1	0			
BEARD, JOHN	1	0			
BEDER, ANTON	1	1	$288 £173	$288 £173	$288 £173
BEDOCCHI, MARIO	2	0			
BELLAROSA, VITTORIO	1	0			
BERNARDEL, GUSTAVE	2	1	$11,750 £7,638	$11,750 £7,638	$11,750 £7,638
BERTELLI, ENZO	1	0			
BERTOLAZZI, GIACINTO	1	1	$3,042 £1,886	$3,042 £1,886	$3,042 £1,886
BETTS	1	1	$15,159 £8,970	$15,159 £8,970	$15,159 £8,970
BETTS, JOHN	1	1	$4,216 £2,990	$4,216 £2,990	$4,216 £2,990
BEYER, GEORGE W.	2	1	$690 £414	$690 £414	$690 £414
BIANCHI, ROBERTO	1	1	$6,006 £4,200	$6,006 £4,200	$6,006 £4,200
BICKLE, PAUL	1	1	$785 £483	$785 £483	$785 £483
BIGNAMI, OTELLO	2	0			
BIRD, RICHMOND HENRY (attributed to)	2	1	$1,537 £943	$1,537 £943	$1,537 £943
BISSOLOTTI, FRANCESCO	1	1	$4,600 £3,220	$4,600 £3,220	$4,600 £3,220
BISSOLOTTI, VINCENZO	1	1	$2,070 £1,242	$2,070 £1,242	$2,070 £1,242
BLANCHARD, PAUL	2	1	$15,771 £9,919	$15,771 £9,919	$15,771 £9,919
BLANCHI, ALBERTO	2	0			
BLITZ, LOUIS	1	1	$740 £518	$740 £518	$740 £518
BOIANCIUC, ROMAN	1	1	$1,387 £828	$1,387 £828	$1,387 £828
BONETTE, MAURICE K.	1	0			
BOUETTE, MAURICE	1	1	$3,353 £2,185	$3,353 £2,185	$3,353 £2,185
BOULANGEOT, EMILE	1	0			
BOULLANGIER, CHARLES	3	2	$7,951 £5,175	$19,376 £12,650	$13,663 £8,913
BOULLANGIER, CHARLES (attributed to)	1	1	$3,129 £2,070	$3,129 £2,070	$3,129 £2,070
BOURGUIGNON, MAURICE	2	0			
BOYES, ARNOLD	1	1	$1,708 £1,035	$1,708 £1,035	$1,708 £1,035
BRADSHAW, B.L.	2	0			

Maker	Items Bid	Sold	Selling Prices Low	High	Avg
BRAY, E.	1	1	$469 £288	$469 £288	$469 £288
BRETON	1	1	$562 £345	$562 £345	$562 £345
BRETON BREVETE	2	2	$1,629 £1,058	$4,073 £2,645	$2,851 £1,852
BRIGGS, JAMES WILLIAM	1	1	$6,084 £3,772	$6,084 £3,772	$6,084 £3,772
BRUCKNER, WILHELM	1	1	$2,294 £1,495	$2,294 £1,495	$2,294 £1,495
BRYANT, GEORGE E.	1	1	$3,174 £1,968	$3,174 £1,968	$3,174 £1,968
BUCKMAN, GEORGE H.	1	1	$1,310 £782	$1,310 £782	$1,310 £782
BUTHOD	3	1	$3,091 £1,840	$3,091 £1,840	$3,091 £1,840
BUTHOD, CHARLES LOUIS	1	1	$2,560 £1,610	$2,560 £1,610	$2,560 £1,610
CANDI, CESARE	3	0			
CAPELA, ANTONIO	4	1	$7,475 £4,485	$7,475 £4,485	$7,475 £4,485
CAPELA, D.	1	0			
CAPELA, DOMINGOS	1	0			
CAPELLI, ALDO	1	0			
CAPICCHIONI, MARINO	3	3	$19,975 £12,984	$27,209 £16,100	$23,778 £15,061
CARESSA & FRANCAIS	2	1	$5,175 £3,450	$5,175 £3,450	$5,175 £3,450
CARLETTI, CARLO	4	1	$9,718 £6,325	$9,718 £6,325	$9,718 £6,325
CARLETTI, CARLO (attributed to)	1	1	$1,946 £1,380	$1,946 £1,380	$1,946 £1,380
CARLETTI, GENUZIO	3	1	$4,664 £2,760	$4,664 £2,760	$4,664 £2,760
CARLETTI, GENUZIO & JOSEPH SETTIN	1	0			
CARLETTI FAMILY	1	0			
CASINI, SERAFINO	1	0			
CASTELLI, CESARE	4	0			
CAVALAZZI, ANTONIO	1	0			
CAVALINI, DINO	1	0			
CAVANI, GIOVANNI (ascribed to)	1	0			
CAVANI, VINCENZO	3	2	$6,900 £4,209	$10,200 £7,038	$8,550 £5,624
CE, GIORGIO	1	0			
CHANOT, FRANCOIS	1	1	$1,283 £897	$1,283 £897	$1,283 £897
CHAPPUY, NICOLAS AUGUSTIN	3	1	$2,302 £1,610	$2,302 £1,610	$2,302 £1,610
CHEVRIER (attributed to)	3	0			
CHEVRIER, A.	1	0			
CHEVRIER, ANDRE	1	0			
COCKER, LAWRENCE	4	2	$1,007 £690	$1,216 £805	$1,111 £748

| Maker | Items | | Selling Prices | | |
	Bid	Sold	Low	High	Avg
COLLENOT, LOUIS	1	1	$2,471 £1,610	$2,471 £1,610	$2,471 £1,610
COLLIN-MEZIN, CH.J.B.	1	0			
COLLIN-MEZIN, CH I.J.B. (attributed to)	1	1	$5,641 £3,450	$5,641 £3,450	$5,641 £3,450
COLLIN-MEZIN, CH.J.B. (III)	1	0			
CONIA, STEFANO	6	3	$3,738 £2,280	$6,319 £4,025	$5,273 £3,252
CONTAVALLI, PRIMO	1	1	$3,680 £2,208	$3,680 £2,208	$3,680 £2,208
CONTIN, MARIO	1	1	$6,344 £4,140	$6,344 £4,140	$6,344 £4,140
CONTINO, ALFREDO (workshop of)	1	1	$8,050 £4,911	$8,050 £4,911	$8,050 £4,911
COPELAND, JOSEPH N.	1	0			
COPLERE, JEAN	1	1	$1,495 £897	$1,495 £897	$1,495 £897
CRASKE, GEORGE	4	3	$2,889 £1,725	$8,050 £4,974	$5,409 £3,383
CROSS, H. CHARLES	2	2	$466 £288	$652 £403	$559 £345
CURLETTO, ANSELMO	1	0			
CURTIN, JOSEPH	1	0			
CUYPERS, JOHANNES	1	1	$17,140 £10,580	$17,140 £10,580	$17,140 £10,580
DA FIESOLE, MINO	1	0			
DARCHE, HILAIRE	2	0			
DEARLOVE, MARK WILLIAM	1	1	$3,651 £2,415	$3,651 £2,415	$3,651 £2,415
DE BARBIERI, PAOLO	1	0			
DECONET, MICHELE	1	0			
DE JONG, MATTHIJS	1	0			
DELEPLANQUE, GERARD J.	1	1	$3,479 £2,070	$3,479 £2,070	$3,479 £2,070
DERACHE, PAUL	1	1	$1,257 £779	$1,257 £779	$1,257 £779
DERAZEY, HONORE	2	1	$10,247 £6,325	$10,247 £6,325	$10,247 £6,325
DEROUX, SEBASTIEN AUGUSTE	1	1	$7,728 £4,600	$7,728 £4,600	$7,728 £4,600
DE SOUZA, COSMO	1	0			
DE VITOR, PIETRO PAOLO (attributed to)	1	1	$55,028 £33,350	$55,028 £33,350	$55,028 £33,350
DEVONEY, FRANK	1	1	$2,462 £1,610	$2,462 £1,610	$2,462 £1,610
DIDIER, MARIUS	2	0			
DIEUDONNE, AMEDEE	1	0			
DIGIUNI, LUIGI	3	2	$1,837 £1,150	$3,769 £2,314	$2,803 £1,732
DILWORTH, JOHN	1	0			
DOBBS, HARRY	3	1	$568 £403	$568 £403	$568 £403

Maker	Items		Selling Prices		
	Bid	Sold	Low	High	Avg
DODD, THOMAS	1	1	$21,379	$21,379	$21,379
			£12,650	£12,650	£12,650
DODDS, EDWARD	1	1	$5,499	$5,499	$5,499
			£3,571	£3,571	£3,571
DUKE, RICHARD	5	5	$1,944	$3,649	$2,890
			£1,150	£2,185	£1,817
DUREN, WILHELM	1	1	$5,262	$5,262	$5,262
			£3,680	£3,680	£3,680
DVORAK, JAN BAPTISTA	1	0			
EBERLE, EUGENE	1	1	$7,682	$7,682	$7,682
			£4,600	£4,600	£4,600
EBERLE, J.U. (ascribed to)	2	0			
EDLER, ERNEST	2	1	$1,380	$1,380	$1,380
			£842	£842	£842
EMERY, JULIAN	5	0			
ENEL, CHARLES (attributed to)	1	0			
ERDESZ, OTTO	2	1	$4,713	$4,713	$4,713
			£2,910	£2,910	£2,910
ERICAN, MARTIN	1	1	$3,738	$3,738	$3,738
			£2,280	£2,280	£2,280
ERICIAN, MARTIN	1	0			
EVE, J.C.	1	1	$2,336	$2,336	$2,336
			£1,380	£1,380	£1,380
FABIANI, ANTONIO (ascribed to)	1	0			
FAGNOLA, ANNIBALE	3	0			
FAIRFAX, ANNELEEN	2	1	$1,389	$1,389	$1,389
			£920	£920	£920
FANTIN, DOMENICO	1	0			
FAROTTI, CELESTE	1	1	$4,225	$4,225	$4,225
			£2,530	£2,530	£2,530
FAROTTO, CELESTE	4	3	$5,025	$6,613	$5,796
			£2,990	£4,350	£3,597
FENDT, BERNARD SIMON	2	0			
FENDT, BERNARD SIMON JR.	1	1	$13,800	$13,800	$13,800
			£8,280	£8,280	£8,280
FERET-MARCOTTE	1	1	$2,422	$2,422	$2,422
			£1,495	£1,495	£1,495
FERRONI, FERDINANDO	2	1	$2,645	$2,645	$2,645
			£1,587	£1,587	£1,587
FERRONI, FERNANDO	1	1	$4,025	$4,025	$4,025
			£2,818	£2,818	£2,818
FICHTL, JOHANN ULRICH	1	1	$1,910	$1,910	$1,910
			£1,109	£1,109	£1,109
FICKER, JOHANN GOTTLOB	1	1	$3,972	$3,972	$3,972
			£2,530	£2,530	£2,530
FIELDING, A.	1	0			
FIORI BROTHERS (attributed to)	1	0			
FIORINI, RAFFAELE	1	1	$59,606	$59,606	$59,606
			£38,900	£38,900	£38,900
FLETA, IGNACIO	1	1	$5,693	$5,693	$5,693
			£3,450	£3,450	£3,450
FLEURY, BENOIT	1	1	$15,902	$15,902	$15,902
			£10,350	£10,350	£10,350

| Maker | Items | | Selling Prices | | |
	Bid	Sold	Low	High	Avg
FLORENTIN, N.	1	1	$1,380 £838	$1,380 £838	$1,380 £838
FONTANA, ALFREDO	1	1	$2,126 £1,265	$2,126 £1,265	$2,126 £1,265
FORSTER	3	1	$4,225 £2,530	$4,225 £2,530	$4,225 £2,530
FORSTER, WILLIAM	2	2	$3,208 £2,070	$5,831 £3,450	$4,519 £2,760
FORSTER, WILLIAM (workshop of)	1	1	$3,529 £2,300	$3,529 £2,300	$3,529 £2,300
FORSTER, WILLIAM (II)	5	3	$5,410 £3,220	$12,650 £7,590	$9,420 £5,949
FOSCHI, GIORGIO	1	0			
FOSCHINI, GIOVANNI	3	1	$3,887 £2,300	$3,887 £2,300	$3,887 £2,300
FURBER, HENRY	1	0			
GABRIELLI, GIOVANNI BATTISTA (workshop of)	1	1	$30,360 £18,400	$30,360 £18,400	$30,360 £18,400
GAGLIANO, RAFFAELE & ANTONIO (II) (attributed to)	1	0			
GAGLIANO FAMILY (MEMBER OF)	1	0			
GAILLARD, CHARLES	2	2	$7,284 £4,497	$16,068 £9,919	$11,676 £7,208
GALIMBERTI, LUIGI	1	0			
GALLA, ANTON	1	1	$4,832 £2,875	$4,832 £2,875	$4,832 £2,875
GAND, GUILLAUME CHARLES LOUIS	1	1	$12,668 £7,820	$12,668 £7,820	$12,668 £7,820
GAND & BERNARDEL	4	1	$18,288 £10,925	$18,288 £10,925	$18,288 £10,925
GAND & BERNARDEL FRERES	2	0			
GARTNER, EUGEN	1	1	$7,360 £4,629	$7,360 £4,629	$7,360 £4,629
GAVINIES, FRANCOIS	1	1	$13,739 £8,970	$13,739 £8,970	$13,739 £8,970
GEISSENHOF, FRANZ	1	1	$14,719 £9,258	$14,719 £9,258	$14,719 £9,258
GIANOTTI, ALFREDO	1	1	$6,325 £3,741	$6,325 £3,741	$6,325 £3,741
GILKES, SAMUEL (attributed to)	1	1	$1,363 £805	$1,363 £805	$1,363 £805
GIULIANI, R.G.	1	0			
GLOOR, ADOLF	2	1	$860 £529	$860 £529	$860 £529
GOFFRILLER, MATTEO (ascribed to)	1	1	$54,855 £34,500	$54,855 £34,500	$54,855 £34,500
GOTZ, CONRAD	1	1	$848 £506	$848 £506	$848 £506
GOULDING	2	0			
GOUVERNEL, PIERRE	1	1	$2,643 £1,725	$2,643 £1,725	$2,643 £1,725
GRANCINO, GIOVANNI (attributed to)	1	0			
GRANDJON, J.	1	0			

Maker	Items Bid	Sold	Selling Prices Low	High	Avg
GUADAGNINI, GIUSEPPE (ascribed to)	1	0			
GUASTALLA, DANTE (attributed to)	2	0			
GUERRA, ALBERTO	2	2	$6,762	$7,050	$6,906
			£4,025	£4,583	£4,304
GUERRA, ALBERTO (ascribed to)	3	2	$1,495	$1,495	$1,495
			£920	£920	£920
GUTH, AUGUST	1	0			
HAAHTI, NICOLIEN	2	1	$3,887	$3,887	$3,887
			£2,530	£2,530	£2,530
HALLETT, L.C.	1	1	$863	$863	$863
			£529	£529	£529
HALLIDAY, R.L.	1	1	$1,091	$1,091	$1,091
			£713	£713	£713
HANSON, H.E.	1	1	$3,450	$3,450	$3,450
			£2,415	£2,415	£2,415
HARDIE, THOMAS	1	0			
HARRILD, PAUL V.	4	1	$1,478	$1,478	$1,478
			£978	£978	£978
HARRIS, CHARLES	5	3	$2,795	$4,225	$3,571
			£1,725	£2,530	£2,147
HARRIS, RICHARD	3	1	$5,216	$5,216	$5,216
			£3,220	£3,220	£3,220
HEBERLEIN	1	1	$2,875	$2,875	$2,875
			£1,745	£1,745	£1,745
HEBERLEIN, HEINRICH TH. (JR.)	1	1	$2,881	$2,881	$2,881
			£1,725	£1,725	£1,725
HEL, JOSEPH	1	0			
HESKETH, THOMAS EARLE	1	0			
HIGHFIELD	1	0			
HIGHFIELD, IAN	1	1	$1,892	$1,892	$1,892
			£1,190	£1,190	£1,190
HILL, JOSEPH	10	5	$5,762	$23,101	$11,942
			£3,450	£13,800	£7,219
HILL, JOSEPH (attributed to)	3	1	$16,373	$16,373	$16,373
			£9,775	£9,775	£9,775
HILL, JOSEPH & SONS	1	1	$3,887	$3,887	$3,887
			£2,530	£2,530	£2,530
HILL, LOCKEY	1	1	$3,850	$3,850	$3,850
			£2,300	£2,300	£2,300
HILL, W.E. & SONS	3	0			
HOFMANN, MAX	1	1	$2,795	$2,795	$2,795
			£1,725	£1,725	£1,725
HOFMANS, MATHIAS	1	1	$38,958	$38,958	$38,958
			£25,800	£25,800	£25,800
HOFNER, KARL	2	1	$144	$144	$144
			£88	£88	£88
HOFNER & VICKERS	2	0			
HOING, CLIFFORD A.	1	0			
HOMOLKA, FERDINAND AUGUST	1	1	$4,754	$4,754	$4,754
			£2,990	£2,990	£2,990
HOWE, ROBERT	1	1	$963	$963	$963
			£575	£575	£575
HUBER, JOHANN GEORG	1	1	$9,373	$9,373	$9,373
			£5,750	£5,750	£5,750
HUSSON	1	0			

135

| Maker | Items | | Selling Prices | | |
	Bid	Sold	Low	High	Avg
HUSSON FAMILY (MEMBER OF)	1	1	$8,642	$8,642	$8,642
			£5,175	£5,175	£5,175
IGNESTI, ROBERTO	1	0			
JACQUOT, CHARLES	3	1	$5,427	$5,427	$5,427
			£3,795	£3,795	£3,795
JAIS, ANTON	2	1	$1,610	$1,610	$1,610
			£985	£985	£985
JAIS, JOHANN	1	0			
JOMBAR, PAUL	1	0			
JUNG, CURT	1	1	$3,986	$3,986	$3,986
			£2,640	£2,640	£2,640
KAUL, PAUL	1	1	$6,914	$6,914	$6,914
			£4,140	£4,140	£4,140
KENNEDY, T. (attributed to)	1	1	$2,342	$2,342	$2,342
			£1,455	£1,455	£1,455
KENNEDY, THOMAS	1	0			
KENNEDY, THOMAS (attributed to)	1	1	$3,887	$3,887	$3,887
			£2,530	£2,530	£2,530
KERSCHENSTEINER, XAVER	2	1	$2,059	$2,059	$2,059
			£1,440	£1,440	£1,440
KLOTZ, AEGIDIUS (I)	1	1	$5,290	$5,290	$5,290
			£3,280	£3,280	£3,280
KLOTZ, AEGIDIUS (I) (attributed to)	1	1	$3,089	$3,089	$3,089
			£2,160	£2,160	£2,160
KLOTZ, AEGIDIUS (II)	2	2	$4,801	$5,589	$5,195
			£2,875	£3,450	£3,163
KLOTZ, JOHANN CARL	1	1	$2,889	$2,889	$2,889
			£1,840	£1,840	£1,840
KLOTZ, JOSEPH (attributed to)	2	1	$4,609	$4,609	$4,609
			£2,760	£2,760	£2,760
KLOTZ, MATTHIAS	1	0			
KLOTZ FAMILY (MEMBER OF)	1	0			
KONIG, RUDOLF	2	0			
KONYA, LAJOS	2	1	$978	$978	$978
			£578	£578	£578
KRAUSS, KARL	1	1	$684	$684	$684
			£437	£437	£437
KRENN, JOSEF	1	1	$2,347	$2,347	$2,347
			£1,495	£1,495	£1,495
KRUMBHOLZ, LORENZ	1	1	$3,260	$3,260	$3,260
			£2,280	£2,280	£2,280
KUSTER, FREDERICK	2	1	$920	$920	$920
			£544	£544	£544
LABERTE, MARC	5	3	$489	$6,958	$2,712
			£298	£4,140	£1,617
LABERTE, MARC (workshop of)	1	1	$1,725	$1,725	$1,725
			£1,047	£1,047	£1,047
LABERTE-HUMBERT BROS.	2	1	$3,707	$3,707	$3,707
			£2,415	£2,415	£2,415
LABRAM, LEONARD	1	1	$1,502	$1,502	$1,502
			£897	£897	£897
LAMB, JOHN	2	1	$987	$987	$987
			£690	£690	£690

Maker	Items		Selling Prices		
	Bid	Sold	Low	High	Avg
LANARO, ALOISIUS	2	0			
LANARO, UMBERTO	5	2	$3,850	$4,711	$4,281
			£2,300	£3,120	£2,710
LANDOLFI, CARLO FERDINANDO	1	1	$131,541	$131,541	$131,541
			£80,700	£80,700	£80,700
LANGONET, ALFRED CHARLES	3	0			
LANT, ERNEST FRANCIS	2	1	$1,118	$1,118	$1,118
			£690	£690	£690
LANTNER, FERDINAND	1	1	$4,928	$4,928	$4,928
			£3,042	£3,042	£3,042
LASSI, ENZO (attributed to)	2	1	$3,386	$3,386	$3,386
			£2,185	£2,185	£2,185
LAURENT, EMILE	1	0			
LAVAZZA, SANTINO (ascribed to)	1	1	$2,300	$2,300	$2,300
			£1,495	£1,495	£1,495
LECLERC, JOSEPH NICOLAS	1	1	$10,592	$10,592	$10,592
			£6,900	£6,900	£6,900
LEE, PERCY	1	1	$5,654	$5,654	$5,654
			£3,680	£3,680	£3,680
LE FEBVRE, JEAN BAPTISTE (attributed to)	1	1	$6,861	$6,861	$6,861
			£4,370	£4,370	£4,370
LEONI, GUIDO	3	1	$1,490	$1,490	$1,490
			£920	£920	£920
LODGE, JOHN	1	1	$576	$576	$576
			£345	£345	£345
LONGMAN & BRODERIP	1	1	$2,037	$2,037	$2,037
			£1,323	£1,323	£1,323
LONGMAN, LUKEY & CO.	1	1	$3,289	$3,289	$3,289
			£2,300	£2,300	£2,300
LORANGE, PAUL	1	1	$2,257	$2,257	$2,257
			£1,495	£1,495	£1,495
LOVERI BROTHERS	1	1	$3,968	$3,968	$3,968
			£2,460	£2,460	£2,460
LUCA, IOAN	1	1	$963	$963	$963
			£575	£575	£575
LUCCI, GIUSEPPE	3	1	$8,698	$8,698	$8,698
			£5,175	£5,175	£5,175
LYE, HENRY	1	0			
MAAG, HENRY	2	1	$219	$219	$219
			£133	£133	£133
MACHOLD, OSKAR	1	1	$1,236	$1,236	$1,236
			£805	£805	£805
MAGNIERE, GABRIEL	1	1	$3,870	$3,870	$3,870
			£2,513	£2,513	£2,513
MANGENOT, P. (attributed to)	1	1	$1,563	$1,563	$1,563
			£1,035	£1,035	£1,035
MANGIACASALE, SALVATORE	1	0			
MANTEGAZZA, PIETRO GIOVANNI	1	1	$85,170	$85,170	$85,170
			£51,000	£51,000	£51,000
MARAVIGLIA, FRANCESCO	1	1	$4,943	$4,943	$4,943
			£3,220	£3,220	£3,220
MARAVIGLIA, GUIDO	3	1	$2,422	$2,422	$2,422
			£1,495	£1,495	£1,495

| Maker | Items | | Selling Prices | | |
	Bid	Sold	Low	High	Avg
MARCHETTI, ENRICO	1	1	$21,379 £12,650	$21,379 £12,650	$21,379 £12,650
MARCHINI, RUDOLFO	1	1	$4,025 £2,576	$4,025 £2,576	$4,025 £2,576
MARTINI, ORESTE	1	1	$4,252 £2,530	$4,252 £2,530	$4,252 £2,530
MASTERS, JOHN	2	1	$1,725 £1,020	$1,725 £1,020	$1,725 £1,020
MATSUDA, TETSUO	1	1	$6,900 £4,830	$6,900 £4,830	$6,900 £4,830
MATTER, ANITA	1	1	$1,863 £1,150	$1,863 £1,150	$1,863 £1,150
MATTIUZZI, BRUNO	1	0			
MAUCOTEL & DESCHAMPS	1	0			
MCGRATH, DAVID	1	1	$1,006 £633	$1,006 £633	$1,006 £633
MELLONI, SETTIMO	2	1	$2,990 £1,824	$2,990 £1,824	$2,990 £1,824
MENNESSON, EMILE	1	0			
MERMILLOT, MAURICE	1	1	$3,611 £2,300	$3,611 £2,300	$3,611 £2,300
MEYER, MAGNUS ANDREAS	1	1	$3,995 £2,513	$3,995 £2,513	$3,995 £2,513
MILLANT, MAX	1	1	$6,325 £4,111	$6,325 £4,111	$6,325 £4,111
MILLOSLAVSKI, JOSEPH	2	0			
MILNES, JOHN	1	0			
MINO DA FIESOLE	1	0			
MOCKEL, OTTO	1	0			
MOINEL & CHERPITEL	1	1	$3,430 £2,185	$3,430 £2,185	$3,430 £2,185
MONK, JOHN KING	1	0			
MONZETTI, JULIO	1	0			
MORETTI, EGIDO	1	0			
MORIZOT, RENE	1	1	$1,212 £717	$1,212 £717	$1,212 £717
MOUGENOT, GEORGES	1	1	$4,349 £2,880	$4,349 £2,880	$4,349 £2,880
MOUGENOT, LEON (workshop of)	1	1	$1,725 £1,035	$1,725 £1,035	$1,725 £1,035
MOZZANI, LUIGI	1	1	$7,079 £4,370	$7,079 £4,370	$7,079 £4,370
MOZZANI, LUIGI (workshop of)	1	1	$3,361 £2,350	$3,361 £2,350	$3,361 £2,350
MUELLER, KARL	1	1	$345 £213	$345 £213	$345 £213
NEBEL, MARTIN	2	1	$1,587 £984	$1,587 £984	$1,587 £984
NEUNER, LUDWIG	1	0			
NEUNER & HORNSTEINER	7	5	$863 £575	$4,626 £2,910	$2,565 £1,566
NEUNER & HORNSTEINER (workshop of)	2	2	$633 £384	$1,610 £966	$1,121 £675

| Maker | Items | | Selling Prices | | |
	Bid	Sold	Low	High	Avg
NIGGEL, SYMPERT	1	1	$4,428 £2,645	$4,428 £2,645	$4,428 £2,645
NIX, CHARLES WILLIAM	1	0			
NOLLI, FRANCO	1	1	$1,500 £977	$1,500 £977	$1,500 £977
NUPIERI, GIUSEPPE	9	6	$1,030 £621	$1,629 £1,058	$1,268 £793
NURNBERGER, WILHELM	1	1	$1,062 £632	$1,062 £632	$1,062 £632
NUTI, CANO	1	1	$2,118 £1,380	$2,118 £1,380	$2,118 £1,380
ODOARDI, GIUSEPPE	2	1	$3,618 £2,222	$3,618 £2,222	$3,618 £2,222
ODOARDI, GIUSEPPE (ascribed to)	1	1	$17,285 £10,350	$17,285 £10,350	$17,285 £10,350
ODOARDI, GIUSEPPE (attributed to)	1	0			
ORNATI, GIUSEPPE	2	2	$24,705 £16,100	$40,227 £25,300	$32,466 £20,700
OWEN, JOHN W.	1	0			
OZAKI, YUKIO	1	1	$1,150 £736	$1,150 £736	$1,150 £736
PADEWET, CARL	1	1	$1,273 £828	$1,273 £828	$1,273 £828
PALMER	1	0			
PANORMO, GEORGE	1	1	$10,868 £7,245	$10,868 £7,245	$10,868 £7,245
PANORMO, VINCENZO	1	0			
PANORMO, VINCENZO (attributed to)	2	1	$21,379 £12,650	$21,379 £12,650	$21,379 £12,650
PAOLOTTO, GIO. BATTA. (attributed to)	1	1	$1,563 £1,035	$1,563 £1,035	$1,563 £1,035
PARESCHI, GAETANO	2	1	$8,050 £5,233	$8,050 £5,233	$8,050 £5,233
PAUL, ADAM D.	1	0			
PEAT, RICHARD	1	1	$782 £518	$782 £518	$782 £518
PERRY, L.A.	1	1	$880 £518	$880 £518	$880 £518
PERRY, THOMAS	1	1	$6,900 £4,081	$6,900 £4,081	$6,900 £4,081
PETERNELLA, JAGO	1	0			
PEVERE, ERNESTO (ascribed to)	1	1	$3,575 £2,248	$3,575 £2,248	$3,575 £2,248
PFRETZSCHNER, CARL FRIEDRICH	1	1	$7,452 £4,600	$7,452 £4,600	$7,452 £4,600
PFRETZSCHNER, E.R. (workshop of)	1	1	$374 £221	$374 £221	$374 £221
PICKERING, NORMAN	1	1	$805 £483	$805 £483	$805 £483
PILAT, PAUL	1	1	$3,618 £2,530	$3,618 £2,530	$3,618 £2,530
PILLEMENT, FRANCOIS	1	0			
PINEIRO, HORACIO	1	1	$4,715 £2,876	$4,715 £2,876	$4,715 £2,876

| Maker | Items | | Selling Prices | | |
	Bid	Sold	Low	High	Avg
PISTONI, PRIMO	1	0			
PISTUCCI, GIOVANNI	1	0			
PIZZOLINI, MARIO	2	0			
PLOWRIGHT, DENIS G.	2	1	$895	$895	$895
			£552	£552	£552
PRELL, JULIUS HERMANN	2	1	$518	$518	$518
			£345	£345	£345
PROKOP, LADISLAV	1	0			
PUSKAS, JOSEPH	1	0			
QUENOIL, CHARLES	1	1	$3,738	$3,738	$3,738
			£2,211	£2,211	£2,211
RACZ, LORAND	2	1	$3,726	$3,726	$3,726
			£2,300	£2,300	£2,300
RADIGHIERI, OTELLO	1	0			
RAMIREZ, MANUEL	1	1	$12,719	$12,719	$12,719
			£8,050	£8,050	£8,050
RASTELLI, LODOVICO	1	0			
RAYMOND, ROBERT JOHN	2	2	$642	$1,460	$1,051
			£414	£920	£667
REGAZZONI, DANTE	1	0			
REGAZZONI, DANTE (attributed to)	1	0			
RENDERR, THEODOR	1	1	$265	$265	$265
			£184	£184	£184
RENOUX, F.	1	0			
RICHARDSON, ARTHUR	4	1	$2,237	$2,237	$2,237
			£1,380	£1,380	£1,380
RINALDI, GIOFREDO BENEDETTO (ascribed to)	5	1	$5,486	$5,486	$5,486
			£3,450	£3,450	£3,450
RITTER, HERMANN	1	1	$460	$460	$460
			£276	£276	£276
ROBINSON, WILLIAM	6	5	$2,820	$4,225	$3,513
			£1,725	£2,530	£2,180
ROCCA, GIUSEPPE (attributed to)	1	1	$19,734	$19,734	$19,734
			£13,800	£13,800	£13,800
ROCCHI, S.	1	0			
ROCCHI, SESTO	1	0			
RONIG, ADOLF	1	0			
ROSADONI, GIOVANNI	3	2	$2,319	$2,350	$2,335
			£1,380	£1,528	£1,454
ROSSI, GIUSEPPE	2	1	$6,765	$6,765	$6,765
			£4,025	£4,025	£4,025
ROSSI, STELIO	1	1	$5,819	$5,819	$5,819
			£3,608	£3,608	£3,608
ROST, FRANZ GEORG	1	0			
ROTH, ERNST HEINRICH	4	1	$681	$681	$681
			£423	£423	£423
ROTH, ERNST HEINRICH (workshop of)	3	2	$920	$1,323	$1,121
			£544	£820	£682
RUPING, HENRY	1	1	$403	$403	$403
			£265	£265	£265
RUTH, BENJAMIN WARREN	1	1	$2,300	$2,300	$2,300
			£1,360	£1,360	£1,360

| Maker | Items | | Selling Prices | | |
	Bid	Sold	Low	High	Avg
SALF	1	0			
SANAVIA, LEONE	1	1	$7,605	$7,605	$7,605
			£4,715	£4,715	£4,715
SANDERSON, DERICK	2	1	$1,153	$1,153	$1,153
			£690	£690	£690
SANNINO, VINCENZO	1	0			
SCARAMPELLA, STEFANO (attributed to)	2	0			
SCHLOSSER, HERMANN	1	1	$754	$754	$754
			£460	£460	£460
SCHMITT, LUCIEN	1	1	$5,775	$5,775	$5,775
			£3,450	£3,450	£3,450
SCOLARI, GIORGIO	4	2	$6,530	$7,128	$6,829
			£3,910	£4,255	£4,083
SDERCI, IGINO	3	1	$8,777	$8,777	$8,777
			£5,520	£5,520	£5,520
SEGAMIGLIA, GIUSTINO	1	0			
SERDET, PAUL	1	1	$19,205	$19,205	$19,205
			£11,500	£11,500	£11,500
SGARBI, GIUSEPPE	1	0			
SICCARDI, SERGIO	1	0			
SIMONAZZI, AMADEO	7	1	$4,099	$4,099	$4,099
			£2,530	£2,530	£2,530
SIMPSON, THOMAS	1	1	$1,035	$1,035	$1,035
			£690	£690	£690
SIRLETO	1	0			
SIRLETO BROTHERS	1	1	$4,600	$4,600	$4,600
			£2,806	£2,806	£2,806
SMITH, ARTHUR E.	1	1	$16,740	$16,740	$16,740
			£10,925	£10,925	£10,925
SMITH, BERT	1	1	$3,353	$3,353	$3,353
			£2,070	£2,070	£2,070
SMITH, THOMAS	3	2	$1,840	$7,722	$4,781
			£1,150	£5,400	£3,275
SMITH, THOMAS (attributed to)	1	0			
SOFFRITTI, ETTORE	1	1	$14,904	$14,904	$14,904
			£9,200	£9,200	£9,200
SOLOMON, GIMPEL	1	1	$1,892	$1,892	$1,892
			£1,190	£1,190	£1,190
SOMNY, JOSEPH MAURICE	1	1	$2,796	$2,796	$2,796
			£1,725	£1,725	£1,725
SONZOGNI, UMBERTO	1	1	$2,300	$2,300	$2,300
			£1,513	£1,513	£1,513
STADLMANN, MICHAEL IGNAZ	2	0			
STAINER, JACOB	1	1	$67,106	$67,106	$67,106
			£42,205	£42,205	£42,205
STEFANINI, GIUSEPPE	1	0			
STORIONI, CARLO	2	1	$1,933	$1,933	$1,933
			£1,150	£1,150	£1,150
STORIONI, LORENZO	1	0			
STOSS, JOHANN MARTIN	1	1	$2,059	$2,059	$2,059
			£1,440	£1,440	£1,440
STYLES, HAROLD LEICESTER	3	2	$487	$1,237	$862
			£299	£805	£552

| Maker | Items | | Selling Prices | | |
	Bid	Sold	Low	High	Avg
TAYLERSON, PETE	2	0			
TAYLOR, ERIC	3	1	$1,126 £690	$1,126 £690	$1,126 £690
THIBOUVILLE-LAMY, J.	11	8	$658 £414	$4,206 £2,645	$1,964 £1,206
THIR, JOHANN GEORG	1	1	$8,237 £5,760	$8,237 £5,760	$8,237 £5,760
THIR FAMILY (MEMBER OF)	1	0			
THOMSON, GEORGE	1	1	$959 £596	$959 £596	$959 £596
THOMPSON, CHARLES & SAMUEL	1	0			
THOMPSON, CHARLES & SAMUEL (attributed to)	1	1	$11,433 £7,475	$11,433 £7,475	$11,433 £7,475
TRIBBY, SCOTT L.	1	1	$2,415 £1,492	$2,415 £1,492	$2,415 £1,492
TRIMBOLI, PIETRO (ascribed to)	1	1	$2,462 £1,610	$2,462 £1,610	$2,462 £1,610
TURCSAK, TIBOR GABOR	1	1	$1,932 £1,150	$1,932 £1,150	$1,932 £1,150
TYE, J.	1	1	$1,564 £978	$1,564 £978	$1,564 £978
VAN DER GEEST, JACOB JAN (attributed to)	2	0			
VAN DER GRINTEN, JOOST	2	0			
VATELOT, ETIENNE	1	1	$16,068 £9,919	$16,068 £9,919	$16,068 £9,919
VATILIOTIS, C.A.	1	1	$2,444 £1,587	$2,444 £1,587	$2,444 £1,587
VETTORI, CARLO	2	1	$3,105 £2,043	$3,105 £2,043	$3,105 £2,043
VETTORI, PAULO	1	0			
VETTORI, PAULO (attributed to)	1	1	$4,071 £2,513	$4,071 £2,513	$4,071 £2,513
VICKERS, J.E.	3	2	$505 £311	$827 £541	$666 £426
VIDOUDEZ, PIERRE	1	1	$4,600 £2,990	$4,600 £2,990	$4,600 £2,990
VILLA, LUIGI	2	1	$1,824 £1,092	$1,824 £1,092	$1,824 £1,092
VILLAUME, GUSTAVE EUGENE	1	1	$3,884 £2,530	$3,884 £2,530	$3,884 £2,530
VOIGT (attributed to)	2	0			
VOIGT, E.R. & SON	2	2	$2,650 £1,610	$2,721 £1,725	$2,686 £1,668
VOIGT, PAUL	3	0			
VOLLER BROTHERS (attributed to)	1	0			
VUILLAUME, GUSTAVE	1	1	$3,611 £2,300	$3,611 £2,300	$3,611 £2,300
VUILLAUME, NICOLAS FRANCOIS	1	1	$5,463 £3,278	$5,463 £3,278	$5,463 £3,278
WAGNER, SEBASTIAN	1	1	$12,000 £8,280	$12,000 £8,280	$12,000 £8,280

Maker	Items Bid	Sold	Low	Selling Prices High	Avg
WALKER, JOHN	1	1	$2,444 £1,495	$2,444 £1,495	$2,444 £1,495
WARD, ROD	2	2	$288 £175	$743 £437	$515 £306
WELLER, FREDERICK (attributed to)	1	1	$1,224 £782	$1,224 £782	$1,224 £782
WHEDBEE, WILLIAM	2	0			
WHITE, WILFRED	1	0			
WHITMARSH, E.	2	1	$904 £598	$904 £598	$904 £598
WHITMARSH, EDWIN	1	1	$1,233 £863	$1,233 £863	$1,233 £863
WHITMARSH, EMANUEL	1	0			
WILKINSON, JOHN	1	1	$7,079 £4,370	$7,079 £4,370	$7,079 £4,370
WILLER, JOANNES MICHAEL	2	0			
WINTER, ANTON	1	0			
WITTY, E.T.	2	0			
WOLFF BROS.	1	1	$482 £287	$482 £287	$482 £287
WORLE, JOHANN PAUL (attributed to)	1	0			
WULME-HUDSON, GEORGE (attributed to)	1	0			
ZACH, CARL	2	0			
ZANI, ALDO	1	0			
ZANOLI, FRANCESCO	1	0			

VIOLA BOW

Maker	Items Bid	Sold	Low	Selling Prices High	Avg
AUDINOT, JACQUES	1	1	$5,750 £4,025	$5,750 £4,025	$5,750 £4,025
BALINT, GEZA	1	1	$529 £328	$529 £328	$529 £328
BAUSCH	6	2	$293 £173	$309 £184	$301 £178
BAUSCH, LUDWIG	1	1	$863 £518	$863 £518	$863 £518
BAUSCH, LUDWIG CHRISTIAN AUGUST	1	0			
BAZIN	2	2	$3,850 £2,300	$4,081 £2,415	$3,966 £2,358
BAZIN, CHARLES	1	1	$2,588 £1,553	$2,588 £1,553	$2,588 £1,553
BAZIN, CHARLES NICHOLAS	1	1	$3,674 £2,300	$3,674 £2,300	$3,674 £2,300
BAZIN, LOUIS	1	1	$1,806 £1,150	$1,806 £1,150	$1,806 £1,150
BECHINI, RENZO	1	0			
BERNARDEL, LEON	1	1	$1,093 £669	$1,093 £669	$1,093 £669
BLONDELET, EMILE (workshop of)	1	1	$1,840 £1,211	$1,840 £1,211	$1,840 £1,211
BRISTOW, S.E.	2	2	$745 £460	$1,390 £897	$1,068 £679
BRISTOW, STEPHEN	1	0			

Maker	Items		Selling Prices		
	Bid	Sold	Low	High	Avg
BRYANT, PERCIVAL WILFRED	2	1	$1,118 £690	$1,118 £690	$1,118 £690
BULTITUDE, ARTHUR RICHARD	13	11	$875 £518	$4,349 £2,880	$2,510 £1,595
BUTHOD, CHARLES	1	0			
BUTHOD, CHARLES LOUIS	1	1	$1,150 £757	$1,150 £757	$1,150 £757
CHALUPETZKY, F.	1	0			
CLUTTERBUCK, JOHN	1	1	$1,054 £748	$1,054 £748	$1,054 £748
COCKER, L.	1	1	$653 £403	$653 £403	$653 £403
COLAS, PROSPER	1	1	$2,300 £1,380	$2,300 £1,380	$2,300 £1,380
COLTMAN, M.	1	0			
CUNIOT-HURY	1	1	$2,743 £1,725	$2,743 £1,725	$2,743 £1,725
CUNIOT-HURY, EUGENE	2	2	$815 £540	$4,113 £2,673	$2,464 £1,607
DEBLAYE, ALBERT	1	1	$937 £575	$937 £575	$937 £575
DITER BROTHERS	1	0			
DODD	2	1	$1,676 £1,092	$1,676 £1,092	$1,676 £1,092
DODD (attributed to)	1	1	$1,216 £805	$1,216 £805	$1,216 £805
DODD, J.	1	1	$3,291 £2,070	$3,291 £2,070	$3,291 £2,070
DODD, JOHN	1	0			
DODD FAMILY (MEMBER OF)	1	1	$2,530 £1,664	$2,530 £1,664	$2,530 £1,664
DOLLING, HEINZ	1	1	$633 £416	$633 £416	$633 £416
DOLLING, KURT	3	2	$730 £437	$759 £460	$744 £449
DOLLING, MICHAEL	1	0			
DORFLER, EGIDIUS	1	0			
DUGAD, ANDRE	1	1	$1,536 £920	$1,536 £920	$1,536 £920
DUPUY	1	0			
DURRSCHMIDT, OTTO	2	2	$750 £460	$1,422 £862	$1,086 £661
DURRSCHMIDT, WILLI CARL	1	1	$1,426 £828	$1,426 £828	$1,426 £828
ENGLISH, CHRIS	1	1	$596 £369	$596 £369	$596 £369
FETIQUE, JULES	1	1	$1,344 £805	$1,344 £805	$1,344 £805
FETIQUE, MARCEL	1	1	$6,178 £4,320	$6,178 £4,320	$6,178 £4,320
FETIQUE, VICTOR	6	1	$4,801 £2,875	$4,801 £2,875	$4,801 £2,875
FINKEL, JOHANN S.	1	1	$3,304 £1,955	$3,304 £1,955	$3,304 £1,955

	Items			*Selling Prices*	
Maker	Bid	Sold	Low	High	Avg
FINKEL, JOHANNES S.	3	1	$2,743 £1,725	$2,743 £1,725	$2,743 £1,725
FINKEL, SIEGFRIED	2	1	$1,150 £748	$1,150 £748	$1,150 £748
FLEISHER, HARRY	1	1	$633 £391	$633 £391	$633 £391
FONCLAUSE, JOSEPH	1	1	$19,975 £12,984	$19,975 £12,984	$19,975 £12,984
FRITSCH, JEAN	1	1	$1,083 £690	$1,083 £690	$1,083 £690
GAND & BERNARDEL	1	1	$3,693 £2,185	$3,693 £2,185	$3,693 £2,185
GAULARD	1	0			
GAULARD (attributed to)	1	1	$1,986 £1,265	$1,986 £1,265	$1,986 £1,265
GEROME, ROGER	1	1	$1,725 £1,135	$1,725 £1,135	$1,725 £1,135
GILLET, LOUIS	1	1	$2,415 £1,691	$2,415 £1,691	$2,415 £1,691
GOTZ, CONRAD	1	0			
GRANDCHAMP, ERIC	1	1	$2,990 £1,944	$2,990 £1,944	$2,990 £1,944
GRANIER, DENIS	2	0			
GRUNKE, RICHARD	1	1	$1,093 £765	$1,093 £765	$1,093 £765
HEL, PIERRE JOSEPH	1	0			
HERRMANN, EMIL	1	0			
HERRMANN, LOTHAR	3	3	$425 £253	$1,348 £805	$829 £491
HILL, W.E. & SONS	44	38	$707 £460	$5,962 £3,680	$3,038 £1,933
HUSSON, AUGUST	1	1	$3,177 £2,070	$3,177 £2,070	$3,177 £2,070
KUN, JOSEPH	1	0			
LABERTE	1	1	$3,024 £2,115	$3,024 £2,115	$3,024 £2,115
LABERTE, MARC	3	1	$1,632 £977	$1,632 £977	$1,632 £977
LAMY, ALFRED JOSEPH	1	1	$16,767 £10,350	$16,767 £10,350	$16,767 £10,350
LAPIERRE, MARCEL	8	6	$1,059 £690	$3,092 £1,920	$2,049 £1,301
LAUXERROIS, JEAN-PAUL	1	1	$1,527 £991	$1,527 £991	$1,527 £991
LEE, JOHN NORWOOD	1	1	$794 £492	$794 £492	$794 £492
LENOBLE, AUGUSTE	1	1	$2,300 £1,495	$2,300 £1,495	$2,300 £1,495
LIU, LLOYD	1	1	$1,265 £832	$1,265 £832	$1,265 £832
LOTTE, FRANCOIS	4	3	$838 £517	$1,150 £748	$947 £594
LOTTE, ROGER	5	5	$1,366 £859	$1,612 £977	$1,493 £927

| Maker | Items | | Selling Prices | | |
	Bid	Sold	Low	High	Avg
LOTTE, ROGER-FRANCOIS	2	2	$601	$997	$799
			£420	£660	£540
MAIRE (workshop of)	1	1	$3,571	$3,571	$3,571
			£2,214	£2,214	£2,214
MAIRE, N. (attributed to)	1	1	$4,960	$4,960	$4,960
			£3,105	£3,105	£3,105
MAIRE, NICOLAS	1	0			
MAIRE, NICOLAS (attributed to)	1	1	$3,176	$3,176	$3,176
			£2,070	£2,070	£2,070
MALINE, GUILLAUME	3	2	$4,099	$6,385	$5,242
			£2,530	£4,465	£3,498
MALINE, NICOLAS (attributed to)	1	1	$6,146	$6,146	$6,146
			£3,680	£3,680	£3,680
METTAL, WALTER	1	1	$450	$450	$450
			£276	£276	£276
MILLANT, BERNARD	1	1	$2,700	$2,700	$2,700
			£1,863	£1,863	£1,863
MILLANT, JEAN-JACQUES	2	2	$3,450	$5,775	$4,613
			£2,243	£3,450	£2,846
MOINEL, DANIEL	1	0			
MOINIER, A.	2	0			
MOINIER, ALAIN	2	1	$1,265	$1,265	$1,265
			£768	£768	£768
MOLLER, MAX	1	1	$1,921	$1,921	$1,921
			£1,150	£1,150	£1,150
MORIZOT	2	2	$1,762	$1,809	$1,786
			£1,150	£1,265	£1,208
MORIZOT, ANDRE	1	1	$1,344	$1,344	$1,344
			£940	£940	£940
MORIZOT, C.	1	0			
MORIZOT, LOUIS	5	5	$1,625	$3,479	$2,388
			£1,035	£2,070	£1,501
MORIZOT, LOUIS (attributed to)	1	1	$975	$975	$975
			£598	£598	£598
MORIZOT, LOUIS (II)	2	2	$2,888	$3,785	$3,336
			£1,725	£2,381	£2,053
NEUDORFER	1	1	$978	$978	$978
			£643	£643	£643
NEUVEVILLE, G.C.	1	0			
NURNBERGER, ALBERT	9	7	$978	$2,875	$1,674
			£632	£1,745	£1,034
NURNBERGER, CHRISTIAN ALBERT	1	1	$2,103	$2,103	$2,103
			£1,323	£1,323	£1,323
NURNBERGER, KARL ALBERT	4	3	$1,312	$2,996	$2,065
			£805	£1,955	£1,360
OUCHARD, EMILE	1	1	$638	$638	$638
			£426	£426	£426
OUCHARD, EMILE A.	2	2	$6,886	$8,400	$7,643
			£4,560	£5,796	£5,178
OUCHARD, JEAN-CLAUDE	3	1	$2,194	$2,194	$2,194
			£1,380	£1,380	£1,380
PAESOLD, RODERICH	2	2	$569	$1,328	$949
			£345	£805	£575

Maker	Items		Selling Prices		
	Bid	Sold	Low	High	Avg
PAJEOT, ETIENNE	4	2	$2,819 £1,840	$7,248 £4,800	$5,034 £3,320
PAULUS, OTTO	1	1	$115 £81	$115 £81	$115 £81
PECCATTE, CHARLES (attributed to)	1	1	$5,055 £3,220	$5,055 £3,220	$5,055 £3,220
PECCATTE, DOMINIQUE	1	1	$42,431 £28,100	$42,431 £28,100	$42,431 £28,100
PECCATTE, FRANCOIS	3	1	$5,589 £3,450	$5,589 £3,450	$5,589 £3,450
PENZEL, K. GERHARD	1	1	$725 £480	$725 £480	$725 £480
PFRETZSCHNER (workshop of)	1	1	$173 £121	$173 £121	$173 £121
PFRETZSCHNER, H.R.	5	3	$906 £600	$2,291 £1,495	$1,749 £1,120
PIERNOT, MARIE LOUIS	2	0			
PRAGER, AUGUST EDWIN	2	2	$1,265 £832	$1,555 £920	$1,410 £876
PRAGER, GUSTAV	1	1	$792 £517	$792 £517	$792 £517
RAUM, WILHELM	1	0			
REICHEL, AUGUST	1	0			
RETFORD, WILLIAM C.	1	1	$5,143 £3,220	$5,143 £3,220	$5,143 £3,220
RICHAUME, ANDRE	1	1	$12,558 £7,475	$12,558 £7,475	$12,558 £7,475
ROTH, ERNST HEINRICH	1	1	$305 £198	$305 £198	$305 £198
SALCHOW, WILLIAM	2	2	$1,125 £690	$1,495 £984	$1,310 £837
SARTORY, EUGENE	5	4	$6,696 £4,370	$23,101 £13,800	$12,111 £7,493
SCHICKER, HORST	3	2	$461 £276	$870 £576	$665 £426
SCHMIDT, C. HANS CARL	1	1	$1,898 £1,150	$1,898 £1,150	$1,898 £1,150
SCHMIDT, HANS KARL	1	1	$2,138 £1,265	$2,138 £1,265	$2,138 £1,265
SCHUSTER, ADOLPH CURT	2	2	$1,255 £747	$1,495 £897	$1,375 £822
SCHUSTER, ALBERT	2	1	$1,035 £621	$1,035 £621	$1,035 £621
SEIFERT, LOTHAR	2	2	$576 £345	$2,888 £1,725	$1,732 £1,035
SERDET, PAUL	1	1	$2,827 £1,840	$2,827 £1,840	$2,827 £1,840
SIMON (workshop of)	1	0			
SIMPSON	2	0			
STAGG, JOHN W.	1	0			
TAYLOR, MALCOLM	3	2	$669 £437	$1,944 £1,265	$1,306 £851
TEPHO, GEORGES	1	1	$2,300 £1,610	$2,300 £1,610	$2,300 £1,610

| Maker | Items | | Selling Prices | | |
	Bid	Sold	Low	High	Avg
THIBOUVILLE-LAMY, J.	6	1	$1,219	$1,219	$1,219
			£748	£748	£748
THIBOUVILLE-LAMY, J. (workshop of)	1	0			
THOMACHOT, STEPHANE	1	0			
THOMASSIN, CLAUDE	3	2	$6,578	$9,775	$8,177
			£4,600	£6,843	£5,721
THOMASSIN, VICTOR	1	1	$3,529	$3,529	$3,529
			£2,300	£2,300	£2,300
TUBBS (ascribed to)	1	1	$916	$916	$916
			£598	£598	£598
TUBBS, J.	1	1	$10,805	$10,805	$10,805
			£6,670	£6,670	£6,670
TUBBS, JAMES	10	8	$922	$11,560	$6,792
			£552	£6,900	£4,216
TUBBS, JAMES (attributed to)	2	0			
TUBBS, WILLIAM	1	0			
UEBEL, K. WERNER	2	1	$1,265	$1,265	$1,265
			£832	£832	£832
UEBEL, KLAUS W.	1	0			
VIDOUDEZ, PIERRE	2	1	$3,785	$3,785	$3,785
			£2,381	£2,381	£2,381
VIGNERON, A.	1	1	$3,430	$3,430	$3,430
			£2,185	£2,185	£2,185
VIGNERON, ANDRE	1	1	$6,722	$6,722	$6,722
			£4,025	£4,025	£4,025
VIGNERON, JOSEPH ARTHUR	1	1	$6,722	$6,722	$6,722
			£4,025	£4,025	£4,025
VILLAUME, GUSTAVE EUGENE	1	1	$1,677	$1,677	$1,677
			£1,035	£1,035	£1,035
VOIGT, ARNOLD	2	1	$1,584	$1,584	$1,584
			£978	£978	£978
VOIRIN, F.N.	1	0			
VUILLAUME, JEAN BAPTISTE	2	2	$2,300	$18,400	$10,350
			£1,610	£12,880	£7,245
WATSON, D.	1	1	$4,801	$4,801	$4,801
			£2,875	£2,875	£2,875
WEICHOLD, R.	1	1	$1,863	$1,863	$1,863
			£1,150	£1,150	£1,150
WEICHOLD, RICHARD	1	1	$940	$940	$940
			£611	£611	£611
WEIDHAAS, PAUL	2	2	$944	$1,262	$1,103
			£660	£747	£704
WERNER, E.	2	1	$580	$580	$580
			£345	£345	£345
WILSON, GARNER	8	6	$894	$2,377	$1,462
			£555	£1,495	£910
WITHERS, EDWARD	1	1	$1,004	$1,004	$1,004
			£633	£633	£633
WURLITZER, REMBERT	1	0			

VIOLIN

ACHNER, PHILIP	1	0			
ACHNER, PHILIP (attributed to)	1	0			

Maker	Items		Selling Prices		
	Bid	*Sold*	*Low*	*High*	*Avg*
ACOULON, A. (attributed to)	2	1	$2,049	$2,049	$2,049
			£1,265	£1,265	£1,265
ACOULON, ALFRED (attributed to)	5	2	$1,219	$2,050	$1,635
			£748	£1,265	£1,007
AERTS	1	0			
AERTS, MARCEL	1	1	$2,527	$2,527	$2,527
			£1,495	£1,495	£1,495
ALBANELLI, FRANCO	5	2	$2,990	$3,286	$3,138
			£1,794	£1,955	£1,875
ALBANI, JOSEPH	3	3	$987	$18,092	$7,894
			£690	£11,109	£5,006
ALBANI, MATTEO	1	1	$16,822	$16,822	$16,822
			£10,580	£10,580	£10,580
ALBANI, MATTHIAS	3	3	$7,825	$8,411	$8,130
			£4,830	£5,400	£5,173
ALBANI, MATTHIAS (attributed to)	1	0			
ALBERT, CHARLES F.	4	0			
ALBERT, J.	2	2	$661	$1,610	$1,136
			£410	£995	£702
ALBERTI, FERDINANDO (attributed to)	1	0			
ALDRIC, JEAN FRANCOIS (attributed to)	3	1	$5,401	$5,401	$5,401
			£3,450	£3,450	£3,450
ALEKSA, JOHN	1	0			
ALF, GREGG	2	2	$9,200	$12,353	$10,776
			£5,585	£8,050	£6,817
ALLEN, JOSEPH S.	1	1	$3,335	$3,335	$3,335
			£2,001	£2,001	£2,001
ALLETSEE, PAULUS (attributed to)	1	1	$3,738	$3,738	$3,738
			£2,459	£2,459	£2,459
ALLISON, JOHN L.	1	1	$518	$518	$518
			£311	£311	£311
ALOISI, G. (attributed to)	1	0			
ALTAVILLA, ARMANDO	8	4	$4,609	$13,122	$8,968
			£2,760	£8,050	£5,596
AMATI, ANTONIO & GIROLAMO	5	5	$29,836	$142,299	$93,286
			£21,160	£87,300	£61,121
AMATI, ANTONIO & GIROLAMO (workshop of)	1	1	$11,213	$11,213	$11,213
			£7,849	£7,849	£7,849
AMATI, DOM NICOLO	4	3	$6,325	$42,251	$27,618
			£4,161	£25,300	£16,874
AMATI, GIROLAMO (II)	2	1	$26,503	$26,503	$26,503
			£17,250	£17,250	£17,250
AMATI, NICOLO	6	2	$107,250	$207,360	$157,305
			£75,000	£128,000	£101,500
AMATI, NICOLO (ascribed to)	1	1	$33,749	$33,749	$33,749
			£22,350	£22,350	£22,350
AMATI FAMILY (MEMBER OF)	1	0			
AMEDO, SIMONAZZI	2	1	$7,314	$7,314	$7,314
			£4,600	£4,600	£4,600
AMIGHETTI, CLAUDIO	2	2	$5,520	$5,750	$5,635
			£3,265	£3,491	£3,378
ANASTASIO, VINCENZO	2	0			
ANCIAUME, BERNARD	1	0			

Maker	Items		Selling Prices		
	Bid	Sold	Low	High	Avg
ANDERSON, A.	2	1	$300	$300	$300
			£184	£184	£184
ANDREWS, EDWARD	1	1	$374	$374	$374
			£230	£230	£230
ANDREWS, M.H.	1	1	$431	$431	$431
			£255	£255	£255
ANGARD, MAXIME	1	1	$855	$855	$855
			£555	£555	£555
ANGERER, FRANZ	1	1	$1,955	$1,955	$1,955
			£1,208	£1,208	£1,208
ANTONELLI, G.	1	1	$1,131	$1,131	$1,131
			£694	£694	£694
ANTONIAZZI (workshop of)	2	1	$8,154	$8,154	$8,154
			£5,400	£5,400	£5,400
ANTONIAZZI, GAETANO	1	1	$11,684	$11,684	$11,684
			£7,175	£7,175	£7,175
ANTONIAZZI, GAETANO (attributed to)	1	1	$56,235	$56,235	$56,235
			£34,500	£34,500	£34,500
ANTONIAZZI, RICCARDO	8	6	$6,914	$39,721	$17,958
			£4,140	£25,300	£11,136
ANTONIAZZI, ROMEO	13	12	$4,900	$33,922	$18,903
			£3,009	£20,829	£11,638
ANTONIAZZI, ROMEO (ascribed to)	2	1	$7,991	$7,991	$7,991
			£5,026	£5,026	£5,026
ANTONIAZZI, ROMEO (attributed to)	1	0			
ANTONIAZZI, ROMEO (workshop of)	1	1	$10,925	$10,925	$10,925
			£6,555	£6,555	£6,555
APPARUT, G.	3	2	$336	$2,167	$1,251
			£230	£1,380	£805
APPARUT, G. (workshop of)	1	0			
APPARUT, GEORGES	9	7	$1,467	$4,686	$2,720
			£897	£2,875	£1,656
APPARUT, GEORGES (workshop of)	1	1	$1,583	$1,583	$1,583
			£977	£977	£977
ARASSI, ENZO	4	2	$4,111	$4,370	$4,241
			£2,841	£2,875	£2,858
ARASSI, ENZO (workshop of)	1	1	$3,738	$3,738	$3,738
			£2,243	£2,243	£2,243
ARBUCKLE, WILLIAM	1	1	$1,917	$1,917	$1,917
			£1,150	£1,150	£1,150
ARBUCKLE, WILLIAM (attributed to)	1	1	$283	$283	$283
			£184	£184	£184
ARCANGELI, LORENZO	1	1	$21,202	$21,202	$21,202
			£13,800	£13,800	£13,800
ARCANGELI, ULDERICO	3	1	$22,770	$22,770	$22,770
			£13,800	£13,800	£13,800
ARCANGELI, ULDERICO (attributed to)	1	1	$6,146	$6,146	$6,146
			£3,680	£3,680	£3,680
ARDERN, JOB	10	5	$870	$2,240	$1,462
			£518	£1,455	£910
AREZIO, CLAUDIO	1	0			
ARMBRUSTER, ADOLF	1	1	$730	$730	$730
			£437	£437	£437

| Maker | Items | | Selling Prices | | |
	Bid	Sold	Low	High	Avg
ARTHUR & JOHNSON	1	1	$1,150 £702	$1,150 £702	$1,150 £702
ASHFORD, LAWRENCE (attributed to)	2	1	$974 £644	$974 £644	$974 £644
ASKEW, JOHN	2	2	$971 £633	$1,589 £1,035	$1,280 £834
ASPINALL, JAMES	1	0			
ASSUNTO, CARLONI	1	1	$1,128 £690	$1,128 £690	$1,128 £690
ATKINSON, WILLIAM	18	8	$1,886 £1,150	$4,250 £2,530	$3,139 £1,915
AUBRY, JOSEPH	3	1	$4,060 £2,645	$4,060 £2,645	$4,060 £2,645
AUCIELLO, LUIGI	1	1	$4,470 £2,645	$4,470 £2,645	$4,470 £2,645
AUDINOT, JUSTIN (attributed to)	1	1	$1,880 £1,150	$1,880 £1,150	$1,880 £1,150
AUDINOT, NESTOR	7	4	$9,516 £5,750	$21,425 £13,225	$14,793 £9,171
AUDINOT, NESTOR (ascribed to)	1	0			
AUDINOT, NESTOR (attributed to)	1	1	$4,673 £2,760	$4,673 £2,760	$4,673 £2,760
AUDINOT, VICTOR	3	2	$3,643 £2,530	$9,315 £5,750	$6,479 £4,140
AUDINOT-MOUROT, V.	1	0			
AUDINOT-MOUROT, V. (workshop of)	1	1	$3,192 £2,232	$3,192 £2,232	$3,192 £2,232
AZZOLA, LUIGI	3	0			
AZZOLA, LUIGI (attributed to)	1	1	$4,485 £2,915	$4,485 £2,915	$4,485 £2,915
BAADER, J. (workshop of)	1	1	$546 £328	$546 £328	$546 £328
BAADER, J.A.	1	1	$2,300 £1,495	$2,300 £1,495	$2,300 £1,495
BAADER & CO., J.A.	1	1	$403 £246	$403 £246	$403 £246
BADALASSI, PIERO	1	0			
BADALASSI, PIERO (attributed to)	1	1	$3,473 £2,300	$3,473 £2,300	$3,473 £2,300
BADARELLO, CARLO	2	2	$5,962 £3,680	$9,179 £5,980	$7,570 £4,830
BAILLY (workshop of)	1	0			
BAILLY, CHARLES	10	5	$1,748 £1,093	$4,694 £2,990	$2,983 £1,881
BAILLY, CHARLES (attributed to)	1	1	$2,512 £1,495	$2,512 £1,495	$2,512 £1,495
BAILLY, CHARLES (workshop of)	3	3	$1,264 £805	$2,760 £1,684	$2,070 £1,267
BAILLY, JENNY	6	4	$450 £276	$2,286 £1,438	$1,567 £1,003
BAILLY, JENNY (attributed to)	1	1	$1,211 £748	$1,211 £748	$1,211 £748
BAILLY, PAUL	23	13	$1,668 £1,035	$10,755 £6,440	$6,833 £4,196

Maker	Items Bid	Sold	Selling Prices Low	High	Avg
BAILLY, PAUL (attributed to)	9	7	$1,703 £1,127	$5,249 £3,220	$3,034 £1,976
BAILLY, PAUL (workshop of)	1	1	$4,025 £2,381	$4,025 £2,381	$4,025 £2,381
BAILLY, RENE	1	1	$1,380 £828	$1,380 £828	$1,380 £828
BALAZS, ISTVAN	2	2	$1,610 £966	$1,955 £1,208	$1,783 £1,087
BALESTRIERI, TOMMASO	7	1	$113,611 £69,700	$113,611 £69,700	$113,611 £69,700
BALL, HARVEY	1	1	$1,150 £690	$1,150 £690	$1,150 £690
BALLANTYNE, ROBERT	1	1	$714 £437	$714 £437	$714 £437
BALLERINI, PIETRO	1	0			
BALTZERSON, PETER E.	1	0			
BANKS, BENJAMIN	11	6	$1,687 £1,035	$9,930 £6,325	$4,886 £3,124
BANKS, JAMES & HENRY	3	2	$3,220 £1,990	$12,483 £7,475	$7,852 £4,732
BARBE, F.	1	1	$892 £633	$892 £633	$892 £633
BARBE, F. (attributed to)	4	1	$1,118 £690	$1,118 £690	$1,118 £690
BARBE, FRANCOIS	1	0			
BARBE, JACQUES (SR.)	1	1	$460 £284	$460 £284	$460 £284
BARBE, TELESPHORE AMABLE	2	1	$4,801 £2,875	$4,801 £2,875	$4,801 £2,875
BARBE FAMILY	1	0			
BARBE FAMILY (MEMBER OF)	2	0			
BARBIERI, BRUNO	3	2	$2,705 £1,610	$6,997 £4,140	$4,851 £2,875
BARBIERI, ENZO	4	0			
BARREL	1	0			
BARRETT, JOHN	3	1	$3,518 £2,300	$3,518 £2,300	$3,518 £2,300
BARRETT, JOHN (ascribed to)	2	0			
BARRI, ROBERT	2	1	$556 £368	$556 £368	$556 £368
BARROWMAN, DAN	2	0			
BARTON, GEORGE	4	3	$192 £115	$3,882 £2,530	$1,558 £1,004
BARTON, J.E.	1	0			
BARTON FAMILY	2	1	$940 £575	$940 £575	$940 £575
BARZONI, FRANCOIS	13	7	$1,273 £828	$1,857 £1,208	$1,536 £986
BARZONI, FRANCOIS (attributed to)	2	1	$1,390 £897	$1,390 £897	$1,390 £897
BASILE, PIETRO	1	1	$2,824 £1,840	$2,824 £1,840	$2,824 £1,840
BASSOT, JOSEPH	3	2	$2,899 £1,725	$7,728 £4,600	$5,314 £3,163

Maker	Items Bid	Sold	Selling Prices Low	High	Avg
BASSOT, JOSEPH (attributed to)	1	1	$2,920 £1,725	$2,920 £1,725	$2,920 £1,725
BATCHELDER, A.M.	1	1	$431 £259	$431 £259	$431 £259
BATELLI, ALFIO	1	0			
BAUER, JEAN	3	2	$4,252 £2,530	$5,405 £3,297	$4,829 £2,914
BAUR, ADOLF	1	1	$4,590 £2,990	$4,590 £2,990	$4,590 £2,990
BAZIN, GUSTAVE	5	2	$662 £460	$2,108 £1,495	$1,385 £978
BAZIN, GUSTAVE (attributed to)	2	1	$987 £690	$987 £690	$987 £690
BEARE & SON	1	1	$690 £460	$690 £460	$690 £460
BECCHINI, RENZO	1	0			
BECKER, CARL	1	1	$26,625 £18,371	$26,625 £18,371	$26,625 £18,371
BECKER, ROBERT	1	1	$3,000 £1,955	$3,000 £1,955	$3,000 £1,955
BEDOCCHI, MARIO	3	1	$10,350 £6,283	$10,350 £6,283	$10,350 £6,283
BEEBE, E.W.	2	2	$748 £462	$3,795 £2,657	$2,271 £1,559
BELLAFONTANA, LORENZO	4	2	$5,998 £3,680	$8,085 £4,830	$7,042 £4,255
BELLAFONTANA, LORENZO (ascribed to)	1	1	$1,759 £1,150	$1,759 £1,150	$1,759 £1,150
BELLAROSA, VITTORIO	4	2	$9,775 £5,865	$11,485 £7,475	$10,630 £6,670
BELLAROSA, VITTORIO (attributed to)	1	1	$4,206 £2,645	$4,206 £2,645	$4,206 £2,645
BELLINGHAM, THOMAS J.	2	1	$973 £690	$973 £690	$973 £690
BELTRAMI, GIUSEPPE	4	3	$2,310 £1,380	$12,483 £7,475	$6,889 £4,225
BELTRAMI, GIUSEPPE (attributed to)	1	0			
BENEDEK, JOANNES	2	0			
BENOZZATI, GIROLAMO	2	0			
BENOZZATI, GIROLAMO (attributed to)	1	1	$1,885 £1,157	$1,885 £1,157	$1,885 £1,157
BERGER, KARL AUGUST	2	2	$4,025 £2,381	$4,113 £2,673	$4,069 £2,527
BERGER & CO., JOSEPH	1	1	$149 £104	$149 £104	$149 £104
BERGONZI, LORENZO	1	1	$2,708 £1,725	$2,708 £1,725	$2,708 £1,725
BERGONZI, MICHAEL ANGELO	1	1	$113,543 £74,100	$113,543 £74,100	$113,543 £74,100
BERGONZI, RICCARDO	1	1	$4,991 £2,898	$4,991 £2,898	$4,991 £2,898
BERINI, MARCUS	1	0			
BERNADELL, ERNEST	1	0			

	Items		Selling Prices		
Maker	Bid	Sold	Low	High	Avg
BERNARD, ANDRE	1	1	$2,471	$2,471	$2,471
			£1,610	£1,610	£1,610
BERNARD, ANDRE (attributed to)	1	0			
BERNARDEL (attributed to)	1	1	$2,249	$2,249	$2,249
			£1,380	£1,380	£1,380
BERNARDEL (workshop of)	3	2	$3,565	$28,194	$15,880
			£2,139	£18,400	£10,270
BBERNARDEL, AUGUST SEBASTIEN PHILIPPE	8	4	$19,550	$32,499	$24,327
			£11,730	£20,700	£15,151
BERNARDEL, AUGUST SEBASTIEN PHILIPPE (attributed to)	4	0			
ERNARDEL, AUGUST SEBASTIEN & ERNEST AUGUST	3	0			
BERNARDEL, GUSTAVE	1	0			
BERNARDEL, GUSTAVE (workshop of)	1	1	$546	$546	$546
			£338	£338	£338
BERNARDEL, GUSTAVE ADOLPHE	4	2	$14,400	$22,094	$18,247
			£9,936	£15,450	£12,693
BERNARDEL, GUSTAVE ADOLPHE (attributed to)	1	1	$9,060	$9,060	$9,060
			£6,000	£6,000	£6,000
BERNARDEL, LEON	15	10	$1,320	$5,762	$3,132
			£805	£3,450	£1,936
BERNARDEL, LEON (attributed to)	4	2	$1,026	$1,118	$1,072
			£656	£690	£673
BERNARDEL, LEON (workshop of)	5	3	$470	$1,840	$1,153
			£306	£1,137	£711
BERNARDEL (PERE) (attributed to)	1	0			
BERNARDEL FAMILY (attributed to)	1	1	$2,999	$2,999	$2,999
			£1,852	£1,852	£1,852
BERTHOLINI, NICOLAS	1	1	$549	$549	$549
			£345	£345	£345
BERTOLAZZI, GIACINTO	2	1	$5,654	$5,654	$5,654
			£3,472	£3,472	£3,472
BETTS	10	2	$332	$717	$525
			£196	£437	£316
BETTS, JOHN	15	11	$321	$11,485	$4,334
			£196	£7,475	£2,731
BEUSCHER, PAUL	3	2	$951	$2,347	$1,649
			£598	£1,495	£1,047
BEUSCHER, PAUL (attributed to)	3	2	$1,188	$1,233	$1,211
			£736	£759	£748
BEUSCHER, PAUL (workshop of)	1	1	$1,725	$1,725	$1,725
			£1,035	£1,035	£1,035
BEYER, NEUMANN	1	0			
BIANCHI, CHRISTOPHER	1	0			
BIANCHI, NICOLO	1	1	$5,851	$5,851	$5,851
			£3,680	£3,680	£3,680
BIANCHI, PASQUALE	1	1	$863	$863	$863
			£526	£526	£526
BIGNAMI, OTELLO	3	1	$8,050	$8,050	$8,050
			£5,635	£5,635	£5,635
BIMBI, BARTOLOMEO	2	0			

	Items		Selling Prices		
Maker	Bid	Sold	Low	High	Avg
BIMBI, BARTOLOMEO (ascribed to)	1	1	$7,538 £4,629	$7,538 £4,629	$7,538 £4,629
BIMBI, BARTOLOMEO (attributed to)	2	0			
BINI, LUCIANO	3	2	$1,265 £810	$2,062 £1,265	$1,663 £1,037
BIRD, RICHMOND HENRY	7	4	$1,782 £1,093	$4,713 £2,910	$3,104 £1,914
BISCH, PAUL (workshop of)	1	1	$1,725 £1,035	$1,725 £1,035	$1,725 £1,035
BISIACH (attributed to)	1	0			
BISIACH (workshop of)	1	0			
BISIACH, CARLO	9	4	$21,942 £13,800	$28,750 £17,765	$24,536 £15,256
BISIACH, LEANDRO	15	8	$7,161 £4,397	$47,134 £29,095	$26,116 £16,558
BISIACH, LEANDRO (attributed to)	6	3	$8,228 £5,175	$18,170 £11,500	$12,987 £8,050
BISIACH, LEANDRO (workshop of)	1	1	$25,300 £15,358	$25,300 £15,358	$25,300 £15,358
BISIACH, LEANDRO & GIACOMO	5	2	$24,675 £16,039	$32,586 £21,160	$28,631 £18,599
BISIACH, LEANDRO (II) & GIACOMO	4	2	$16,308 £10,800	$26,565 £16,100	$21,437 £13,450
BISIACH, LEANDRO (JR.)	1	1	$21,379 £12,650	$21,379 £12,650	$21,379 £12,650
BISIACH, LEANDRO (JR.) (workshop of)	2	1	$12,061 £7,406	$12,061 £7,406	$12,061 £7,406
BISIACH FAMILY	1	1	$29,808 £18,400	$29,808 £18,400	$29,808 £18,400
BISIACH FAMILY (MEMBER OF) (attributed to)	2	1	$13,138 £7,820	$13,138 £7,820	$13,138 £7,820
BITTERER, JOSEPH	1	1	$460 £276	$460 £276	$460 £276
BITTNER, ALOIS	1	1	$2,898 £1,725	$2,898 £1,725	$2,898 £1,725
BLANCHARD, PAUL	10	3	$11,454 £7,475	$18,211 £11,241	$14,596 £9,305
BLANCHARD, PAUL (workshop of)	1	1	$6,997 £4,140	$6,997 £4,140	$6,997 £4,140
BLANCHI, ALBERTO	4	3	$5,831 £3,450	$11,923 £7,360	$8,855 £5,520
BLONDELET, EMILE	6	5	$1,424 £897	$2,999 £1,840	$2,055 £1,289
BLONDELET, EMILE (workshop of)	1	1	$1,490 £920	$1,490 £920	$1,490 £920
BLONDELET, H. EMILE	25	11	$1,042 £690	$3,498 £2,070	$1,841 £1,129
BLYTH, WILLIAMSON	3	1	$576 £368	$576 £368	$576 £368
BLYTH, WILLIAMSON (attributed to)	1	1	$452 £299	$452 £299	$452 £299
BOCQUAY, JACQUES	1	1	$17,285 £10,350	$17,285 £10,350	$17,285 £10,350

Maker	Items		Selling Prices		
	Bid	Sold	Low	High	Avg
BOCQUAY, JACQUES (attributed to)	4	2	$868	$1,646	$1,257
			£575	£1,035	£805
BODOR, JOHN JR.	1	1	$2,875	$2,875	$2,875
			£1,725	£1,725	£1,725
BOERNER, LAWRENCE E.	2	0			
BOFILL, SALVATORE	1	1	$8,694	$8,694	$8,694
			£5,175	£5,175	£5,175
BOFILL, SALVATORE (attributed to)	1	0			
BOLLER, MICHAEL (ascribed to)	1	0			
BONDANELLI, CHIARISSIMO	1	1	$2,249	$2,249	$2,249
			£1,380	£1,380	£1,380
BONNAVENTURE, G. (attributed to)	1	1	$1,596	$1,596	$1,596
			£943	£943	£943
BONNEL, EMILE	2	0			
BONNEL, EMILE (workshop of)	1	1	$2,115	$2,115	$2,115
			£1,375	£1,375	£1,375
BOOSEY & HAWKES (workshop of)	1	1	$1,233	$1,233	$1,233
			£747	£747	£747
BOQUAY, JACQUES	2	2	$6,694	$15,456	$11,075
			£4,370	£9,200	£6,785
BORRIERO, FRANCESCO	1	0			
BOSI, CARLO (attributed to)	2	1	$4,397	$4,397	$4,397
			£2,875	£2,875	£2,875
BOSSI, GIUSEPPE	2	0			
BOSSI, GIUSEPPE (attributed to)	1	1	$4,801	$4,801	$4,801
			£2,875	£2,875	£2,875
BOTTURI, BENVENUTO	2	1	$8,942	$8,942	$8,942
			£5,520	£5,520	£5,520
BOTTURI, BENVENUTO (ascribed to)	1	1	$704	$704	$704
			£460	£460	£460
BOULANGEOT, EMILE	5	3	$966	$5,624	$2,733
			£575	£3,450	£1,659
BOULANGEOT, EMILE (workshop of)	1	1	$2,049	$2,049	$2,049
			£1,265	£1,265	£1,265
BOULANGEOT, JULES CAMILLE	1	1	$3,671	$3,671	$3,671
			£2,185	£2,185	£2,185
BOULLANGIER, C.	1	0			
BOULLANGIER, CHARLES	14	8	$3,265	$15,836	$8,568
			£1,955	£9,775	£5,449
BOULLANGIER, CHARLES (attributed to)	2	1	$2,340	$2,340	$2,340
			£1,495	£1,495	£1,495
BOULLANGIER, CHARLES (FILS)	1	1	$1,725	$1,725	$1,725
			£1,058	£1,058	£1,058
BOURLIER	1	1	$1,090	$1,090	$1,090
			£690	£690	£690
BOYES, ARNOLD	2	0			
BRAN, MARSINO	1	1	$1,410	$1,410	$1,410
			£920	£920	£920
BRANDNER, JOHANN	1	1	$529	$529	$529
			£345	£345	£345
BRAUND, FREDERICK T.	3	3	$552	$1,592	$967
			£345	£1,035	£621
BRETON	6	4	$169	$3,091	$1,343
			£104	£1,840	£802

Maker	Items Bid	Sold	Selling Prices Low	High	Avg
BRETON (workshop of)	5	4	$431 £262	$686 £437	$574 £361
BRETON BREVETE	2	1	$187 £115	$187 £115	$187 £115
BRETON, FRANCOIS (workshop of)	3	2	$690 £426	$920 £544	$805 £485
BRETON FAMILY (MEMBER OF)	1	1	$1,588 £978	$1,588 £978	$1,588 £978
BREUT, KARL WERNER	1	1	$3,289 £2,300	$3,289 £2,300	$3,289 £2,300
BRIGGS, JAMES WILLIAM	10	4	$1,316 £805	$6,578 £4,600	$4,439 £2,904
BROLIO, V. STEPHANO	2	0			
BROSCHI, CARLO	1	1	$2,638 £1,620	$2,638 £1,620	$2,638 £1,620
BROWN, J.	4	3	$672 £437	$1,759 £1,150	$1,121 £721
BROWN, JAMES	5	2	$1,829 £1,150	$3,498 £2,070	$2,663 £1,610
BRUCKNER, E. (attributed to)	1	0			
BRUCKNER, ERICH (attributed to)	1	1	$790 £483	$790 £483	$790 £483
BRUET, NICOLAS	2	1	$736 £460	$736 £460	$736 £460
BRUGERE, CHARLES GEORGES	2	0			
BRUGERE, P.	1	1	$3,353 £2,070	$3,353 £2,070	$3,353 £2,070
BRULLO, LORENZO R.	1	0			
BRUNEAU, SIMON	1	1	$2,185 £1,350	$2,185 £1,350	$2,185 £1,350
BRUNO, CARLO	3	1	$9,373 £5,750	$9,373 £5,750	$9,373 £5,750
BRUSSEAU, ALFRED	1	0			
BRYANT, GEORGE E.	1	0			
BRYANT, L.D.	1	1	$489 £293	$489 £293	$489 £293
BRYANT, OLE H.	2	2	$1,645 £1,069	$6,325 £4,111	$3,985 £2,590
BUCHSTETTER, GABRIEL DAVID	4	2	$1,380 £842	$2,856 £1,997	$2,118 £1,419
BUCKMAN, GEORGE H.	3	2	$1,500 £977	$1,632 £977	$1,566 £977
BULLARD, OLIN	1	1	$920 £552	$920 £552	$920 £552
BUTHOD	2	2	$1,128 £690	$1,641 £977	$1,385 £834
BUTHOD (workshop of)	1	1	$1,610 £995	$1,610 £995	$1,610 £995
BUTHOD, CHARLES LOUIS	3	3	$357 £230	$2,648 £1,725	$1,577 £1,035
BYROM, JOHN	1	1	$7,668 £4,600	$7,668 £4,600	$7,668 £4,600
CAHUSAC	5	2	$1,062 £632	$1,427 £920	$1,244 £776

Maker	Items		Selling Prices		
	Bid	Sold	Low	High	Avg
CAHUSAC (attributed to)	1	1	$1,604 £1,035	$1,604 £1,035	$1,604 £1,035
CAHUSAC, THOMAS (SR.)	1	1	$2,471 £1,610	$2,471 £1,610	$2,471 £1,610
CAIL, LOUIS	1	1	$920 £598	$920 £598	$920 £598
CAIRNS, PETER	2	1	$338 £207	$338 £207	$338 £207
CALACE, RAFFAELE	2	2	$1,181 £748	$3,618 £2,222	$2,400 £1,485
CALCAGNI, BERNARDO	2	2	$22,356 £13,800	$25,709 £15,870	$24,033 £14,835
CALCAGNI, BERNARDO (ascribed to)	1	1	$7,930 £5,175	$7,930 £5,175	$7,930 £5,175
CALCAGNI, BERNARDO (workshop of)	1	1	$26,803 £17,750	$26,803 £17,750	$26,803 £17,750
CALLIER, FRANK	1	1	$690 £414	$690 £414	$690 £414
CALOT, JOSEPH	1	0			
CALVAROLA, BARTOLOMEO	1	1	$2,865 £1,759	$2,865 £1,759	$2,865 £1,759
CAMILLI, CAMILLO	9	6	$40,886 £24,150	$134,435 £80,500	$70,980 £43,861
CAMILLI, CAMILLO (attributed to)	4	2	$13,800 £8,280	$16,000 £9,600	$14,900 £8,940
CANDI, CESARE	3	2	$24,078 £14,375	$26,422 £17,250	$25,250 £15,813
CANDI, CESARE (attributed to)	1	0			
CANDI, ORESTE	2	0			
CANTOV, JULIUS (attributed to)	1	1	$845 £506	$845 £506	$845 £506
CAPELA, ANTONIO	3	3	$5,589 £3,450	$8,811 £5,750	$7,463 £4,742
CAPELA, DOMINGOS	1	0			
CAPELLINI, VIRGILIO	1	0			
CAPICCHIONI, MARINO	3	3	$13,800 £8,280	$59,989 £37,030	$33,996 £21,213
CAPICCHIONI, MARINO (attributed to)	1	1	$12,650 £7,717	$12,650 £7,717	$12,650 £7,717
CAPICCHIONI, MARIO	3	2	$9,603 £5,750	$27,336 £17,193	$18,469 £11,471
CAPPA, GIOFFREDO	3	1	$50,253 £29,900	$50,253 £29,900	$50,253 £29,900
CAPPA, GIOFFREDO (ascribed to)	1	0			
CAPPICHIONI, MARINO (attributed to)	1	1	$5,750 £3,738	$5,750 £3,738	$5,750 £3,738
CARBONARE, ALAIN	1	1	$5,999 £3,703	$5,999 £3,703	$5,999 £3,703
CARCASSI, LORENZO	4	2	$14,375 £8,798	$26,082 £16,100	$20,229 £12,449
CARCASSI, LORENZO (attributed to)	2	1	$7,783 £5,520	$7,783 £5,520	$7,783 £5,520
CARCASSI, LORENZO & TOMMASO	14	10	$29,808 £18,400	$55,890 £34,500	$40,144 £24,825

| Maker | Items | | Selling Prices | | |
	Bid	Sold	Low	High	Avg
CARCASSI, LORENZO & TOMMASO					
(ascribed to)	1	1	$9,400	$9,400	$9,400
			£6,110	£6,110	£6,110
CARCASSI, LORENZO & TOMMASO					
(attributed to)	1	0			
CARCASSI, VINCENZO	1	1	$32,913	$32,913	$32,913
			£20,700	£20,700	£20,700
CARDI, LUIGI (ascribed to)	2	1	$3,163	$3,163	$3,163
			£2,024	£2,024	£2,024
CARDI, LUIGI (attributed to)	2	1	$4,481	$4,481	$4,481
			£2,910	£2,910	£2,910
CARDINET, D.	1	1	$1,321	$1,321	$1,321
			£863	£863	£863
CARESSA, ALBERT	4	1	$3,749	$3,749	$3,749
			£2,300	£2,300	£2,300
CARESSA & FRANCAIS	2	1	$6,521	$6,521	$6,521
			£4,560	£4,560	£4,560
CARLETTI, CARLO	6	2	$10,247	$10,563	$10,405
			£6,325	£6,325	£6,325
CARLETTI, CARLO (ascribed to)	1	1	$8,625	$8,625	$8,625
			£5,329	£5,329	£5,329
CARLETTI, CARLO (attributed to)	5	1	$4,054	$4,054	$4,054
			£2,875	£2,875	£2,875
CARLETTI, GABRIELE	1	0			
CARLETTI, GENUZIO	2	1	$4,744	$4,744	$4,744
			£2,875	£2,875	£2,875
CARLETTI, GENUZIO (ascribed to)	1	1	$4,888	$4,888	$4,888
			£2,933	£2,933	£2,933
CARLETTI, GENUZIO & JOSEPH SETTIN	1	1	$9,400	$9,400	$9,400
			£6,110	£6,110	£6,110
CARLETTI, ORFEO	2	1	$14,621	$14,621	$14,621
			£8,970	£8,970	£8,970
CARLISLE, JAMES REYNOLD	1	1	$3,450	$3,450	$3,450
			£2,094	£2,094	£2,094
CARLONI, ASSUNTO	2	2	$2,917	$3,220	$3,069
			£1,905	£2,040	£1,972
CARMICHAEL, R.	1	0			
CARROLL, JOHN	1	1	$531	$531	$531
			£322	£322	£322
CARSLAW, ROBERT	1	1	$559	$559	$559
			£345	£345	£345
CARTWRIGHT, CHARLES D.	4	2	$460	$690	$575
			£303	£421	£362
CARY, ALPHONSE	2	0			
CASELLA, MARIO	1	0			
CASINI, LAPO	2	0			
CASTAGNERI, ANDREA	3	2	$1,840	$6,400	$4,120
			£1,211	£4,025	£2,618
CASTAGNERI, ANDREA (ascribed to)	1	0			
CASTAGNINO, GIUSEPPE	3	3	$10,220	$17,140	$14,088
			£6,670	£10,580	£8,817
CASTELLO, PAOLO	6	4	$5,750	$62,514	$24,254
			£3,783	£41,400	£15,838

Maker	Items		Selling Prices		
	Bid	Sold	Low	High	Avg
CASTELLO, PAOLO (ascribed to)	1	1	$31,866	$31,866	$31,866
			£19,550	£19,550	£19,550
CASTELLO, PAOLO (attributed to)	1	0			
CASTURELLI, ANTONIO (ascribed to)	1	0			
CATENARI, ENRICO	4	1	$49,450	$49,450	$49,450
			£32,533	£32,533	£32,533
CAUSSIN, F. (attributed to)	1	1	$4,713	$4,713	$4,713
			£2,910	£2,910	£2,910
CAUSSIN, F.N.	2	1	$2,422	$2,422	$2,422
			£1,495	£1,495	£1,495
CAUSSIN, FRANCOIS	4	2	$7,728	$9,673	$8,700
			£4,600	£6,084	£5,342
CAUSSIN, FRANCOIS (attributed to)	3	2	$960	$2,049	$1,505
			£575	£1,265	£920
CAUSSIN FAMILY (MEMBER OF)	2	1	$1,075	$1,075	$1,075
			£667	£667	£667
CAVALAZZI, ANTONIO	4	1	$2,812	$2,812	$2,812
			£1,725	£1,725	£1,725
CAVALERI, JOSEPH	2	1	$24,705	$24,705	$24,705
			£16,100	£16,100	£16,100
CAVALLI, ARISTIDE	8	8	$1,960	$6,572	$3,451
			£1,203	£3,910	£2,091
CAVALLI, ARISTIDE (workshop of)	2	2	$1,255	$3,105	$2,180
			£747	£2,043	£1,395
CAVALLO, LUIGI	1	0			
CAVANI, G.	1	0			
CAVANI, GIOVANNI	1	0			
CAVANI, GIOVANNI (ascribed to)	1	1	$2,796	$2,796	$2,796
			£1,725	£1,725	£1,725
CAVANI, GIOVANNI (II)	1	0			
CAVANI, VINCENZO	4	2	$2,300	$5,442	$3,871
			£1,610	£3,220	£2,415
CAYFORD, FREDERICK	1	1	$3,187	$3,187	$3,187
			£1,955	£1,955	£1,955
CELANI, EMEDIO (attributed to)	1	0			
CELESTINI, ANTONIO	1	0			
CELONIATO, GIOVANNI FRANCESCO	4	2	$30,925	$33,534	$32,229
			£18,400	£20,700	£19,550
CERMAK, JOSEF ANTONIN	1	1	$3,220	$3,220	$3,220
			£1,955	£1,955	£1,955
CERMAK, JOSEF ANTONIN (attributed to)	1	1	$530	$530	$530
			£345	£345	£345
CERUTI, RICARDO	1	0			
CERUTI, ENRICO	5	2	$36,708	$61,851	$49,280
			£21,850	£38,900	£30,375
CERUTI, ENRICO (ascribed to)	3	3	$8,625	$31,688	$18,138
			£5,329	£18,975	£11,156
CERUTI, GIOVANNI BATTISTA (attributed to)	2	2	$1,610	$7,680	$4,645
			£966	£4,830	£2,898
CERUTI, GIUSEPPE	1	0			
CERUTI FAMILY (MEMBER OF)	1	1	$40,572	$40,572	$40,572
			£24,150	£24,150	£24,150

Maker	Items		Selling Prices		
	Bid	Sold	Low	High	Avg
CHAMPION, RENE	1	1	$1,585 £1,035	$1,585 £1,035	$1,585 £1,035
CHANNON, FREDERICK WILLIAM	1	1	$4,321 £2,588	$4,321 £2,588	$4,321 £2,588
CHANOT	1	0			
CHANOT, FRANCOIS	2	0			
CHANOT, FREDERICK WILLIAM	5	5	$4,660 £2,875	$10,833 £6,900	$7,337 £4,692
CHANOT, FREDERICK WILLIAM (attributed to)	1	1	$2,952 £1,955	$2,952 £1,955	$2,952 £1,955
CHANOT, G.A.	4	4	$1,671 £1,093	$5,511 £3,450	$3,488 £2,199
CHANOT, GEORGE ADOLPH	5	1	$3,498 £2,070	$3,498 £2,070	$3,498 £2,070
CHANOT, GEORGE ADOLPH (workshop of)	1	1	$4,600 £2,760	$4,600 £2,760	$4,600 £2,760
CHANOT, GEORGES	13	11	$2,996 £1,955	$40,331 £24,150	$20,719 £12,759
CHANOT, GEORGES (attributed to)	1	0			
CHANOT, GEORGES (II)	2	2	$1,925 £1,150	$10,971 £6,900	$6,448 £4,025
CHANOT, JOSEPH ANTHONY	2	1	$4,341 £2,875	$4,341 £2,875	$4,341 £2,875
CHANOT FAMILY (MEMBER OF)	1	0			
CHAPMAN	2	1	$537 £368	$537 £368	$537 £368
CHAPPUY	4	4	$155 £92	$5,189 £3,680	$1,972 £1,337
CHAPPUY (attributed to)	1	1	$679 £414	$679 £414	$679 £414
CHAPPUY, A.	1	1	$1,266 £748	$1,266 £748	$1,266 £748
CHAPPUY, AUGUSTIN	2	0			
CHAPPUY, N.	1	0			
CHAPPUY, N.A. (attributed to)	1	1	$2,142 £1,323	$2,142 £1,323	$2,142 £1,323
CHAPPUY, NICOLAS	1	1	$3,214 £1,984	$3,214 £1,984	$3,214 £1,984
CHAPPUY, NICOLAS AUGUSTIN	9	5	$696 £483	$4,258 £2,645	$2,354 £1,456
CHAROTTE	2	2	$867 £552	$1,139 £690	$1,003 £621
CHAROTTE, CLAUDE (attributed to)	1	1	$1,297 £920	$1,297 £920	$1,297 £920
CHAROTTE, VICTOR JOSEPH	2	0			
CHAROTTE-MILLOT, JOSEPH	4	2	$1,102 £690	$3,290 £2,139	$2,196 £1,414
CHAROTTE-MILLOT, JOSEPH (workshop of)	1	1	$575 £355	$575 £355	$575 £355
CHERPITEL, GEORGE	2	0			
CHERPITEL, L.	1	0			

Maker	Items		Selling Prices		
	Bid	Sold	Low	High	Avg
CHERPITEL, LOUIS	4	2	$3,250	$3,335	$3,292
			£2,070	£2,134	£2,102
CHERPITEL, N.E. (attributed to)	1	1	$2,999	$2,999	$2,999
			£1,852	£1,852	£1,852
CHEVRIER (ascribed to)	1	1	$282	$282	$282
			£173	£173	£173
CHEVRIER, ANDRE (ascribed to)	1	0			
CHEVRIER, CLAUDE	3	2	$1,093	$1,265	$1,179
			£656	£748	£702
CHIESA, CARLO	2	1	$2,823	$2,823	$2,823
			£1,840	£1,840	£1,840
CHIOCCHI, GAETANO	1	0			
CHIOCCHI, GAETANO (attributed to)	1	1	$12,184	$12,184	$12,184
			£7,475	£7,475	£7,475
CHIPOT, P. (attributed to)	1	1	$2,385	$2,385	$2,385
			£1,553	£1,553	£1,553
CHIPOT, PAUL	1	1	$4,844	$4,844	$4,844
			£2,990	£2,990	£2,990
CHIPOT-VUILLAUME	24	19	$677	$2,608	$1,670
			£414	£1,553	£1,021
CHIPOT-VUILLAUME (workshop of)	2	2	$1,380	$1,955	$1,668
			£828	£1,173	£1,001
CICILIATI, ALESSANDRO	1	1	$5,216	$5,216	$5,216
			£3,220	£3,220	£3,220
CIOAMI, LASANO	1	1	$2,537	$2,537	$2,537
			£1,680	£1,680	£1,680
CIOFFI, A.	1	0			
CLARK, HOMER H.	1	1	$5,796	$5,796	$5,796
			£3,450	£3,450	£3,450
CLAUDOT, ALBERT	1	1	$4,945	$4,945	$4,945
			£3,016	£3,016	£3,016
CLAUDOT, AUGUSTIN	1	1	$4,888	$4,888	$4,888
			£3,174	£3,174	£3,174
CLAUDOT, CHARLES	4	2	$863	$3,416	$2,139
			£533	£2,070	£1,301
CLAUDOT, CHARLES (workshop of)	1	0			
CLAUDOT, CHARLES II	2	2	$1,131	$2,313	$1,722
			£694	£1,455	£1,075
CLEMENS, ROBERT	1	1	$1,380	$1,380	$1,380
			£838	£838	£838
CLEMENT, JEAN LAMBERT (attributed to)	1	1	$4,099	$4,099	$4,099
			£2,530	£2,530	£2,530
CLEMENT, JEAN LAURENT	1	1			
CLOUGH, GEORGE	3	1	$1,272	$1,272	$1,272
			£828	£828	£828
COCCHIONI, ERALDO (ascribed to)	1	0			
COCKCROFT, W.	1	1	$825	$825	$825
			£506	£506	£506
COCKER, LAWRENCE	3	1	$2,113	$2,113	$2,113
			£1,265	£1,265	£1,265
COFFMANN, C.R.	1	0			
COLAPIETRO, FRANCESCO	2	0			
COLE, JAMES	1	1	$1,590	$1,590	$1,590
			£1,035	£1,035	£1,035

Maker	Items		Selling Prices		
	Bid	Sold	Low	High	Avg
COLEMAN, EDWARD E.	1	1	$1,265 £782	$1,265 £782	$1,265 £782
COLIN, JEAN BAPTISTE	27	22	$863 £533	$2,824 £1,840	$1,693 £1,038
COLIN, JEAN BAPTISTE (attributed to)	1	1	$1,078 £713	$1,078 £713	$1,078 £713
COLIN, JEAN BAPTISTE (workshop of)	1	1	$633 £391	$633 £391	$633 £391
COLLENOT, LOUIS	1	1	$364 £253	$364 £253	$364 £253
COLLIER & DAVIS	1	1	$1,252 £828	$1,252 £828	$1,252 £828
COLLIN, J.B. (workshop of)	1	1	$690 £408	$690 £408	$690 £408
COLLIN-MEZIN	1	1	$4,658 £2,875	$4,658 £2,875	$4,658 £2,875
COLLIN-MEZIN (attributed to)	3	1	$2,249 £1,380	$2,249 £1,380	$2,249 £1,380
COLLIN-MEZIN (workshop of)	5	4	$546 £359	$2,523 £1,587	$1,400 £869
COLLIN-MEZIN, CH.J.B.	84	63	$734 £437	$7,700 £4,600	$3,803 £2,372
COLLIN-MEZIN, CH.J.B. (attributed to)	9	6	$691 £426	$3,710 £2,415	$2,098 £1,303
COLLIN-MEZIN, CH.J.B. (workshop of)	10	8	$1,444 £920	$3,972 £2,530	$2,142 £1,372
COLLIN-MEZIN, CH.J.B. (FILS)	15	11	$884 £575	$5,467 £3,439	$3,419 £2,086
COLLIN-MEZIN, CH.J.B. (FILS) (attributed to)	2	1	$1,407 £863	$1,407 £863	$1,407 £863
COLLIN-MEZIN, CH.J.B. (II)	11	7	$1,586 £1,035	$2,648 £1,725	$2,107 £1,385
COLLIN-MEZIN, CH.J.B. (III)	6	2	$2,467 £1,495	$2,467 £1,610	$2,467 £1,553
COLLINS, GLEN	2	2	$5,436 £3,600	$27,852 £17,193	$16,644 £10,396
COLOMBO, CAMILLO	1	0			
COLT, E.W.	1	0			
COMBS, JOHN	1	1	$230 £140	$230 £140	$230 £140
COMSTOCK, WILMER E.	1	0			
COMUNI, ANTONIO (ascribed to)	1	1	$8,698 £5,760	$8,698 £5,760	$8,698 £5,760
CONANT, WILLIAM A.	4	4	$374 £246	$1,175 £764	$818 £519
CONE, GEORGES	2	2	$1,196 £748	$6,721 £4,700	$3,959 £2,724
CONE, GEORGES (workshop of)	1	1	$1,610 £952	$1,610 £952	$1,610 £952
CONE, GEORGES & FILS	1	1	$3,353 £2,070	$3,353 £2,070	$3,353 £2,070
CONIA, STEFANO	7	3	$1,651 £977	$6,160 £3,680	$4,137 £2,483

Maker	Items		Selling Prices		
	Bid	Sold	Low	High	Avg
CONNELAN, MICHAEL	1	1	$384	$384	$384
			£230	£230	£230
CONTAVALLI	1	0			
CONTAVALLI, LUIGI	1	1	$3,392	$3,392	$3,392
			£2,083	£2,083	£2,083
CONTAVALLI, PRIMO	2	1	$16,822	$16,822	$16,822
			£10,580	£10,580	£10,580
CONTINO, ALFREDO	6	6	$8,625	$22,356	$16,444
			£5,329	£13,800	£10,162
CONTINO, ALFREDO (attributed to)	1	1	$5,451	$5,451	$5,451
			£3,220	£3,220	£3,220
CONTRERAS, JOSE	2	2	$14,117	$25,310	$19,714
			£9,200	£14,950	£12,075
COOPER, HUGH W.	1	1	$636	$636	$636
			£403	£403	£403
CORATTI, IVANO	1	1	$6,561	$6,561	$6,561
			£4,025	£4,025	£4,025
CORDANO, GIACOMO FILIPPO	3	1	$24,967	$24,967	$24,967
			£14,950	£14,950	£14,950
CORNELLISSEN, MARTEN	1	0			
CORSBY, GEORGE	3	0			
CORSINI, GIORGIO	1	0			
COSSU, FRANCESCO	2	0			
COSTA, FELIX MORI	2	2	$10,051	$43,332	$26,691
			£5,980	£27,600	£16,790
COSTA, FELIX MORI (attributed to)	1	1	$5,463	$5,463	$5,463
			£3,824	£3,824	£3,824
COSTARDI, BRUNO	1	1	$2,070	$2,070	$2,070
			£1,325	£1,325	£1,325
COUCH, C.M.	1	1	$345	$345	$345
			£207	£207	£207
COURTIER, LOUIS	3	2	$2,115	$2,350	$2,233
			£1,375	£1,528	£1,451
COUTURIEUX, M.	4	4	$518	$932	$756
			£345	£575	£469
CRAIG, JOHN	1	1	$1,546	$1,546	$1,546
			£920	£920	£920
CRAMOND	4	2	$402	$710	$556
			£253	£437	£345
CRAMOND, CHARLES	2	1	$987	$987	$987
			£690	£690	£690
CRASKE, G.	1	0			
CRASKE, GEORGE	32	21	$2,782	$8,280	$5,518
			£1,840	£5,520	£3,434
CREMONINI, VIRGILIO	1	0			
CROSS, NATHANIEL	1	1	$1,932	$1,932	$1,932
			£1,150	£1,150	£1,150
CROSS, NATHANIEL (attributed to)	1	1	$4,481	$4,481	$4,481
			£2,910	£2,910	£2,910
CROUT, THOMAS FARROW (attributed to)	1	1	$486	$486	$486
			£311	£311	£311
CROWTHER (attributed to)	1	1	$1,006	$1,006	$1,006
			£633	£633	£633

Maker	Items		Selling Prices		
	Bid	Sold	Low	High	Avg
CUNAULT, GEORGES	4	2	$1,840	$12,617	$7,228
			£1,117	£7,935	£4,526
CUNAULT, GEORGES (workshop of)	1	0			
CUNE, RENE (workshop of)	1	1	$2,115	$2,115	$2,115
			£1,375	£1,375	£1,375
CUNIN, ALBERT (attributed to)	1	1	$1,594	$1,594	$1,594
			£978	£978	£978
CUNY (attributed to)	1	1	$3,986	$3,986	$3,986
			£2,640	£2,640	£2,640
CURLETTO, ANSELMO	2	0			
CURTIL, ANTOINE	1	1	$2,847	$2,847	$2,847
			£1,783	£1,783	£1,783
CURTIN, JOSEPH	2	2	$15,902	$25,709	$20,806
			£10,350	£15,870	£13,110
CURTIS, ROGER	1	1	$1,160	$1,160	$1,160
			£690	£690	£690
CUTHBERT, ROBERT	1	1	$9,143	$9,143	$9,143
			£5,750	£5,750	£5,750
CUYPERS, JOHANNES	9	6	$16,353	$44,988	$30,683
			£10,350	£27,600	£19,081
CUYPERS, JOHANNES (attributed to)	1	1	$5,639	$5,639	$5,639
			£3,680	£3,680	£3,680
CUYPERS, JOHANNES BERNARD	1	1	$14,496	$14,496	$14,496
			£9,600	£9,600	£9,600
CUYPERS, JOHANNES FRANCIS	1	1	$19,205	$19,205	$19,205
			£11,500	£11,500	£11,500
CUYPERS, JOHANNES THEODORUS	2	2	$28,808	$31,542	$30,175
			£17,250	£19,838	£18,544
CUYPERS, J.T. (attributed to)	2	1	$857	$857	$857
			£529	£529	£529
CUYPERS FAMILY (MEMBER OF)	1	1	$10,588	$10,588	$10,588
			£6,900	£6,900	£6,900
CUYPERS FAMILY (MEMBER OF) (ascribed to)	1	1	$10,284	$10,284	$10,284
			£6,348	£6,348	£6,348
DAHLEN, FRANS WALDEMAR	2	2	$1,344	$2,113	$1,728
			£805	£1,265	£1,035
DAILEY, ISRAEL A.	1	1	$1,150	$1,150	$1,150
			£702	£702	£702
D'ALAGLIO, JOSEPH	1	1	$44,085	$44,085	$44,085
			£27,600	£27,600	£27,600
DAL CANTO, GIUSTINO	3	2	$2,313	$6,955	$4,634
			£1,455	£4,140	£2,797
DALINGER, SEBASTIAN (attributed to)	1	0			
DALLA COSTA, PIETRO ANTONIO	3	2	$44,806	$56,925	$50,866
			£29,095	£34,500	£31,798
DALLA COSTA, PIETRO ANTONIO (attributed to)	1	1	$20,700	$20,700	$20,700
			£12,420	£12,420	£12,420
DALL'AGLIO, GIUSEPPE	4	1	$22,094	$22,094	$22,094
			£15,450	£15,450	£15,450
DALL'AGLIO, GIUSEPPE (ascribed to)	2	2	$26,082	$29,994	$28,038
			£16,100	£18,515	£17,308
DALLINGER, SEBASTIAN	2	0			

Maker	Items Bid	Sold	Selling Prices Low	High	Avg
DANIELS, SAMUEL WESLEY	1	1	$240 £166	$240 £166	$240 £166
DARBEY, GEORGE	3	3	$2,888 £1,725	$5,972 £3,565	$4,243 £2,607
DARBY	1	0			
DARCHE, HILAIRE	7	3	$6,427 £3,968	$11,523 £6,900	$8,483 £5,156
DARCHE, NICHOLAS	2	1	$1,610 £985	$1,610 £985	$1,610 £985
D'ARIA, VINCENZO	1	1	$11,178 £6,900	$11,178 £6,900	$11,178 £6,900
DARTE, A.	1	1	$2,785 £1,719	$2,785 £1,719	$2,785 £1,719
DARTE, AUGUSTE	1	0			
DA RUB, ANGELO (attributed to)	1	1	$12,633 £7,475	$12,633 £7,475	$12,633 £7,475
DAY, JOHN	1	1	$6,900 £4,081	$6,900 £4,081	$6,900 £4,081
DAY, W.S.	1	1	$336 £235	$336 £235	$336 £235
DAY, WILLIAM	2	0			
DEARLOVE, MARK	1	1	$5,403 £3,335	$5,403 £3,335	$5,403 £3,335
DEAS, WILLIAM	2	1	$282 £173	$282 £173	$282 £173
DE BARBIERI, PAOLO	4	0			
DE BARBIERI, PAOLO (attributed to)	1	1	$12,719 £8,050	$12,719 £8,050	$12,719 £8,050
DEBLAYE, ALBERT	11	9	$1,725 £1,150	$2,981 £1,840	$2,360 £1,497
DEBLAYE, ALBERT (attributed to)	6	3	$1,034 £667	$2,474 £1,610	$1,591 £1,035
DEBLAYE, ALBERT (workshop of)	1	1	$1,495 £884	$1,495 £884	$1,495 £884
DEBLAYE, ALBERT JOSEPH	1	1	$1,242 £863	$1,242 £863	$1,242 £863
DEBLAYE, ALBERT JOSEPH (workshop of)	1	1	$1,680 £1,175	$1,680 £1,175	$1,680 £1,175
DE BONIS, ROCCO DONI (attributed to)	1	0			
DE COMBLE, AMBROISE	1	1	$7,668 £4,600	$7,668 £4,600	$7,668 £4,600
DE COMBLE, AMBROISE (attributed to)	1	1	$6,184 £4,025	$6,184 £4,025	$6,184 £4,025
DECONET, MICHELE	2	1	$12,684 £8,400	$12,684 £8,400	$12,684 £8,400
DECONET, MICHELE (attributed to)	1	0			
DEGANI, DOMENICO	1	1	$19,550 £13,685	$19,550 £13,685	$19,550 £13,685
DEGANI, DOMENICO (attributed to)	1	1	$7,590 £4,600	$7,590 £4,600	$7,590 £4,600
DEGANI, EUGENIO	16	11	$21,861 £13,423	$35,337 £23,000	$29,656 £18,334

Maker	Items Bid	Sold	Selling Prices Low	High	Avg
DEGANI, GIULIO	17	11	$5,175 £3,198	$30,360 £18,400	$18,952 £11,796
DE JONG, MATTHIJS	1	0			
DEL BUSSETTO, GIOVANNI MARIA	1	1	$248,711 £153,525	$248,711 £153,525	$248,711 £153,525
DEL CANTO, GIUSTINO (attributed to)	1	0			
DELEPLANQUE, GERARD J.	2	2	$2,599 £1,553	$5,654 £3,680	$4,126 £2,616
DELFOUR, DANIEL	1	0			
DEL FREDE, ANTONIO (attributed to)	1	1	$4,111 £2,875	$4,111 £2,875	$4,111 £2,875
DEL HIERRO, JOSE	1	1	$3,562 £2,185	$3,562 £2,185	$3,562 £2,185
DELIGNON, LOUIS (attributed to)	1	1	$1,151 £805	$1,151 £805	$1,151 £805
DELIVET, AUGUSTE	2	1	$2,070 £1,279	$2,070 £1,279	$2,070 £1,279
DELLA CORTE, ALFONSO	2	1	$9,692 £6,325	$9,692 £6,325	$9,692 £6,325
DELLA CORTE, ALFONSO (attributed to)	1	0			
DEL LUNGO, ALFREDO	2	2	$1,783 £1,035	$8,832 £5,555	$5,307 £3,295
DE MEGLIO, GIOVANNI	1	0			
DE MUZIO, FRANCESCO (attributed to)	1	1	$1,885 £1,157	$1,885 £1,157	$1,885 £1,157
DENNIS, JESSE	1	0			
DENTI, ALBERTO	2	1	$1,955 £1,251	$1,955 £1,251	$1,955 £1,251
DE PLANIS, AUGUST	1	1	$38,823 £25,300	$38,823 £25,300	$38,823 £25,300
DERAZEY (workshop of)	1	1	$1,159 £805	$1,159 £805	$1,159 £805
DERAZEY, H.	7	5	$2,818 £1,840	$8,694 £5,175	$4,908 £3,042
DERAZEY, HONORE	21	14	$1,410 £920	$21,416 £12,650	$9,106 £5,756
DERAZEY, HONORE (attributed to)	1	1	$4,465 £2,902	$4,465 £2,902	$4,465 £2,902
DERAZEY, HONORE (workshop of)	5	3	$1,840 £1,104	$3,250 £2,070	$2,369 £1,528
DERAZEY, JUSTIN	14	8	$2,528 £1,610	$10,708 £6,325	$5,101 £3,112
DERAZEY, JUSTIN (attributed to)	5	1	$2,257 £1,495	$2,257 £1,495	$2,257 £1,495
DERAZEY, JUSTIN (workshop of)	4	3	$705 £458	$1,427 £998	$1,061 £706
DERAZEY FAMILY (MEMBER OF)	2	1	$3,936 £2,415	$3,936 £2,415	$3,936 £2,415
DEROUX, AUGUST S. (attributed to)	2	0			
DE RUB, A.	2	0			
DE RUB, ANGELO	2	1	$13,892 £9,200	$13,892 £9,200	$13,892 £9,200
DESIATO, GIUSEPPE (attributed to)	3	3	$3,220 £1,932	$4,776 £2,990	$4,006 £2,484

Maker	Items Bid	Sold	Selling Prices Low	High	Avg
DESIATO, VINCENZO (ascribed to)	1	1	$1,472 £926	$1,472 £926	$1,472 £926
DESIATO, VINCENZO (attributed to)	1	0			
DESIDERI, PIETRO PAOLO	1	1	$13,041 £8,050	$13,041 £8,050	$13,041 £8,050
D'ESPINE, ALESSANDRO	3	0			
DE TOPPANI, ANGELO	2	2	$7,490 £4,485	$12,633 £7,475	$10,061 £5,980
DEULIN, JOSEF	1	1	$403 £238	$403 £238	$403 £238
DEVEAU, JOHN G.	1	1	$1,495 £972	$1,495 £972	$1,495 £972
DEVONEY, FRANK	1	0			
DE ZORZI, VALENTINO	4	3	$14,950 £8,970	$29,390 £18,400	$19,763 £12,313
DE ZORZI, VALENTINO (workshop of)	1	1	$5,463 £3,231	$5,463 £3,231	$5,463 £3,231
DICKENSON, EDWARD	2	1	$1,344 £805	$1,344 £805	$1,344 £805
DICONET, MICHAEL (attributed to)	1	1	$3,620 £2,248	$3,620 £2,248	$3,620 £2,248
DIDCZENKO, DIMITRO	2	1	$9,600 £6,624	$9,600 £6,624	$9,600 £6,624
DIDELOT, J.	1	0			
DIDION, G.	1	0			
DIEUDONNE	2	2	$1,555 £920	$3,123 £1,955	$2,339 £1,438
DIEUDONNE (workshop of)	1	0			
DIEUDONNE, A. (attributed to)	2	1	$1,863 £1,150	$1,863 £1,150	$1,863 £1,150
DIEUDONNE, AMEDEE	20	12	$1,725 £1,035	$9,462 £5,951	$3,513 £2,193
DIEUDONNE, AMEDEE (attributed to)	6	5	$1,847 £1,127	$3,518 £2,300	$2,499 £1,571
DIEUDONNE, AMEDEE (workshop of)	1	1	$2,688 £1,880	$2,688 £1,880	$2,688 £1,880
DI LELIO, ARMANDO	2	1	$5,467 £3,439	$5,467 £3,439	$5,467 £3,439
DI SANTO CELLINI, MARCELLO	1	1	$2,291 £1,495	$2,291 £1,495	$2,291 £1,495
DITER, JUSTIN	1	1	$6,325 £3,840	$6,325 £3,840	$6,325 £3,840
DIX, DAVID	3	2	$626 £414	$782 £518	$704 £466
DIXON, ALFRED THOMAS	1	1	$1,160 £690	$1,160 £690	$1,160 £690
DOBBIE, WILLIAM	1	1	$937 £575	$937 £575	$937 £575
DOBRESOVITCH, MARCO (attributed to)	1	1	$2,070 £1,380	$2,070 £1,380	$2,070 £1,380
DOBRITCHCOV, FILIP	1	1	$2,588 £1,553	$2,588 £1,553	$2,588 £1,553
DODD, THOMAS	1	1	$12,710 £8,280	$12,710 £8,280	$12,710 £8,280

| Maker | Items | | Selling Prices | | |
	Bid	Sold	Low	High	Avg
DODD, THOMAS (attributed to)	1	1	$9,664 £5,750	$9,664 £5,750	$9,664 £5,750
DOERFFEL	1	1	$504 £322	$504 £322	$504 £322
DOLLENZ, GIOVANNI (attributed to)	3	2	$2,306 £1,380	$4,865 £3,450	$3,585 £2,415
DOLLENZ, GIUSEPPE	1	0			
DOLLING, HERMANN	1	0			
DOLLING, HERMANN (JR.)	2	2	$1,585 £1,035	$1,610 £1,047	$1,598 £1,041
DOLLING, ROBERT A.	3	3	$1,116 £725	$1,495 £984	$1,369 £869
DOLLING, ROBERT A. (workshop of)	1	1	$1,093 £675	$1,093 £675	$1,093 £675
DOOLEY, J.W.	1	1	$1,404 £897	$1,404 £897	$1,404 £897
DORELLI, GIOVANNI (ascribed to)	1	0			
DORFEL, ADOLF PAUL	2	2	$3,080 £2,040	$3,986 £2,640	$3,533 £2,340
DOTSCH, MICHAEL	1	1	$10,247 £6,325	$10,247 £6,325	$10,247 £6,325
DOTSCH, MICHAEL (attributed to)	1	1	$4,298 £2,673	$4,298 £2,673	$4,298 £2,673
DOW, WILLIAM HENRY	1	0			
DROUIN, CHARLES	1	0			
DROUIN, ETIENNE	1	1	$1,739 £1,035	$1,739 £1,035	$1,739 £1,035
DROZEN, F.X.	2	1	$3,467 £2,070	$3,467 £2,070	$3,467 £2,070
DUCHENE, NICOLAS	2	2	$690 £426	$1,234 £805	$962 £616
DUCHENE, NICOLAS (ascribed to)	1	0			
DUERER, WILHELM	4	2	$154 £92	$518 £316	$336 £204
DUKE (workshop of)	1	0			
DUKE, RICHARD	25	14	$493 £345	$11,597 £6,900	$5,339 £3,291
DUKE, RICHARD (ascribed to)	1	1	$2,823 £1,840	$2,823 £1,840	$2,823 £1,840
DUKE, RICHARD (attributed to)	2	0			
DUKE, RICHARD (workshop of)	1	1	$3,571 £2,214	$3,571 £2,214	$3,571 £2,214
DUKE, RICHARD (JR.) (attributed to)	2	1	$1,181 £748	$1,181 £748	$1,181 £748
DUKE FAMILY	2	0			
DUMAS, HENRY	1	0			
DUNCAN, GEORGE	1	1	$2,605 £1,725	$2,605 £1,725	$2,605 £1,725
DUNCAN, ROBERT	1	1	$1,294 £863	$1,294 £863	$1,294 £863
DUNLOP, JOHN	3	2	$357 £219	$704 £437	$531 £328
DURRSCHMIDT, WILHELM	1	1	$2,415 £1,492	$2,415 £1,492	$2,415 £1,492

Maker	Items		Selling Prices		
	Bid	Sold	Low	High	Avg
DUWAER, H.G.	2	1	$3,473 £2,300	$3,473 £2,300	$3,473 £2,300
DVORAK, CAREL BOROMAUS	2	1	$3,304 £1,955	$3,304 £1,955	$3,304 £1,955
DVORAK, JAN BAPTISTA	6	5	$3,657 £2,300	$6,110 £3,968	$5,134 £3,220
DVORAK, KARL	1	1	$2,300 £1,513	$2,300 £1,513	$2,300 £1,513
DYKES, ARTHUR WILLIAM	2	1	$1,229 £736	$1,229 £736	$1,229 £736
DYKES, GEORGE	2	1	$4,609 £2,760	$4,609 £2,760	$4,609 £2,760
EATON, ERIC S.	1	1	$869 £517	$869 £517	$869 £517
EBERLE, EUGENE	1	1	$3,286 £1,955	$3,286 £1,955	$3,286 £1,955
EBERLE, JOHANN ULRICH	5	4	$2,990 £1,824	$9,641 £5,951	$6,493 £3,956
EBERLE, TOMASO	5	4	$26,450 £16,399	$65,297 £39,100	$37,680 £23,219
EBERLE, TOMASO (attributed to)	2	1	$2,513 £1,563	$2,513 £1,563	$2,513 £1,563
ECKLAND, DONALD	3	2	$4,025 £2,487	$4,364 £2,706	$4,195 £2,596
EHRICKE, CHARLES	1	0			
EHRLICH	1	1	$4,252 £2,530	$4,252 £2,530	$4,252 £2,530
EKLID, ARNDT O.	1	1	$411 £267	$411 £267	$411 £267
EKSTRAND, GUSTAF	2	0			
ELLIOT, WILLIAM	2	2	$1,150 £714	$2,600 £1,553	$1,875 £1,133
EMERSON, ELIJAH	1	1	$2,300 £1,360	$2,300 £1,360	$2,300 £1,360
EMERY, JULIAN	2	1	$840 £575	$840 £575	$840 £575
ERBA, PAOLO	1	0			
ERDESZ, OTTO	2	1	$3,738 £2,280	$3,738 £2,280	$3,738 £2,280
ERDESZ, OTTO ALEXANDER	1	1	$3,220 £2,118	$3,220 £2,118	$3,220 £2,118
ERTZ, NEIL	1	1	$1,491 £920	$1,491 £920	$1,491 £920
ESPOSITO, RAFFAELE (attributed to)	1	1	$1,093 £666	$1,093 £666	$1,093 £666
ESPOSTI, PIERGIUSEPPE	1	1	$2,875 £1,840	$2,875 £1,840	$2,875 £1,840
EURSOLO, JOHANN GEORG	1	1	$2,898 £1,725	$2,898 £1,725	$2,898 £1,725
EUSCHEN, KARL	1	1	$1,802 £1,092	$1,802 £1,092	$1,802 £1,092
EVANS & CO., GEORGE	1	1	$1,746 £1,058	$1,746 £1,058	$1,746 £1,058

Maker	Items Bid	Sold	Selling Prices Low	High	Avg
EWAN, D.	1	1	$225 £138	$225 £138	$225 £138
EWAN, DAVID	1	0			
EWBANK, HENRY	1	1	$345 £207	$345 £207	$345 £207
FABRICATORE, GENNARO	3	0			
FABRIS, LUIGI	2	1	$16,520 £9,775	$16,520 £9,775	$16,520 £9,775
FABRIS, LUIGI (attributed to)	1	1	$8,777 £5,520	$8,777 £5,520	$8,777 £5,520
FAGNOLA, ANNIBALE	8	5	$33,098 £19,550	$64,998 £41,400	$51,756 £31,954
FAGNOLA, ANNIBALE (ascribed to)	1	1	$18,630 £11,500	$18,630 £11,500	$18,630 £11,500
FAGNOLA, ANNIBALE (attributed to)	4	2	$12,121 £7,038	$12,350 £7,671	$12,235 £7,354
FAGNOLA, H.	1	1	$72,979 £43,700	$72,979 £43,700	$72,979 £43,700
FAGNOLA, H. (attributed to)	1	0			
FALISSE, A.	6	2	$3,887 £2,300	$6,325 £4,161	$5,106 £3,231
FALISSE, AUGUSTE & GEORGES	1	1	$3,450 £2,300	$3,450 £2,300	$3,450 £2,300
FANTIN, DOMENICO	2	2	$4,523 £2,777	$5,999 £3,703	$5,261 £3,240
FARINA, ERMINIO	1	1	$17,699 £10,925	$17,699 £10,925	$17,699 £10,925
FARLEY, CHARLES E.	3	3	$529 £328	$1,265 £768	$790 £480
FAROTTI, CELESTE	3	3	$17,112 £9,936	$23,500 £15,275	$20,016 £12,237
FAROTTI, CELESTE (ascribed to)	1	0			
FAROTTO, CELESTE (attributed to)	2	2	$10,925 £7,101	$12,330 £8,050	$11,628 £7,576
FEBBRARI, DIPENDENTE	2	0			
FENDT, BERNARD	1	0			
FENDT, BERNARD SIMON	2	1	$29,325 £19,550	$29,325 £19,550	$29,325 £19,550
FENDT, BERNARD SIMON (attributed to)	4	2	$2,914 £1,783	$11,178 £6,900	$7,046 £4,341
FENDT, FRANCOIS (attributed to)	1	0			
FENGA, GIULIANO (ascribed to)	1	0			
FENT, FRANCOIS	4	2	$4,235 £2,530	$8,223 £5,750	$6,229 £4,140
FERENCZY-TOMASOWSKY, CHARLES	1	1	$4,934 £3,450	$4,934 £3,450	$4,934 £3,450
FERRARI, LUIGI	1	0			
FERRONI, FERDINANDO	1	1	$4,600 £3,026	$4,600 £3,026	$4,600 £3,026
FETIQUE, EMILE (attributed to)	1	1	$5,570 £3,439	$5,570 £3,439	$5,570 £3,439
FETIQUE, VICTOR	1	0			
FEYZEAU (attributed to)	2	1	$470 £288	$470 £288	$470 £288

Maker	Bid	Sold	Low	High	Avg
		Items		Selling Prices	
FICHTL, JOHANN ULRICH	2	1	$1,620 £1,035	$1,620 £1,035	$1,620 £1,035
FICKER, JOHANN CHRISTIAN	8	5	$2,037 £1,265	$5,041 £3,525	$3,177 £2,060
FICKER, JOHANN GOTTLOB	6	5	$920 £605	$3,856 £2,381	$2,285 £1,411
FIKER, JOHANN CHRISTIAN	1	1	$3,968 £2,460	$3,968 £2,460	$3,968 £2,460
FILANO, LUIGI	1	1	$6,176 £4,025	$6,176 £4,025	$6,176 £4,025
FILIPPI, VITTORIO	1	1	$3,080 £1,840	$3,080 £1,840	$3,080 £1,840
FILLION, G.	1	0			
FIORINI, GIUSEPPE	4	2	$35,305 £23,000	$47,134 £29,095	$41,219 £26,048
FIORINI, GIUSEPPE (ascribed to)	1	0			
FIORINI, PAOLO	3	3	$1,220 £767	$2,138 £1,495	$1,832 £1,176
FIORINI, RAFFAELE	2	2	$2,444 £1,495	$8,082 £5,060	$5,263 £3,278
FIORINI, RAFFAELE (attributed to)	1	1	$15,077 £9,258	$15,077 £9,258	$15,077 £9,258
FISCHER	1	0			
FISCHER, A.E.	1	1	$781 £518	$781 £518	$781 £518
FISCHER, CARL	1	1	$1,035 £690	$1,035 £690	$1,035 £690
FISCHER, LORENZ	1	0			
FISCHER, RAY	1	0			
FISCHER, ZACHARIAS	2	2	$74 £46	$2,523 £1,587	$1,299 £817
FLEURY, BENOIT	2	1	$1,563 £1,035	$1,563 £1,035	$1,563 £1,035
FORBERGER, ROBERT	1	0			
FORD, JACOB	4	2	$3,286 £1,955	$6,980 £4,370	$5,133 £3,163
FORD, JOSEPH W.	2	1	$425 £253	$425 £253	$425 £253
FORST, HANS (workshop of)	2	1	$978 £587	$978 £587	$978 £587
FORSTER, W.	1	0			
FORSTER, W. (attributed to)	1	1	$2,933 £1,955	$2,933 £1,955	$2,933 £1,955
FORSTER, WILLIAM	7	2	$1,725 £1,208	$7,298 £4,370	$4,511 £2,789
FORSTER, WILLIAM (II)	1	1	$3,226 £1,955	$3,226 £1,955	$3,226 £1,955
FORSTER, WILLIAM (III)	2	1	$5,436 £3,600	$5,436 £3,600	$5,436 £3,600
FOSCHI, GIORGIO	2	1	$5,005 £2,990	$5,005 £2,990	$5,005 £2,990
FOSCHINI, GIOVANNI	1	0			
FRACASSI, ARTURO	1	1	$10,046 £5,980	$10,046 £5,980	$10,046 £5,980

| Maker | Items | | Selling Prices | | |
	Bid	Sold	Low	High	Avg
FRANK, MEINRADUS (attributed to)	1	0			
FRANKE, PAUL	1	1	$3,728	$3,728	$3,728
			£2,300	£2,300	£2,300
FRANOT, P.	1	1	$1,267	$1,267	$1,267
			£782	£782	£782
FRANOT, PATRICE	1	1	$1,380	$1,380	$1,380
			£838	£838	£838
FREDI, RODOLFO	5	3	$4,235	$19,550	$12,634
			£2,530	£12,862	£8,197
FREDI, RODOLFO (ascribed to)	1	0			
FREDI, RODOLFO (attributed to)	3	1	$2,138	$2,138	$2,138
			£1,265	£1,265	£1,265
FREYMADL, SEBASTIAN	1	0			
FRIEDL, GUSTAVE	2	2	$298	$994	$646
			£207	£690	£449
FRIEDRICH, JOHN & BROS.	1	1	$1,265	$1,265	$1,265
			£768	£768	£768
FRIEDRICH, JOHN & BROS. (workshop of)	2	2	$460	$690	$575
			£279	£454	£367
FULLER, HENRY	1	1	$1,592	$1,592	$1,592
			£1,035	£1,035	£1,035
FURBER	3	1	$3,666	$3,666	$3,666
			£2,381	£2,381	£2,381
FURBER (attributed to)	1	1	$134	$134	$134
			£80	£80	£80
FURBER, JOHN	3	2	$3,353	$3,385	$3,369
			£2,070	£2,070	£2,070
FURBER, MATTHEW	2	1	$6,184	$6,184	$6,184
			£4,025	£4,025	£4,025
FUREY, WILLIAM	1	0			
GABBITAS, EDWIN	1	0			
GABOR, ANRISAK TIBOR	2	2	$1,412	$1,546	$1,479
			£920	£920	£920
GABRIELLI, GIOVANNI BATTISTA	5	4	$19,435	$50,531	$34,594
			£11,500	£29,900	£20,988
GABRIELLI, GIOVANNI BATTISTA (ascribed to)	2	1	$4,832	$4,832	$4,832
			£2,875	£2,875	£2,875
GADDA, GAETANO	3	3	$10,925	$19,435	$15,019
			£6,664	£12,650	£9,505
GADDA, GAETANO (attributed to)	4	1	$10,284	$10,284	$10,284
			£6,348	£6,348	£6,348
GADDA, GAETANO (workshop of)	1	0			
GADDA, MARIO	1	1	$8,154	$8,154	$8,154
			£5,400	£5,400	£5,400
GAFFINO, ANDREA	1	1	$8,998	$8,998	$8,998
			£5,555	£5,555	£5,555
GAFFINO, GIUSEPPE (attributed to)	2	0			
GAGGINI (ascribed to)	1	1	$2,898	$2,898	$2,898
			£1,725	£1,725	£1,725
GAGGINI, PIETRO	2	0			
GAGGINI, PIETRO (attributed to)	5	1	$2,049	$2,049	$2,049
			£1,265	£1,265	£1,265

| Maker | Items | | Selling Prices | | |
	Bid	Sold	Low	High	Avg
GAGLIANO (workshop of)	1	0			
GAGLIANO, ALESSANDRO	4	3	$61,851	$230,575	$137,914
			£38,900	£142,957	£86,052
GAGLIANO, FERDINAND	9	5	$25,026	$68,500	$38,568
			£14,950	£44,525	£23,744
GAGLIANO, FERDINAND (attributed to)	2	2	$41,125	$44,850	$42,988
			£26,731	£26,910	£26,821
GAGLIANO, GENNARO	2	1	$125,632	$125,632	$125,632
			£74,750	£74,750	£74,750
GAGLIANO, GIUSEPPE	7	2	$46,750	$54,050	$50,400
			£32,257	£32,430	£32,344
GAGLIANO, GIUSEPPE (attributed to)	1	0			
GAGLIANO, GIUSEPPE & ANTONIO	6	2	$21,150	$76,597	$48,874
			£13,748	£49,900	£31,824
GAGLIANO, GIUSEPPE & ANTONIO (ascribed to)	1	0			
GAGLIANO, JOHANNES (attributed to)	1	1	$6,900	$6,900	$6,900
			£4,140	£4,140	£4,140
GAGLIANO, NICOLA	21	12	$21,150	$163,293	$102,970
			£13,748	£102,700	£63,431
GAGLIANO, NICOLA (attributed to)	2	2	$11,470	$25,026	$18,248
			£7,475	£14,950	£11,213
GAGLIANO, NICOLA (I) (attributed to)	1	1	$86,664	$86,664	$86,664
			£55,200	£55,200	£55,200
GAGLIANO, NICOLO (II)	2	0			
GAGLIANO, RAFFAELE & ANTONIO (II)	3	0			
GAGLIANO, RAFFAELE & ANTONIO (II) (attributed to)	1	1	$30,728	$30,728	$30,728
			£18,400	£18,400	£18,400
GAGLIANO FAMILY (MEMBER OF)	4	2	$20,563	$34,652	$27,607
			£13,366	£20,700	£17,033
GAGLIANO FAMILY (MEMBER OF) (attributed to)	1	1	$73,286	$73,286	$73,286
			£47,700	£47,700	£47,700
GAIANI, ROMANO	2	0			
GAIBISSO, GIOVANNI BATTISTA	4	2	$9,488	$10,971	$10,229
			£5,750	£6,900	£6,325
GAIBISSO, GIOVANNI BATTISTA (attributed to)	1	1	$9,867	$9,867	$9,867
			£6,900	£6,900	£6,900
GAIDA, GIOVANNI	7	6	$8,280	$21,252	$14,992
			£5,520	£12,650	£9,258
GAIDA, SILVIO (attributed to)	1	0			
GAILLARD, CHARLES	5	2	$2,332	$2,899	$2,616
			£1,380	£1,725	£1,553
GAILLARD, CHARLES (attributed to)	4	1	$183	$183	$183
			£115	£115	£115
GALEAZZI, ADELINO	1	1	$1,055	$1,055	$1,055
			£648	£648	£648
GALEO	1	1	$1,294	$1,294	$1,294
			£863	£863	£863
GALIMBERTI, LUIGI	1	0			
GALLA, ANTON	3	3	$1,555	$2,760	$2,197
			£920	£1,656	£1,319

Maker	Items Bid	Sold	Selling Prices Low	High	Avg
GALLINOTTI, PIETRO	2	1	$9,867 £6,900	$9,867 £6,900	$9,867 £6,900
GALRAM, J.J.	1	0			
GAND, ADOLPHE CHARLES	1	0			
GAND, CHARLES (attributed to)	1	1	$13,524 £8,050	$13,524 £8,050	$13,524 £8,050
GAND, CHARLES ADOLPHE	2	0			
GAND, CHARLES FRANCOIS	3	2	$10,689 £6,325	$23,000 £14,030	$16,845 £10,178
GAND BROS.	3	3	$10,626 £6,325	$19,205 £11,500	$15,267 £9,248
GAND FAMILY (MEMBER OF)	1	1	$5,589 £3,450	$5,589 £3,450	$5,589 £3,450
GAND & BERNARDEL	12	10	$7,452 £4,600	$19,975 £12,984	$12,706 £7,884
GAND & BERNARDEL (workshop of)	1	1	$3,353 £2,070	$3,353 £2,070	$3,353 £2,070
GAND & BERNARDEL FRERES	2	2	$14,400 £9,936	$19,282 £11,903	$16,841 £10,919
GARIMBERTI, FERDINANDO	2	2	$33,570 £21,850	$36,927 £21,850	$35,248 £21,850
GARIMBERTI, FERDINANDO (attributed to)	1	0			
GARTNER, EUGEN	2	1	$1,380 £842	$1,380 £842	$1,380 £842
GASPARRI, MARIO	1	0			
GATTI, GEORGIO	3	0			
GEESMAN, EDWARD	1	0			
GEIPEL, HERMANN	1	1	$1,175 £764	$1,175 £764	$1,175 £764
GEISSENHOF, FRANZ	14	8	$3,450 £2,094	$20,165 £12,075	$10,840 £6,608
GEISSER, NICOLAUS	2	0			
GEMUNDER, AUGUST	2	2	$3,167 £1,955	$5,175 £3,061	$4,171 £2,508
GEMUNDER, AUGUST (workshop of)	1	0			
GEMUNDER, AUGUST & SONS	3	1	$575 £345	$575 £345	$575 £345
GEMUNDER, AUGUST & SONS (workshop of)	2	1	$1,035 £628	$1,035 £628	$1,035 £628
GEMUNDER, GEORGE (SR.)	2	1	$13,973 £8,625	$13,973 £8,625	$13,973 £8,625
GENIN, LOUIS (attributed to)	1	1	$1,391 £920	$1,391 £920	$1,391 £920
GENOVA, GIOVANNI BATTISTA	1	0			
GENOVESE, RICCARDO	2	0			
GERMAIN, EMILE	4	3	$6,935 £4,140	$8,998 £5,555	$7,919 £4,842
GERMAIN, LOUIS JOSEPH (attributed to)	1	1	$3,968 £2,460	$3,968 £2,460	$3,968 £2,460
GIAMBERINI, SIMONE	2	1	$18,925 £11,903	$18,925 £11,903	$18,925 £11,903

| Maker | Items | | Selling Prices | | |
	Bid	Sold	Low	High	Avg
GIANOTTI, ALFREDO	2	2	$3,680 £2,274	$4,830 £2,946	$4,255 £2,610
GIBBONS, ARTHUR W.	1	0			
GIBSON CO.	2	2	$794 £492	$978 £636	$886 £564
GIGLI, GIULIO CESARE	2	2	$13,024 £8,625	$21,107 £12,961	$17,065 £10,793
GILBERT, JEFFREY J.	5	3	$638 £437	$2,138 £1,495	$1,631 £1,104
GILBERT, JEFFREY JAMES	2	2	$1,490 £1,035	$1,822 £1,265	$1,656 £1,150
GILCHRIST, JAMES	1	1	$1,127 £667	$1,127 £667	$1,127 £667
GILKES, WILLIAM	1	1	$2,471 £1,610	$2,471 £1,610	$2,471 £1,610
GIORDANI, ENRICO	1	0			
GIORGIS, NICOLAUS	1	1	$8,642 £5,175	$8,642 £5,175	$8,642 £5,175
GIRARDI, MARIO	3	0			
GIUDICI, CARLO	1	0			
GLADSTONE, R.	1	1	$531 £345	$531 £345	$531 £345
GLAESEL, EDMUND	1	1	$2,513 £1,558	$2,513 £1,558	$2,513 £1,558
GLAESEL, ERNST	1	1	$934 £575	$934 £575	$934 £575
GLAESEL, LUDWIG	1	1	$2,332 £1,380	$2,332 £1,380	$2,332 £1,380
GLASS, FRANZ JOHANN	1	1	$2,523 £1,587	$2,523 £1,587	$2,523 £1,587
GLASS, FRIEDRICH AUGUST	1	1	$403 £246	$403 £246	$403 £246
GLASS, JOHANN (workshop of)	1	1	$2,070 £1,362	$2,070 £1,362	$2,070 £1,362
GLENISTER, WILLIAM	12	6	$580 £345	$3,030 £1,955	$1,569 £974
GLIER, AUGUST CLEMENS	1	0			
GLIER, ROBERT	3	2	$1,495 £897	$2,400 £1,656	$1,948 £1,277
GLIER & SOHN, C.G.	2	2	$1,863 £1,150	$2,142 £1,323	$2,003 £1,236
GLIGA, VASILE	1	1	$963 £595	$963 £595	$963 £595
GLOOR, ADOLF	3	2	$561 £345	$635 £391	$598 £368
GOBETTI, FRANCESCO	1	1	$79,651 £55,700	$79,651 £55,700	$79,651 £55,700
GOFFRILLER, MATTEO	3	1	$76,895 £45,500	$76,895 £45,500	$76,895 £45,500
GOFFRILLER, MATTEO (ascribed to)	3	3	$21,942 £13,800	$64,274 £39,675	$47,369 £29,325
GOLL, CAROLUS	1	1	$7,452 £4,600	$7,452 £4,600	$7,452 £4,600
GONZALEZ, FERNANDO SOLAR	2	0			

Maker	Items		Selling Prices		
	Bid	Sold	Low	High	Avg
GORRIE, ANDREW	1	1	$730 £460	$730 £460	$730 £460
GOSS, PHILIP (attributed to)	2	1	$624 £403	$624 £403	$624 £403
GOSS, WALTER S.	7	7	$575 £403	$3,335 £2,335	$1,758 £1,166
GOTTI, ANSELMO	1	1	$16,100 £9,821	$16,100 £9,821	$16,100 £9,821
GOTTI, ORSOLO	3	2	$5,467 £3,439	$6,708 £4,370	$6,088 £3,904
GOTZ, C.A.	2	1	$207 £127	$207 £127	$207 £127
GOTZ, CONRAD	1	0			
GOULD, JOHN ALFRED	2	0			
GOULDING	4	4	$975 £598	$2,332 £1,380	$1,590 £978
GOULDING & CO.	3	2	$1,643 £978	$2,318 £1,380	$1,981 £1,179
GOWAR, E. (attributed to)	5	1	$263 £161	$263 £161	$263 £161
GRAGNANI, ANTONIO	8	6	$7,970 £4,830	$64,136 £38,900	$37,204 £22,909
GRAHAM, ROBERT	1	0			
GRANCINO, FRANCESCO (attributed to)	1	0			
GRANCINO, GIOVANNI	8	4	$68,154 £44,400	$207,725 £128,225	$108,227 £68,019
GRANCINO, GIOVANNI (attributed to)	1	0			
GRANCINO, GIOVANNI (II) (attributed to)	1	1	$32,499 £20,700	$32,499 £20,700	$32,499 £20,700
GRANCINO FAMILY (ascribed to)	1	1	$2,605 £1,725	$2,605 £1,725	$2,605 £1,725
GRANDINI, GERONIMO	1	1	$1,380 £920	$1,380 £920	$1,380 £920
GRANDJON (attributed to)	1	1	$1,059 £690	$1,059 £690	$1,059 £690
GRANDJON, J.	1	1	$2,332 £1,380	$2,332 £1,380	$2,332 £1,380
GRANDJON, J. (workshop of)	1	1	$470 £306	$470 £306	$470 £306
GRANDJON, JULES (attributed to)	1	1	$1,389 £920	$1,389 £920	$1,389 £920
GRANDJON, JULES (FILS)	4	3	$1,198 £713	$7,248 £4,800	$3,905 £2,528
GRANDJON, JULES (FILS) (attributed to)	2	2	$2,049 £1,265	$4,761 £2,952	$3,405 £2,108
GRANDJON, PROSPER GERARD	1	1	$1,495 £908	$1,495 £908	$1,495 £908
GRANGEAUD, M.	1	1	$450 £288	$450 £288	$450 £288
GRANT, DANIEL P.	1	1	$518 £306	$518 £306	$518 £306
GRATER & SON, T.	2	2	$660 £403	$1,460 £920	$1,060 £661

Maker	Items Bid	Sold	Low	Selling Prices High	Avg
GRATER, THOMAS	1	1	$787 £483	$787 £483	$787 £483
GREENWOOD, GEORGE WILLIAM	1	1	$3,000 £1,955	$3,000 £1,955	$3,000 £1,955
GRIFFIN, WOODBURY	1	1	$1,265 £748	$1,265 £748	$1,265 £748
GROBITZ	1	0			
GUADAGNINI, ANTONIO	1	1	$40,986 £25,300	$40,986 £25,300	$40,986 £25,300
GUADAGNINI, CARLO (attributed to)	1	1	$44,158 £27,773	$44,158 £27,773	$44,158 £27,773
GUADAGNINI, FELICE	2	1	$56,925 £34,500	$56,925 £34,500	$56,925 £34,500
GUADAGNINI, FRANCESCO	4	1	$45,230 £27,773	$45,230 £27,773	$45,230 £27,773
GUADAGNINI, FRANCESCO (ascribed to)	1	1	$21,150 £13,748	$21,150 £13,748	$21,150 £13,748
GUADAGNINI, GIOVANNI BATTISTA	13	8	$77,751 £47,700	$401,775 £243,500	$236,622 £148,479
GUADAGNINI, GIOVANNI BATTISTA (attributed to)	1	1	$11,474 £7,475	$11,474 £7,475	$11,474 £7,475
GUADAGNINI, GIUSEPPE	2	1	$63,269 £41,900	$63,269 £41,900	$63,269 £41,900
GUADAGNINI, GIUSEPPE (attributed to)	3	1	$32,137 £19,838	$32,137 £19,838	$32,137 £19,838
GUADAGNINI BROTHERS (ascribed to)	1	0			
GUADAGNINI FAMILY (MEMBER OF)	1	0			
GUADAGNINI FAMILY (MEMBER OF) (ascribed to)	1	1	$103,540 £62,000	$103,540 £62,000	$103,540 £62,000
GUADAGNINI FAMILY (MEMBER OF) (attributed to)	3	1	$10,689 £6,325	$10,689 £6,325	$10,689 £6,325
GUADO, LORENZO FRASSINO	1	1	$3,795 £2,300	$3,795 £2,300	$3,795 £2,300
GUADO, LORENZO FRASSINO (attributed to)	1	0			
GUARNERI, ANDREA	10	6	$43,125 £28,750	$162,640 £100,395	$112,006 £69,529
GUARNERI, ANDREA (attributed to)	1	1	$44,712 £27,600	$44,712 £27,600	$44,712 £27,600
GUARNERI, GIUSEPPE (FILIUS ANDREAE)	2	1	$278,055 £166,500	$278,055 £166,500	$278,055 £166,500
GUARNERI, GIUSEPPE (FILIUS ANDREAE) (ascribed to)	1	1	$4,600 £2,760	$4,600 £2,760	$4,600 £2,760
GUARNERI, JOSEPH (DEL GESU)	3	2	$444,730 £311,000	$932,035 £551,500	$688,383 £431,250
GUARNERI, PIETRO (OF MANTUA)	2	2	$26,803 £17,750	$64,800 £40,000	$45,801 £28,875
GUARNERI, PIETRO (OF VENICE)	5	0			
GUARNERI FAMILY (ascribed to)	1	0			
GUASTALLA, ALFREDO (attributed to)	2	1	$5,837 £4,140	$5,837 £4,140	$5,837 £4,140

| Maker | Items | | Selling Prices | | |
	Bid	Sold	Low	High	Avg
GUASTALLA, DANTE & ALFREDO	1	1	$13,414 £8,280	$13,414 £8,280	$13,414 £8,280
GUASTALLA, DANTE & ALFREDO (attributed to)	2	0			
GUERRA, EVASIO EMILE	7	6	$14,904 £9,200	$33,922 £20,829	$20,802 £13,063
GUERSAN, LOUIS	7	5	$822 £506	$11,512 £8,050	$5,098 £3,347
GUERSAN, LOUIS (attributed to)	1	0			
GUIDANTE, FLORENO (ascribed to)	1	1	$2,645 £1,645	$2,645 £1,645	$2,645 £1,645
GUIDANTE, GIOVANNI FLORENO	2	1	$9,664 £5,750	$9,664 £5,750	$9,664 £5,750
GUIDANTE, GIOVANNI FLORENO (ascribed to)	1	0			
GUIDANTE, GIOVANNI FLORENO (attributed to)	2	1	$24,967 £14,950	$24,967 £14,950	$24,967 £14,950
GUILLAMI, JUAN	2	2	$14,531 £8,970	$16,711 £10,316	$15,621 £9,643
GUINDON, H.	1	1	$298 £185	$298 £185	$298 £185
GUTH, AUGUST	2	1	$2,915 £1,725	$2,915 £1,725	$2,915 £1,725
GUTH, PAUL (attributed to)	1	1	$3,575 £2,248	$3,575 £2,248	$3,575 £2,248
GUTTER, GEORG ADAM	1	0			
GUTTER, JOHANN GEORG	1	0			
GUTTER, JOHANN GEORG (attributed to)	2	2	$635 £391	$1,291 £771	$963 £581
GYULA, CSISZAR	1	1	$1,495 £884	$1,495 £884	$1,495 £884
HAAHTI, EERO	1	1	$3,262 £2,013	$3,262 £2,013	$3,262 £2,013
HADDEN, ROBERT	1	1	$690 £414	$690 £414	$690 £414
HAKKERT, JACQUES	1	0			
HALL, GEORGE S.	1	1	$633 £391	$633 £391	$633 £391
HALL, R.G.	2	2	$431 £280	$920 £605	$676 £443
HALL, WILLIAM	2	1	$309 £184	$309 £184	$309 £184
HALLIDAY, R.L.	3	3	$360 £230	$588 £380	$492 £318
HAMM, ALBAN (workshop of)	1	1	$518 £340	$518 £340	$518 £340
HAMM, JOHANN GOTTFRIED	2	1	$1,150 £698	$1,150 £698	$1,150 £698
HAMM, JOHANN GOTTFRIED (workshop of)	1	1	$173 £105	$173 £105	$173 £105
HAMMIG, LIPPOLD	1	0			

Maker	Items		Selling Prices		
	Bid	Sold	Low	High	Avg
HAMMOND, JOHN	2	1	$185	$185	$185
			£115	£115	£115
HANSEN, SVERRE	2	2	$1,583	$3,166	$2,375
			£1,035	£2,070	£1,553
HARDIE (attributed to)	1	1	$727	$727	$727
			£460	£460	£460
HARDIE, JAMES (attributed to)	2	0			
HARDIE, JAMES & SONS	1	1	$580	$580	$580
			£345	£345	£345
HARDIE, JAMES & SONS (attributed to)	3	1	$1,118	$1,118	$1,118
			£690	£690	£690
HARDIE, JOHN	2	1	$537	$537	$537
			£368	£368	£368
HARDIE, MATTHEW	5	2	$3,864	$5,677	$4,771
			£2,300	£3,571	£2,935
HARDIE, MATTHEW (attributed to)	5	3	$695	$8,554	$5,009
			£460	£5,555	£3,155
HARDIE, MATTHEW & SON	1	1	$5,216	$5,216	$5,216
			£3,220	£3,220	£3,220
HARDIE, THOMAS	1	1	$973	$973	$973
			£575	£575	£575
HARDWICK, JOHN E.	2	2	$530	$707	$619
			£345	£460	£403
HARLOW, FRANK	2	1	$672	$672	$672
			£437	£437	£437
HARRIS, CHARLES	3	2	$6,185	$7,728	$6,956
			£3,680	£4,600	£4,140
HARRIS, CHARLES (II)	1	1	$3,416	$3,416	$3,416
			£2,070	£2,070	£2,070
HARRIS, HENRY	1	1	$805	$805	$805
			£491	£491	£491
HARRIS, J.E.	2	1	$3,220	$3,220	$3,220
			£2,093	£2,093	£2,093
HART & SON	5	5	$1,609	$4,285	$3,108
			£1,012	£2,645	£1,925
HART & SON (workshop of)	1	1	$1,898	$1,898	$1,898
			£1,150	£1,150	£1,150
HAUSMANN, OTTOMAR	2	2	$1,093	$1,840	$1,467
			£710	£1,137	£924
HAVEMANN, CARL FRIEDRICH	1	1	$210	$210	$210
			£126	£126	£126
HAWKES & SON	2	2	$580	$943	$761
			£403	£575	£489
HAWKES & SONS	1	0			
HAYNES & CO.	1	1	$1,997	$1,997	$1,997
			£1,256	£1,256	£1,256
HAZELL, LEONARD W.	4	1	$186	$186	$186
			£115	£115	£115
HEATON, WILLIAM	3	2	$668	$797	$733
			£437	£483	£460
HEBERLEIN (workshop of)	3	2	$616	$1,497	$1,057
			£402	£977	£690
HEBERLEIN, ALBERT (JR.)	1	1	$3,306	$3,306	$3,306
			£2,056	£2,056	£2,056

Maker	Items		Selling Prices		
	Bid	*Sold*	*Low*	*High*	*Avg*
HEBERLEIN, ALBERT AUGUST (JR.)	2	2	$575	$1,874	$1,225
			£374	£1,150	£762
HEBERLEIN, FRIEDRICH	2	1	$508	$508	$508
			£330	£330	£330
HEBERLEIN, G.F. (JR.)	1	1	$978	$978	$978
			£587	£587	£587
HEBERLEIN, HEINRICH E. (JR.) (workshop of)	1	1	$518	$518	$518
			£340	£340	£340
HEBERLEIN, HEINRICH TH. (workshop of)	2	2	$1,150	$1,840	$1,495
			£757	£1,088	£922
HEBERLEIN, HEINRICH TH. (JR.)	6	5	$805	$2,875	$1,820
			£483	£1,869	£1,124
HEBERLEIN, HEINRICH TH. (JR.) (workshop of)	8	7	$431	$2,070	$1,208
			£255	£1,224	£726
HEBERLEIN, L. FRITZ (attributed to)	1	1	$809	$809	$809
			£483	£483	£483
HEBERLEIN FAMILY (MEMBER OF)	1	0			
HEINEL, OSKAR BERNHARD	1	1	$805	$805	$805
			£483	£483	£483
HEINEL, OSKAR ERICH	3	1	$2,695	$2,695	$2,695
			£1,610	£1,610	£1,610
HEINICKE, MATHIAS	8	2	$3,353	$3,887	$3,620
			£2,070	£2,300	£2,185
HEL, J.	1	1	$16,324	$16,324	$16,324
			£9,775	£9,775	£9,775
HEL, JOSEPH	11	7	$3,540	$18,975	$10,655
			£2,185	£12,650	£6,851
HEL, JOSEPH (attributed to)	1	1	$16,295	$16,295	$16,295
			£9,775	£9,775	£9,775
HEL, PIERRE	1	1	$11,711	$11,711	$11,711
			£7,274	£7,274	£7,274
HEL, PIERRE JEAN HENRI	4	3	$12,650	$18,211	$15,565
			£8,322	£11,241	£9,780
HEL, PIERRE JOSEPH	5	2	$14,404	$16,764	$15,584
			£8,625	£10,925	£9,775
HELLMER, JOHANN GEORG	2	2	$2,944	$4,605	$3,774
			£1,852	£3,220	£2,536
HELLMER, JOHANN GEORG (attributed to)	2	1	$3,187	$3,187	$3,187
			£1,955	£1,955	£1,955
HELLMER, KARL	1	1	$489	$489	$489
			£289	£289	£289
HEMPEL, JULIUS	1	1	$1,093	$1,093	$1,093
			£675	£675	£675
HENDERSHOT, JOHN C.	1	1	$345	$345	$345
			£204	£204	£204
HENDERSON, F.V.	1	1	$518	$518	$518
			£311	£311	£311
HENDERSON, HAROLD A.	1	1	$2,415	$2,415	$2,415
			£1,466	£1,466	£1,466
HENNING, GUSTAV	1	1	$690	$690	$690
			£414	£414	£414

| Maker | Items | | Selling Prices | | |
	Bid	Sold	Low	High	Avg
HENRY	1	1	$7,321 £4,370	$7,321 £4,370	$7,321 £4,370
HENRY, CHARLES	1	0			
HENRY, EUGENE	2	1	$7,941 £5,175	$7,941 £5,175	$7,941 £5,175
HENRY, J.B.	1	1	$3,183 £2,070	$3,183 £2,070	$3,183 £2,070
HENTSCHEL, JOHANN JOSEPH	1	0			
HERBRIG, CHARLES EDWARD	1	1	$805 £493	$805 £493	$805 £493
HERCLIK, FR.	1	0			
HERCLIK, JOSEF BOHUMIL	1	1	$2,960 £2,070	$2,960 £2,070	$2,960 £2,070
HERCLIK, LADISLAV	1	1	$1,802 £1,092	$1,802 £1,092	$1,802 £1,092
HERMANN (workshop of)	1	1	$196 £119	$196 £119	$196 £119
HEROLD, RICHARD	1	1	$132 £92	$132 £92	$132 £92
HERRMANN, EMIL (workshop of)	1	1	$2,350 £1,528	$2,350 £1,528	$2,350 £1,528
HERRMANN, HEINRICH (attributed to)	1	1	$530 £345	$530 £345	$530 £345
HERRMANN, KARL (workshop of)	1	1	$1,150 £757	$1,150 £757	$1,150 £757
HERTL, ANTON	4	2	$571 £391	$854 £518	$712 £454
HESKETH	1	1	$4,993 £2,990	$4,993 £2,990	$4,993 £2,990
HESKETH, THOMAS EARLE	15	12	$1,733 £1,035	$8,580 £6,000	$5,097 £3,274
HEYLIGERS, MATHIJS	3	0			
HILAIRE, PAUL	1	0			
HILAIRE, PAUL (workshop of)	1	1	$1,725 £1,066	$1,725 £1,066	$1,725 £1,066
HILL, JOSEPH	7	6	$3,565 £2,175	$8,066 £4,830	$5,847 £3,659
HILL, JOSEPH (ascribed to)	1	1	$811 £575	$811 £575	$811 £575
HILL, JOSEPH (attributed to)	3	2	$748 £460	$2,120 £1,380	$1,434 £920
HILL, LOCKEY	1	1	$1,546 £920	$1,546 £920	$1,546 £920
HILL, W.E. & SONS	22	12	$5,436 £3,335	$19,282 £11,903	$10,630 £6,674
HILL, W.E. & SONS (workshop of)	1	1	$2,251 £1,389	$2,251 £1,389	$2,251 £1,389
HILL FAMILY (MEMBER OF)	5	3	$2,409 £1,495	$3,479 £2,300	$3,082 £1,955
HJORTH, A.	3	1	$1,398 £978	$1,398 £978	$1,398 £978
HJORTH, EMIL	2	0			
HJORTH, KNUD	1	0			

Maker	Items		Selling Prices		
	Bid	Sold	Low	High	Avg
HOFFMANN, EDUARD	1	1	$1,058	$1,058	$1,058
			£656	£656	£656
HOFMANN, G. WILLIAM	1	1	$3,214	$3,214	$3,214
			£1,984	£1,984	£1,984
HOFMANN, GEORG PHILIP	2	0			
HOFMANS, MATHIAS (attributed to)	1	1	$1,679	$1,679	$1,679
			£1,092	£1,092	£1,092
HOFNER, KARL	2	2	$1,060	$1,263	$1,162
			£690	£748	£719
HOLDER, T.J.	1	1	$5,780	$5,780	$5,780
			£3,450	£3,450	£3,450
HOLDER, T.J. (attributed to)	3	0			
HOLDER, THOMAS	1	0			
HOLDER, THOMAS (attributed to)	3	0			
HOLLISTER, W.	1	0			
HOLST, JOHANNES (attributed to)	2	1	$883	$883	$883
			£529	£529	£529
HOMENICK BROTHERS	2	2	$1,175	$3,220	$2,198
			£822	£1,990	£1,406
HOMOLKA, EMANUEL ADAM	1	1	$7,991	$7,991	$7,991
			£5,026	£5,026	£5,026
HOMOLKA, FERDINAND AUGUST	1	1	$7,951	$7,951	$7,951
			£5,175	£5,175	£5,175
HOMOLKA, FERDINAND JOS.	1	1	$1,034	$1,034	$1,034
			£633	£633	£633
HOPF	8	4	$212	$875	$580
			£138	£598	£368
HOPF (attributed to)	1	1	$691	$691	$691
			£414	£414	£414
HOPF, DAVID	1	1	$1,380	$1,380	$1,380
			£828	£828	£828
HOPF, L.	1	0			
HOPF FAMILY (MEMBER OF)	5	1	$1,536	$1,536	$1,536
			£920	£920	£920
HORNSTEINER	5	5	$394	$789	$565
			£242	£483	£347
HORNSTEINER (ascribed to)	1	1	$1,344	$1,344	$1,344
			£805	£805	£805
HORNSTEINER (attributed to)	1	0			
HORNSTEINER (workshop of)	1	1	$345	$345	$345
			£210	£210	£210
HORNSTEINER, J.	2	1	$489	$489	$489
			£299	£299	£299
HORNSTEINER, JOSEPH	2	1	$1,360	$1,360	$1,360
			£805	£805	£805
HORNSTEINER, JOSEPH (II)	3	3	$1,410	$3,866	$2,359
			£920	£2,300	£1,437
HORNSTEINER, MATHIAS	2	1	$5,175	$5,175	$5,175
			£3,061	£3,061	£3,061
HORNSTEINER FAMILY	4	2	$309	$466	$388
			£184	£288	£236
HOWARD, CLARK	1	1	$1,725	$1,725	$1,725
			£1,047	£1,047	£1,047

| Maker | Items | | Selling Prices | | |
	Bid	Sold	Low	High	Avg
HOWE, R.	1	1	$204	$204	$204
			£127	£127	£127
HOWE, ROBERT	2	0			
HOWELL, T.	1	1	$1,114	$1,114	$1,114
			£667	£667	£667
HOYER, ANDREAS	1	0			
HOYER, FRIEDRICH	2	2	$537	$1,380	$958
			£322	£816	£569
HUDSON, GEORGE	3	1	$1,883	$1,883	$1,883
			£1,127	£1,127	£1,127
HUDSON, GEORGE WULME	3	2	$8,942	$9,200	$9,071
			£5,520	£5,612	£5,566
HULINSKY, THOMAS	1	1	$3,887	$3,887	$3,887
			£2,300	£2,300	£2,300
HUMBERT	1	1	$1,211	$1,211	$1,211
			£748	£748	£748
HUME, ALEXANDER	2	1	$5,286	$5,286	$5,286
			£3,450	£3,450	£3,450
HUMS, ALBIN	1	1	$1,035	$1,035	$1,035
			£621	£621	£621
HUNGER, C.F.	1	1	$3,073	$3,073	$3,073
			£1,840	£1,840	£1,840
HURE, HARRY	2	1	$794	$794	$794
			£492	£492	£492
JACOBS, H.	1	1	$28,808	$28,808	$28,808
			£17,250	£17,250	£17,250
JACOBS, HENDRIK	5	4	$11,500	$24,369	$16,857
			£7,015	£14,950	£10,494
JACQUEMIN, RENE (attributed to)	2	0			
JACQUEMIN, RENE (workshop of)	1	1	$863	$863	$863
			£518	£518	£518
JACQUOT, CHARLES	5	5	$3,726	$8,942	$6,703
			£2,300	£5,520	£4,251
JACQUOT, CHARLES (ascribed to)	1	1	$4,771	$4,771	$4,771
			£3,105	£3,105	£3,105
JACQUOT, FERNAND	2	2	$2,820	$5,175	$3,998
			£1,725	£3,105	£2,415
JAEGER, HANS	1	1	$182	$182	$182
			£127	£127	£127
JAIS, ANDREAS	2	1	$4,694	$4,694	$4,694
			£2,990	£2,990	£2,990
JAIS, ANTON	2	1	$5,636	$5,636	$5,636
			£3,335	£3,335	£3,335
JAIS, JOHANN (attributed to)	1	0			
JAIS, JOHANNES	1	1	$13,200	$13,200	$13,200
			£9,108	£9,108	£9,108
JAMIESON	1	0			
JAUCK, JOHANNES (ascribed to)	2	1	$2,876	$2,876	$2,876
			£1,725	£1,725	£1,725
JAY, HENRY (ascribed to)	1	1	$2,702	$2,702	$2,702
			£1,668	£1,668	£1,668
JAY, HENRY (attributed to)	1	1	$2,544	$2,544	$2,544
			£1,610	£1,610	£1,610

Maker	Items		Selling Prices		
	Bid	Sold	Low	High	Avg
JIROWSKY, HANS	2	1	$914	$914	$914
			£575	£575	£575
JOHN, WILLIAM	1	1	$9,028	$9,028	$9,028
			£5,750	£5,750	£5,750
JOHNSON, GEORGE	2	1	$863	$863	$863
			£510	£510	£510
JOHNSON, JOHN	12	6	$920	$5,962	$3,904
			£558	£3,680	£2,479
JOHNSON, PETER ANDREAS	1	1	$1,265	$1,265	$1,265
			£886	£886	£886
JOLLY, LEON	4	2	$597	$1,145	$871
			£368	£748	£558
JOLY, LOUIS	1	0			
JOMBAR, PAUL	7	2	$2,889	$3,882	$3,386
			£1,840	£2,530	£2,185
JOMBAR, PAUL (attributed to)	2	1	$2,881	$2,881	$2,881
			£1,725	£1,725	£1,725
JONES, WILLIAM H.	3	1	$820	$820	$820
			£529	£529	£529
JORIO, VINCENZO (ascribed to)	1	0			
JORIO, VINCENZO (attributed to)	3	2	$8,050	$13,156	$10,603
			£5,152	£9,200	£7,176
JUZEK, JOHN	5	5	$546	$1,955	$1,473
			£328	£1,208	£910
JUZEK, JOHN (workshop of)	5	5	$431	$2,990	$1,409
			£263	£1,848	£866
KAGANSKY, VALERY	1	1	$2,999	$2,999	$2,999
			£1,852	£1,852	£1,852
KALTENBRUNNER, K. RICHARD	1	1	$5,750	$5,750	$5,750
			£3,553	£3,553	£3,553
KAMPFFE, AUGUST	1	0			
KARNER, BARTHOLOMAUS	2	1	$960	$960	$960
			£575	£575	£575
KARNER, BARTHOLOMAUS (II)	2	0			
KAUL, PAUL	7	5	$2,990	$8,998	$7,237
			£1,794	£5,555	£4,552
KEANE	1	1	$1,097	$1,097	$1,097
			£690	£690	£690
KEFFER, JOANNES (attributed to)	1	1	$1,740	$1,740	$1,740
			£1,035	£1,035	£1,035
KEMPTER, ANDREAS	2	1	$5,467	$5,467	$5,467
			£3,439	£3,439	£3,439
KEMPTER, ANDREAS (attributed to)	2	0			
KENNEDY, THOMAS	9	3	$5,962	$6,856	$6,467
			£3,680	£4,232	£4,017
KENNEDY, THOMAS (attributed to)	2	1	$2,236	$2,236	$2,236
			£1,380	£1,380	£1,380
KERSCHENSTEINER, XAVER	2	1	$2,059	$2,059	$2,059
			£1,440	£1,440	£1,440
KESSEL, M.J.H.	1	1	$2,313	$2,313	$2,313
			£1,455	£1,455	£1,455
KESSLER, W. AUGUST (JR.)	1	1	$3,457	$3,457	$3,457
			£2,070	£2,070	£2,070

| Maker | Items | | Selling Prices | | |
	Bid	Sold	Low	High	Avg
KINGMAN, GORDON MAURY	2	2	$840	$1,080	$960
			£580	£745	£662
KLEIN & CIE., A.	1	1	$497	$497	$497
			£345	£345	£345
KLEINMAN, CORNELIUS (attributed to)	1	0			
KLINTH, ALBERT W.	1	1	$431	$431	$431
			£259	£259	£259
KLOTZ	1	1	$1,693	$1,693	$1,693
			£1,058	£1,058	£1,058
KLOTZ, AEGIDIUS (I)	7	4	$3,841	$5,412	$4,635
			£2,300	£3,220	£2,760
KLOTZ, AEGIDIUS (I) (attributed to)	1	1	$3,374	$3,374	$3,374
			£2,070	£2,070	£2,070
KLOTZ, AEGIDIUS (II)	5	3	$2,530	$4,255	$3,527
			£1,543	£2,553	£2,132
KLOTZ, AEGIDIUS (II) (attributed to)	2	0			
KLOTZ, CARL FREDRICH (attributed to)	1	0			
KLOTZ, GEORG	5	4	$1,890	$3,910	$2,740
			£1,208	£2,374	£1,672
KLOTZ, GEORG (attributed to)	1	1	$4,934	$4,934	$4,934
			£3,450	£3,450	£3,450
KLOTZ, GEORG (II)	8	2	$8,551	$19,282	$13,917
			£5,060	£11,903	£8,481
KLOTZ, JOHANN CARL	6	5	$2,476	$6,072	$3,567
			£1,610	£3,680	£2,215
KLOTZ, JOSEPH	9	3	$4,237	$8,092	$6,283
			£2,760	£4,830	£3,872
KLOTZ, JOSEPH (attributed to)	1	1	$4,025	$4,025	$4,025
			£2,415	£2,415	£2,415
KLOTZ, MATHIAS (I)	3	1	$9,664	$9,664	$9,664
			£5,750	£5,750	£5,750
KLOTZ, MATHIAS (I) (attributed to)	3	1	$5,841	$5,841	$5,841
			£3,450	£3,450	£3,450
KLOTZ, MATHIAS (II)	1	0			
KLOTZ, MICHAEL	4	2	$1,273	$7,067	$4,170
			£828	£4,600	£2,714
KLOTZ, SEBASTIAN	11	7	$2,174	$27,945	$8,692
			£1,440	£17,250	£5,469
KLOTZ, SEBASTIAN (attributed to)	1	1	$3,802	$3,802	$3,802
			£2,473	£2,473	£2,473
KLOTZ, SEBASTIAN (II)	3	1	$3,457	$3,457	$3,457
			£2,070	£2,070	£2,070
KLOTZ FAMILY (MEMBER OF)	29	18	$810	$8,118	$2,276
			£518	£4,830	£1,416
KNEDLER, VILMOS	1	1	$920	$920	$920
			£558	£558	£558
KNIGHT, FRANK R.	1	1	$1,724	$1,724	$1,724
			£1,127	£1,127	£1,127
KNILLING, JOHANN	1	1	$2,796	$2,796	$2,796
			£1,955	£1,955	£1,955
KNOPF, HENRY RICHARD	4	4	$1,725	$3,163	$2,573
			£1,047	£1,898	£1,551
KNOPF, W.	1	1	$1,397	$1,397	$1,397
			£863	£863	£863

Maker	Items Bid	Sold	Low	Selling Prices High	Avg
KNORR, ALBERT	4	4	$1,495 £912	$3,738 £2,243	$2,455 £1,545
KNORR, P.	1	1	$5,417 £3,450	$5,417 £3,450	$5,417 £3,450
KNUPFER, ALBERT	2	1	$936 £598	$936 £598	$936 £598
KOCH, FRANZ JOSEPH	2	2	$1,150 £704	$2,608 £1,610	$1,879 £1,157
KOCHLY, J. (attributed to)	1	0			
KONIG, PAUL & HERMANN	2	1	$2,915 £1,725	$2,915 £1,725	$2,915 £1,725
KONYA, ISTVAN	2	1	$2,400 £1,656	$2,400 £1,656	$2,400 £1,656
KOSTLER, WILLY	1	1	$265 £184	$265 £184	$265 £184
KRELL, ALBERT	3	2	$1,380 £897	$1,840 £1,104	$1,610 £1,001
KREUTZINGER, ANTON (attributed to)	1	0			
KREUZINGER, JOSEPH (II)	1	1	$1,325 £920	$1,325 £920	$1,325 £920
KRILOV, ALESSANDRO	1	0			
KRILOV, ALESSANDRO (attributed to)	2	1	$1,081 £667	$1,081 £667	$1,081 £667
KRINER, HANS B.	2	2	$1,380 £842	$2,122 £1,380	$1,751 £1,111
KRINER, JOSEPH	3	1	$1,139 £690	$1,139 £690	$1,139 £690
KRIZ, FRANTISEK	1	0			
KROGH, CHRISTIAN	1	0			
KRUMBHOLZ, LORENZ	5	4	$1,687 £1,035	$7,298 £4,370	$4,634 £2,846
KUCHARSKI, B.	1	0			
KUDANOWSKI, JAN	11	7	$1,328 £805	$3,575 £2,248	$2,658 £1,635
KUGLER, FERDINAND	1	1	$4,369 £3,055	$4,369 £3,055	$4,369 £3,055
KULIK, JAN	2	2	$6,555 £4,261	$8,237 £5,760	$7,396 £5,010
KULIK, JOHANN	3	3	$4,071 £2,513	$8,625 £5,101	$6,006 £3,640
KUN, JOSEPH	1	1	$2,645 £1,606	$2,645 £1,606	$2,645 £1,606
KUNTZE-FECHNER, MARTIN	1	1	$7,452 £4,600	$7,452 £4,600	$7,452 £4,600
KUNZE, WILHELM PAUL	3	2	$1,179 £728	$4,658 £2,875	$2,918 £1,801
KVAMME, MAGNE	1	1	$575 £345	$575 £345	$575 £345
L'HUMBERT, E.	1	1	$6,178 £4,025	$6,178 £4,025	$6,178 £4,025
LABERTE	5	4	$475 £299	$1,363 £863	$884 £558
LABERTE, MARC	8	5	$1,145 £747	$4,060 £2,645	$2,276 £1,438

Maker	Items		Selling Prices		
	Bid	Sold	Low	High	Avg
LABERTE, MARC (attributed to)	1	1	$1,519 £897	$1,519 £897	$1,519 £897
LABERTE, MARC (workshop of)	5	3	$940 £611	$2,645 £1,640	$2,019 £1,287
LABERTE-HUMBERT BROS.	8	5	$911 £633	$2,527 £1,495	$1,517 £932
LABERTE-MAGNIE	3	0			
LAFLEUR, J.	1	1	$937 £575	$937 £575	$937 £575
LAJOS, KONYA	1	0			
LAMBERT	2	2	$3,080 £1,840	$4,754 £2,990	$3,917 £2,415
LAMBERT, JEAN NICOLAS	1	0			
LAMBERTON, JAMES	1	0			
LAMY, THIBOUVILLE	1	0			
LANARO, UMBERTO	1	1	$4,874 £2,990	$4,874 £2,990	$4,874 £2,990
LANDOLFI, CARLO FERDINANDO	6	3	$13,800 £8,418	$70,458 £46,000	$38,740 £25,589
LANDOLFI, CARLO FERDINANDO (attributed to)	2	0			
LANDOLFI, PIETRO ANTONIO	2	1	$46,261 £29,095	$46,261 £29,095	$46,261 £29,095
LANDOLFI, PIETRO ANTONIO (ascribed to)	1	1	$35,650 £24,955	$35,650 £24,955	$35,650 £24,955
LANDOLFI, PIETRO ANTONIO (attributed to)	2	1	$13,235 £8,625	$13,235 £8,625	$13,235 £8,625
LANDON, CHRISTOPHE	1	0			
LANGE, H. FRANCIS	1	1	$748 £449	$748 £449	$748 £449
LANGONET, EUGENE	5	2	$3,703 £2,296	$6,706 £4,370	$5,204 £3,333
LANINI, LORIS	1	1	$2,657 £1,610	$2,657 £1,610	$2,657 £1,610
LANTNER, FERDINAND MARTIN	1	1	$1,235 £767	$1,235 £767	$1,235 £767
LARCHER, JEAN	2	2	$1,344 £805	$1,921 £1,150	$1,632 £978
LARCHER, JEAN (attributed to)	4	1	$805 £506	$805 £506	$805 £506
LARGOWARD, RAYBURN	1	1	$796 £518	$796 £518	$796 £518
LASSI, FRANCESCO	3	2	$2,194 £1,380	$8,826 £5,750	$5,510 £3,565
LATTERELL, GEORGE	1	1	$1,380 £845	$1,380 £845	$1,380 £845
LAUMANN, ROBERT	1	1	$6,355 £4,140	$6,355 £4,140	$6,355 £4,140
LAURENT, EMILE	2	1	$7,682 £4,600	$7,682 £4,600	$7,682 £4,600
LAURENT, EMILE (II)	1	1	$2,819 £1,840	$2,819 £1,840	$2,819 £1,840

Maker	Items Bid	Sold	Low	Selling Prices High	Avg
LAVEST, J.	1	1	$3,450 £2,041	$3,450 £2,041	$3,450 £2,041
LAVEST, J. (attributed to)	2	0			
LEAR, M.D.	1	0			
LEAVITT, F.A.	1	1	$518 £311	$518 £311	$518 £311
LECCHI, BERNARDO GIUSEPPE	1	1	$8,473 £5,520	$8,473 £5,520	$8,473 £5,520
LECCHI, GUISEPPE	3	1	$13,251 £8,625	$13,251 £8,625	$13,251 £8,625
LECCI, G. (attributed to)	1	0			
LECHI	1	1	$754 £460	$754 £460	$754 £460
LECHI, ANTONIO	9	8	$654 £417	$1,944 £1,150	$1,146 £700
LECHLEITNER, CHRISTIAN (attributed to)	1	1	$2,571 £1,587	$2,571 £1,587	$2,571 £1,587
LECLERC, JOSEPH NICOLAS	3	1	$3,601 £2,300	$3,601 £2,300	$3,601 £2,300
LECYR, JAMES F.	1	1	$1,955 £1,156	$1,955 £1,156	$1,955 £1,156
LEE, PERCY	1	1	$4,609 £2,760	$4,609 £2,760	$4,609 £2,760
LEEB, ANDREAS CARL	1	1	$2,356 £1,560	$2,356 £1,560	$2,356 £1,560
LEEB, JOHANN GEORG	2	1	$2,062 £1,265	$2,062 £1,265	$2,062 £1,265
LEIDOLFF, JOHANN CHRISTOPH	3	1	$920 £644	$920 £644	$920 £644
LEIDOLFF, JOSEPH FERDINAND	1	1	$1,651 £977	$1,651 £977	$1,651 £977
LE LYONNAIS, CHARLES	1	0			
LEMBOCK, GABRIEL	1	1	$5,295 £3,439	$5,295 £3,439	$5,295 £3,439
LENTZ, JOHANN NICOLAUS	1	1	$973 £690	$973 £690	$973 £690
LEONORI, PAOLO	1	1	$5,962 £3,680	$5,962 £3,680	$5,962 £3,680
LEWIS, WILLIAM & SON	1	0			
LIESSEM, R.	2	2	$2,346 £1,438	$4,803 £2,875	$3,575 £2,156
LIESSEM, REMERUS	1	0			
LINDORFER, WILLI	1	0			
LINDSAY, DAVID	1	1	$1,234 £805	$1,234 £805	$1,234 £805
LINDSAY, DAVID (attributed to)	1	1	$459 £299	$459 £299	$459 £299
LIPPOLD, CARL FREDERICK (attributed to)	1	0			
LOGAN, JOHN	1	1	$1,069 £690	$1,069 £690	$1,069 £690
LONDERO, RAFFAELE	1	0			
LONGIARU, GIOVANNI	1	1	$3,042 £1,886	$3,042 £1,886	$3,042 £1,886

Maker	Items		Selling Prices		
	Bid	Sold	Low	High	Avg
LONGMAN	4	2	$245	$566	$405
			£150	£345	£247
LONGMAN & CO.	1	1	$1,676	$1,676	$1,676
			£1,093	£1,093	£1,093
LONGMAN & BRODERIP	1	1	$3,281	$3,281	$3,281
			£2,013	£2,013	£2,013
LONGMAN, LUKEY & CO.	1	1	$768	$768	$768
			£460	£460	£460
LONGSON, F.H.	2	1	$3,243	$3,243	$3,243
			£2,300	£2,300	£2,300
LORANGE, PAUL	2	1	$1,380	$1,380	$1,380
			£863	£863	£863
LORANGE, PAUL (attributed to)	1	1	$2,467	$2,467	$2,467
			£1,725	£1,725	£1,725
LORENZ FAMILY (attributed to)	1	0			
LOTT, JOHN	2	2	$23,621	$31,706	$27,664
			£14,950	£20,700	£17,825
LOTT, JOHN (ascribed to)	1	0			
LOTT, JOHN (attributed to)	1	0			
LOTT, JOHN (SR.)	1	1	$11,141	$11,141	$11,141
			£7,245	£7,245	£7,245
LOTT, JOHN FREDERICK	1	1	$45,540	$45,540	$45,540
			£27,600	£27,600	£27,600
LOTT, JOHN FREDERICK (ascribed to)	1	0			
LOTT, JOHN FREDERICK (attributed to)	1	0			
LOTT, JOHN FREDERICK (PERE) (attributed to)	1	1	$3,856	$3,856	$3,856
			£2,381	£2,381	£2,381
LOUGHTON, A.J.	2	1	$251	$251	$251
			£150	£150	£150
LOWENDALL	5	4	$386	$1,450	$866
			£230	£943	£552
LOWENDALL, HERMANN (workshop of)	1	1	$1,265	$1,265	$1,265
			£748	£748	£748
LOWENDALL, LOUIS	17	13	$282	$1,159	$773
			£173	£713	£479
LOWENDALL, LOUIS (workshop of)	2	2	$230	$1,118	$674
			£136	£690	£413
LUCCA, ANTONIO	3	3	$5,216	$16,698	$9,366
			£3,220	£10,120	£5,673
LUCCI, GIUSEPPE	9	8	$7,512	$16,250	$11,282
			£4,485	£10,350	£6,955
LUCCI, GIUSEPPE (attributed to)	1	1	$5,463	$5,463	$5,463
			£3,375	£3,375	£3,375
LUDWIG, L. (workshop of)	1	1	$230	$230	$230
			£151	£151	£151
LUFF, WILLIAM H.	9	5	$3,167	$7,345	$5,245
			£1,955	£4,370	£3,177
LUPOT, FRANCOIS	1	0			
LUPOT, NICOLAS	7	3	$31,938	$134,769	$90,082
			£19,838	£80,700	£54,179
LUPOT, NICOLAS (attributed to)	3	0			
LUTHER, ANDREAS	1	0			

Maker	Items Bid	Sold	Selling Prices Low	High	Avg
LUTZ, IGNAZ	1	1	$4,485 £2,691	$4,485 £2,691	$4,485 £2,691
LUTZ, LOUIS (attributed to)	1	0			
LUZZATTI, GIACOMO	1	0			
LYE, HENRY	1	1	$2,297 £1,495	$2,297 £1,495	$2,297 £1,495
LYON, U.	2	1	$578 £368	$578 £368	$578 £368
MAAG, HENRY	7	5	$115 £70	$460 £281	$212 £129
MACCARTHY, J.L.T.	1	0			
MACVEAN, ALEXANDER	1	0			
MADAY, EDWARD	1	1	$863 £533	$863 £533	$863 £533
MAGGINI, GIOVANNI PAOLO	5	3	$42,405 £27,600	$168,368 £100,500	$88,907 £55,569
MAGIALI, CAESAR	1	1	$5,798 £3,450	$5,798 £3,450	$5,798 £3,450
MAGNIERE, GABRIEL	7	6	$1,344 £805	$4,694 £2,990	$2,748 £1,699
MAGNIERE, GABRIEL (attributed to)	1	1	$2,474 £1,610	$2,474 £1,610	$2,474 £1,610
MAICH, JOHN P.	1	1	$345 £213	$345 £213	$345 £213
MAINARDI, GIOVANNI	1	0			
MALAGUTI, ERMINIO	1	1	$3,439 £2,132	$3,439 £2,132	$3,439 £2,132
MALINE	1	1	$3,477 £2,300	$3,477 £2,300	$3,477 £2,300
MALINE FAMILY (MEMBER OF)	1	0			
MALVOLTI, PIETRO ANTONIO	1	1	$6,784 £4,166	$6,784 £4,166	$6,784 £4,166
MANDELLI, CAMILLO	2	1	$23,000 £13,800	$23,000 £13,800	$23,000 £13,800
MANGENOT, AMATI	4	1	$3,534 £2,300	$3,534 £2,300	$3,534 £2,300
MANGENOT, AMATI (workshop of)	1	1	$2,233 £1,451	$2,233 £1,451	$2,233 £1,451
MANGENOT, P.	1	1	$1,216 £805	$1,216 £805	$1,216 £805
MANGENOT, PAUL	6	5	$811 £529	$2,608 £1,610	$1,576 £968
MANSUY	1	1	$1,835 £1,093	$1,835 £1,093	$1,835 £1,093
MANTEGAZZA, PIETRO GIOVANNI	3	2	$20,125 £12,075	$68,609 £43,700	$44,367 £27,888
MANTEGAZZA, PIETRO GIOVANNI (attributed to)	1	0			
MARAVELLI	1	1	$920 £598	$920 £598	$920 £598
MARAVIGLIA, FRANCESCO	1	0			
MARAVIGLIA, GUIDO	2	1	$2,706 £1,610	$2,706 £1,610	$2,706 £1,610

Maker	Items Bid	Sold	Selling Prices Low	High	Avg
MARCHAND, EUGENE	1	1	$7,123 £4,370	$7,123 £4,370	$7,123 £4,370
MARCHETTI, EDUARDO	1	0			
MARCHETTI, EDUARDO (ascribed to)	1	0			
MARCHETTI, ENRICO	6	3	$5,290 £3,227	$17,699 £10,925	$10,724 £6,634
MARCHETTI, ENRICO (attributed to)	4	0			
MARCHETTI, ENRICO (workshop of)	1	0			
MARCHI, GIOVANNI (attributed to)	1	1	$13,605 £8,050	$13,605 £8,050	$13,605 £8,050
MARCHI, GIOVANNI ANTONIO	2	1	$54,418 £32,200	$54,418 £32,200	$54,418 £32,200
MARCHINI, RUDOLFO	1	1	$4,025 £2,576	$4,025 £2,576	$4,025 £2,576
MARCONCINI, JOSEPH	2	1	$48,737 £29,900	$48,737 £29,900	$48,737 £29,900
MARCONCINI, JOSEPH (attributed to)	2	0			
MARCONCINI, LUIGI ALOISIO	1	0			
MARDULA, FRANCISZEK & STANISLAW	2	1	$690 £421	$690 £421	$690 £421
MARGINI, RENZO	1	0			
MARIANI (attributed to)	1	0			
MARIANI, ANTONIO	1	0			
MARIANI, ANTONIO (ascribed to)	1	0			
MARISSAL, O. (workshop of)	1	1	$969 £598	$969 £598	$969 £598
MARISSAL, OLIVIER	1	0			
MARSHALL, JOHN (attributed to)	1	1	$3,853 £2,300	$3,853 £2,300	$3,853 £2,300
MARSIGLIESE, BIAGIO	1	0			
MARTIN	1	0			
MARTIN, E.	1	1	$403 £242	$403 £242	$403 £242
MARTIN, E. (workshop of)	12	11	$201 £132	$705 £458	$448 £277
MARTINENGHI, MARCELLO G.B.	1	1	$9,176 £5,980	$9,176 £5,980	$9,176 £5,980
MARTINI, ORESTE	1	1	$10,902 £6,900	$10,902 £6,900	$10,902 £6,900
MARTINI, ORESTE (attributed to)	1	1	$3,220 £1,990	$3,220 £1,990	$3,220 £1,990
MARTINO, GIUSEPPE	1	1	$2,990 £1,848	$2,990 £1,848	$2,990 £1,848
MASON, GEORGE	1	1	$451 £276	$451 £276	$451 £276
MASON, WALTER	1	1	$3,523 £2,300	$3,523 £2,300	$3,523 £2,300
MAST, JEAN LAURENT (attributed to)	1	0			
MAST, JOSEPH LAURENT	5	2	$1,118 £690	$1,285 £794	$1,202 £742
MATTER, ANITA	3	1	$934 £575	$934 £575	$934 £575
MATTIUZZI, BRUNO	1	0			

Maker	Items Bid	Sold	Low	Selling Prices High	Avg
MONTANARI, LUIGI (attributed to)	1	1	$13,978 £9,775	$13,978 £9,775	$13,978 £9,775
MONTEIRO, HENRIQUE	2	1	$3,304 £1,955	$3,304 £1,955	$3,304 £1,955
MONTERUMICI, ARMANDO (ascribed to)	1	0			
MONTEVECCHI, LUIGI (attributed to)	1	1	$3,172 £2,070	$3,172 £2,070	$3,172 £2,070
MONTEVERDE, CLAUDIO	6	3	$1,102 £690	$4,332 £2,818	$2,330 £1,476
MONZANI (attributed to)	2	0			
MONZINO, ANTONIO	1	0			
MONZINO & FIGLI	2	1	$1,955 £1,150	$1,955 £1,150	$1,955 £1,150
MOORE, ALFRED	4	1	$1,501 £920	$1,501 £920	$1,501 £920
MORARA, PAOLO	1	1	$1,312 £805	$1,312 £805	$1,312 £805
MORASSI, GIOVANNI BATTISTA	3	2	$7,059 £4,600	$11,945 £7,130	$9,502 £5,865
MORITZ, ALFRED	1	1	$730 £437	$730 £437	$730 £437
MORIZOT, RENE	3	1	$3,450 £2,270	$3,450 £2,270	$3,450 £2,270
MORLOT	1	1	$1,031 £633	$1,031 £633	$1,031 £633
MORLOT, NICOLAS	1	1	$575 £355	$575 £355	$575 £355
MORRISON, ARCHIBALD	1	1	$926 £575	$926 £575	$926 £575
MORSE, JOHN	1	1	$1,380 £816	$1,380 £816	$1,380 £816
MORTIMER, JOHN WILLIAM	1	1	$430 £253	$430 £253	$430 £253
MOSCHELLA, SALVATORE	1	1	$1,586 £1,035	$1,586 £1,035	$1,586 £1,035
MOSHER, ALEX H.	2	0			
MOUGEL	1	0			
MOUGENOT	1	1	$2,167 £1,380	$2,167 £1,380	$2,167 £1,380
MOUGENOT, GEORGES	9	9	$2,125 £1,265	$10,934 £6,877	$5,060 £3,166
MOUGENOT, GEORGES (attributed to)	2	1	$1,308 £805	$1,308 £805	$1,308 £805
MOUGENOT, LEON	17	11	$1,242 £863	$7,222 £4,600	$2,676 £1,732
MOUGENOT, LEON (attributed to)	4	4	$932 £575	$2,705 £1,610	$1,837 £1,136
MOUGENOT, LEON (workshop of)	2	1	$2,350 £1,528	$2,350 £1,528	$2,350 £1,528
MOUGENOT, P. & L. PRONIER	1	1	$4,694 £2,990	$4,694 £2,990	$4,694 £2,990
MOYA, HIDALGO	7	6	$1,641 £977	$3,055 £1,984	$2,516 £1,580
MOYA, HIDALGO (attributed to)	1	0			

Maker	Items		Selling Prices		
	Bid	Sold	Low	High	Avg
MOZZANI, LUIGI	13	8	$2,310	$8,570	$6,319
			£1,380	£5,520	£3,939
MOZZANI, LUIGI (attributed to)	2	1	$3,853	$3,853	$3,853
			£2,300	£2,300	£2,300
MOZZANI, LUIGI (workshop of)	1	0			
MUIR, HAROLD	2	0			
MULLER, JOSEPH	1	0			
MULLER, KARL	1	0			
MULLER, KARL (attributed to)	1	1	$1,212	$1,212	$1,212
			£782	£782	£782
MUMBY, ERNEST	1	0			
MUNCHER, ROMEDIO	4	4	$2,437	$6,900	$4,541
			£1,495	£4,189	£2,806
MUNCHER, ROMEDIO (attributed to)	1	1	$2,138	$2,138	$2,138
			£1,265	£1,265	£1,265
MUNCHER, ROMEDIO (workshop of)	1	0			
MURDOCH, JOHN	1	1	$1,156	$1,156	$1,156
			£690	£690	£690
MURDOCH & CO.	2	1	$143	$143	$143
			£98	£98	£98
MURRAY, THOMAS	1	1	$1,441	$1,441	$1,441
			£863	£863	£863
MUSCHIETTI, UMBERTO	2	1	$4,664	$4,664	$4,664
			£2,760	£2,760	£2,760
MUTTI, VITTORIO	3	0			
NAFISSI, CARLO (ascribed to)	1	1	$2,467	$2,467	$2,467
			£1,610	£1,610	£1,610
NALDI, A.	1	0			
NATIONAL DOBRO CORP.	1	1	$1,150	$1,150	$1,150
			£680	£680	£680
NELSON FAMILY	1	0			
NEMESSANYI, SAMUEL FELIX	1	1	$35,250	$35,250	$35,250
			£24,322	£24,322	£24,322
NEUBAUER, GERHARD	2	1	$1,725	$1,725	$1,725
			£1,020	£1,020	£1,020
NEUDORFER, ALFRED	1	1	$1,218	$1,218	$1,218
			£747	£747	£747
NEUMANN, ADOLPH (workshop of)	1	1	$345	$345	$345
			£207	£207	£207
NEUNER (workshop of)	3	3	$403	$748	$527
			£244	£462	£323
NEUNER, LUDWIG	1	1	$364	$364	$364
			£218	£218	£218
NEUNER, MATHIAS	8	7	$345	$2,236	$889
			£207	£1,380	£544
NEUNER & HORNSTEINER	46	35	$81	$4,928	$889
			£52	£3,042	£561
NEUNER & HORNSTEINER (workshop of)	5	4	$288	$748	$561
			£173	£454	£338
NICHOLLS, COLIN	2	2	$2,070	$5,880	$3,975
			£1,380	£4,112	£2,746
NICOLAS	1	1	$2,999	$2,999	$2,999
			£1,852	£1,852	£1,852

Maker	Items Bid	Sold	Low	Selling Prices High	Avg
NICOLAS, DIDIER (L'AINE)	46	24	$489 £293	$4,888 £2,981	$1,448 £906
NICOLAS, DIDIER (L'AINE) (attributed to)	1	1	$1,283 £828	$1,283 £828	$1,283 £828
NICOLAS, DIDIER (L'AINE) (workshop of)	1	1	$1,093 £656	$1,093 £656	$1,093 £656
NICOLAS FAMILY (MEMBER OF)	1	1	$9,930 £6,325	$9,930 £6,325	$9,930 £6,325
NOBILE, FRANCESCO (attributed to)	1	1	$4,620 £2,760	$4,620 £2,760	$4,620 £2,760
NOEBE, LOUIS	2	2	$1,767 £1,150	$2,785 £1,719	$2,276 £1,435
NOLLI, MARCO	1	1	$2,467 £1,495	$2,467 £1,495	$2,467 £1,495
NORMAN, BARAK (ascribed to)	1	1	$963 £575	$963 £575	$963 £575
NOSEK, VACLAV	3	0			
NOVELLI, NATALE	1	1	$15,887 £10,350	$15,887 £10,350	$15,887 £10,350
NOVELLI, NATALE (ascribed to)	1	0			
NUPIERI, GIUSEPPE	5	4	$712 £437	$1,495 £897	$1,127 £679
ODDONE, CARLO GIUSEPPE	5	3	$26,887 £16,100	$45,230 £27,773	$36,883 £22,291
ODDONE, CARLO GIUSEPPE (ascribed to)	2	0			
ODOARDI, GIUSEPPE	1	1	$21,593 £14,300	$21,593 £14,300	$21,593 £14,300
ODOARDI, GIUSEPPE (attributed to)	2	2	$2,261 £1,389	$3,241 £2,070	$2,751 £1,729
OLDFIELD, W.	1	1	$162 £104	$162 £104	$162 £104
OLIVER, BARRY	1	1	$2,528 £1,610	$2,528 £1,610	$2,528 £1,610
OLIVIER & BISCH	3	3	$2,305 £1,380	$2,332 £1,380	$2,318 £1,380
OLIVIER & BISCH (attributed to)	1	1	$525 £322	$525 £322	$525 £322
OLRY, J. (attributed to)	4	0			
OMOND, JAMES	2	0			
ORLANDINI, A.	2	1	$3,887 £2,300	$3,887 £2,300	$3,887 £2,300
ORLANDINI, ARCHIMEDE	1	1	$9,000 £6,210	$9,000 £6,210	$9,000 £6,210
ORMOND, JAMES	1	1	$805 £564	$805 £564	$805 £564
ORNATI, GIUSEPPE	6	4	$15,887 £10,350	$40,986 £25,300	$24,967 £16,168
ORNATI, GIUSEPPE (workshop of)	1	1	$10,592 £6,900	$10,592 £6,900	$10,592 £6,900
ORSELLI, ENRICO	2	2	$3,565 £2,345	$6,061 £3,519	$4,813 £2,932
ORY, F.	3	1	$601 £368	$601 £368	$601 £368

Maker	Items		Selling Prices		
	Bid	Sold	Low	High	Avg
OSMANEK, A.	1	1	$1,057	$1,057	$1,057
			£690	£690	£690
OTTO, C.W.F.	1	1	$2,209	$2,209	$2,209
			£1,438	£1,438	£1,438
OTTO, CARL AUGUST	1	1	$2,645	$2,645	$2,645
			£1,613	£1,613	£1,613
OTTO, LOUIS	1	0			
OWEN, JOHN W.	2	2	$2,347	$3,864	$3,106
			£1,495	£2,300	£1,898
PACHERELE, PIERRE	3	1	$26,887	$26,887	$26,887
			£16,100	£16,100	£16,100
PACHERELE, PIERRE (ascribed to)	2	1	$15,902	$15,902	$15,902
			£10,350	£10,350	£10,350
PACHERELE, PIERRE (attributed to)	3	2	$3,699	$3,761	$3,730
			£2,185	£2,300	£2,243
PAESOLD, RODERICH	1	1	$938	$938	$938
			£575	£575	£575
PAINE, ARTHUR	1	1	$1,840	$1,840	$1,840
			£1,104	£1,104	£1,104
PAINE, THOMAS D.	3	2	$288	$431	$359
			£173	£280	£226
PAJEOT (FILS) (workshop of)	1	1	$932	$932	$932
			£575	£575	£575
PALLAVER, GIOVANNI	1	0			
PALLOTTA, PIETRO	1	0			
PALMIERI, ALESSANDRO	1	1	$12,353	$12,353	$12,353
			£8,050	£8,050	£8,050
PAMPHILON, EDWARD	4	3	$4,333	$13,800	$8,447
			£2,760	£9,200	£5,667
PANORMO, GEORGE	2	1	$19,435	$19,435	$19,435
			£11,500	£11,500	£11,500
PANORMO, J. (attributed to)	1	1	$8,118	$8,118	$8,118
			£5,290	£5,290	£5,290
PANORMO, JOSEPH	1	1	$40,986	$40,986	$40,986
			£25,300	£25,300	£25,300
PANORMO, JOSEPH (attributed to)	1	1	$4,111	$4,111	$4,111
			£2,875	£2,875	£2,875
PANORMO, VINCENZO	9	7	$33,741	$66,742	$45,504
			£20,700	£44,200	£28,756
PANORMO, VINCENZO (ascribed to)	1	1	$18,745	$18,745	$18,745
			£11,500	£11,500	£11,500
PANORMO, VINCENZO (attributed to)	7	5	$1,737	$58,600	$21,239
			£1,150	£34,660	£13,012
PANORMO FAMILY (MEMBER OF) (ascribed to)	1	0			
PANORMO FAMILY (MEMBER OF) (attributed to)	1	1	$16,376	$16,376	$16,376
			£9,775	£9,775	£9,775
PAOLETTI, SILVIO VEZIO	3	3	$3,618	$4,620	$4,158
			£2,222	£2,760	£2,581
PAQUOTTE, JEAN BAPTIST	1	1	$7,739	$7,739	$7,739
			£5,026	£5,026	£5,026
PARALUPI, RODOLFO (attributed to)	1	0			

SAMUEL FELIX NEMESSANYI | Violin: Budapest, 1871 | Sotheby's, October 6, 2000, Lot 21

SABASTIAN WAGNER | Viola: Meersbourg, second half 18th C. | Sotheby's, October 6, 2000, Lot 79

CHARLES AND ELMER STROMBERG
Fine American Archtop Guitar: Boston, 1947 | Skinner, November 5, 2000, Lot 8

GIOVANNI BATTISTA GUADAGNINI | Fine Italian Violin: Parma, c. 1770 | Skinner, May 7, 2000, Lot 128

LEON BERNARDEL | French Violoncello: Paris, c. 1918 | Skinner, May 7, 2000, Lot 29

ANTONIO & GIROLAMO AMATI | Fine, Rare Italian Violin: Cremona, 1608 | Skinner, November 5, 2000, Lot 84

CARLO TONONI | Violin: Venice, 1725 | Sotheby's, October 6, 2000, Lot 24

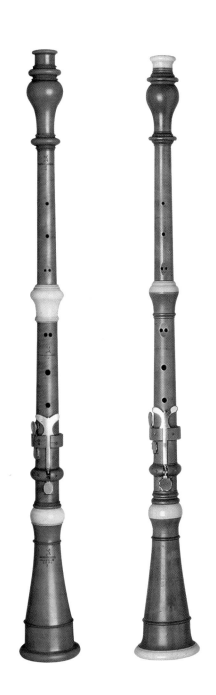

JAKOB FREDERICH GRUNDMANN
Two-Keyed Boxwood Oboe: Dresden, 1774 | Sotheby's, November 16, 2000, lot 312
GOULDING & CO | Two-Keyed Boxwood Oboe: London, c. 1800 | Sotheby's, November 16, 2000, lot 314

Maker	Items		Selling Prices		
	Bid	Sold	Low	High	Avg
MAUCOTEL, CHARLES	5	2	$13,041	$18,925	$15,983
			£8,050	£11,903	£9,976
MAULE, GIOVANNI (attributed to)	1	0			
MAURIZI, FRANCESCO	3	2	$14,980	$23,046	$19,013
			£8,970	£13,800	£11,385
MAYSON, WALTER H.	24	16	$730	$3,195	$1,519
			£460	£1,955	£945
MCCALLUM, ALEX	1	1	$232	$232	$232
			£161	£161	£161
MCLAREN, JOHN (attributed to)	1	1	$1,216	$1,216	$1,216
			£805	£805	£805
MEARES, RICHARD (attributed to)	1	1	$822	$822	$822
			£575	£575	£575
MEDIO-FINO	1	1	$174	$174	$174
			£104	£104	£104
MEIER, KARL	1	1	$1,093	$1,093	$1,093
			£719	£719	£719
MEINEL, FRIEDRICH WILHELM	1	1	$748	$748	$748
			£442	£442	£442
MEINEL, OSKAR	1	1	$920	$920	$920
			£552	£552	£552
MEISEL, FRIEDRICH WILHELM	1	1	$558	$558	$558
			£357	£357	£357
MEISEL, JOHANN GEORG	1	1	$575	$575	$575
			£345	£345	£345
MEISEL, KARL	1	1	$259	$259	$259
			£155	£155	£155
MEISEL, KARL (workshop of)	2	2	$633	$920	$776
			£380	£552	£466
MEISEL, LOTHAR	1	1	$1,265	$1,265	$1,265
			£748	£748	£748
MEISSNER, JOHANN FRIEDERICH	1	0			
MELEGARI, MICHELE & PIETRO	1	0			
MELZL, JOHANN GEORG	3	1	$1,024	$1,024	$1,024
			£632	£632	£632
MENICHETTI, MARTINO	2	0			
MENNEGAND, CHARLES (attributed to)	1	1	$2,999	$2,999	$2,999
			£1,840	£1,840	£1,840
MENNESSON, EMILE	10	6	$1,929	$4,594	$3,054
			£1,208	£2,990	£1,971
MENNESSON, EMILE (attributed to)	1	1	$1,770	$1,770	$1,770
			£1,093	£1,093	£1,093
MENZINGER, GUSTAV	1	1	$1,380	$1,380	$1,380
			£828	£828	£828
MERCIOLLE, JULES (workshop of)	2	1	$2,415	$2,415	$2,415
			£1,449	£1,449	£1,449
MERIOTTE, CHARLES	1	0			
MERMILLOT, MAURICE	10	6	$3,457	$11,178	$6,318
			£2,070	£6,900	£3,979
MERMILLOT, MAURICE (attributed to)	1	1	$3,452	$3,452	$3,452
			£2,185	£2,185	£2,185
MERRETT, H.W.	1	1	$209	$209	$209
			£138	£138	£138

| Maker | Items | | Selling Prices | | |
	Bid	Sold	Low	High	Avg
MESSON, E.	1	1	$1,677	$1,677	$1,677
			£1,035	£1,035	£1,035
MEUCCI, ENZO	1	1	$3,432	$3,432	$3,432
			£2,400	£2,400	£2,400
MEYER, KARL	3	2	$193	$1,005	$599
			£115	£598	£357
MEZZADRI, ALESSANDRO (ascribed to)	1	1	$5,796	$5,796	$5,796
			£3,450	£3,450	£3,450
MICELLI, CARLO	1	1	$230	$230	$230
			£138	£138	£138
MICHETTI, PLINIO	2	2	$7,475	$14,973	$11,224
			£4,485	£8,694	£6,590
MIGAZZI, LUIGI	1	1	$4,416	$4,416	$4,416
			£2,777	£2,777	£2,777
MILES, ROLF	1	0			
MILITELLA, MARIANO	1	0			
MILLANT, ROGER & MAX	1	0			
MILNE, PATRICK G.	1	1	$1,933	$1,933	$1,933
			£1,150	£1,150	£1,150
MILTON, LOUIS	2	2	$2,142	$2,631	$2,387
			£1,323	£1,840	£1,581
MINNOZZI, MARCO	1	1	$2,881	$2,881	$2,881
			£1,725	£1,725	£1,725
MIRAUCOURT, N.	1	1	$1,806	$1,806	$1,806
			£1,150	£1,150	£1,150
MIREMONT, CLAUDE AUGUSTIN	10	7	$4,801	$17,193	$9,393
			£2,875	£10,659	£5,826
MOCKEL, OSWALD	2	0			
MOCKEL, OTTO	2	0			
MODAUDO, G.	1	0			
MOENNIG, WILLIAM (workshop of)	1	1	$805	$805	$805
			£489	£489	£489
MOINEL, CHARLES	2	0			
MOINEL, DANIEL	1	1	$1,344	$1,344	$1,344
			£805	£805	£805
MOINEL & CHERPITEL	3	1	$3,726	$3,726	$3,726
			£2,300	£2,300	£2,300
MOINEL & CHERPITEL (workshop of)	1	1	$2,184	$2,184	$2,184
			£1,527	£1,527	£1,527
MOINIER, ALAIN	1	1	$3,672	$3,672	$3,672
			£2,185	£2,185	£2,185
MOITESSIER, LOUIS	2	0			
MOLLER, MAX	1	1	$5,041	$5,041	$5,041
			£3,525	£3,525	£3,525
MONK	1	1	$556	$556	$556
			£368	£368	£368
MONK, JOHN KING	5	2	$460	$1,091	$776
			£276	£748	£512
MONNIG, FRITZ	4	2	$933	$2,204	$1,569
			£552	£1,380	£966
MONTAGNANA, DOMENICO	2	0			
MONTAGNANA, DOMENICO (attributed to)	1	1	$2,300	$2,300	$2,300
			£1,472	£1,472	£1,472

| Maker | Items | | Selling Prices | | |
---	Bid	Sold	Low	High	Avg
PARESCHI, GAETANO	7	2	$4,592 £2,875	$15,077 £9,258	$9,834 £6,066
PARKER, DANIEL	3	1	$13,714 £8,625	$13,714 £8,625	$13,714 £8,625
PARMEGGIANI, ROMOLA	2	1	$3,015 £1,852	$3,015 £1,852	$3,015 £1,852
PASSAU, SIMON SCHODLER	1	1	$1,151 £805	$1,151 £805	$1,151 £805
PASSAURO-ZUCCARO, RAYMOND	2	2	$805 £483	$1,265 £759	$1,035 £621
PASTA, GAETANO	3	1	$20,407 £12,075	$20,407 £12,075	$20,407 £12,075
PATERSON, J.B.	1	0			
PATOCKA, BENJAMIN	1	1	$1,938 £1,265	$1,938 £1,265	$1,938 £1,265
PATOCKA, BENJAMIN (attributed to)	1	1	$2,120 £1,380	$2,120 £1,380	$2,120 £1,380
PATZELT, FERDINAND (attributed to)	2	0			
PAULI, JOSEPH	1	1	$1,265 £832	$1,265 £832	$1,265 £832
PAULSEN, P.C.	1	0			
PAULUS, ALBIN LUDWIG	4	2	$1,059 £690	$1,118 £690	$1,089 £690
PAULUS, KONRAD (attributed to)	2	0			
PAWLIKOWSKI, JAN	1	1	$1,725 £1,035	$1,725 £1,035	$1,725 £1,035
PAYNE, ALAN	1	0			
PEARCE, WILLIAM	2	1	$1,739 £1,035	$1,739 £1,035	$1,739 £1,035
PEDRAZZINI, GIUSEPPE	27	15	$10,872 £7,200	$57,615 £34,500	$30,000 £18,679
PEDRAZZINI, GIUSEPPE (ascribed to)	1	0			
PEDRAZZINI, GIUSEPPE (attributed to)	2	1	$5,511 £3,450	$5,511 £3,450	$5,511 £3,450
PEDRAZZINI, GIUSEPPE (workshop of)	2	2	$4,025 £2,616	$8,625 £5,520	$6,325 £4,068
PELLACANI, GIUSEPPE	3	1	$6,440 £4,508	$6,440 £4,508	$6,440 £4,508
PELLACANI, GIUSEPPE (ascribed to)	1	0			
PELLACANI, GIUSEPPE (attributed to)	1	0			
PELLERANI, ANTONIO	1	1	$9,163 £5,980	$9,163 £5,980	$9,163 £5,980
PELLIZON, ANTONIO (I)	1	1	$9,423 £5,786	$9,423 £5,786	$9,423 £5,786
PEREGO, FLAVIO	1	0			
PERESSON, SERGIO	3	2	$18,463 £10,925	$23,194 £13,800	$20,828 £12,363
PEROTTI, ENEA	1	0			
PERR, MICHAEL	1	0			
PERRIN, E.J. (FILS)	1	1	$397 £276	$397 £276	$397 £276
PERRIN, ETIENNE	1	0			

Maker	Items		Selling Prices		
	Bid	Sold	Low	High	Avg
PERRY	2	1	$251	$251	$251
			£150	£150	£150
PERRY, JAMES	3	0			
PERRY, L.A.	1	1	$668	$668	$668
			£437	£437	£437
PERRY, THOMAS	6	3	$1,219	$1,932	$1,664
			£748	£1,211	£1,036
PERRY, THOMAS & WM. WILKINSON	6	3	$922	$4,711	$2,341
			£552	£3,120	£1,523
PERRY, WILLIAM (attributed to)	1	1	$731	$731	$731
			£460	£460	£460
PERRY & WILKINSON	10	6	$748	$4,025	$1,983
			£460	£2,463	£1,210
PERRY & WILKINSON (attributed to)	1	1	$1,013	$1,013	$1,013
			£605	£605	£605
PETERNELLA, JAGO	3	1	$6,907	$6,907	$6,907
			£4,830	£4,830	£4,830
PETERS, WILLIAM L.	1	1	$1,610	$1,610	$1,610
			£966	£966	£966
PETERSON, P.A.	2	1	$578	$578	$578
			£368	£368	£368
PETZOLD, PAUL	1	0			
PFRETZSCHNER	1	0			
PFRETZSCHNER, E.R.	1	1	$92	$92	$92
			£56	£56	£56
PFRETZSCHNER, G.A. (workshop of)	1	1	$201	$201	$201
			£121	£121	£121
PFRETZSCHNER, JOHANN GOTTLOB	1	1	$900	$900	$900
			£575	£575	£575
PICCAGLIANI, ARMANDO	1	1	$1,960	$1,960	$1,960
			£1,203	£1,203	£1,203
PICKARD, H.	1	1	$3,105	$3,105	$3,105
			£1,919	£1,919	£1,919
PICKSTONE, HARRY	2	2	$230	$332	$281
			£138	£196	£167
PIERCE, WILLIAM	1	1	$403	$403	$403
			£242	£242	£242
PIEROTTE, JULES	2	1	$559	$559	$559
			£345	£345	£345
PIERRAY, CLAUDE	2	2	$5,442	$5,750	$5,596
			£3,220	£3,450	£3,335
PILAR, KAREL	3	2	$1,360	$4,388	$2,874
			£805	£2,760	£1,783
PILAR, VLADIMIR	2	2	$2,467	$2,907	$2,687
			£1,495	£1,840	£1,668
PILAT, PAUL	4	4	$6,707	$11,903	$8,578
			£4,140	£7,380	£5,327
PILLEMENT	1	1	$1,302	$1,302	$1,302
			£863	£863	£863
PILLEMENT, FRANCOIS	3	2	$1,267	$2,277	$1,772
			£782	£1,380	£1,081
PINEAU, JOSEPH	1	1	$690	$690	$690
			£414	£414	£414

Maker	Items Bid	Sold	Selling Prices Low	High	Avg
PIQUE (ascribed to)	1	0			
PIQUE, F. (attributed to)	1	0			
PIQUE, FRANCOIS LOUIS (ascribed to)	1	1	$3,473 £2,300	$3,473 £2,300	$3,473 £2,300
PIQUE, FRANCOIS LOUIS (attributed to)	1	1	$4,600 £2,721	$4,600 £2,721	$4,600 £2,721
PIRETTI, ENRICO	2	1	$1,586 £1,035	$1,586 £1,035	$1,586 £1,035
PIROT, CLAUDE	3	1	$17,250 £10,350	$17,250 £10,350	$17,250 £10,350
PIVA, GIOVANNI	1	0			
PLIVERICS, EMIL	1	1	$6,523 £4,320	$6,523 £4,320	$6,523 £4,320
PLOWRIGHT, DENIS G.	2	1	$765 £506	$765 £506	$765 £506
POEHLAND & FUCHS	2	2	$863 £533	$3,450 £2,270	$2,156 £1,401
POGGI, ANSALDO	3	3	$29,956 £19,550	$40,601 £26,450	$34,904 £22,233
POGGI, ANSALDO (attributed to)	1	1	$1,725 £1,035	$1,725 £1,035	$1,725 £1,035
POIROT, A.	1	1	$1,131 £694	$1,131 £694	$1,131 £694
POIROT, AINE	1	0			
POIRSON	1	0			
POIRSON, ELOPHE	1	1	$15,525 £9,315	$15,525 £9,315	$15,525 £9,315
POLITI, ENRICO & RAUL	1	1	$14,576 £8,625	$14,576 £8,625	$14,576 £8,625
POLITI, ENRICO & RAUL (attributed to)	1	1	$3,290 £2,139	$3,290 £2,139	$3,290 £2,139
POLITI, EUGENIO	1	0			
POLITI, RAUL	3	2	$6,641 £4,025	$10,689 £6,325	$8,665 £5,175
POLLASTRI, GAETANO	10	5	$14,719 £9,258	$42,757 £25,300	$27,556 £17,331
POLLASTRI, GAETANO (ascribed to)	4	3	$6,521 £4,025	$10,925 £6,555	$8,315 £5,070
POLLASTRI, GAETANO (attributed to)	3	3	$6,900 £4,830	$9,641 £5,951	$8,308 £5,319
POSCH, ANTON	1	1	$5,216 £3,220	$5,216 £3,220	$5,216 £3,220
POSTACCHINI, ANDREA	2	1	$7,161 £4,397	$7,161 £4,397	$7,161 £4,397
POSTACCHINI, ANDREA (attributed to)	5	4	$4,388 £2,760	$27,600 £16,755	$17,709 £11,246
POSTIGLIONE, VINCENZO	11	7	$10,350 £6,314	$43,315 £28,290	$28,020 £17,360
POSTIGLIONE, VINCENZO (attributed to)	7	2	$7,800 £5,382	$31,719 £20,700	$19,759 £13,041
POSTIGLIONE, VINCENZO (workshop of)	1	1	$15,882 £10,350	$15,882 £10,350	$15,882 £10,350
POSTIGLIONE, VINCENZO & GIOVANNI PISTUCCI	1	0			

Maker	Items		Selling Prices		
	Bid	Sold	Low	High	Avg
POUZOL, EMILE (attributed to)	1	1	$1,971 £1,217	$1,971 £1,217	$1,971 £1,217
POWERS, LINCOLN	1	1	$374 £246	$374 £246	$374 £246
POWLOSKI, PATRICIA	1	0			
POWLOSKI-BANCHERO, PATRICIA	1	1	$1,840 £1,104	$1,840 £1,104	$1,840 £1,104
PRAGA, EUGENIO	3	2	$8,539 £5,175	$48,438 £29,900	$28,488 £17,538
PRAGA, EUGENIO (workshop of)	1	1	$9,775 £6,354	$9,775 £6,354	$9,775 £6,354
PRAGER, AUGUST EDWIN	1	0			
PRAILL, RONALD WILLIAM	5	1	$1,118 £690	$1,118 £690	$1,118 £690
PRATT, ARTHUR	1	1	$705 £458	$705 £458	$705 £458
PRESSENDA, GIOVANNI FRANCESCO	6	4	$141,120 £84,000	$196,134 £128,000	$158,663 £99,813
PRESTON, JAMES	1	1	$1,360 £805	$1,360 £805	$1,360 £805
PRIER, PETER PAUL	2	2	$840 £580	$5,999 £3,703	$3,419 £2,141
PRIESTNALL, J.	1	1	$1,060 £690	$1,060 £690	$1,060 £690
PRIESTNALL, JOHN	1	1	$538 £322	$538 £322	$538 £322
PRIMAVERA, ALFREDO (workshop of)	1	0			
PRINCE, W.B.	2	1	$1,316 £805	$1,316 £805	$1,316 £805
PROKOP, LADISLAV	3	3	$288 £178	$6,856 £4,232	$2,506 £1,547
PROKOP, LADISLAV (attributed to)	1	1	$695 £460	$695 £460	$695 £460
PROKOP, LADISLAV (II)	2	0			
PUGLISI (attributed to)	1	1	$2,952 £1,955	$2,952 £1,955	$2,952 £1,955
PUGLISI, CONCETTO	1	0			
PUGLISI, MICHELANGELO	2	1	$5,700 £3,933	$5,700 £3,933	$5,700 £3,933
PUGLISI, MICHELANGELO (attributed to)	1	1	$5,301 £3,450	$5,301 £3,450	$5,301 £3,450
PUGLISI, REALE	4	3	$3,850 £2,300	$5,356 £3,306	$4,621 £2,827
PULPANECK, FRITZ	1	0			
PUOZZO, EDSON	1	0			
PUPUNAT, FRANCOIS MARIE	2	1	$1,440 £920	$1,440 £920	$1,440 £920
PURDAY, T.E.	1	1	$1,018 £661	$1,018 £661	$1,018 £661
PUSKAS, JOSEPH	2	2	$2,875 £1,760	$3,450 £2,070	$3,163 £1,915
PYNE, GEORGE	17	13	$1,809 £1,265	$6,165 £3,910	$4,017 £2,483

| Maker | Items | | Selling Prices | | |
---	Bid	Sold	Low	High	Avg
QUAN, SHEN FEI ZHENG	1	1	$2,142	$2,142	$2,142
			£1,323	£1,323	£1,323
QUENOIL, VICTOR	2	0			
RABASSINI, MASSIMO	1	1	$1,725	$1,725	$1,725
			£1,104	£1,104	£1,104
RADIGHIERI, OTELLO	1	1	$2,185	$2,185	$2,185
			£1,333	£1,333	£1,333
RAE, JOHN	5	2	$559	$777	$668
			£345	£460	£403
RAEBURN, JOHN	1	1	$1,348	$1,348	$1,348
			£805	£805	£805
RAMBAUX, CLAUDE VICTOR	1	1	$4,229	$4,229	$4,229
			£2,760	£2,760	£2,760
RAMBAUX, CLAUDE VICTOR (attributed to)	1	1	$4,754	$4,754	$4,754
			£2,990	£2,990	£2,990
RAMIREZ, MANUEL (ascribed to)	1	1	$7,638	$7,638	$7,638
			£4,715	£4,715	£4,715
RASTELLI, LODOVICO	1	0			
RATHBONE, A. (attributed to)	1	1	$848	$848	$848
			£552	£552	£552
RAUTENBERG, NICOLE	1	1	$2,588	$2,588	$2,588
			£1,656	£1,656	£1,656
RAVIZZA, CARLO	2	1	$4,893	$4,893	$4,893
			£3,034	£3,034	£3,034
RAVIZZA, CARLO (attributed to)	1	1	$6,642	$6,642	$6,642
			£4,100	£4,100	£4,100
RAYMOND, ROBERT JOHN	2	1	$468	$468	$468
			£299	£299	£299
REED, JOSEPH	1	1	$1,273	$1,273	$1,273
			£828	£828	£828
REGAZZONI, DANTE	2	1	$5,591	$5,591	$5,591
			£3,910	£3,910	£3,910
REGAZZONI, DANTE PAOLO	2	2	$3,187	$8,177	$5,682
			£1,955	£5,175	£3,565
REICHEL	1	0			
REICHEL, E.O.	1	1	$460	$460	$460
			£276	£276	£276
REICHEL, J.G. (attributed to)	1	0			
REICHEL, JOHANN GOTTFRIED	1	1	$278	$278	$278
			£173	£173	£173
REICHERT, EDUARD	4	3	$316	$575	$441
			£190	£345	£265
REICHERT, EDUARD (workshop of)	1	1	$489	$489	$489
			£293	£293	£293
REITER, JOHANN	2	1	$1,610	$1,610	$1,610
			£995	£995	£995
REMENYI, MIHALY	1	1	$6,308	$6,308	$6,308
			£3,968	£3,968	£3,968
REMY (FILS)	1	1	$1,354	$1,354	$1,354
			£863	£863	£863
REMY, JEAN MATHURIN	1	0			
RENAUDIN, LEOPOLD	1	1	$5,055	$5,055	$5,055
			£3,220	£3,220	£3,220

Maker	Items Bid	Sold	Selling Prices Low	High	Avg
RENAUDIN, LEOPOLD (ascribed to)	1	0			
RENAULT & CHATELAIN (attributed to)	2	0			
RESUCHE, CHARLES	1	1	$3,524 £2,300	$3,524 £2,300	$3,524 £2,300
RESUCHE, CHARLES (attributed to)	2	1	$3,834 £2,300	$3,834 £2,300	$3,834 £2,300
REUTER, GUNTHER	1	1	$4,313 £2,837	$4,313 £2,837	$4,313 £2,837
RICARD, ALEXANDER	3	2	$920 £558	$920 £598	$920 £578
RICHARDSON, ARTHUR	15	11	$3,278 £2,185	$8,666 £5,520	$6,083 £3,837
RICHARDSON, FRANK	1	1	$920 £605	$920 £605	$920 £605
RICHELME, ANTOINE MARIUS	2	0			
RIEGER, PAUL	1	1	$1,677 £1,035	$1,677 £1,035	$1,677 £1,035
RIEGER & FIORINI (attributed to)	2	1	$999 £598	$999 £598	$999 £598
RINALDI, GIOFREDO BENEDETTO	1	1	$22,908 £14,950	$22,908 £14,950	$22,908 £14,950
RINALDI, MARENGO ROMANUS (ascribed to)	1	1	$23,046 £13,800	$23,046 £13,800	$23,046 £13,800
RIVA, CARLO "SEVERINO"	1	0			
RIVIERE & HAWKES	2	1	$677 £414	$677 £414	$677 £414
RIVOLTA, GIACOMO	5	0			
ROBB, THOMAS	1	0			
ROBIN, M.	1	0			
ROBINSON	1	1	$296 £196	$296 £196	$296 £196
ROBINSON, A.G.	2	2	$407 £265	$608 £403	$508 £334
ROBINSON, STANLEY	1	0			
ROBINSON, WILLIAM	25	14	$1,259 £863	$4,600 £2,806	$2,721 £1,681
ROBINSON, WILLIAM & STANLEY	1	1	$1,069 £690	$1,069 £690	$1,069 £690
ROCCA, ENRICO	6	4	$29,900 £18,299	$79,152 £51,750	$43,173 £27,920
ROCCA, ENRICO (ascribed to)	2	1	$2,700 £1,863	$2,700 £1,863	$2,700 £1,863
ROCCA, ENRICO (attributed to)	1	0			
ROCCA, GIUSEPPE	8	4	$130,845 £91,500	$238,464 £147,200	$192,006 £126,113
ROCCA, GIUSEPPE (attributed to)	2	2	$25,709 £15,870	$28,750 £17,250	$27,230 £16,560
ROCCA, GIUSEPPE (workshop of)	1	0			
ROCCHI, S.	1	0			
ROCCHI, SESTO	5	4	$8,642 £5,175	$14,438 £8,625	$11,355 £7,021
ROCKWELL, JOSEPH H.	2	0			

Maker	Items Bid	Sold	Selling Prices Low	High	Avg
ROGERI, PIETRO GIACOMO	1	1	$132,158 £78,200	$132,158 £78,200	$132,158 £78,200
ROMBOUTS, PIETER	4	2	$9,930 £6,325	$16,353 £10,350	$13,142 £8,338
ROMBOUTS, PIETER (attributed to)	1	0			
ROMER, ADOLF	2	0			
ROOT-DUERER	1	1	$316 £193	$316 £193	$316 £193
ROPE, ALFRED JAMES	1	1	$608 £403	$608 £403	$608 £403
ROPES, WALTER S.	1	1	$1,265 £832	$1,265 £832	$1,265 £832
ROSADONI, GIOVANNI	1	1	$5,005 £2,990	$5,005 £2,990	$5,005 £2,990
ROSCHER, CHRISTIAN HEINRICH WILHELM	1	1	$3,220 £1,932	$3,220 £1,932	$3,220 £1,932
ROSSI, DOMENICO	3	0			
ROSSI, GIOVANNI	1	1	$39,468 £27,600	$39,468 £27,600	$39,468 £27,600
ROSSI, GIUSEPPE	4	2	$6,168 £3,680	$6,182 £4,025	$6,175 £3,853
ROTH	1	0			
ROTH (ascribed to)	2	0			
ROTH (attributed to)	1	1	$3,671 £2,185	$3,671 £2,185	$3,671 £2,185
ROTH, ERNST HEINRICH	30	24	$546 £332	$6,388 £3,968	$2,776 £1,740
ROTH, ERNST HEINRICH (workshop of)	8	8	$460 £276	$2,645 £1,851	$941 £604
ROTH & LEDERER	3	1	$518 £311	$518 £311	$518 £311
ROUMEN, JOHANNES ARNOLDUS	1	0			
ROUMEN, L.W. (attributed to)	1	1	$4,285 £2,645	$4,285 £2,645	$4,285 £2,645
ROVATTI, LUIGI	1	1	$5,216 £3,220	$5,216 £3,220	$5,216 £3,220
ROVESCALLI, A.	2	1	$5,589 £3,450	$5,589 £3,450	$5,589 £3,450
ROVESCALLI, AZZO (ascribed to)	1	1	$3,290 £2,139	$3,290 £2,139	$3,290 £2,139
ROVESCALLI, MANLIO	1	0			
ROVESCALLI, TULLIO	1	1	$9,400 £6,110	$9,400 £6,110	$9,400 £6,110
ROWINSKI, STANISLAV	2	0			
RUBUS, RIGART	3	3	$115 £70	$288 £184	$203 £127
RUDDIMAN, JOSEPH	1	0			
RUFFE, CARL	1	1	$4,287 £2,645	$4,287 £2,645	$4,287 £2,645
RUGGIERI, FRANCESCO	8	4	$62,800 £40,000	$151,302 £90,600	$100,044 £63,221
RUGGIERI, FRANCESCO (ascribed to)	1	0			
RUGGIERI, FRANCESCO (attributed to)	1	0			

Maker	Items		Selling Prices		
	Bid	Sold	Low	High	Avg
RUSHWORTH & DREAPER	6	5	$495 £322	$2,608 £1,610	$1,516 £938
RUTH, BENJAMIN WARREN	1	1	$2,415 £1,428	$2,415 £1,428	$2,415 £1,428
RUZIEKA, JOSEPHUS	1	1	$3,285 £2,070	$3,285 £2,070	$3,285 £2,070
RUZIEKA, JOSEPHUS (attributed to)	1	1	$2,357 £1,455	$2,357 £1,455	$2,357 £1,455
SACCANI, BENIGNO (workshop of)	1	1	$1,840 £1,137	$1,840 £1,137	$1,840 £1,137
SALOMON	2	2	$1,643 £978	$6,388 £3,968	$4,015 £2,473
SALOMON, J.B.	2	2	$3,478 £2,070	$7,728 £4,600	$5,603 £3,335
SALOMON, JEAN BAPTISTE DESHAYES	4	1	$3,600 £2,484	$3,600 £2,484	$3,600 £2,484
SALSEDO, LUIGI	2	1	$2,743 £1,725	$2,743 £1,725	$2,743 £1,725
SALVADORI, GIUSEPPE	1	0			
SANNINO, V.	1	0			
SANNINO, VINCENZO	12	6	$19,411 £12,650	$63,342 £39,100	$40,550 £24,913
SANNINO, VINCENZO (ascribed to)	1	1	$7,498 £4,600	$7,498 £4,600	$7,498 £4,600
SANNINO, VINCENZO (attributed to)	3	1	$5,123 £3,105	$5,123 £3,105	$5,123 £3,105
SANTAGIULIANA, GIACINTO	1	0			
SARACINI, ANTONIO (attributed to)	1	0			
SARFATI, GERARDO	1	0			
SAUNDERS, ERNEST	1	1	$588 £411	$588 £411	$588 £411
SAUNDERS, S.	2	1	$544 £322	$544 £322	$544 £322
SAUNIER	1	1	$748 £442	$748 £442	$748 £442
SCARAMPELLA, GIUSEPPE	1	1	$48,438 £29,900	$48,438 £29,900	$48,438 £29,900
SCARAMPELLA, STEFANO	10	7	$13,973 £8,625	$53,903 £32,200	$35,310 £22,051
SCARAMPELLA, STEFANO (ascribed to)	1	1	$9,200 £5,520	$9,200 £5,520	$9,200 £5,520
SCARAMPELLA, STEFANO (attributed to)	4	2	$4,713 £2,910	$14,404 £8,625	$9,559 £5,767
SCARTABELLI, MAURO	2	2	$1,034 £633	$1,357 £833	$1,195 £733
SCHAUPP, PAUL E.	3	2	$345 £227	$374 £246	$359 £236
SCHAUPP, PAUL & CHARLES	1	0			
SCHETELIG, ERNST	2	0			
SCHEVERLE, JOANNES	1	1	$920 £544	$920 £544	$920 £544
SCHILBACH, OSWALD A.	1	1	$920 £544	$920 £544	$920 £544

Maker	Items		Selling Prices		
	Bid	Sold	Low	High	Avg
SCHIRMER, HANS (workshop of)	1	1	$1,410 £917	$1,410 £917	$1,410 £917
SCHLEGEL, KLAUS	1	1	$1,687 £1,035	$1,687 £1,035	$1,687 £1,035
SCHLEMMER, JOCHEN	1	1	$540 £345	$540 £345	$540 £345
SCHLOSSER, HERMANN	2	2	$615 £368	$1,262 £747	$938 £558
SCHMIDT, E.R. & CO.	3	1	$244 £150	$244 £150	$244 £150
SCHMIDT, ERNST REINHOLD	3	2	$2,070 £1,242	$2,070 £1,242	$2,070 £1,242
SCHMIDT, ERNST REINHOLD (workshop of)	2	1	$1,093 £719	$1,093 £719	$1,093 £719
SCHMIDT, MAX WILLIBALD	1	1	$1,560 £1,076	$1,560 £1,076	$1,560 £1,076
SCHMIDT, REINHOLD	1	1	$1,150 £690	$1,150 £690	$1,150 £690
SCHMITT, LUCIEN	4	2	$2,631 £1,840	$4,658 £2,875	$3,644 £2,358
SCHOLL, H. (attributed to)	1	1	$366 £219	$366 £219	$366 £219
SCHONFELDER, HERBERT EMIL	1	1	$978 £643	$978 £643	$978 £643
SCHONFELDER, JOHANN GEORG	4	3	$575 £374	$3,125 £2,185	$1,586 £1,072
SCHONFELDER, JOHANN GEORG (II)	2	2	$781 £518	$3,172 £2,070	$1,977 £1,294
SCHROETTER, A.	3	2	$92 £56	$316 £192	$204 £124
SCHULTZ, HENRY Y.	1	1	$2,185 £1,350	$2,185 £1,350	$2,185 £1,350
SCHUSTER, EDOUARD	4	2	$1,926 £1,150	$6,319 £4,025	$4,123 £2,588
SCHUSTER, MAX	1	1	$1,955 £1,271	$1,955 £1,271	$1,955 £1,271
SCHUSTER, MAX K.	2	2	$1,380 £828	$3,850 £2,300	$2,615 £1,564
SCHUSTER BROS. (workshop of)	1	1	$1,495 £984	$1,495 £984	$1,495 £984
SCHUSTER & CO.	1	1	$360 £230	$360 £230	$360 £230
SCHUSTER & CO. (workshop of)	1	1	$546 £332	$546 £332	$546 £332
SCHWAICHER, LEOPOLD (attributed to)	1	1	$1,118 £690	$1,118 £690	$1,118 £690
SCHWARTZ, ANTON	1	1	$1,265 £832	$1,265 £832	$1,265 £832
SCHWARZ, HEINRICH	1	1	$783 £483	$783 £483	$783 £483
SCHWEITZER, JOHANN BAPTISTE (attributed to)	1	1	$794 £494	$794 £494	$794 £494

Maker	Items Bid	Sold	Selling Prices Low	High	Avg
SCIALE, GIUSEPPE	1	1	$23,046 £13,800	$23,046 £13,800	$23,046 £13,800
SCOGGINS, MICHAEL GENE	1	1	$2,415 £1,449	$2,415 £1,449	$2,415 £1,449
SCOLARI, GIORGIO	1	1	$7,311 £4,485	$7,311 £4,485	$7,311 £4,485
SDERCI, IGINO	5	2	$13,444 £8,050	$14,100 £9,165	$13,772 £8,608
SDERCI, LUCIANO	2	2	$10,592 £6,900	$11,551 £6,900	$11,071 £6,900
SEBASTIEN, JEAN	2	1	$748 £478	$748 £478	$748 £478
SEIFERT, GEORGE	1	1	$1,853 £1,150	$1,853 £1,150	$1,853 £1,150
SEIFERT, OTTO	1	1	$4,943 £3,220	$4,943 £3,220	$4,943 £3,220
SEITZ, ANTON	1	1	$2,115 £1,380	$2,115 £1,380	$2,115 £1,380
SEITZ, JOHANNES	1	0			
SEITZ, NICOLAS	1	1	$1,282 £782	$1,282 £782	$1,282 £782
SERAPHIN, SANCTUS	1	1	$43,332 £27,600	$43,332 £27,600	$43,332 £27,600
SERAPHIN, SANTO	4	2	$118,260 £73,000	$135,999 £83,950	$127,130 £78,475
SERDET, PAUL	5	2	$2,933 £1,955	$6,886 £4,560	$4,909 £3,258
SERDET, PAUL (workshop of)	1	1	$2,167 £1,380	$2,167 £1,380	$2,167 £1,380
SGARABOTTO, GAETANO	8	4	$26,450 £15,870	$36,490 £21,850	$32,098 £19,636
SGARABOTTO, GAETANO (attributed to)	5	4	$5,796 £3,450	$12,834 £7,452	$9,624 £5,767
SGARABOTTO, PIETRO	3	2	$18,463 £10,925	$23,000 £14,950	$20,732 £12,938
SGARBI, ANTONIO	2	2	$3,795 £2,300	$15,462 £9,200	$9,629 £5,750
SGARBI, ANTONIO (attributed to)	3	2	$3,177 £1,955	$4,146 £2,546	$3,661 £2,250
SGARBI, GIUSEPPE	1	0			
SHAPIRO, OSCAR	1	0			
SHARLET, STACY	1	1	$920 £605	$920 £605	$920 £605
SHEARER, THOMAS	1	1	$661 £410	$661 £410	$661 £410
SHELMERDINE, ANTHONY	2	1	$1,054 £748	$1,054 £748	$1,054 £748
SHELMERDINE, ANTHONY (attributed to)	1	1	$732 £437	$732 £437	$732 £437
SHELTON, JOHN F.	1	0			
SHIPMAN, MARGARET	1	1	$2,300 £1,380	$2,300 £1,380	$2,300 £1,380
SIEGA, ETTORE & SON	2	2	$7,825 £4,830	$8,998 £5,555	$8,411 £5,192

Maker	Items Bid	Sold	Low	Selling Prices High	Avg
SIEGA, IGINIO	2	1	$10,654 £6,670	$10,654 £6,670	$10,654 £6,670
SIGNORINI, SERAFINO (attributed to)	1	0			
SILVESTRE, HIPPOLYTE	1	1	$15,364 £9,200	$15,364 £9,200	$15,364 £9,200
SILVESTRE, HIPPOLYTE CHRETIEN	9	4	$6,361 £4,140	$15,795 £9,430	$12,307 £7,561
SILVESTRE, HIPPOLYTE CHRETIEN (attributed to)	2	2	$6,613 £3,968	$21,379 £14,950	$13,996 £9,459
SILVESTRE, PIERRE	4	3	$9,060 £5,865	$26,503 £17,250	$15,113 £9,705
SILVESTRE, PIERRE (attributed to)	1	1	$26,450 £16,399	$26,450 £16,399	$26,450 £16,399
SILVESTRE, PIERRE & HIPPOLYTE	7	4	$7,825 £4,830	$28,513 £18,515	$16,168 £10,163
SILVESTRE & MAUCOTEL	4	2	$5,589 £3,450	$6,613 £4,140	$6,101 £3,795
SILVESTRE & MAUCOTEL (attributed to workshop of)	1	0			
SILVESTRE & MAUCOTEL (workshop of)	1	1	$4,113 £2,673	$4,113 £2,673	$4,113 £2,673
SIMEONI, GIANNANDREA (attributed to)	1	1	$4,240 £2,760	$4,240 £2,760	$4,240 £2,760
SIMON, PIERRE	1	1	$8,570 £5,290	$8,570 £5,290	$8,570 £5,290
SIMONAZZI, AMADEO	3	2	$6,154 £3,685	$11,141 £6,877	$8,647 £5,281
SIMONAZZI, AMADEO (ascribed to)	1	1	$6,000 £4,140	$6,000 £4,140	$6,000 £4,140
SIMONAZZI, AMADEO (attributed to)	1	1	$5,055 £3,220	$5,055 £3,220	$5,055 £3,220
SIMONIN, CHARLES	1	1	$3,167 £1,955	$3,167 £1,955	$3,167 £1,955
SIMONIN, CHARLES (attributed to)	5	0			
SIMOUTRE, NICHOLAS EUGENE	1	0			
SIMOUTRE, NICOLAS	1	1	$3,693 £2,185	$3,693 £2,185	$3,693 £2,185
SIMPSON, JAMES & JOHN	3	2	$1,676 £1,093	$2,588 £1,553	$2,132 £1,323
SIMS, BARRY	2	1	$692 £414	$692 £414	$692 £414
SINCLAIR, WILLIAM	1	0			
SIRONI, AMBROGIO	2	2	$3,392 £2,083	$12,061 £7,406	$7,727 £4,744
SIVORI	1	1	$1,104 £690	$1,104 £690	$1,104 £690
SMALLEY, G.B.	1	1	$713 £437	$713 £437	$713 £437
SMILLIE, ALEXANDER	4	4	$1,247 £747	$4,993 £3,290	$3,748 £2,418
SMILLIE, ANDREW Y. (attributed to)	3	1	$1,054 £748	$1,054 £748	$1,054 £748

Maker	Items Bid	Sold	Low	Selling Prices High	Avg
SMITH, ARTHUR E.	2	2	$9,633 £5,750	$12,721 £8,280	$11,177 £7,015
SMITH, BERT	5	4	$923 £633	$2,236 £1,380	$1,707 £1,093
SMITH, JOHN	9	5	$1,134 £667	$3,524 £2,300	$1,817 £1,139
SMITH, JOHN (attributed to)	1	1	$919 £598	$919 £598	$919 £598
SMITH, THOMAS	2	2	$201 £121	$2,119 £1,265	$1,160 £693
SMITH, THOMAS (attributed to)	4	3	$1,863 £1,150	$3,936 £2,415	$2,643 £1,629
SMITH, WILLIAM (attributed to)	1	1	$2,889 £1,725	$2,889 £1,725	$2,889 £1,725
SNEIDER, JOSEPH	1	0			
SNEIDER, JOSEPH (attributed to)	1	1	$16,100 £9,660	$16,100 £9,660	$16,100 £9,660
SOFFRITTI, ALOYSIO LUIGI	1	0			
SOFFRITTI, ALOYSIO LUIGI (attributed to)	1	0			
SOFFRITTI, ETTORE	2	0			
SOFFRITTI, LUIGI	1	0			
SOFFRITTI, LUIGI (ascribed to)	1	1	$5,796 £3,450	$5,796 £3,450	$5,796 £3,450
SOLFERINO, REMO	1	0			
SOLIANI, ANGELO	4	0			
SOLIANI, ANGELO (attributed to)	1	0			
SOLLNER, FRANZ JOSEF	3	1	$932 £575	$932 £575	$932 £575
SOLZI, ANDREA	1	1	$3,738 £2,392	$3,738 £2,392	$3,738 £2,392
SOMNY, JOSEPH MAURICE	1	1	$1,159 £805	$1,159 £805	$1,159 £805
SORIOT & DIDION	1	1	$4,637 £2,760	$4,637 £2,760	$4,637 £2,760
SORSANO, SPIRITO	1	1	$53,774 £32,200	$53,774 £32,200	$53,774 £32,200
SORSANO, SPIRITO (attributed to)	1	1	$3,092 £1,840	$3,092 £1,840	$3,092 £1,840
SOUBEYRAN, MARC	1	1	$1,454 £920	$1,454 £920	$1,454 £920
SPATAFFI, GUERRIERO	1	0			
SPIDLEN, FRANTISEK F.	4	1	$10,573 £6,900	$10,573 £6,900	$10,573 £6,900
SPIDLEN, OTAKAR FRANTISEK	4	3	$3,850 £2,300	$6,948 £4,370	$5,127 £3,220
SPIDLEN, OTAKAR FRANTISEK (attributed to)	1	0			
SPIDLEN, PREMYSL OTAKAR	2	0			
SPIELMANN, RUDOLF	1	1	$4,462 £3,120	$4,462 £3,120	$4,462 £3,120
SQUIER, JEROME BONAPARTE	2	2	$1,093 £710	$3,795 £2,497	$2,444 £1,604
SQUIER, VICTOR CARROLL	3	2	$978 £604	$1,560 £1,076	$1,269 £840

Maker	Bid	Sold	Low	High	Avg
SQUIRE, V.C.	1	1	$374 £224	$374 £224	$374 £224
STADLMANN, JOHANN JOSEPH	3	1	$3,726 £2,300	$3,726 £2,300	$3,726 £2,300
STADLMANN, JOHANN JOSEPH (attributed to)	3	0			
STADLMANN, MICHAEL IGNAZ	1	1	$5,216 £3,220	$5,216 £3,220	$5,216 £3,220
STAINER, JACOB	3	1	$57,615 £34,500	$57,615 £34,500	$57,615 £34,500
STANLEY, C.F.	1	1	$1,840 £1,104	$1,840 £1,104	$1,840 £1,104
STANLEY, ROBERT A.	2	1	$470 £322	$470 £322	$470 £322
STAUFFER, JOHANN GEORG	1	0			
STEFANINI	2	0			
STEFANINI, GIUSEPPE	5	5	$4,255 £2,629	$10,296 £7,200	$8,006 £5,012
STIEBER, ERNST	1	1	$2,812 £1,725	$2,812 £1,725	$2,812 £1,725
STIRRAT, DAVID	3	1	$4,514 £2,875	$4,514 £2,875	$4,514 £2,875
STIRRAT, DAVID (attributed to)	1	1	$2,726 £1,725	$2,726 £1,725	$2,726 £1,725
STONEMAN, HENRY (attributed to)	1	1	$989 £644	$989 £644	$989 £644
STORIONI, CARLO	6	5	$668 £437	$2,332 £1,380	$1,636 £989
STORIONI, LORENZO	1	1	$70,146 £43,300	$70,146 £43,300	$70,146 £43,300
STOSS, IGNAZ GEORG	1	1	$1,348 £805	$1,348 £805	$1,348 £805
STOTT, GEORGE T. (attributed to)	1	1	$684 £437	$684 £437	$684 £437
STRADIVARI, ANTONIO	10	4	$226,688 £147,200	$1,582,325 £947,500	$1,004,820 £621,525
STRADIVARI, FRANCESCO	1	0			
STRAINER, J.	1	1	$348 £230	$348 £230	$348 £230
STRAUB, JOSEPH	1	1	$5,377 £3,220	$5,377 £3,220	$5,377 £3,220
STRELLINI	1	1	$3,354 £2,185	$3,354 £2,185	$3,354 £2,185
STRIEBIG, JEAN	3	3	$604 £414	$4,592 £2,875	$2,131 £1,346
STRNAD, CASPAR	1	1	$11,523 £6,900	$11,523 £6,900	$11,523 £6,900
STROBL, MICHAEL	2	0			
STUBER, JOHANN	1	0			
STUMPEL, H.C.	1	1	$403 £242	$403 £242	$403 £242
SUCHY, FRANZ	1	1	$1,043 £621	$1,043 £621	$1,043 £621

Maker	Items Bid	Sold	Selling Prices Low	High	Avg
SUZUKI	1	1	$104 £63	$104 £63	$104 £63
SYSKA, JACEK	1	0			
SZEPESSY, BELA	9	6	$3,110 £1,840	$9,085 £5,750	$6,258 £3,904
TARANTINO, GIUSEPPE	1	1	$6,417 £3,726	$6,417 £3,726	$6,417 £3,726
TARASCONI, G.	1	1	$19,435 £11,500	$19,435 £11,500	$19,435 £11,500
TARR, SHELLEY	1	0			
TARR, THOMAS	2	1	$1,176 £713	$1,176 £713	$1,176 £713
TARR, WILLIAM	3	1	$2,415 £1,466	$2,415 £1,466	$2,415 £1,466
TARTAGLIA, FRANCESCO	1	0			
TASSINI, MARCO	2	2	$3,864 £2,300	$4,276 £2,530	$4,070 £2,415
TAUSCHER, EDUARD	3	2	$500 £299	$720 £460	$610 £380
TAYLOR, GULIELMUS (attributed to)	2	2	$267 £173	$2,827 £1,840	$1,547 £1,006
TECCHLER, DAVID	7	3	$23,005 £13,800	$30,309 £18,975	$27,506 £16,675
TELLER, ROMAN (workshop of)	1	1	$863 £567	$863 £567	$863 £567
TENUCCI, EUGEN	1	1	$3,657 £2,300	$3,657 £2,300	$3,657 £2,300
TERRANA, GERLANDO	2	1	$2,243 £1,495	$2,243 £1,495	$2,243 £1,495
TERRY, JOHN	1	1	$2,645 £1,634	$2,645 £1,634	$2,645 £1,634
TESTORE, CARLO ANTONIO	10	7	$30,728 £18,400	$79,500 £51,675	$51,822 £32,354
TESTORE, CARLO ANTONIO (attributed to)	3	2	$14,950 £9,238	$16,324 £9,775	$15,637 £9,506
TESTORE, CARLO GIUSEPPE	2	2	$37,824 £26,450	$72,345 £45,500	$55,084 £35,975
TESTORE, CARLO GIUSEPPE (ascribed to)	1	0			
TESTORE, PAOLO ANTONIO	5	3	$6,784 £4,166	$15,771 £9,919	$10,040 £6,458
TESTORE, PAOLO ANTONIO (attributed to)	1	0			
TESTORE FAMILY (MEMBER OF)	3	2	$11,523 £6,900	$32,258 £19,550	$21,890 £13,225
THEODORAN, JACOB	1	1	$646 £420	$646 £420	$646 £420
THIBOUT, JACQUES PIERRE	4	2	$12,633 £7,475	$23,421 £15,209	$18,027 £11,342
THIBOUT, JACQUES PIERRE (attributed to)	1	1	$4,462 £3,120	$4,462 £3,120	$4,462 £3,120
THIBOUVILLE-LAMY, J.	139	112	$134 £80	$8,834 £5,750	$877 £549

Maker	Items Bid	Sold	Selling Prices Low	High	Avg
THIBOUVILLE-LAMY, J. (workshop of)	11	9	$288 £170	$1,150 £698	$598 £367
THIBOUVILLE-LAMY, JEROME	15	13	$166 £115	$2,231 £1,560	$610 £415
THIER (attributed to)	1	1	$1,445 £863	$1,445 £863	$1,445 £863
THIER, JOSEPH	3	3	$1,745 £1,092	$2,467 £1,495	$1,997 £1,227
THIR, ANTON	2	0			
THIR, ANTON (attributed to)	1	1	$1,398 £978	$1,398 £978	$1,398 £978
THIR, JOHANN GEORG	3	2	$1,555 £920	$3,353 £2,070	$2,454 £1,495
THIR, MATHIAS	3	2	$4,175 £2,530	$4,934 £2,990	$4,554 £2,760
THIR, MATHIAS (attributed to)	2	1	$781 £518	$781 £518	$781 £518
THOMASSIN	1	1	$8,349 £5,060	$8,349 £5,060	$8,349 £5,060
THOMPSON, CHARLES & SAMUEL	24	18	$205 £127	$3,450 £2,270	$1,377 £871
THOMPSON, E.A.	1	1	$288 £175	$288 £175	$288 £175
THOMPSON & SON	4	3	$1,216 £805	$1,955 £1,208	$1,491 £958
THOUVENEL	1	0			
THOUVENEL, CHARLES	1	1	$559 £345	$559 £345	$559 £345
THOUVENEL, HENRY	1	1	$863 £567	$863 £567	$863 £567
THUMHARD, JOHANN STEPHAN	1	1	$1,391 £920	$1,391 £920	$1,391 £920
TIEDEMANN, JAKOB	3	1	$1,682 £1,035	$1,682 £1,035	$1,682 £1,035
TILLER, C.W.	1	1	$375 £230	$375 £230	$375 £230
TILLER, C.W. (attributed to)	1	1	$450 £276	$450 £276	$450 £276
TILLER, WILFRED	1	1	$656 £403	$656 £403	$656 £403
TIM	1	1	$1,280 £805	$1,280 £805	$1,280 £805
TIMTONE	1	1	$1,150 £702	$1,150 £702	$1,150 £702
TINSLEY, CHARLES	1	1	$250 £149	$250 £149	$250 £149
TIPPER, J.W.	1	1	$1,191 £713	$1,191 £713	$1,191 £713
TOBIN, RICHARD	4	1	$13,414 £8,280	$13,414 £8,280	$13,414 £8,280
TOBIN, RICHARD (ascribed to)	1	0			
TOMASHOV, DANIEL	1	0			
TONONI, CARLO	5	3	$51,198 £32,200	$173,250 £119,542	$94,399 £63,310

Maker	Items Bid	Sold	Selling Prices Low	High	Avg
TONONI, GIOVANNI	1	1	$43,884 £27,600	$43,884 £27,600	$43,884 £27,600
TONONI, GIOVANNI (attributed to)	1	0			
TONONI, JOANNES (attributed to)	1	1	$9,200 £5,612	$9,200 £5,612	$9,200 £5,612
TOOMEY, T.	1	1	$559 £345	$559 £345	$559 £345
TOSELLO, BENITO (ascribed to)	2	0			
TOTH, A.	1	1	$589 £368	$589 £368	$589 £368
TOTH, JOANNES	1	1	$2,990 £1,815	$2,990 £1,815	$2,990 £1,815
TRAPANI, RAFFAELE	1	1	$35,397 £21,850	$35,397 £21,850	$35,397 £21,850
TRAPP, HERMANN	1	0			
TRAUTNER, HANS	1	1	$4,285 £2,645	$4,285 £2,645	$4,285 £2,645
TROIANI, CARLO	2	1	$3,651 £2,415	$3,651 £2,415	$3,651 £2,415
TUA, SILVIO	1	0			
TUBBS, C.E.	1	0			
TURCSAK, TIBOR GABOR	2	2	$1,730 £1,124	$2,785 £1,719	$2,258 £1,421
TURNER, W. (attributed to)	1	0			
TURRINI, GAETANO	1	0			
TWEEDALE, CHARLES L.	6	3	$805 £489	$949 £575	$896 £546
TYSON, HERBERT W.	1	1	$1,378 £897	$1,378 £897	$1,378 £897
UDALRICUS, JOHANNES (attributed to)	1	0			
ULCIGRAI, NICOLO	1	0			
ULLMANN, GIORGIO	1	1	$13,122 £8,050	$13,122 £8,050	$13,122 £8,050
URBINO, RICHARD ALEXANDER	1	0			
URFF, WILLIAM	1	1	$431 £259	$431 £259	$431 £259
UTILI, NICOLO	1	0			
VACCARI, ALBERTO	1	0			
VACCARI, GIUSEPPE	2	2	$2,126 £1,265	$2,513 £1,495	$2,320 £1,380
VACCARI, RAFFAELLO	5	1	$11,272 £6,670	$11,272 £6,670	$11,272 £6,670
VAN DER GEEST, JACOB JAN	4	1	$3,091 £1,840	$3,091 £1,840	$3,091 £1,840
VANGELISTI, PIER LORENZO (ascribed to)	1	1	$14,400 £9,936	$14,400 £9,936	$14,400 £9,936
VAN HOOF, ALPHONS	3	3	$4,658 £2,875	$6,930 £4,140	$5,996 £3,680
VAROTTO, GIAMPIETRO (attributed to)	1	0			
VATELOT, MARCEL	3	0			
VAUTRIN, JOSEPH	5	3	$1,035 £640	$3,069 £1,955	$2,300 £1,440

Maker	Items		Selling Prices		
	Bid	Sold	Low	High	Avg
VAUTRIN, JOSEPH (attributed to)	1	1	$868 £575	$868 £575	$868 £575
VAVRA, JAN BAPTISTA	1	0			
VAVRA, KAREL (I)	1	1	$2,185 £1,437	$2,185 £1,437	$2,185 £1,437
VEDRAL, JOSEPH	1	0			
VENTAPANE, LORENZO	9	4	$39,721 £25,300	$51,198 £32,200	$47,904 £29,785
VENTAPANE, LORENZO (ascribed to)	1	0			
VENTAPANE, LORENZO (attributed to)	3	2	$8,118 £4,830	$16,584 £10,183	$12,351 £7,507
VENTAPANE, PASQUALE	2	1	$4,033 £2,415	$4,033 £2,415	$4,033 £2,415
VENTAPANE, PASQUALE (attributed to)	1	0			
VENTAPANE, VINCENZO (attributed to)	1	1	$18,400 £12,105	$18,400 £12,105	$18,400 £12,105
VENTURINI, LUCIANO	2	0			
VETTORI, CARLO	6	5	$3,457 £2,070	$6,784 £4,166	$5,110 £3,247
VETTORI, DARIO	1	0			
VETTORI, PAULO	4	4	$3,565 £2,345	$5,047 £3,174	$4,237 £2,689
VICKERS, E.	2	1	$320 £196	$320 £196	$320 £196
VICKERS, J.E.	3	1	$375 £230	$375 £230	$375 £230
VIDOUDEZ, ALFRED	1	0			
VIEDENHOFER, BERNHARD	1	1	$2,585 £1,680	$2,585 £1,680	$2,585 £1,680
VIGNALI, GIUSEPPE	1	1	$4,689 £3,105	$4,689 £3,105	$4,689 £3,105
VILLA, LUIGI	3	2	$1,824 £1,092	$3,073 £1,840	$2,448 £1,466
VILLAUME, GUSTAVE EUGENE	6	4	$1,687 £1,035	$3,110 £1,840	$2,374 £1,479
VINACCIA, GAETANO	1	0			
VINACCIA, GENNARO	3	2	$11,551 £6,900	$31,740 £19,679	$21,645 £13,289
VINACCIA FAMILY (MEMBER OF)	1	1	$5,175 £3,622	$5,175 £3,622	$5,175 £3,622
VINACCIA FAMILY (MEMBER OF) (ascribed to)	1	1	$32,900 £21,385	$32,900 £21,385	$32,900 £21,385
VINCENT, ALFRED	18	12	$1,096 £713	$5,962 £3,680	$3,859 £2,463
VINCENT, ARTHUR	1	1	$6,936 £4,140	$6,936 £4,140	$6,936 £4,140
VISTOLI, LUIGI	3	1	$9,718 £5,750	$9,718 £5,750	$9,718 £5,750
VITERBO, AUGUSTO DA RUB	3	0			
VOIGT, ARNOLD	3	3	$541 £322	$1,610 £977	$1,055 £640
VOIGT, JOHANN CHRISTIAN (II)	1	1	$1,035 £631	$1,035 £631	$1,035 £631

Maker	Items		Selling Prices		
	Bid	Sold	Low	High	Avg
VOIGT, JOHANN GEORG	2	1	$768 £460	$768 £460	$768 £460
VOIGT, PAUL	1	1	$900 £552	$900 £552	$900 £552
VOIGT, WERNER	3	1	$1,926 £1,150	$1,926 £1,150	$1,926 £1,150
VOLLER BROTHERS	1	0			
VRANCKO, JULIUS	1	1	$1,385 £860	$1,385 £860	$1,385 £860
VUILLAUME (workshop of)	1	1	$5,216 £3,200	$5,216 £3,200	$5,216 £3,200
VUILLAUME, F.N. (attributed to)	1	1	$8,722 £5,520	$8,722 £5,520	$8,722 £5,520
VUILLAUME, GUSTAVE	1	0			
VUILLAUME, JEAN BAPTISTE	38	25	$3,749 £2,300	$117,555 £72,565	$54,770 £33,736
VUILLAUME, JEAN BAPTISTE (attributed to)	4	1	$13,629 £8,050	$13,629 £8,050	$13,629 £8,050
VUILLAUME, JEAN BAPTISTE (workshop of)	4	2	$23,500 £14,950	$25,126 £15,275	$24,313 £15,113
VUILLAUME, N. (attributed to)	1	0			
VUILLAUME, NICHOLAS & J.B.	1	1	$20,493 £12,650	$20,493 £12,650	$20,493 £12,650
VUILLAUME, NICOLAS	10	5	$1,784 £1,265	$6,334 £3,910	$4,211 £2,622
VUILLAUME, NICOLAS (attributed to)	2	2	$2,084 £1,380	$5,383 £3,565	$3,733 £2,473
VUILLAUME, NICOLAS (workshop of)	1	1	$5,025 £2,990	$5,025 £2,990	$5,025 £2,990
VUILLAUME, NICOLAS FRANCOIS	6	3	$12,483 £7,475	$21,107 £13,800	$16,977 £10,542
VUILLAUME, SEBASTIAN	3	1	$8,551 £5,060	$8,551 £5,060	$8,551 £5,060
WADE, H.F.	1	1	$690 £414	$690 £414	$690 £414
WAGNER & GEORGE	2	2	$4,099 £2,530	$4,713 £2,910	$4,406 £2,720
WAHLBERG, LEIF	1	1	$2,778 £1,840	$2,778 £1,840	$2,778 £1,840
WALKER, JOHN	2	2	$2,250 £1,438	$3,303 £2,185	$2,777 £1,811
WALKER, WILLIAM	1	0			
WALMSLEY, P. (attributed to)	1	1	$2,062 £1,265	$2,062 £1,265	$2,062 £1,265
WALMSLEY, PETER	4	1	$1,220 £748	$1,220 £748	$1,220 £748
WAMSLEY, PETER	7	3	$1,025 £633	$2,718 £1,800	$2,085 £1,309
WARD, GEORGE	1	1	$2,705 £1,610	$2,705 £1,610	$2,705 £1,610
WARD, GEORGE (ascribed to)	1	1	$1,159 £747	$1,159 £747	$1,159 £747

Maker	Items Bid	Sold	Selling Prices Low	High	Avg
WARD, GEORGE (attributed to)	1	0			
WARD, ROBERT	1	0			
WARRICK, A.	1	1	$3,634 £2,300	$3,634 £2,300	$3,634 £2,300
WARWICK, A.	2	1	$1,191 £713	$1,191 £713	$1,191 £713
WASSERMANN, JOSEPH	2	0			
WATSON, FRANK	1	1	$2,305 £1,380	$2,305 £1,380	$2,305 £1,380
WATT, WALTER	1	1	$1,440 £862	$1,440 £862	$1,440 £862
WEBB, R.J.	1	1	$6,569 £3,910	$6,569 £3,910	$6,569 £3,910
WEBSTER, GEORGE	1	1	$1,212 £713	$1,212 £713	$1,212 £713
WEICHOLD, RICHARD	2	1	$828 £518	$828 £518	$828 £518
WEISS, EUGENIO	3	2	$1,121 £748	$2,412 £1,481	$1,767 £1,114
WELLBY, CHARLES	1	0			
WELLER, F.W.	1	1	$1,463 £920	$1,463 £920	$1,463 £920
WELLER, FREDERICK	4	1	$1,632 £977	$1,632 £977	$1,632 £977
WELLER, FREDERICK (attributed to)	4	1	$307 £184	$307 £184	$307 £184
WELLER, MICHAEL	1	1	$2,300 £1,360	$2,300 £1,360	$2,300 £1,360
WERLE, J. PAUL (attributed to)	1	1	$1,153 £690	$1,153 £690	$1,153 £690
WERRO, JEAN	2	1	$4,605 £3,220	$4,605 £3,220	$4,605 £3,220
WESTON, A.T.	1	1	$863 £528	$863 £528	$863 £528
WHEELER, A.H.	1	1	$805 £491	$805 £491	$805 £491
WHITE, ASA WARREN	6	6	$489 £322	$2,645 £1,613	$1,653 £1,018
WHITE, IRA	1	1	$1,725 £1,020	$1,725 £1,020	$1,725 £1,020
WHITE, NEHEMIAH	1	1	$805 £489	$805 £489	$805 £489
WHITMARSH, E.	3	3	$1,800 £1,150	$1,932 £1,150	$1,865 £1,150
WHITMARSH, EDWIN (attributed to)	1	1	$1,759 £1,150	$1,759 £1,150	$1,759 £1,150
WHITMARSH, EMANUEL	12	8	$874 £517	$2,471 £1,610	$1,840 £1,154
WHITMARSH, EMANUEL (attributed to)	1	1	$2,226 £1,449	$2,226 £1,449	$2,226 £1,449
WIDHALM, LEOPOLD	8	4	$5,400 £3,401	$7,728 £4,600	$6,646 £4,082
WIDHALM, MARTIN LEOPOLD	2	2	$9,000 £5,750	$9,603 £6,210	$9,301 £5,980

225

| Maker | Items | | Selling Prices | | |
	Bid	Sold	Low	High	Avg
WIDHALM, MARTIN LEOPOLD					
(attributed to)	1	1	$3,540	$3,540	$3,540
			£2,185	£2,185	£2,185
WIEBE, DAVID	1	1	$4,713	$4,713	$4,713
			£2,910	£2,910	£2,910
WIEGANET, A.G.	1	1	$1,035	$1,035	$1,035
			£681	£681	£681
WILD, ANDREA (ascribed to)	1	0			
WILD, FRANZ ANTON (attributed to)	1	0			
WILDSTEINBONER, HERMANN	1	1	$258	$258	$258
			£161	£161	£161
WILKANOWSKI, W.	8	8	$460	$1,035	$681
			£279	£673	£429
WILKANOWSKI, WILLIAM	1	0			
WILKINSON (attributed to)	1	1	$3,428	$3,428	$3,428
			£2,116	£2,116	£2,116
WILKINSON, JOHN	2	1	$4,175	$4,175	$4,175
			£2,530	£2,530	£2,530
WILKINSON, JOHN (ascribed to)	1	1	$1,594	$1,594	$1,594
			£978	£978	£978
WILKINSON, JOHN (attributed to)	2	1	$1,789	$1,789	$1,789
			£1,127	£1,127	£1,127
WILLARD, ELI A.	1	1	$489	$489	$489
			£293	£293	£293
WILLIAMS, F.C.	1	1	$920	$920	$920
			£552	£552	£552
WILMET, F.J.	1	1	$2,444	$2,444	$2,444
			£1,495	£1,495	£1,495
WILSON	1	1	$336	$336	$336
			£230	£230	£230
WILSON, H.	1	0			
WINDER, J.	2	1	$1,151	$1,151	$1,151
			£805	£805	£805
WINTER & SON (attributed to)	2	1	$927	$927	$927
			£598	£598	£598
WINTERLING, GEORG	2	2	$6,765	$8,085	$7,425
			£4,025	£4,830	£4,428
WITHERS, GEORGE	3	2	$2,319	$5,294	$3,807
			£1,380	£3,450	£2,415
WITHERS, GEORGE & SONS	3	2	$1,329	$3,467	$2,398
			£782	£2,070	£1,426
WITHERS, JOSEPH	3	2	$2,068	$5,356	$3,712
			£1,265	£3,306	£2,286
WITTMANN, ANTON	1	1	$4,934	$4,934	$4,934
			£3,220	£3,220	£3,220
WOLFF BROS.	21	16	$339	$3,291	$943
			£219	£2,070	£590
WOOD, OTIS W.	1	1	$431	$431	$431
			£259	£259	£259
WOOD, WILLIAM HOWARD	1	1	$1,125	$1,125	$1,125
			£697	£697	£697
WORLE, MATHIAS	1	1	$1,159	$1,159	$1,159
			£805	£805	£805
WORNLE, GEORG (attributed to)	1	1	$2,812	$2,812	$2,812

Maker	Items Bid	Sold	Low	Selling Prices High	Avg
			£1,725	£1,725	£1,725
WOULDHAVE, JOHN	2	1	$728	$728	$728
			£451	£451	£451
WULME-HUDSON, GEORGE	14	10	$1,737	$9,410	$6,226
			£1,150	£5,635	£3,755
WULME-HUDSON, GEORGE (ascribed to)	1	1	$8,050	$8,050	$8,050
			£5,233	£5,233	£5,233
WULME-HUDSON, GEORGE (attributed to)	1	1	$3,467	$3,467	$3,467
			£2,070	£2,070	£2,070
WURLITZER, REMBERT	1	1	$4,500	$4,500	$4,500
			£3,105	£3,105	£3,105
WURLITZER CO., RUDOLPH	1	1	$403	$403	$403
			£242	£242	£242
YOUNG, JOHN	1	1	$695	$695	$695
			£460	£460	£460
ZACH & CO., CARL	1	1	$7,788	$7,788	$7,788
			£4,600	£4,600	£4,600
ZAHN, UTE	2	1	$935	$935	$935
			£552	£552	£552
ZANI, ALDO	1	1	$7,211	$7,211	$7,211
			£4,370	£4,370	£4,370
ZANISI, FILIPPO	1	0			
ZANISI, FILIPPO (ascribed to)	1	1	$2,115	$2,115	$2,115
			£1,375	£1,375	£1,375
ZANOLI, FRANCESCO	1	1	$2,734	$2,734	$2,734
			£1,719	£1,719	£1,719
ZANOLI, GIACOMO	2	1	$28,750	$28,750	$28,750
			£17,250	£17,250	£17,250
ZANOLI, GIACOMO (ascribed to)	1	1	$16,800	$16,800	$16,800
			£11,592	£11,592	£11,592
ZANOLI, GIACOMO (attributed to)	2	0			
ZIMMER, K. OTTO	1	1	$10,833	$10,833	$10,833
			£6,900	£6,900	£6,900
ZIMMERMANN, JULIUS HEINRICH (attributed to)	1	1	$1,061	$1,061	$1,061
			£690	£690	£690
ZURLINI, NICOLO	1	0			
ZUST, J.E.	1	1	$4,313	$4,313	$4,313
			£2,875	£2,875	£2,875

VIOLIN BOW

Maker	Items Bid	Sold	Low	Selling Prices High	Avg
ACKERMANN, GOTTFRIED	1	1	$1,392	$1,392	$1,392
			£859	£859	£859
ADAM (attributed to)	3	1	$6,338	$6,338	$6,338
			£3,795	£3,795	£3,795
ADAM, J.D.	1	1	$10,247	$10,247	$10,247
			£6,325	£6,325	£6,325
ADAM, JEAN	1	1	$11,163	$11,163	$11,163
			£7,256	£7,256	£7,256
ADAM, JEAN (attributed to)	2	1	$1,380	$1,380	$1,380
			£838	£838	£838
ADAM, JEAN DOMINIQUE	1	0			
ADAM FAMILY (attributed to)	1	1	$2,062	$2,062	$2,062
			£1,265	£1,265	£1,265

Maker	Items		Selling Prices		
	Bid	Sold	Low	High	Avg
ALLEN, SAMUEL	5	2	$3,657 £2,300	$4,605 £3,220	$4,131 £2,760
ALLEN, SAMUEL (ascribed to)	1	1	$7,050 £4,583	$7,050 £4,583	$7,050 £4,583
ALLEN, SAMUEL (attributed to)	1	1	$5,654 £3,680	$5,654 £3,680	$5,654 £3,680
ALVEY, BRIAN	1	0			
AMES, ROBERT	1	1	$2,415 £1,473	$2,415 £1,473	$2,415 £1,473
ASHMEAD, RALPH	1	0			
AUBRY, JOSEPH	3	3	$525 £322	$3,177 £2,070	$1,554 £989
AUDINOT, JACQUES	1	1	$1,155 £690	$1,155 £690	$1,155 £690
AUDINOT, NESTOR	1	0			
BAILEY, G.E.	1	1	$971 £633	$971 £633	$971 £633
BAILLY, CHARLES	1	1	$1,646 £1,035	$1,646 £1,035	$1,646 £1,035
BARBE, AUGUSTE	1	1	$4,252 £2,530	$4,252 £2,530	$4,252 £2,530
BASTIEN, E.	2	1	$1,348 £805	$1,348 £805	$1,348 £805
BAUSCH	5	4	$122 £81	$1,175 £805	$545 £354
BAUSCH (workshop of)	2	1	$230 £150	$230 £150	$230 £150
BAUSCH, L.	1	1	$403 £246	$403 £246	$403 £246
BAUSCH, L. (workshop of)	1	1	$518 £340	$518 £340	$518 £340
BAUSCH, LUDWIG	3	3	$690 £414	$894 £552	$796 £486
BAUSCH, LUDWIG & SOHN	5	3	$673 £402	$949 £575	$766 £464
BAUSCH, LUDWIG (II)	1	1	$1,234 £805	$1,234 £805	$1,234 £805
BAUSCH, LUDWIG CHRISTIAN AUGUST	1	1	$863 £533	$863 £533	$863 £533
BAUSCH, LUDWIG CHRISTIAN AUGUST (workshop of)	1	1	$374 £227	$374 £227	$374 £227
BAUSCH, OTTO	1	1	$805 £491	$805 £491	$805 £491
BAUSCH, OTTO (workshop of)	1	1	$805 £476	$805 £476	$805 £476
BAZIN	22	11	$232 £138	$5,356 £3,306	$1,462 £890
BAZIN (workshop of)	4	2	$633 £443	$2,113 £1,265	$1,373 £854
BAZIN, C.	1	1	$2,332 £1,380	$2,332 £1,380	$2,332 £1,380
BAZIN, CHARLES	16	12	$1,093 £656	$5,412 £3,220	$2,215 £1,396

Maker	Items		Selling Prices		
	Bid	Sold	Low	High	Avg
BAZIN, CHARLES (workshop of)	2	1	$2,070	$2,070	$2,070
			£1,346	£1,346	£1,346
BAZIN, CHARLES (II)	3	1	$559	$559	$559
			£345	£345	£345
BAZIN, CHARLES ALFRED	3	2	$1,540	$1,955	$1,748
			£1,020	£1,193	£1,106
BAZIN, CHARLES NICHOLAS	25	17	$1,152	$6,521	$2,312
			£690	£4,025	£1,444
BAZIN, CHARLES NICHOLAS (workshop of)	1	1	$2,233	$2,233	$2,233
			£1,451	£1,451	£1,451
BAZIN, LOUIS	25	22	$518	$4,416	$2,012
			£320	£2,777	£1,263
BAZIN, LOUIS (workshop of)	1	1	$374	$374	$374
			£224	£224	£224
BAZIN, LOUIS (II)	5	3	$347	$1,396	$954
			£207	£862	£586
BAZIN FAMILY (MEMBER OF)	3	1	$1,612	$1,612	$1,612
			£977	£977	£977
BAZIN FAMILY (MEMBER OF) (attributed to)	1	0			
BEARE, JOHN & ARTHUR	6	5	$1,588	$5,442	$3,156
			£1,035	£3,220	£1,897
BERNARD, J.P.	1	1	$1,009	$1,009	$1,009
			£635	£635	£635
BERNARDEL, GUSTAVE (workshop of)	1	1	$3,680	$3,680	$3,680
			£2,234	£2,234	£2,234
BERNARDEL, GUSTAVE ADOLPHE	1	1	$1,518	$1,518	$1,518
			£920	£920	£920
BERNARDEL, LEON	10	5	$412	$1,944	$970
			£253	£1,150	£591
BERNARDEL, LEON (workshop of)	2	2	$2,530	$4,025	$3,278
			£1,536	£2,443	£1,990
BETTS	1	1	$2,497	$2,497	$2,497
			£1,495	£1,495	£1,495
BETTS, JOHN	2	2	$1,786	$2,721	$2,254
			£1,124	£1,610	£1,367
BETTS, JOHN (ascribed to)	1	0			
BISHOP, EDGAR	1	1	$2,070	$2,070	$2,070
			£1,380	£1,380	£1,380
BLONDELET, H. EMILE	3	2	$1,942	$2,207	$2,074
			£1,265	£1,388	£1,327
BOLLINGER, JOSEPH	1	1	$920	$920	$920
			£552	£552	£552
BOURGUIGNON, MAURICE	1	1	$878	$878	$878
			£552	£552	£552
BOUVIN, JEAN	1	0			
BOVIS, FRANCOIS	1	1	$878	$878	$878
			£552	£552	£552
BRAMBACH, P. OTTO	1	0			
BRISTOW, S.E.	1	1	$883	$883	$883
			£575	£575	£575
BRISTOW, STEPHEN	2	2	$777	$1,845	$1,311
			£460	£1,092	£776

Maker	Items		Selling Prices		
	Bid	Sold	Low	High	Avg
BRUGERE FAMILY	1	1	$1,769	$1,769	$1,769
			£1,092	£1,092	£1,092
BRYANT	2	0			
BRYANT, P.W.	1	1	$1,316	$1,316	$1,316
			£920	£920	£920
BRYANT, PERCIVAL WILFRED	3	3	$1,057	$1,210	$1,131
			£690	£747	£709
BULTITUDE, ARTHUR RICHARD	20	18	$453	$5,390	$2,604
			£276	£3,335	£1,625
BUTHOD	2	2	$155	$169	$162
			£92	£104	£98
BUTHOD, CHARLES	1	0			
BUTHOD, CHARLES LOUIS	5	3	$1,125	$2,204	$1,638
			£690	£1,380	£1,035
BYROM, H.	1	1	$691	$691	$691
			£414	£414	£414
BYRON, J.	2	1	$468	$468	$468
			£299	£299	£299
CALLIER, FRANK	4	4	$331	$863	$543
			£205	£567	£349
CALLIER, PAUL J.	1	1	$1,495	$1,495	$1,495
			£984	£984	£984
CAPELA, ANTONIO	1	0			
CARESSA, ALBERT	6	4	$1,024	$3,304	$1,926
			£632	£1,955	£1,179
CARESSA & FRANCAIS	3	3	$1,749	$3,354	$2,423
			£1,035	£2,185	£1,533
CHALUPETZKY, F.	1	1	$1,057	$1,057	$1,057
			£690	£690	£690
CHANOT	1	1	$675	$675	$675
			£414	£414	£414
CHANOT (attributed to)	1	1	$12,523	$12,523	$12,523
			£7,475	£7,475	£7,475
CHANOT, G.A.	2	0			
CHANOT, GEORGE ADOLPH	1	1	$3,995	$3,995	$3,995
			£2,513	£2,513	£2,513
CHANOT & CHARDON	2	2	$914	$1,490	$1,202
			£575	£920	£748
CHARDON, ANDRE	1	1	$1,579	$1,579	$1,579
			£943	£943	£943
CHARDON, JOSEPH MARIE	1	0			
CHIPOT-VUILLAUME	2	0			
CLARK, JULIAN B.	2	1	$972	$972	$972
			£575	£575	£575
CLASQUIN, G.	3	2	$1,508	$2,185	$1,846
			£926	£1,311	£1,118
CLAUDOT, ALBERT	1	0			
CLUTTERBUCK, JOHN	1	1	$1,058	$1,058	$1,058
			£632	£632	£632
COCKER, L.	2	1	$174	$174	$174
			£104	£104	£104
COCKER, LAWRENCE	2	0			
COLAS, PROSPER	8	6	$693	$3,089	$1,650
			£414	£2,160	£1,091

Maker	Items		Selling Prices		
	Bid	Sold	Low	High	Avg
COLAS, PROSPER (attributed to)	2	0			
COLLENOT, LOUIS	1	1	$1,463	$1,463	$1,463
			£920	£920	£920
COLLIN-MEZIN	3	1	$2,113	$2,113	$2,113
			£1,265	£1,265	£1,265
COLLIN-MEZIN, CH.J.B.	3	3	$960	$2,915	$1,817
			£575	£1,725	£1,081
COLLIN-MEZIN, CH.J.B. (FILS)	1	0			
COLLIN-MEZIN, CH.J.B. (II)	2	0			
CONE, GEORGES & FILS	1	0			
CORSBY, GEORGE	1	1	$3,416	$3,416	$3,416
			£2,070	£2,070	£2,070
CUNIOT-HURY	8	6	$1,135	$2,113	$1,527
			£805	£1,265	£947
CUNIOT-HURY, EUGENE	18	13	$578	$1,630	$943
			£357	£1,140	£586
DARBEY, GEORGE	6	4	$838	$2,555	$1,310
			£518	£1,587	£814
DARCHE, HILAIRE	5	5	$214	$1,733	$1,173
			£124	£1,035	£703
DARCHE, NICHOLAS	1	1	$968	$968	$968
			£632	£632	£632
DELIVET, AUGUSTE	1	1	$2,467	$2,467	$2,467
			£1,495	£1,495	£1,495
DIDIER, PAUL	2	0			
DITER, PAUL FRANCOIS	1	0			
DITER BROTHERS	1	0			
DODD	11	6	$822	$1,944	$1,231
			£575	£1,150	£757
DODD (attributed to)	5	4	$700	$2,362	$1,428
			£414	£1,495	£909
DODD, J.	4	2	$556	$960	$758
			£345	£575	£460
DODD, JAMES	7	5	$863	$6,463	$2,431
			£561	£4,201	£1,555
DODD, JOHN	25	20	$651	$6,613	$2,913
			£402	£4,113	£1,837
DODD, JOHN (attributed to)	1	1	$989	$989	$989
			£644	£644	£644
DODD, JOHN KEW	2	2	$2,116	$2,645	$2,381
			£1,316	£1,719	£1,518
DODD, THOMAS	1	1	$2,400	$2,400	$2,400
			£1,656	£1,656	£1,656
DODD FAMILY	1	0			
DODD FAMILY (MEMBER OF)	2	1	$1,998	$1,998	$1,998
			£1,299	£1,299	£1,299
DOLLING, BERND	1	1	$740	$740	$740
			£483	£483	£483
DOLLING, HEINZ	10	7	$169	$1,472	$910
			£104	£926	£570
DOLLING, KURT	2	0			
DORFLER, EGIDIUS	1	1	$1,150	$1,150	$1,150
			£690	£690	£690

Maker	Items		Selling Prices		
	Bid	Sold	Low	High	Avg
DOTSCHKAIL, R.	1	0			
DUBOIS, VICTOR	1	1	$39	$39	$39
			£23	£23	£23
DUCHAINE	1	0			
DUCHAINE, NICHOLAS	1	0			
DUCHENE, NICOLAS	1	1	$1,480	$1,480	$1,480
			£1,035	£1,035	£1,035
DUGAD, ANDRE	3	1	$637	$637	$637
			£391	£391	£391
DUPREE, EMILE	1	0			
DUPUY	4	2	$1,760	$1,771	$1,765
			£1,035	£1,093	£1,064
DUPUY, GEORGE	2	1	$2,261	$2,261	$2,261
			£1,389	£1,389	£1,389
DUPUY, GEORGE (workshop of)	1	1	$1,725	$1,725	$1,725
			£1,047	£1,047	£1,047
DURRSCHMIDT, OTTO	5	3	$500	$604	$544
			£299	£368	£337
DURRSCHMIDT, WOLFGANG	2	0			
ENEL, CHARLES	5	5	$570	$1,631	$1,279
			£331	£1,080	£819
EURY, FRANCOIS	1	0			
EURY, FRANCOIS (ascribed to)	1	1	$1,412	$1,412	$1,412
			£920	£920	£920
EURY, NICOLAS	5	2	$3,534	$7,508	$5,521
			£2,300	£4,485	£3,393
EURY, NICOLAS (ascribed to)	1	1	$3,693	$3,693	$3,693
			£2,185	£2,185	£2,185
FAROTTO, CELESTINO	1	0			
FERRON & KROEPLIN	1	0			
FETIQUE, CHARLES	3	2	$863	$4,081	$2,472
			£517	£2,415	£1,466
FETIQUE, JULES	4	4	$5,750	$7,348	$6,281
			£3,450	£4,600	£4,025
FETIQUE, MARCEL	10	8	$3,154	$7,583	$4,156
			£1,984	£4,830	£2,644
FETIQUE, V.	1	1	$2,743	$2,743	$2,743
			£1,725	£1,725	£1,725
FETIQUE, VICTOR	59	45	$374	$15,614	$4,592
			£262	£9,775	£2,898
FETIQUE, VICTOR (ascribed to)	1	1	$2,574	$2,574	$2,574
			£1,800	£1,800	£1,800
FETIQUE, VICTOR (attributed to)	2	1	$4,844	$4,844	$4,844
			£2,990	£2,990	£2,990
FETIQUE, VICTOR (workshop of)	1	1	$978	$978	$978
			£587	£587	£587
FINKEL	4	2	$304	$1,259	$781
			£184	£863	£523
FINKEL (workshop of)	2	2	$705	$823	$764
			£458	£535	£497
FINKEL, JOHANN S.	1	0			
FINKEL, JOHANN S. (workshop of)	2	2	$316	$345	$331
			£187	£204	£196

Maker	Items Bid	Sold	Low	Selling Prices High	Avg
FINKEL, JOHANNES S.	4	2	$2,695 £1,610	$8,141 £5,026	$5,418 £3,318
FINKEL, SIEGFRIED	5	3	$772 £540	$1,898 £1,150	$1,325 £832
FLEURY, H.	3	2	$169 £104	$407 £265	$288 £184
FONCLAUSE, JOSEPH	3	1	$3,353 £2,070	$3,353 £2,070	$3,353 £2,070
FORSTER, WILLIAM	1	0			
FORSTER, WILLIAM (II)	2	1	$2,846 £1,725	$2,846 £1,725	$2,846 £1,725
FRANCAIS, EMILE	3	3	$600 £368	$2,467 £1,610	$1,463 £934
FRANCAIS, LUCIEN	3	1	$1,921 £1,150	$1,921 £1,150	$1,921 £1,150
FRITSCH, JEAN	3	2	$932 £575	$1,071 £661	$1,001 £618
GAND, CHARLES NICOLAS EUGENE	1	1	$2,528 £1,610	$2,528 £1,610	$2,528 £1,610
GAND BROS.	2	2	$525 £322	$1,944 £1,150	$1,234 £736
GAND & BERNARDEL	13	7	$1,312 £805	$5,301 £3,450	$2,759 £1,709
GAULARD	3	2	$2,875 £1,840	$5,053 £2,990	$3,964 £2,415
GAUTIE, P. & SON	1	1	$4,694 £2,990	$4,694 £2,990	$4,694 £2,990
GERMAIN, EMILE	1	1	$9,315 £5,750	$9,315 £5,750	$9,315 £5,750
GEROME, ROGER	10	8	$960 £575	$2,185 £1,333	$1,311 £819
GILLET	1	0			
GILLET, LOUIS	2	2	$1,677 £1,035	$1,928 £1,190	$1,802 £1,113
GOHDE, GREGORY	1	1	$540 £345	$540 £345	$540 £345
GOTZ, CONRAD	3	2	$428 £253	$745 £460	$586 £357
GOTZ, CONRAD (workshop of)	1	1	$1,093 £663	$1,093 £663	$1,093 £663
GRAND ADAM	3	0			
GREEN, HOWARD	3	3	$691 £414	$963 £575	$795 £475
GRIMM	2	2	$789 £483	$1,880 £1,150	$1,335 £817
GRUNKE, RICHARD	5	5	$920 £552	$2,185 £1,420	$1,503 £967
HART & SON	4	4	$706 £460	$2,357 £1,495	$1,835 £1,140
HART & SON (workshop of)	2	1	$1,610 £977	$1,610 £977	$1,610 £977
HAWKES & SON	1	1	$266 £161	$266 £161	$266 £161

| Maker | Items | | Selling Prices | | |
	Bid	Sold	Low	High	Avg
HEBERLEIN, HEINRICH TH.	1	1	$1,049 £621	$1,049 £621	$1,049 £621
HEL (workshop of)	1	1	$1,680 £1,159	$1,680 £1,159	$1,680 £1,159
HEL, PIERRE JOSEPH	1	0			
HENRY	1	1	$20,226 £12,075	$20,226 £12,075	$20,226 £12,075
HENRY, EUGENE	2	1	$914 £575	$914 £575	$914 £575
HENRY, J.V.	2	0			
HENRY, JOSEPH	6	3	$2,645 £1,645	$14,548 £9,019	$6,671 £4,168
HENRY, JOSEPH (attributed to)	1	1	$6,714 £4,370	$6,714 £4,370	$6,714 £4,370
HERMANN, A.	1	1	$269 £184	$269 £184	$269 £184
HERMANN, ADOLF	1	1	$334 £207	$334 £207	$334 £207
HERNOULT, HENRI (attributed to)	1	1	$1,921 £1,150	$1,921 £1,150	$1,921 £1,150
HERRMANN, A.	6	3	$293 £173	$1,035 £631	$567 £345
HERRMANN, AUGUST FRIEDRICH	1	1	$1,147 £747	$1,147 £747	$1,147 £747
HERRMANN, E.	2	2	$389 £253	$773 £460	$581 £357
HERRMANN, EMIL	4	3	$690 £454	$1,323 £823	$1,093 £683
HERRMANN, EMIL (workshop of)	1	1	$1,380 £908	$1,380 £908	$1,380 £908
HILL	1	1	$684 £437	$684 £437	$684 £437
HILL, W.E. & SONS	340	300	$327 £196	$10,082 £7,050	$2,546 £1,601
HILL, WILLIAM EBSWORTH	1	1	$1,380 £828	$1,380 £828	$1,380 £828
HOUFFLACK, G.	1	1	$1,829 £1,093	$1,829 £1,093	$1,829 £1,093
HOYER (attributed to)	1	1	$1,148 £748	$1,148 £748	$1,148 £748
HOYER, ADOLF	1	1	$849 £552	$849 £552	$849 £552
HOYER, C.A.	7	2	$58 £35	$1,051 £661	$555 £348
HOYER, OTTO	9	8	$173 £121	$1,265 £759	$850 £539
HOYER, OTTO (workshop of)	1	1	$920 £544	$920 £544	$920 £544
HOYER, OTTO A.	25	17	$387 £230	$2,889 £1,840	$1,096 £681
HOYER, OTTO A. (workshop of)	1	1	$661 £410	$661 £410	$661 £410
HUMS, ALBIN	2	2	$792 £517	$794 £517	$793 £517

| Maker | Items | | Selling Prices | | |
	Bid	Sold	Low	High	Avg
HURY, CUNIOT	4	4	$773 £483	$1,826 £1,127	$1,318 £805
HUSSON, AUGUST	4	3	$856 £497	$3,474 £2,185	$2,468 £1,507
HUSSON, CHARLES	1	1	$1,986 £1,265	$1,986 £1,265	$1,986 £1,265
HUSSON, CHARLES CLAUDE	7	4	$713 £414	$1,955 £1,187	$1,330 £797
HUSSON, CHARLES CLAUDE (attributed to)	1	1	$1,324 £862	$1,324 £862	$1,324 £862
HUSSON, CHARLES CLAUDE (II)	2	0			
JOMBAR, P.	1	1	$806 £552	$806 £552	$806 £552
JOMBAR, PAUL	10	5	$1,236 £805	$4,099 £2,530	$2,193 £1,413
KARON, JAN	1	1	$794 £492	$794 £492	$794 £492
KAUL, PAUL	1	0			
KEY, ALBERT E.	1	1	$374 £221	$374 £221	$374 £221
KITTEL (attributed to)	1	0			
KITTEL, NICOLAUS (ascribed to)	2	0			
KITTEL, NICOLAUS (attributed to)	3	3	$2,588 £1,584	$95,013 £58,650	$39,318 £24,266
KNOPF	1	0			
KNOPF (workshop of)	1	1	$748 £449	$748 £449	$748 £449
KNOPF, CHRISTIAN WILHELM	1	1	$6,463 £4,201	$6,463 £4,201	$6,463 £4,201
KNOPF, H.	1	1	$1,304 £805	$1,304 £805	$1,304 £805
KNOPF, H.R.	1	0			
KNOPF, HEINRICH	6	5	$616 £368	$2,812 £1,725	$1,483 £902
KNOPF, HENRY RICHARD	1	0			
KOLSTEIN, SAMUEL	2	2	$535 £330	$1,714 £1,058	$1,124 £694
KOUCKY, WILLIAM H.	1	1	$633 £391	$633 £391	$633 £391
KOVANDA, FRANK	1	0			
KREUSLER, ERNST	1	1	$360 £230	$360 £230	$360 £230
KUEHNL, EMIL	3	2	$115 £69	$1,495 £884	$805 £477
KUHNLA, STEFFEN	1	1	$315 £198	$315 £198	$315 £198
KUN, JOSEPH	1	1	$1,495 £884	$1,495 £884	$1,495 £884
LABERTE	5	3	$549 £345	$1,125 £690	$806 £498
LABERTE (attributed to)	1	0			
LABERTE, MARC	11	7	$187 £115	$2,528 £1,610	$1,066 £679

Maker	Items		Selling Prices		
	Bid	Sold	Low	High	Avg
LABERTE, MARC (workshop of)	3	1	$115	$115	$115
			£70	£70	£70
LAFLEUR	1	0			
LAFLEUR, JOSEPH RENE	4	3	$1,997	$3,841	$3,121
			£1,256	£2,300	£1,952
LAFLEUR, JOSEPH RENE (attributed to)	2	1	$631	$631	$631
			£397	£397	£397
LAMBERT, N.	2	2	$1,518	$1,646	$1,582
			£920	£1,035	£978
LAMY, A.	13	8	$4,225	$12,483	$7,815
			£2,530	£7,475	£4,765
LAMY, A. (ascribed to)	1	1	$1,175	$1,175	$1,175
			£822	£822	£822
LAMY, A. (attributed to)	3	1	$749	$749	$749
			£483	£483	£483
LAMY, A.J.	1	0			
LAMY, ALFRED	18	15	$920	$7,682	$4,839
			£561	£4,830	£3,010
LAMY, ALFRED (attributed to)	1	1	$1,265	$1,265	$1,265
			£774	£774	£774
LAMY, ALFRED JOSEPH	41	33	$1,087	$14,576	$5,881
			£667	£8,625	£3,612
LAMY, HIPPOLYTE CAMILLE	3	0			
LAMY, JULES	2	1	$3,069	$3,069	$3,069
			£1,955	£1,955	£1,955
LAMY, LOUIS	1	1	$1,765	$1,765	$1,765
			£1,150	£1,150	£1,150
LAMY, LOUIS (attributed to)	1	1	$835	$835	$835
			£506	£506	£506
LAMY FAMILY (MEMBER OF)	1	0			
LANDON, CHRISTOPHE	1	1	$3,525	$3,525	$3,525
			£2,291	£2,291	£2,291
LANGONET, EUGENE	1	0			
LANGONET, EUGENE (workshop of)	1	1	$1,955	$1,955	$1,955
			£1,187	£1,187	£1,187
LAPIERRE	2	2	$633	$1,151	$892
			£386	£805	£596
LAPIERRE, MARCEL	6	6	$1,265	$3,172	$1,771
			£759	£2,070	£1,116
LATOUR, ARMAND	1	1	$905	$905	$905
			£555	£555	£555
LAURY, N.	2	1	$1,697	$1,697	$1,697
			£1,035	£1,035	£1,035
LAUXERROIS, JEAN-PAUL	2	2	$1,145	$1,453	$1,299
			£747	£897	£822
LAVEST, MICHEL	1	1	$551	$551	$551
			£345	£345	£345
LECCHI, BERNARDO GIUSEPPE	1	0			
LEE, JOHN NORWOOD	7	4	$978	$2,357	$1,524
			£626	£1,455	£951
LEICHT, MAX	3	3	$673	$1,210	$866
			£402	£747	£533
LENOBLE, AUGUSTE	2	1	$7,498	$7,498	$7,498
			£4,600	£4,600	£4,600

| Maker | Items | | Selling Prices | | |
	Bid	Sold	Low	High	Avg
LORANGE, PAUL	1	0			
LOTTE, FRANCOIS	14	10	$1,116	$2,305	$1,493
			£690	£1,380	£902
LOTTE, ROGER	4	2	$2,523	$7,731	$5,127
			£1,587	£4,600	£3,094
LOTTE, ROGER-FRANCOIS	10	6	$822	$3,055	$1,862
			£517	£1,984	£1,149
LUCCHI, GIOVANNI	1	0			
LUPOT	4	3	$845	$7,398	$3,514
			£518	£4,830	£2,243
LUPOT, F. (attributed to)	2	0			
LUPOT, FRANCOIS	2	0			
LUPOT, FRANCOIS (II)	4	3	$2,648	$10,833	$6,437
			£1,725	£6,900	£4,025
LUPOT, NICOLAS	1	0			
MACKENZIE, D.C.	2	2	$705	$940	$823
			£458	£611	£535
MAGNIERE, GABRIEL	1	0			
MAIRE (workshop of)	1	1	$2,999	$2,999	$2,999
			£1,840	£1,840	£1,840
MAIRE, N. (workshop of)	2	2	$676	$5,762	$3,219
			£403	£3,450	£1,926
MAIRE, NICOLAS	7	5	$5,750	$25,300	$16,342
			£3,508	£14,964	£9,835
MAIRE, NICOLAS (attributed to)	1	0			
MAIRE, NICOLAS (workshop of)	1	1	$3,877	$3,877	$3,877
			£2,530	£2,530	£2,530
MAIRE, NICOLAS (II)	1	1	$6,729	$6,729	$6,729
			£4,232	£4,232	£4,232
MALINE (attributed to)	1	1	$3,947	$3,947	$3,947
			£2,760	£2,760	£2,760
MALINE (workshop of)	1	1	$4,388	$4,388	$4,388
			£2,760	£2,760	£2,760
MALINE, GUILLAUME	11	7	$3,531	$25,126	$10,242
			£2,300	£14,950	£6,232
MALINE, GUILLAUME (workshop of)	1	0			
MARCOLTE	1	0			
MARISSAL, OLIVIER	1	1	$858	$858	$858
			£600	£600	£600
MARTIN, J.	1	1	$758	$758	$758
			£483	£483	£483
MARTIN, J. (attributed to)	2	1	$1,782	$1,782	$1,782
			£1,093	£1,093	£1,093
MARTIN, JEAN JOSEPH	8	6	$2,167	$5,486	$3,668
			£1,380	£3,450	£2,292
MATTHEWS, PHILIP	1	0			
MAUCOTEL & DESCHAMPS	4	3	$347	$1,236	$895
			£207	£805	£567
MCGILL, A.	1	0			
MEINEL, F.	1	0			
MENNESSON, EMILE	2	0			
METTAL, WALTER	2	1	$690	$690	$690
			£422	£422	£422

Maker	Items		Selling Prices		
	Bid	Sold	Low	High	Avg
MILLANT, B.	2	1	$2,899	$2,899	$2,899
			£1,725	£1,725	£1,725
MILLANT, JEAN-JACQUES	1	1	$3,887	$3,887	$3,887
			£2,300	£2,300	£2,300
MILLANT, M.	2	1	$1,360	$1,360	$1,360
			£805	£805	£805
MILLANT, ROGER	1	1	$1,829	$1,829	$1,829
			£1,150	£1,150	£1,150
MILLANT, ROGER & MAX	6	4	$823	$2,657	$1,432
			£518	£1,610	£910
MIQUEL, E.	2	1	$1,160	$1,160	$1,160
			£690	£690	£690
MIQUEL FAMILY (MEMBER OF)	1	0			
MOHR, RODNEY D.	1	1	$690	$690	$690
			£414	£414	£414
MOINEL & CHERPITEL	1	1	$2,167	$2,167	$2,167
			£1,380	£1,380	£1,380
MOLLER, M.	1	1	$1,642	$1,642	$1,642
			£977	£977	£977
MOLLER & ZOON	2	1	$1,635	$1,635	$1,635
			£977	£977	£977
MONNIG, A. HERMANN	2	1	$450	$450	$450
			£276	£276	£276
MORIZOT (attributed to)	1	0			
MORIZOT, L.	6	5	$740	$3,947	$1,802
			£518	£2,760	£1,215
MORIZOT, LOUIS	31	23	$615	$5,700	$2,105
			£368	£3,933	£1,343
MORIZOT, LOUIS (attributed to)	1	1	$1,495	$1,495	$1,495
			£912	£912	£912
MORIZOT, LOUIS (II)	16	11	$944	$4,571	$2,413
			£660	£2,875	£1,517
MORIZOT (FRERES), LOUIS	5	4	$731	$1,344	$1,134
			£460	£805	£690
MORIZOT FRERES	1	0			
MORIZOT FAMILY	8	6	$748	$2,530	$1,379
			£456	£1,518	£835
MORTH	1	0			
MOUGENOT, LEON	2	1	$794	$794	$794
			£517	£517	£517
MULLER, FRIEDRICH KARL	1	1	$1,928	$1,928	$1,928
			£1,190	£1,190	£1,190
NAVEA-VERA, DANIEL	1	1	$1,725	$1,725	$1,725
			£1,104	£1,104	£1,104
NEHR, J.P.	1	0			
NEUDORFER, RUDOLPH	2	1	$2,746	$2,746	$2,746
			£1,920	£1,920	£1,920
NEUVILLE	1	1	$396	$396	$396
			£253	£253	£253
NORRIS & BARNES	1	1	$1,359	$1,359	$1,359
			£900	£900	£900
NURNBERGER	1	1	$1,125	$1,125	$1,125
			£697	£697	£697

Maker	Items Bid	Sold	Low	Selling Prices High	Avg
NURNBERGER (workshop of)	4	4	$144 £101	$1,265 £759	$714 £462
NURNBERGER, ALBERT	63	54	$288 £175	$3,462 £2,248	$1,355 £854
NURNBERGER, ALBERT (attributed to)	3	1	$1,121 £690	$1,121 £690	$1,121 £690
NURNBERGER, ALBERT (workshop of)	3	2	$403 £282	$805 £497	$604 £390
NURNBERGER, CH.	1	1	$575 £378	$575 £378	$575 £378
NURNBERGER, CHRISTIAN ALBERT	6	4	$1,536 £920	$2,523 £1,587	$1,828 £1,133
NURNBERGER, FRANZ ALBERT (II)	1	1	$1,440 £994	$1,440 £994	$1,440 £994
NURNBERGER, KARL ALBERT	33	27	$865 £517	$3,457 £2,070	$1,778 £1,100
NURNBERGER, KARL ALBERT (II)	1	1	$2,295 £1,495	$2,295 £1,495	$2,295 £1,495
NURNBERGER-SUESS, AUGUST	1	1	$1,162 £713	$1,162 £713	$1,162 £713
OUCHARD, B.	2	2	$3,785 £2,381	$5,693 £3,450	$4,739 £2,915
OUCHARD, BERNARD	2	1	$3,540 £2,185	$3,540 £2,185	$3,540 £2,185
OUCHARD, E.	3	1	$4,592 £2,875	$4,592 £2,875	$4,592 £2,875
OUCHARD, EMILE	23	15	$904 £632	$6,038 £3,623	$2,811 £1,699
OUCHARD, EMILE (FILS)	1	1	$6,856 £4,232	$6,856 £4,232	$6,856 £4,232
OUCHARD, EMILE A.	17	13	$519 £310	$12,855 £7,935	$5,832 £3,617
OUCHARD, EMILE FRANCOIS	16	14	$1,405 £862	$11,141 £6,877	$3,579 £2,263
OUCHARD, J.CL. (attributed to)	2	0			
OUDINOT	1	0			
PAESOLD, RODERICH	1	0			
PAJEOT	5	3	$6,217 £3,910	$11,765 £7,130	$9,055 £5,597
PAJEOT, E.	2	1	$4,830 £3,220	$4,830 £3,220	$4,830 £3,220
PAJEOT, ETIENNE	16	10	$2,291 £1,495	$19,150 £13,213	$9,655 £6,196
PAJEOT, LOUIS SIMON	6	3	$1,682 £1,058	$13,926 £8,596	$8,860 £5,518
PAJEOT, LOUIS SIMON (attributed to)	1	0			
PAJEOT FAMILY (MEMBER OF)	1	0			
PAJEOT-MAIRE	1	1	$4,462 £3,120	$4,462 £3,120	$4,462 £3,120
PANORMO	1	0			
PANORMO, LOUIS	3	1	$960 £575	$960 £575	$960 £575
PASSA, FRANK	1	1	$690 £454	$690 £454	$690 £454

Maker	Items Bid	Sold	Selling Prices Low	High	Avg
PATIGNY, PIERRE	4	3	$3,009 £1,840	$5,570 £3,439	$4,288 £2,641
PAULUS, GUNTER A.	2	1	$1,344 £805	$1,344 £805	$1,344 £805
PAULUS, JOHANNES O.	2	1	$792 £517	$792 £517	$792 £517
PAULUS, OTTO	1	1	$792 £517	$792 £517	$792 £517
PECCATTE, C.	1	0			
PECCATTE, CHARLES	8	7	$2,138 £1,265	$14,097 £9,200	$6,749 £4,366
PECCATTE, D. & HENRY, J.	1	1	$7,682 £4,600	$7,682 £4,600	$7,682 £4,600
PECCATTE, DOMINIQUE	9	7	$5,286 £3,450	$41,527 £28,290	$25,938 £16,691
PECCATTE, DOMINIQUE (ascribed to)	2	1	$27,209 £16,100	$27,209 £16,100	$27,209 £16,100
PECCATTE, FRANCOIS	1	1	$27,852 £17,193	$27,852 £17,193	$27,852 £17,193
PECCATTE FAMILY (MEMBER OF)	4	2	$15,836 £9,775	$21,666 £13,800	$18,751 £11,788
PENZEL	1	1	$367 £219	$367 £219	$367 £219
PENZEL, E.	1	1	$436 £305	$436 £305	$436 £305
PENZEL, E.M.	1	1	$863 £524	$863 £524	$863 £524
PENZEL, GERHARD	1	1	$518 £336	$518 £336	$518 £336
PENZEL, K. GERHARD	3	2	$870 £576	$2,118 £1,380	$1,494 £978
PERSOIS	4	2	$20,165 £12,075	$34,305 £21,850	$27,235 £16,963
PERSOIS, JEAN (attributed to)	1	1	$4,805 £3,360	$4,805 £3,360	$4,805 £3,360
PERSOIS, JEAN-PIERRE-MARIE	1	1	$56,868 £35,258	$56,868 £35,258	$56,868 £35,258
PFRETZSCHNER	4	3	$469 £288	$756 £518	$565 £376
PFRETZSCHNER (attributed to)	1	1	$940 £575	$940 £575	$940 £575
PFRETZSCHNER (workshop of)	1	1	$1,150 £805	$1,150 £805	$1,150 £805
PFRETZSCHNER, C.F.	1	0			
PFRETZSCHNER, E.R.	1	1	$1,035 £673	$1,035 £673	$1,035 £673
PFRETZSCHNER, G.A.	5	5	$460 £276	$1,380 £828	$765 £461
PFRETZSCHNER, H.R.	52	41	$259 £181	$3,785 £2,381	$1,241 £778
PFRETZSCHNER, H.R. (workshop of)	1	1	$489 £293	$489 £293	$489 £293
PFRETZSCHNER, HERMANN RICHARD	1	1	$1,736 £1,092	$1,736 £1,092	$1,736 £1,092

Maker	Items		Selling Prices		
	Bid	Sold	Low	High	Avg
PFRETZSCHNER, L.	3	1	$1,208 £805	$1,208 £805	$1,208 £805
PFRETZSCHNER, L. (attributed to)	1	1	$1,007 £656	$1,007 £656	$1,007 £656
PFRETZSCHNER, W.	2	1	$442 £276	$442 £276	$442 £276
PFRETZSCHNER, W.A.	4	4	$280 £172	$1,610 £982	$838 £506
PFRETZSCHNER, WILHELM AUGUST	2	1	$1,353 £862	$1,353 £862	$1,353 £862
PILLOT	2	2	$736 £460	$1,728 £1,035	$1,232 £748
POIRSON	3	0			
POIRSON, JUSTIN	8	4	$294 £185	$3,430 £2,185	$2,035 £1,294
POIRSON, JUSTIN (attributed to)	1	1	$2,185 £1,333	$2,185 £1,333	$2,185 £1,333
PRAGA, EUGENIO	1	0			
PRAGER, AUGUST EDWIN	13	12	$576 £345	$2,310 £1,495	$1,432 £869
PRAGER, GUSTAV	8	6	$352 £219	$829 £517	$585 £381
PRAGER, GUSTAV OSKAR	2	2	$922 £552	$1,093 £688	$1,008 £620
PRELL, HERMAN WILHELM	9	6	$380 £253	$1,114 £725	$688 £428
RAHM, WILHELM	1	1	$1,412 £920	$1,412 £920	$1,412 £920
RAPOPORT, HAIM (attributed to)	6	2	$338 £207	$338 £207	$338 £207
RAU	1	0			
RAU, AUGUST	9	6	$375 £230	$2,233 £1,451	$1,280 £800
REICHEL	1	1	$226 £138	$226 £138	$226 £138
REIDEL, E.	1	1	$460 £272	$460 £272	$460 £272
RETFORD, WILLIAM	1	0			
RETFORD, WILLIAM C.	1	0			
RICHAUME	1	0			
RICHAUME, ANDRE	5	5	$3,348 £2,185	$8,998 £5,555	$6,325 £3,940
ROBICHAUD	1	1	$1,536 £920	$1,536 £920	$1,536 £920
ROCKWELL, DAVID BAILEY	1	1	$403 £238	$403 £238	$403 £238
ROLLAND	1	1	$5,762 £3,450	$5,762 £3,450	$5,762 £3,450
ROLLAND, BENOIT	2	2	$1,177 £727	$1,380 £853	$1,279 £790
ROLLAND, S.	1	0			
ROTH, ERNST HEINRICH	1	1	$201 £141	$201 £141	$201 £141

| Maker | Items | | Selling Prices | | |
	Bid	Sold	Low	High	Avg
ROTH, ERNST HEINRICH (workshop of)	1	1	$805	$805	$805
			£489	£489	£489
SANDNER, A.L.	1	0			
SARTORY, E.	10	8	$6,210	$18,630	$10,479
			£4,140	£11,500	£6,922
SARTORY, EUGENE	124	103	$734	$21,850	$8,442
			£437	£13,264	£5,306
SARTORY, EUGENE (attributed to)	2	2	$2,689	$3,498	$3,094
			£1,610	£2,070	£1,840
SARTORY, EUGENE (workshop of)	2	2	$3,226	$3,658	$3,442
			£1,955	£2,185	£2,070
SCHICKER, HORST	2	0			
SCHINDLER, GUSTAV	1	1	$863	$863	$863
			£604	£604	£604
SCHMIDT, HANS KARL	1	0			
SCHMITT, LUCIEN	1	1	$1,518	$1,518	$1,518
			£920	£920	£920
SCHUBERT, PAUL	1	1	$149	$149	$149
			£92	£92	£92
SCHULLER	1	1	$601	$601	$601
			£391	£391	£391
SCHULTZ, T.	1	1	$348	$348	$348
			£230	£230	£230
SCHUSTER, ADOLF	5	3	$839	$1,150	$971
			£587	£711	£648
SCHUSTER, ADOLF C.	1	1	$1,848	$1,848	$1,848
			£1,292	£1,292	£1,292
SCHUSTER, ADOLPH CURT	3	3	$916	$1,490	$1,128
			£593	£920	£704
SCHUSTER, ALBERT	1	1	$489	$489	$489
			£318	£318	£318
SCHUSTER, GOTHARD	4	3	$186	$1,210	$788
			£115	£747	£479
SCHUSTER, M.K.	1	0			
SCHUSTER, MAX K.	1	1	$1,035	$1,035	$1,035
			£621	£621	£621
SCHUSTER, W.R.	1	1	$431	$431	$431
			£288	£288	£288
SCHUSTER, WILHELM R.	1	1	$805	$805	$805
			£489	£489	£489
SEIFERT, LOTHAR	16	10	$288	$2,999	$1,213
			£173	£1,852	£746
SEIFERT, W.	1	1	$487	$487	$487
			£322	£322	£322
SERDET, PAUL	4	2	$575	$1,631	$1,103
			£345	£1,080	£713
SILVESTRE & MAUCOTEL	5	2	$2,422	$2,819	$2,621
			£1,495	£1,840	£1,668
SILVESTRE & MAUCOTEL (workshop of)	2	1	$1,725	$1,725	$1,725
			£1,047	£1,047	£1,047
SIMON, F.R.	1	0			
SIMON, PAUL	7	5	$2,118	$13,978	$6,254
			£1,380	£9,775	£4,094

| Maker | Items | | Selling Prices | | |
	Bid	Sold	Low	High	Avg
SIMON, PAUL (ascribed to)	1	1	$4,664 £2,760	$4,664 £2,760	$4,664 £2,760
SIMON, PAUL (attributed to)	1	1	$4,140 £2,484	$4,140 £2,484	$4,140 £2,484
SIMON, PIERRE	4	4	$13,200 £9,108	$38,125 £26,306	$22,564 £15,407
SIMON BROS.	2	1	$1,874 £1,150	$1,874 £1,150	$1,874 £1,150
SMITH, THOMAS	1	1	$4,071 £2,513	$4,071 £2,513	$4,071 £2,513
STOHR, H.A.	1	1	$207 £127	$207 £127	$207 £127
STOSS, ARNOLD	1	1	$1,323 £820	$1,323 £820	$1,323 £820
STUBER, JOHANN	1	1	$1,234 £805	$1,234 £805	$1,234 £805
SUESS, AUGUST NURNBERGER	1	1	$410 £253	$410 £253	$410 £253
SUSS, CARL	1	1	$632 £379	$632 £379	$632 £379
TAYLOR, MALCOLM	6	2	$805 £489	$1,643 £978	$1,224 £733
TAYLOR, MICHAEL J.	1	1	$2,295 £1,495	$2,295 £1,495	$2,295 £1,495
THIBOUT, JACQUES PIERRE	1	1	$3,001 £1,955	$3,001 £1,955	$3,001 £1,955
THIBOUVILLE-LAMY, J.	18	12	$428 £253	$1,646 £1,035	$838 £525
THIBOUVILLE-LAMY, JEROME	4	2	$1,371 £862	$1,677 £1,035	$1,524 £949
THOMA, A.	1	1	$151 £104	$151 £104	$151 £104
THOMA, ADOLF	1	1	$1,018 £661	$1,018 £661	$1,018 £661
THOMA, ARTHUR	4	0			
THOMA, MATHIAS	1	1	$1,304 £805	$1,304 £805	$1,304 £805
THOMASSIN	2	1	$1,068 £632	$1,068 £632	$1,068 £632
THOMASSIN (attributed to)	1	0			
THOMASSIN, C.	12	9	$411 £288	$6,762 £4,025	$2,412 £1,524
THOMASSIN, CLAUDE	35	28	$673 £414	$5,198 £3,105	$2,539 £1,582
THOMASSIN, CLAUDE (attributed to)	1	0			
THOMASSIN, CLAUDE (workshop of)	1	0			
TILLOTSON, J.	1	1	$730 £460	$730 £460	$730 £460
TOURNIER, JOSEPH ALEXIS	1	1	$3,416 £2,070	$3,416 £2,070	$3,416 £2,070
TOURNIER, JOSEPH ALEXIS (workshop of)	1	1	$2,530 £1,536	$2,530 £1,536	$2,530 £1,536
TOURTE, FRANCOIS	2	1	$76,684 £49,795	$76,684 £49,795	$76,684 £49,795

Maker	Items		Selling Prices		
	Bid	Sold	Low	High	Avg
TOURTE, FRANCOIS (ascribed to)	1	0			
TOURTE, FRANCOIS (attributed to)	1	1	$9,775	$9,775	$9,775
			£5,934	£5,934	£5,934
TOURTE, FRANCOIS XAVIER	4	3	$49,276	$68,372	$59,212
			£30,418	£42,205	£36,551
TOURTE, LOUIS (PERE)	3	3	$5,589	$20,353	$10,790
			£3,450	£12,564	£6,660
TOURTE, XAVIER (ascribed to)	2	1	$5,303	$5,303	$5,303
			£3,335	£3,335	£3,335
TOURTE, XAVIER (L'AINE) (ascribed to)	1	0			
TOURTE FAMILY	1	0			
TOURTE FAMILY (ascribed to)	1	0			
TUA, SILVIO	2	0			
TUBBS	2	2	$664	$1,312	$988
			£403	£805	£604
TUBBS (attributed to)	1	0			
TUBBS, ALFRED	2	1	$2,608	$2,608	$2,608
			£1,610	£1,610	£1,610
TUBBS, C.E.	2	0			
TUBBS, EDWARD	2	2	$1,725	$1,840	$1,783
			£1,104	£1,122	£1,113
TUBBS, J.	4	2	$2,981	$3,353	$3,167
			£1,840	£2,070	£1,955
TUBBS, JAMES	125	93	$729	$18,000	$4,647
			£483	£12,420	£2,911
TUBBS, JAMES (attributed to)	5	4	$720	$1,480	$1,120
			£460	£874	£699
TUBBS, T. (attributed to)	4	2	$103	$1,397	$750
			£63	£863	£463
TUBBS, THOMAS	2	2	$2,248	$3,348	$2,798
			£1,394	£2,185	£1,789
TUBBS, WILLIAM	4	1	$1,579	$1,579	$1,579
			£1,104	£1,104	£1,104
TUBBS, WILLIAM (attributed to)	3	3	$2,109	$2,926	$2,385
			£1,265	£1,840	£1,495
UEBEL, K. WERNER	2	0			
ULLMANN, GIORGIO	3	1	$856	$856	$856
			£497	£497	£497
VAN DER MEER, KAREL	5	3	$91	$2,236	$1,262
			£57	£1,380	£819
VEDRAL, JOSEPH	2	2	$1,118	$1,285	$1,202
			£690	£794	£742
VICKERS, J.E.	4	2	$226	$244	$235
			£138	£150	£144
VICTOR, T.	1	1	$1,864	$1,864	$1,864
			£1,150	£1,150	£1,150
VIDOUDEZ, PIERRE	5	3	$480	$2,588	$1,580
			£287	£1,553	£977
VIGNERON, A.	17	12	$1,280	$7,079	$4,368
			£805	£4,370	£2,808
VIGNERON, A. (attributed to)	2	0			
VIGNERON, ANDRE	13	10	$841	$6,722	$4,517
			£529	£4,140	£2,849

Maker	Items		Selling Prices		
	Bid	Sold	Low	High	Avg
VIGNERON, ARTHUR	1	1	$8,694 £5,175	$8,694 £5,175	$8,694 £5,175
VIGNERON, JOSEPH ARTHUR	36	30	$589 £370	$13,283 £8,200	$4,722 £2,899
VIGNERON, JOSEPH ARTHUR (attributed to)	1	1	$2,049 £1,265	$2,049 £1,265	$2,049 £1,265
VOIGT, ARNOLD	8	6	$675 £402	$1,320 £805	$832 £507
VOIGT, WERNER	1	1	$451 £276	$451 £276	$451 £276
VOIRIN, F.N.	9	5	$5,288 £3,437	$12,110 £7,475	$7,899 £4,930
VOIRIN, FRANCOIS NICOLAS	79	52	$1,009 £635	$42,849 £26,450	$7,438 £4,657
VOIRIN, FRANCOIS NICOLAS (ascribed to)	1	0			
VOIRIN, J.	5	1	$1,031 £633	$1,031 £633	$1,031 £633
VOIRIN, JOSEPH	7	5	$1,304 £805	$4,590 £2,990	$2,521 £1,611
VUILLAUME	1	1	$168 £115	$168 £115	$168 £115
VUILLAUME (workshop of)	3	2	$2,560 £1,610	$4,081 £2,415	$3,321 £2,013
VUILLAUME, JEAN BAPTISTE	31	23	$1,059 £690	$12,633 £7,935	$6,491 £4,014
VUILLAUME, JEAN BAPTISTE (attributed to)	1	0			
VUILLAUME, JEAN BAPTISTE (workshop of)	2	2	$2,990 £1,824	$3,220 £1,964	$3,105 £1,894
VUILLAUME, NICOLAS (workshop of)	1	1	$1,264 £805	$1,264 £805	$1,264 £805
WATSON, WILLIAM	6	5	$1,344 £805	$3,000 £2,070	$2,032 £1,332
WEICHOLD	7	5	$283 £173	$863 £517	$562 £340
WEICHOLD, R.	2	2	$1,025 £633	$2,585 £1,680	$1,805 £1,156
WEICHOLD, RICHARD	24	19	$489 £293	$1,725 £1,056	$959 £590
WEIDEMANN, R.	1	1	$696 £414	$696 £414	$696 £414
WEIDHAAS, PAUL	3	2	$1,415 £920	$1,682 £1,058	$1,548 £989
WEIMER, CARL	1	1	$900 £555	$900 £555	$900 £555
WEISCHOLD, R.	1	1	$495 £322	$495 £322	$495 £322
WERNER, EMIL	3	2	$542 £345	$1,687 £1,035	$1,114 £690
WERRO, HENRY	2	0			
WILSON, GARNER	9	7	$684 £437	$1,751 £1,092	$1,319 £837

Maker	Items		Selling Prices		
	Bid	Sold	Low	High	Avg
WINKLER, F.	3	3	$205	$588	$456
			£127	£403	£302
WITHERS, EDWARD	1	1	$576	$576	$576
			£368	£368	£368
WITHERS, EDWARD & SONS	1	0			
WITHERS, GEORGE	2	2	$705	$811	$758
			£460	£529	£495
WITHERS, GEORGE & SONS	3	3	$773	$1,829	$1,381
			£460	£1,150	£843
WUNDERLICH	1	1	$302	$302	$302
			£207	£207	£207
WUNDERLICH, F.R.	1	1	$451	$451	$451
			£276	£276	£276
WUNDERLICH, FRIEDRICH	7	6	$403	$1,500	$994
			£276	£977	£626
WURLITZER, REMBERT	1	1	$651	$651	$651
			£402	£402	£402
YOUNG, DAVID RUSSELL	1	0			
ZABINSKI, ROGER ALFONS	2	2	$518	$546	$532
			£311	£328	£319
ZAPF, H. WALTER	2	0			
ZIMMERMANN, JULIUS HEINRICH	1	0			

VIOLONCELLO

Maker	Items		Selling Prices		
	Bid	Sold	Low	High	Avg
ALBANI, MICHAEL	1	0			
ALBERTI, FERDINANDO (attributed to)	2	1	$1,852	$1,852	$1,852
			£1,152	£1,152	£1,152
ALLETSEE, PAULUS	1	1	$15,882	$15,882	$15,882
			£10,350	£10,350	£10,350
ANTONIAZZI, RICCARDO (attributed to)	1	0			
APPARUT, GEORGES (workshop of)	3	1	$9,315	$9,315	$9,315
			£5,750	£5,750	£5,750
ARCANGELI, ULDERICO	1	0			
BAADER, J.A. (attributed to)	1	1	$2,608	$2,608	$2,608
			£1,610	£1,610	£1,610
BACZYNSKI, LADISLAUS	1	0			
BAILEY, G.E.	1	0			
BAILLY, CHARLES	1	1	$6,914	$6,914	$6,914
			£4,140	£4,140	£4,140
BAILLY, PAUL	2	0			
BANDINI, MARIO	2	2	$5,589	$6,738	$6,163
			£3,450	£4,025	£3,738
BANKS, BENJAMIN	1	0			
BANKS, JAMES & HENRY	1	0			
BANKS, STEPHENSON (attributed to)	2	1	$1,738	$1,738	$1,738
			£1,150	£1,150	£1,150
BARBE, F.J.	1	1	$46,575	$46,575	$46,575
			£28,750	£28,750	£28,750
BARKER	1	1	$1,217	$1,217	$1,217
			£805	£805	£805
BARRETT, JOHN	2	0			

| Maker | Items | | Selling Prices | | |
	Bid	Sold	Low	High	Avg
BERNARDEL, AUGUST SEBASTIEN PHILIPPE	1	1	$61,289 £36,700	$61,289 £36,700	$61,289 £36,700
BERNARDEL, GUSTAVE	3	1	$24,714 £16,100	$24,714 £16,100	$24,714 £16,100
BERNARDEL, GUSTAVE (workshop of)	1	1	$20,700 £12,627	$20,700 £12,627	$20,700 £12,627
BERNARDEL, GUSTAVE ADOLPHE	1	0			
BERNARDEL, LEON	4	3	$11,500 £7,475	$22,770 £13,800	$16,615 £10,158
BERNARDEL, LEON (workshop of)	1	1	$4,694 £2,990	$4,694 £2,990	$4,694 £2,990
BETTS	3	2	$23,771 £14,950	$34,983 £20,700	$29,377 £17,825
BETTS (ascribed to)	1	1	$5,262 £3,680	$5,262 £3,680	$5,262 £3,680
BETTS, JOHN	3	1	$3,353 £2,070	$3,353 £2,070	$3,353 £2,070
BINA, J.	1	1	$6,165 £4,025	$6,165 £4,025	$6,165 £4,025
BISIACH (workshop of)	1	1	$37,950 £23,000	$37,950 £23,000	$37,950 £23,000
BISIACH, LEANDRO & GIACOMO	2	1	$34,983 £20,700	$34,983 £20,700	$34,983 £20,700
BLANCHI, ALBERTO	1	1	$28,117 £17,250	$28,117 £17,250	$28,117 £17,250
BLONDELET, H. EMILE	2	1	$10,925 £7,101	$10,925 £7,101	$10,925 £7,101
BOLINK, JAAP	1	1	$4,947 £3,220	$4,947 £3,220	$4,947 £3,220
BONORA, GIUSEPPE (ascribed to)	1	1	$10,925 £6,462	$10,925 £6,462	$10,925 £6,462
BOULLANGIER, CHARLES	1	0			
BOURLIER, NICOLAS	1	1	$10,296 £7,200	$10,296 £7,200	$10,296 £7,200
BOUSSU, JOSEPH BENOIT	1	1	$20,700 £12,627	$20,700 £12,627	$20,700 £12,627
BRIGGS, JAMES WILLIAM	2	2	$16,429 £9,775	$23,194 £13,800	$19,811 £11,788
BRYANT, PAUL	1	1	$1,604 £1,035	$1,604 £1,035	$1,604 £1,035
BUCHESTETTER, GABRIEL DAVID	1	1	$13,782 £8,970	$13,782 £8,970	$13,782 £8,970
BUTHOD, CHARLES LOUIS	4	4	$3,889 £2,530	$21,202 £13,800	$11,287 £7,188
CALCAGNI, BERNARDO	2	2	$34,466 £21,275	$156,500 £95,778	$95,483 £58,527
CARCASSI, LORENZO & TOMMASO	3	3	$73,220 £47,700	$176,985 £109,250	$134,702 £83,983
CARCASSI, TOMMASO	1	0			
CASINI, ANTONIO	1	0			
CASINI, SERAFINO	1	0			
CATENI, PIETRO	2	0			

Maker	Items Bid	Sold	Selling Prices Low	High	Avg
CAUSSIN, FRANCOIS	1	1	$6,176 £4,025	$6,176 £4,025	$6,176 £4,025
CAVALLI, ARISTIDE	1	1	$14,059 £8,625	$14,059 £8,625	$14,059 £8,625
CAVANI, GIOVANNI	1	1	$26,450 £18,515	$26,450 £18,515	$26,450 £18,515
CERUTI, GIUSEPPE (ascribed to)	3	1	$16,203 £10,350	$16,203 £10,350	$16,203 £10,350
CHANOT, FRANCOIS	1	1	$4,276 £2,990	$4,276 £2,990	$4,276 £2,990
CHANOT, GEORGES (II)	2	1	$56,775 £35,708	$56,775 £35,708	$56,775 £35,708
CHANOT, JOSEPH ANTHONY	1	1	$17,874 £11,241	$17,874 £11,241	$17,874 £11,241
CHARDON & FILS	2	1	$9,373 £5,750	$9,373 £5,750	$9,373 £5,750
CHARETTE, PIERRE	1	1	$2,300 £1,403	$2,300 £1,403	$2,300 £1,403
CHAROTTE, VICTOR JOSEPH	1	1	$3,457 £2,070	$3,457 £2,070	$3,457 £2,070
CHRISTA, JOSEPH PAULUS	1	0			
COCKER, LAWRENCE	1	1	$5,659 £3,680	$5,659 £3,680	$5,659 £3,680
COINUS, ANDRE	2	1	$2,960 £2,070	$2,960 £2,070	$2,960 £2,070
COLAS, PROSPER	1	1	$12,563 £7,475	$12,563 £7,475	$12,563 £7,475
COLLIN-MEZIN, CH.J.B.	5	3	$21,107 £13,800	$26,422 £17,250	$23,191 £14,950
COLLIN-MEZIN, CH.J.B. (workshop of)	1	1	$4,888 £2,891	$4,888 £2,891	$4,888 £2,891
COLLIN-MEZIN, CH.J.B. (III)	2	1	$2,305 £1,380	$2,305 £1,380	$2,305 £1,380
CONIA, STEFANO	1	1	$16,740 £10,925	$16,740 £10,925	$16,740 £10,925
COSTA, FELIX MORI (attributed to)	1	1	$57,500 £35,075	$57,500 £35,075	$57,500 £35,075
CRASKE, GEORGE	5	2	$14,490 £8,625	$20,700 £13,800	$17,595 £11,213
CUISSET, A.	4	1	$4,715 £2,875	$4,715 £2,875	$4,715 £2,875
CURLETTO, ANSELMO	2	1	$11,385 £6,900	$11,385 £6,900	$11,385 £6,900
CUTHBERT, ROBERT	1	1	$11,811 £7,475	$11,811 £7,475	$11,811 £7,475
CUYPERS, JOHANNES	3	1	$9,538 £6,670	$9,538 £6,670	$9,538 £6,670
DARCHE, HILAIRE	3	1	$13,605 £8,050	$13,605 £8,050	$13,605 £8,050
DEARLOVE	1	1	$4,862 £3,220	$4,862 £3,220	$4,862 £3,220
DEARLOVE, MARK WILLIAM	1	1	$9,853 £5,865	$9,853 £5,865	$9,853 £5,865
DEARLOVE, WILLIAM	2	1	$2,768 £1,719	$2,768 £1,719	$2,768 £1,719

Maker	Items		Selling Prices		
	Bid	Sold	Low	High	Avg
DECONET, MICHELE	2	0			
DECONET, MICHELE (ascribed to)	1	0			
DEGANI, EUGENIO	2	2	$32,200	$59,700	$45,950
			£19,896	£36,241	£28,069
DE MARCH, CARLO	1	1	$23,472	$23,472	$23,472
			£14,950	£14,950	£14,950
DERAZEY, HONORE	1	1	$36,992	$36,992	$36,992
			£21,850	£21,850	£21,850
DERAZEY, JUSTIN	1	0			
DIEUDONNE, A. (attributed to)	2	1	$3,820	$3,820	$3,820
			£2,530	£2,530	£2,530
DIEUDONNE, AMEDEE	1	0			
DODD, THOMAS	4	1	$34,776	$34,776	$34,776
			£20,700	£20,700	£20,700
DOLLENZ, GIOVANNI	2	0			
DOLLENZ, GIUSEPPE	1	0			
DOLLING, AUGUST	1	1	$4,658	$4,658	$4,658
			£2,875	£2,875	£2,875
DOLLING, HERMANN (JR.)	2	2	$2,846	$3,289	$3,068
			£1,725	£2,300	£2,013
DUKE, RICHARD (attributed to)	2	2	$7,284	$16,376	$11,830
			£4,497	£9,775	£7,136
DYKES, GEORGE L. (workshop of)	1	1	$5,463	$5,463	$5,463
			£3,332	£3,332	£3,332
ELLERSIECK, ALBERT	1	1	$4,844	$4,844	$4,844
			£2,990	£2,990	£2,990
EMDE, J.F.C.	1	1	$1,945	$1,945	$1,945
			£1,265	£1,265	£1,265
EMERY, JULIAN	1	1	$5,796	$5,796	$5,796
			£3,450	£3,450	£3,450
ENZENSPERGER, BERNARD (II)	1	1	$7,315	$7,315	$7,315
			£4,370	£4,370	£4,370
FANTIN, DOMENICO	1	0			
FARINA, ERMINIO	1	1	$32,649	$32,649	$32,649
			£19,550	£19,550	£19,550
FAROTTI, CELESTE	1	1	$68,500	$68,500	$68,500
			£41,100	£41,100	£41,100
FENDT, BERNARD SIMON	1	1	$31,706	$31,706	$31,706
			£20,700	£20,700	£20,700
FICKER, GUSTAVE AUGUST	1	1	$1,200	$1,200	$1,200
			£828	£828	£828
FIORI BROTHERS	1	0			
FIORINI, PAOLO	1	1	$9,438	$9,438	$9,438
			£6,600	£6,600	£6,600
FORSTER, SIMON ANDREW	1	1	$38,410	$38,410	$38,410
			£23,000	£23,000	£23,000
FORSTER, WILLIAM	8	6	$16,445	$46,202	$29,819
			£11,500	£27,600	£18,362
FORSTER, WILLIAM (II)	2	2	$17,395	$30,728	$24,062
			£10,350	£18,400	£14,375
FRANCAIS, LUCIEN (attributed to)	1	1	$4,816	$4,816	$4,816
			£2,875	£2,875	£2,875
FRANKS, RAY	1	1	$4,194	$4,194	$4,194
			£2,588	£2,588	£2,588

Violoncello

| Maker | Items | | Selling Prices | | |
	Bid	Sold	Low	High	Avg
FUCHS, WENZEL	1	1	$2,990 £1,794	$2,990 £1,794	$2,990 £1,794
FURBER, JOHN	1	1	$4,530 £3,000	$4,530 £3,000	$4,530 £3,000
FURBER FAMILY	1	0			
GAGLIANO, GENNARO	1	1	$409,860 £253,000	$409,860 £253,000	$409,860 £253,000
GAGLIANO, JOSEPH	2	0			
GAGLIANO, RAFFAELE & ANTONIO (II)	2	2	$74,924 £46,006	$115,968 £69,000	$95,446 £57,503
GAGLIANO FAMILY (MEMBER OF)	1	0			
GAILLARD-LAJOUS, JULES	1	1	$19,102 £12,650	$19,102 £12,650	$19,102 £12,650
GALIMBERTI, LUIGI	1	1	$20,700 £12,420	$20,700 £12,420	$20,700 £12,420
GALLA, ANTON	2	2	$3,353 £2,070	$3,856 £2,381	$3,605 £2,225
GAND BROS.	4	0			
GARINI	1	1	$1,025 £633	$1,025 £633	$1,025 £633
GEISSENHOF, FRANZ (attributed to)	1	1	$13,973 £8,625	$13,973 £8,625	$13,973 £8,625
GIANOTTI, ALFREDO (attributed to)	1	1	$3,082 £1,840	$3,082 £1,840	$3,082 £1,840
GIBERTINI, ANTONIO	1	0			
GILBERT, JEFFREY J.	2	1	$7,342 £4,370	$7,342 £4,370	$7,342 £4,370
GILBERT, JEFFREY JAMES	1	0			
GLENISTER, WILLIAM	1	1	$4,285 £2,645	$4,285 £2,645	$4,285 £2,645
GLOOR, ADOLF	4	2	$1,028 £633	$2,504 £1,495	$1,766 £1,064
GOATER, MICHAEL	1	0			
GODDARD, CHARLES (attributed to)	1	1	$784 £506	$784 £506	$784 £506
GOTZ, C.A.	1	1	$1,230 £759	$1,230 £759	$1,230 £759
GOULDING & CO.	2	2	$4,830 £2,875	$14,801 £8,970	$9,815 £5,923
GRANCINO, FRANCESCO & GIOVANNI (ascribed to)	1	1	$4,025 £2,381	$4,025 £2,381	$4,025 £2,381
GRANCINO, GIOVANNI	6	1	$307,280 £184,000	$307,280 £184,000	$307,280 £184,000
GRANDJON, J. (attributed to)	1	1	$10,601 £6,900	$10,601 £6,900	$10,601 £6,900
GROSSMANN, MAX	1	1	$4,341 £2,875	$4,341 £2,875	$4,341 £2,875
GRULLI, PIETRO	1	1	$27,553 £17,250	$27,553 £17,250	$27,553 £17,250
GUERRA, ALBERTO	1	0			
GUERSAN, LOUIS	2	1	$2,277 £1,380	$2,277 £1,380	$2,277 £1,380

Maker	Bid	Sold	Low	High	Avg
GUERSAN, LOUIS (attributed to)	1	1	$4,276 / £2,990	$4,276 / £2,990	$4,276 / £2,990
HAIDE, JAY	1	0			
HAMMIG, W.H.	2	1	$7,825 / £4,830	$7,825 / £4,830	$7,825 / £4,830
HAMMIG, WIHELM HERMAN	1	1	$10,872 / £7,200	$10,872 / £7,200	$10,872 / £7,200
HARDIE, MATTHEW	2	2	$18,170 / £10,925	$18,354 / £11,500	$18,262 / £11,213
HARRIS, CHARLES	3	3	$4,285 / £2,645	$13,216 / £8,625	$8,410 / £5,290
HARRIS, CHARLES (attributed to)	1	1	$9,209 / £6,440	$9,209 / £6,440	$9,209 / £6,440
HAUSMANN, OTTOMAR	1	1	$3,910 / £2,416	$3,910 / £2,416	$3,910 / £2,416
HEINICKE, MATHIAS	2	2	$6,486 / £4,600	$7,452 / £4,600	$6,969 / £4,600
HEL, JOSEPH	1	1	$67,012 / £40,000	$67,012 / £40,000	$67,012 / £40,000
HEL, PIERRE JOSEPH	1	1	$11,474 / £7,475	$11,474 / £7,475	$11,474 / £7,475
HELLMER, JOHANN GEORG (ascribed to)	1	1	$2,497 / £1,495	$2,497 / £1,495	$2,497 / £1,495
HERRMANN, KARL (workshop of)	1	1	$1,610 / £977	$1,610 / £977	$1,610 / £977
HILL, HENRY LOCKEY	2	0			
HILL, JOSEPH	4	3	$25,041 / £14,950	$36,599 / £23,000	$32,315 / £19,933
HILL, JOSEPH (ascribed to)	1	1	$6,641 / £4,025	$6,641 / £4,025	$6,641 / £4,025
HILL, LOCKEY	8	3	$6,002 / £3,910	$25,266 / £14,950	$13,246 / £7,973
HILL, W.E. & SONS	1	1	$7,894 / £5,520	$7,894 / £5,520	$7,894 / £5,520
HILL, WILLIAM EBSWORTH	1	0			
HILL FAMILY (MEMBER OF)	1	1	$2,823 / £1,840	$2,823 / £1,840	$2,823 / £1,840
HORNSTEINER	1	1	$3,961 / £2,415	$3,961 / £2,415	$3,961 / £2,415
HORNSTEINER, JOSEPH (attributed to)	1	1	$13,449 / £8,050	$13,449 / £8,050	$13,449 / £8,050
HORNUNG, PASQUALE	1	1	$4,600 / £2,944	$4,600 / £2,944	$4,600 / £2,944
HULL, ROBERT	1	0			
JACQUEMIN, RENE	1	1	$6,139 / £3,910	$6,139 / £3,910	$6,139 / £3,910
JAY, HENRY (attributed to)	1	1	$7,268 / £4,600	$7,268 / £4,600	$7,268 / £4,600
JOHNSON, JOHN	1	1	$10,350 / £6,728	$10,350 / £6,728	$10,350 / £6,728
JONES, EDWARD B. (attributed to)	1	1	$2,721 / £1,610	$2,721 / £1,610	$2,721 / £1,610
JORIO, VINCENZO	1	0			

| Maker | Items | | Selling Prices | | |
	Bid	Sold	Low	High	Avg
JUZEK, JOHN	3	2	$1,455	$2,777	$2,116
			£902	£1,722	£1,312
KAUL, PAUL	1	1	$18,630	$18,630	$18,630
			£11,500	£11,500	£11,500
KENNEDY, THOMAS	10	9	$15,426	$46,092	$26,622
			£9,522	£27,600	£16,781
KENNEDY, THOMAS (ascribed to)	1	0			
KENNEDY, THOMAS (attributed to)	1	1	$5,630	$5,630	$5,630
			£3,450	£3,450	£3,450
KLIER, OTTO JOSEPH	1	1	$1,518	$1,518	$1,518
			£920	£920	£920
KLOTZ, AEGIDIUS (I)	1	1	$3,465	$3,465	$3,465
			£2,070	£2,070	£2,070
KLOTZ, JOSEPH	1	0			
KLOTZ, SEBASTIAN (II) (attributed to)	1	0			
KLOTZ FAMILY (MEMBER OF)	1	0			
KONYA (workshop of)	1	0			
KRUMBHOLZ, LORENZ	1	0			
LABERTE	2	1	$7,497	$7,497	$7,497
			£4,715	£4,715	£4,715
LABERTE, MARC (attributed to)	2	1	$6,167	$6,167	$6,167
			£3,795	£3,795	£3,795
LABERTE-HUMBERT BROS.	2	1	$9,673	$9,673	$9,673
			£6,084	£6,084	£6,084
LAJOS, KONYA	1	1	$4,658	$4,658	$4,658
			£2,875	£2,875	£2,875
LAMBERT, JEAN NICOLAS	1	1	$18,330	$18,330	$18,330
			£11,903	£11,903	£11,903
LANG, BENEDIKT	3	1	$2,138	$2,138	$2,138
			£1,265	£1,265	£1,265
LANG, RUDOLF	1	1	$2,827	$2,827	$2,827
			£1,840	£1,840	£1,840
LECAVELLE, FRANCOIS	1	1	$5,377	$5,377	$5,377
			£3,220	£3,220	£3,220
LECHI, ANTONIO	1	1	$3,634	$3,634	$3,634
			£2,300	£2,300	£2,300
LECHI, ANTONIO (attributed to)	1	1	$6,900	$6,900	$6,900
			£4,600	£4,600	£4,600
LE LIEVRE, PIERRE	1	1	$9,718	$9,718	$9,718
			£6,325	£6,325	£6,325
LONGMAN & BRODERIP	4	3	$752	$6,219	$4,348
			£460	£3,680	£2,607
LONGMAN, LUKEY & CO.	3	1	$6,400	$6,400	$6,400
			£4,025	£4,025	£4,025
LOTT, JOHN FREDERICK (attributed to)	1	0			
LOWENDALL	1	1	$5,475	$5,475	$5,475
			£3,450	£3,450	£3,450
LOWENDALL, L.	1	1	$4,637	$4,637	$4,637
			£2,760	£2,760	£2,760
LOWENDALL, LOUIS	1	1	$1,540	$1,540	$1,540
			£920	£920	£920
MAGNIERE, GABRIEL	1	1	$2,981	$2,981	$2,981
			£1,840	£1,840	£1,840
MANGENOT (workshop of)	1	0			

Maker	Items		Selling Prices		
	Bid	Sold	Low	High	Avg
MARCHETTI, ENRICO	1	1	$75,611 £52,875	$75,611 £52,875	$75,611 £52,875
MARCHETTI, ENRICO (attributed to)	1	0			
MARSIGLIESE, BIAGIO	1	1	$6,900 £4,416	$6,900 £4,416	$6,900 £4,416
MARTIN, E. (workshop of)	1	1	$1,955 £1,208	$1,955 £1,208	$1,955 £1,208
MAYSON, WALTER H.	1	1	$8,692 £5,750	$8,692 £5,750	$8,692 £5,750
MEINEL, OSKAR	1	1	$2,875 £1,725	$2,875 £1,725	$2,875 £1,725
MELLEGARI, ENRICO	1	1	$31,050 £20,700	$31,050 £20,700	$31,050 £20,700
MENNESSON, EMILE	2	0			
MERLIN, JOSEPH	1	1	$27,852 £17,193	$27,852 £17,193	$27,852 £17,193
MERLING, PAULI	1	1	$10,310 £6,325	$10,310 £6,325	$10,310 £6,325
MESSORI, PIETRO	3	1	$3,018 £1,840	$3,018 £1,840	$3,018 £1,840
MILLANT, ROGER & MAX	2	1	$15,444 £10,800	$15,444 £10,800	$15,444 £10,800
MILNES, JOHN	1	1	$2,616 £1,610	$2,616 £1,610	$2,616 £1,610
MORASSI, GIOVANNI BATTISTA	2	2	$21,028 £13,225	$23,005 £13,800	$22,016 £13,513
MORRISON, JOHN	2	0			
MOUGENOT, LEON	4	3	$5,624 £3,450	$11,202 £7,274	$8,080 £5,185
NEUNER, MATHIAS	1	1	$4,030 £2,760	$4,030 £2,760	$4,030 £2,760
NEUNER & HORNSTEINER	12	10	$759 £460	$32,994 £21,850	$6,804 £4,439
NICOLAS, DIDIER (L'AINE)	1	0			
NIX, CHARLES WILLIAM	1	1	$439 £276	$439 £276	$439 £276
NORMAN, BARAK	6	3	$3,018 £1,840	$24,398 £14,950	$10,681 £6,567
NORMAN, BARAK & NATHANIEL CROSS	1	1	$14,444 £9,200	$14,444 £9,200	$14,444 £9,200
NORRIS, ROB	1	1	$756 £518	$756 £518	$756 £518
NOVELLI, NATALE	1	1	$9,200 £5,888	$9,200 £5,888	$9,200 £5,888
NURNBERGER, ALBERT	1	1	$1,265 £748	$1,265 £748	$1,265 £748
OTTO, C.W.F. (attributed to)	1	1	$3,310 £1,955	$3,310 £1,955	$3,310 £1,955
OWEN, JOHN W.	1	1	$9,364 £6,095	$9,364 £6,095	$9,364 £6,095
PADEWET, JOHANN II	2	1	$4,276 £2,530	$4,276 £2,530	$4,276 £2,530
PAESOLD, R.	1	1	$1,297 £920	$1,297 £920	$1,297 £920

| Maker | Items | | Selling Prices | | |
	Bid	Sold	Low	High	Avg
PANORMO, VINCENZO	1	0			
PANORMO, VINCENZO (attributed to)	2	2	$7,668 £4,600	$59,821 £36,700	$33,745 £20,650
PARESCHI, GAETANO	1	1	$16,871 £10,350	$16,871 £10,350	$16,871 £10,350
PARMEGGIANI, ROMOLA	1	1	$26,432 £17,250	$26,432 £17,250	$26,432 £17,250
PEDRAZZINI, GIUSEPPE	3	2	$61,456 £36,800	$62,978 £41,100	$62,217 £38,950
PEDRAZZINI, GIUSEPPE (attributed to)	2	0			
PELLIZON, GIOVANNI	1	0			
PELLIZON FAMILY (MEMBER OF)	1	0			
PETERNELLA, JAGO	2	0			
PEVERE, ERNESTO	1	1	$30,550 £19,858	$30,550 £19,858	$30,550 £19,858
PFAB, FRIEDRICH AUGUST	1	1	$9,438 £6,600	$9,438 £6,600	$9,438 £6,600
PFRETZSCHNER (workshop of)	2	2	$575 £345	$1,380 £828	$978 £587
PIATTELLINI, A.	1	1	$57,615 £34,500	$57,615 £34,500	$57,615 £34,500
PICCAGLIANI (workshop of)	1	0			
PICKARD, H.	1	1	$4,325 £2,645	$4,325 £2,645	$4,325 £2,645
PILLEMENT (workshop of)	1	1	$6,000 £4,140	$6,000 £4,140	$6,000 £4,140
PILLEMENT, FRANCOIS	2	1	$4,862 £3,220	$4,862 £3,220	$4,862 £3,220
PIROT, CLAUDE	2	1	$21,850 £15,295	$21,850 £15,295	$21,850 £15,295
POGGI, ANSALDO	2	2	$59,821 £36,700	$79,850 £47,700	$69,835 £42,200
POGGI, ANSALDO (attributed to)	1	1	$17,336 £10,350	$17,336 £10,350	$17,336 £10,350
POSCH, ANTON	3	1	$17,193 £10,694	$17,193 £10,694	$17,193 £10,694
POSTIGLIONE, VINCENZO	1	0			
PRENTICE, RONALD	2	1	$3,374 £2,070	$3,374 £2,070	$3,374 £2,070
PRESSENDA, GIOVANNI FRANCESCO	1	1	$343,170 £205,000	$343,170 £205,000	$343,170 £205,000
PRESTON, JOHN	1	0			
PRINCE, W.B.	1	1	$5,775 £3,450	$5,775 £3,450	$5,775 £3,450
RAYMAN, JACOB	1	1	$36,966 £25,850	$36,966 £25,850	$36,966 £25,850
REGAZZONI, DANTE PAOLO	1	1	$3,850 £2,300	$3,850 £2,300	$3,850 £2,300
REITER, JOHANN	2	0			
RENAUDIN, LEOPOLD	1	1	$12,357 £8,050	$12,357 £8,050	$12,357 £8,050
RICHARDSON, ARTHUR	3	2	$5,403 £3,335	$13,892 £9,200	$9,647 £6,268

Maker	Items Bid	Sold	Selling Prices Low	High	Avg
RIECHERS, AUGUST (attributed to)	2	1	$3,259 £1,955	$3,259 £1,955	$3,259 £1,955
RIVOLTA, GIACOMO (attributed to)	1	1	$49,933 £29,900	$49,933 £29,900	$49,933 £29,900
ROBINSON, WILLIAM	1	0			
ROCCA, ENRICO	1	1	$73,688 £48,800	$73,688 £48,800	$73,688 £48,800
ROCCA, GIUSEPPE (ascribed to)	1	1	$98,596 £62,800	$98,596 £62,800	$98,596 £62,800
ROSADONI, GIOVANNI	1	1	$8,813 £5,728	$8,813 £5,728	$8,813 £5,728
ROSSI, GIOVANNI	1	1	$33,922 £20,829	$33,922 £20,829	$33,922 £20,829
ROTH, ERNST HEINRICH	1	1	$6,146 £3,680	$6,146 £3,680	$6,146 £3,680
ROUDHLOF, F. & MAUCHAND	2	1	$2,594 £1,840	$2,594 £1,840	$2,594 £1,840
ROUDHLOFF, FRANCOIS	1	0			
ROUGIER, MAURICE	2	0			
RUGGIERI, FRANCESCO	1	1	$193,281 £115,000	$193,281 £115,000	$193,281 £115,000
RUNNACLES, HARRY E.	1	1	$2,120 £1,380	$2,120 £1,380	$2,120 £1,380
SACQUIN, CLAUDE	1	1	$21,202 £13,800	$21,202 £13,800	$21,202 £13,800
SALSEDO, LUIGI	1	1	$7,590 £4,600	$7,590 £4,600	$7,590 £4,600
SANDNER, ANTON	1	1	$4,588 £2,990	$4,588 £2,990	$4,588 £2,990
SANNINO, VINCENZO	3	1	$31,227 £19,550	$31,227 £19,550	$31,227 £19,550
SANTAGIULIANA, GAETANO	1	0			
SCAPPIO, FRANCESCO	2	2	$11,178 £6,900	$12,855 £7,935	$12,016 £7,418
SCARAMPELLA, GIUSEPPE (ascribed to)	2	0			
SCARAMPELLA, STEFANO	1	0			
SCARAMPELLA, STEFANO (ascribed to)	2	1	$14,628 £9,200	$14,628 £9,200	$14,628 £9,200
SCARAMPELLA, STEFANO (attributed to)	1	0			
SCHUSTER, JOSEF	2	1	$1,739 £1,035	$1,739 £1,035	$1,739 £1,035
SCHUSTER, JOSEF (workshop of)	1	1	$3,290 £2,139	$3,290 £2,139	$3,290 £2,139
SCHWARZ BROS.	1	1	$10,514 £6,210	$10,514 £6,210	$10,514 £6,210
SCIORILLI, LUIGI	1	1	$2,113 £1,265	$2,113 £1,265	$2,113 £1,265
SILVESTRE, HIPPOLYTE CHRETIEN	1	1	$36,800 £22,080	$36,800 £22,080	$36,800 £22,080
SILVESTRE & MAUCOTEL	1	1	$15,347 £9,775	$15,347 £9,775	$15,347 £9,775
SMILLIE, ALEXANDER	2	1	$3,093 £1,840	$3,093 £1,840	$3,093 £1,840

Maker	Items		Selling Prices		
	Bid	Sold	Low	High	Avg
SMITH, ARTHUR E.	1	1	$18,529 £12,075	$18,529 £12,075	$18,529 £12,075
SMITH, THOMAS	9	6	$2,555 £1,610	$27,255 £17,250	$12,258 £7,767
SMITH, THOMAS (attributed to)	4	2	$2,632 £1,610	$8,060 £4,945	$5,346 £3,278
SMITH, WILLIAM	1	1	$1,874 £1,150	$1,874 £1,150	$1,874 £1,150
SMITH, WILLIAM EDWARD	1	1	$2,277 £1,380	$2,277 £1,380	$2,277 £1,380
STAINER, JACOB (attributed to)	1	1	$6,900 £4,416	$6,900 £4,416	$6,900 £4,416
STAUDINGER, MATHAUS WENCESLAUS	1	1	$10,833 £6,900	$10,833 £6,900	$10,833 £6,900
STEWART, C.G.	1	0			
STORIONI, LORENZO (attributed to)	1	1	$115,473 £80,750	$115,473 £80,750	$115,473 £80,750
STOSS, JOHANN MARTIN	1	1	$9,664 £5,750	$9,664 £5,750	$9,664 £5,750
STRADIVARI, ANTONIO	1	1	$898,945 £551,500	$898,945 £551,500	$898,945 £551,500
TARASCONI, CAROL	1	0			
TECCHLER, DAVID	1	0			
TECCHLER, DAVID (attributed to)	1	0			
TESTORE, CARLO ANTONIO	1	0			
TESTORE, CARLO ANTONIO (attributed to)	1	1	$66,993 £41,100	$66,993 £41,100	$66,993 £41,100
TESTORE, CARLO GIUSEPPE	1	1	$158,650 £95,000	$158,650 £95,000	$158,650 £95,000
THIBOUT, JACQUES PIERRE	2	1	$19,384 £12,650	$19,384 £12,650	$19,384 £12,650
THIBOUVILLE-LAMY, J.	25	23	$707 £449	$6,486 £4,600	$2,223 £1,397
THIBOUVILLE-LAMY, J. (workshop of)	1	1	$575 £345	$575 £345	$575 £345
THIBOUVILLE-LAMY, JEROME	2	2	$1,280 £805	$9,966 £6,600	$5,623 £3,703
THOMA, MATHIAS (workshop of)	1	1	$575 £340	$575 £340	$575 £340
THOMPSON, ALFRED	1	0			
THOMPSON, ROBERT (attributed to)	1	1	$2,971 £1,783	$2,971 £1,783	$2,971 £1,783
TOMAS, OTIS A.	1	1	$1,610 £995	$1,610 £995	$1,610 £995
TOMASSINI, DOMENICO	1	0			
TRAPP, HERMANN	2	1	$2,610 £1,610	$2,610 £1,610	$2,610 £1,610
UCHIYAMA, MASAYUKI	2	0			
VALENCE (attributed to)	1	1	$10,530 £6,440	$10,530 £6,440	$10,530 £6,440
VAN HOOF, ALPHONS	1	1	$11,454 £7,475	$11,454 £7,475	$11,454 £7,475

Maker	Items		Selling Prices		
	Bid	Sold	Low	High	Avg
VAN VESSEM, JAN	1	1	$3,125 £2,185	$3,125 £2,185	$3,125 £2,185
VENTAPANE, LORENZO	2	2	$85,514 £50,600	$87,458 £51,750	$86,486 £51,175
VENTAPANE, LORENZO (attributed to)	1	0			
VERHASSELT, F.	1	1	$8,746 £5,175	$8,746 £5,175	$8,746 £5,175
VERINI, ANDREA	1	1	$5,467 £3,439	$5,467 £3,439	$5,467 £3,439
VILLA, LUIGI	1	0			
VOIGT, E.R. & SON	1	1	$3,947 £2,415	$3,947 £2,415	$3,947 £2,415
VUILLAUME, JEAN BAPTISTE	6	4	$68,634 £41,000	$130,845 £91,500	$103,240 £65,509
VUILLAUME, SEBASTIAN	1	0			
WAMSLEY, PETER	5	3	$2,118 £1,380	$9,373 £5,750	$6,625 £4,102
WATSON, JOHN	1	1	$2,138 £1,495	$2,138 £1,495	$2,138 £1,495
WEERTMAN, ROELOF	1	0			
WEIGERT, JOHANN BLASIUS	2	0			
WERNER, ERICH	4	0			
WHITAKER, MAURICE	1	1	$11,560 £6,900	$11,560 £6,900	$11,560 £6,900
WHITE, ASA WARREN	1	1	$1,725 £1,052	$1,725 £1,052	$1,725 £1,052
WHITMARSH, EMANUEL	2	1	$3,286 £1,955	$3,286 £1,955	$3,286 £1,955
WILFER, ALBIN	1	1	$9,867 £6,900	$9,867 £6,900	$9,867 £6,900
WILLIS, ALAN	1	1	$3,450 £2,415	$3,450 £2,415	$3,450 £2,415
WINTERLING, GEORG	1	1	$16,302 £11,400	$16,302 £11,400	$16,302 £11,400
WITHERS, EDWARD	1	1	$19,102 £12,650	$19,102 £12,650	$19,102 £12,650
WOLDRING, HENDRIK	1	1	$3,972 £2,530	$3,972 £2,530	$3,972 £2,530
WOLFF BROS.	3	2	$3,749 £2,300	$5,025 £2,990	$4,387 £2,645
ZANI, ALDO	1	0			
ZANOLI, GIACOMO	1	1	$67,815 £41,100	$67,815 £41,100	$67,815 £41,100
ZIMMERMANN, JULIUS HEINRICH	1	1	$972 £575	$972 £575	$972 £575
ZIMMERMANN, JULIUS HEINRICH (attributed to)	2	1	$4,124 £2,530	$4,124 £2,530	$4,124 £2,530

VIOLONCELLO BOW

Maker	Items		Selling Prices		
ADAM, JEAN DOMINIQUE (attributed to)	1	0			
ALVEY, BRIAN	3	1	$274 £161	$274 £161	$274 £161

Maker	Items Bid	Sold	Low	Selling Prices High	Avg
BAILEY, G.E.	3	2	$743 £437	$773 £460	$758 £449
BARBE, AUGUSTE	1	0			
BAUSCH	6	4	$56 £35	$2,011 £1,265	$707 £449
BAUSCH, L.	1	1	$1,380 £816	$1,380 £816	$1,380 £816
BAUSCH, LUDWIG	1	1	$2,049 £1,265	$2,049 £1,265	$2,049 £1,265
BAZIN	5	4	$1,610 £952	$3,936 £2,415	$2,797 £1,719
BAZIN (attributed to)	2	1	$2,236 £1,380	$2,236 £1,380	$2,236 £1,380
BAZIN (workshop of)	1	1	$1,765 £1,150	$1,765 £1,150	$1,765 £1,150
BAZIN, CHARLES	3	2	$2,070 £1,346	$3,401 £2,013	$2,736 £1,679
BAZIN, CHARLES NICHOLAS	12	10	$570 £331	$4,404 £2,875	$2,605 £1,610
BAZIN, LOUIS	7	3	$1,062 £632	$3,364 £2,116	$1,837 £1,146
BAZIN, LOUIS (workshop of)	2	1	$768 £460	$768 £460	$768 £460
BAZIN, LOUIS (II)	1	1	$1,677 £1,035	$1,677 £1,035	$1,677 £1,035
BEARE, JOHN & ARTHUR	3	2	$849 £518	$3,055 £1,984	$1,952 £1,251
BEARE & SON	1	1	$1,155 £690	$1,155 £690	$1,155 £690
BECHINI, RENZO	1	0			
BEILKE, MARTIN O.	1	1	$1,398 £863	$1,398 £863	$1,398 £863
BELLIS, ANDREW	1	0			
BERNARDEL, GUSTAVE	3	3	$1,462 £897	$2,875 £1,760	$2,107 £1,295
BERNARDEL, GUSTAVE ADOLPHE	1	1	$637 £391	$637 £391	$637 £391
BERNARDEL, LEON	5	2	$428 £248	$1,733 £1,035	$1,080 £642
BOUMAN, WILLIAM	1	1	$720 £497	$720 £497	$720 £497
BOURGUIGNON, MAURICE	1	1	$2,118 £1,265	$2,118 £1,265	$2,118 £1,265
BRISTOW, S.E.	1	1	$411 £253	$411 £253	$411 £253
BRISTOW, STEPHEN	1	0			
BRYANT, PERCIVAL WILFRED	1	1	$1,540 £920	$1,540 £920	$1,540 £920
BULTITUDE, ARTHUR RICHARD	12	9	$705 £460	$4,832 £2,875	$2,252 £1,431
BUTHOD	2	1	$87 £58	$87 £58	$87 £58
BUTHOD, CHARLES	2	2	$787 £483	$822 £575	$805 £529

| Maker | Items | | Selling Prices | | |
	Bid	Sold	Low	High	Avg
BUTHOD, CHARLES LOUIS	1	1	$1,892 £1,190	$1,892 £1,190	$1,892 £1,190
BUTHOD, CHARLES LOUIS (workshop of)	1	1	$1,380 £908	$1,380 £908	$1,380 £908
BYROM, GEORGE	1	1	$970 £632	$970 £632	$970 £632
CARESSA, ALBERT	1	1	$1,152 £690	$1,152 £690	$1,152 £690
CHANOT & CHARDON	1	0			
CHERPITEL, MOINEL	1	0			
CLUTTERBUCK, J.	1	1	$1,216 £863	$1,216 £863	$1,216 £863
CLUTTERBUCK, JOHN	1	0			
COCKER, L.	2	2	$348 £230	$463 £299	$406 £265
COCKER, LAWRENCE	1	1	$1,149 £748	$1,149 £748	$1,149 £748
COLAS, PROSPER	9	5	$475 £299	$2,319 £1,380	$1,473 £894
COLLIN-MEZIN (workshop of)	1	1	$3,450 £2,132	$3,450 £2,132	$3,450 £2,132
COLLIN-MEZIN, CH.J.B.	1	0			
COLLINS, ROY	1	1	$442 £288	$442 £288	$442 £288
CONIA, STEFANO	1	0			
CUNIOT-HURY	4	2	$1,271 £759	$1,271 £759	$1,271 £759
DABER, J.F.	1	1	$1,495 £972	$1,495 £972	$1,495 £972
DARCHE, HILAIRE	1	1	$1,938 £1,265	$1,938 £1,265	$1,938 £1,265
DARTE, AUGUSTE (workshop of)	1	1	$2,990 £1,815	$2,990 £1,815	$2,990 £1,815
DAVIS	1	1	$2,497 £1,495	$2,497 £1,495	$2,497 £1,495
DODD	8	7	$1,031 £633	$7,700 £4,600	$4,932 £2,965
DODD, EDWARD	1	0			
DODD, J.	3	1	$2,823 £1,840	$2,823 £1,840	$2,823 £1,840
DODD, JAMES	1	1	$1,371 £862	$1,371 £862	$1,371 £862
DODD, JOHN	7	7	$1,590 £977	$7,498 £4,600	$3,339 £2,084
DODD, JOHN (attributed to)	2	0			
DODD, JOHN KEW	1	0			
DODD FAMILY	1	1	$777 £460	$777 £460	$777 £460
DOLLING, HEINZ	1	1	$1,055 £690	$1,055 £690	$1,055 £690
DUPUY, GEORGE	1	1	$1,612 £977	$1,612 £977	$1,612 £977
DURRSCHMIDT, OTTO (workshop of)	1	1	$633 £384	$633 £384	$633 £384

Maker	Items		Selling Prices		
	Bid	Sold	Low	High	Avg
EURY, NICOLAS	2	0			
FETIQUE, MARCEL	1	0			
FETIQUE, MARCEL (attributed to)	1	0			
FETIQUE, VICTOR	15	13	$1,555	$8,066	$3,997
			£920	£4,830	£2,488
FETIQUE, VICTOR (ascribed to)	1	1	$1,210	$1,210	$1,210
			£747	£747	£747
FINKEL, JOHANN S.	2	2	$1,352	$1,944	$1,648
			£805	£1,265	£1,035
FINKEL, JOHANNES S.	2	0			
FINKEL, SIEGFRIED	1	1	$972	$972	$972
			£575	£575	£575
FORSTER	1	1	$3,887	$3,887	$3,887
			£2,530	£2,530	£2,530
FORSTER, WILLIAM (II)	1	1	$2,422	$2,422	$2,422
			£1,495	£1,495	£1,495
FRANCAIS, EMILE	2	2	$1,502	$4,146	$2,824
			£897	£2,546	£1,721
FRITSCH, JEAN	1	1	$1,840	$1,840	$1,840
			£1,088	£1,088	£1,088
GAND BROS.	1	1	$2,496	$2,496	$2,496
			£1,449	£1,449	£1,449
GAND & BERNARDEL	3	2	$1,676	$3,529	$2,603
			£1,092	£2,300	£1,696
GEROME, ROGER	2	2	$1,561	$1,725	$1,643
			£978	£1,035	£1,006
GILLET, LOUIS	4	3	$862	$5,762	$2,835
			£529	£3,450	£1,734
GOTZ, CONRAD	1	1	$424	$424	$424
			£276	£276	£276
GRAND ADAM (attributed to)	1	0			
GRANDCHAMP, ERIC	1	1	$1,540	$1,540	$1,540
			£920	£920	£920
GRUNKE	3	0			
HAMMIG, W.H.	1	1	$869	$869	$869
			£517	£517	£517
HART	1	1	$2,041	$2,041	$2,041
			£1,208	£1,208	£1,208
HART & SON	2	1	$526	$526	$526
			£322	£322	£322
HAWKES & SON	1	1	$1,068	$1,068	$1,068
			£632	£632	£632
HEBERLIN, FRIEDRICH	1	1	$1,412	$1,412	$1,412
			£920	£920	£920
HEL, PIERRE	1	0			
HEL, PIERRE JEAN HENRI	1	1	$2,889	$2,889	$2,889
			£1,840	£1,840	£1,840
HEL, PIERRE JOSEPH (workshop of)	1	1	$1,093	$1,093	$1,093
			£663	£663	£663
HENDERSON, F.V.	1	0			
HENRY (attributed to)	1	0			
HENRY, EUGENE	2	0			
HENRY, J.V.	1	0			

Maker	Items		Selling Prices		
	Bid	Sold	Low	High	Avg
HENRY, JOSEPH	2	2	$21,706 £14,375	$31,671 £19,550	$26,689 £16,963
HENRY, JOSEPH (attributed to)	1	1	$5,055 £3,220	$5,055 £3,220	$5,055 £3,220
HERRMANN, EDWIN OTTO	2	2	$883 £575	$1,938 £1,265	$1,410 £920
HERRMANN, PAUL	1	1	$773 £460	$773 £460	$773 £460
HILAIRE, PAUL	1	0			
HILL	1	1	$336 £219	$336 £219	$336 £219
HILL, W.E. & SONS	89	73	$168 £104	$8,400 £5,796	$2,369 £1,497
HILL, W.E. & SONS (attributed to)	1	1	$2,347 £1,495	$2,347 £1,495	$2,347 £1,495
HURY, CUNIOT	1	0			
HUSSON, CHARLES CLAUDE	2	2	$2,236 £1,380	$3,534 £2,300	$2,885 £1,840
JOMBAR, PAUL	2	1	$192 £115	$192 £115	$192 £115
KNOPF, CHRISTIAN WILHELM	1	1	$2,016 £1,410	$2,016 £1,410	$2,016 £1,410
KOLSTEIN, SAMUEL	1	1	$1,380 £908	$1,380 £908	$1,380 £908
KOVANDA, FRANK	1	1	$667 £467	$667 £467	$667 £467
KUDANOWSKI	3	1	$519 £368	$519 £368	$519 £368
LABERTE	1	1	$782 £483	$782 £483	$782 £483
LABERTE, MARC	1	1	$1,234 £805	$1,234 £805	$1,234 £805
LAFLEUR, JACQUES	1	0			
LAFLEUR, JACQUES RENE	1	1	$22,770 £13,800	$22,770 £13,800	$22,770 £13,800
LAMY, A.	4	2	$3,290 £2,139	$4,776 £2,990	$4,033 £2,564
LAMY, ALFRED	9	5	$2,300 £1,421	$7,475 £4,619	$4,292 £2,701
LAMY, ALFRED JOSEPH	19	15	$2,236 £1,380	$16,457 £10,350	$5,895 £3,642
LAMY, JULES	2	0			
LANGONET, EUGENE	1	1	$542 £345	$542 £345	$542 £345
LAPIERRE, MARCEL	3	1	$575 £351	$575 £351	$575 £351
LAPIERRE, MARCEL (attributed to)	1	1	$2,889 £1,725	$2,889 £1,725	$2,889 £1,725
LEE, JOHN NORWOOD	3	1	$1,265 £782	$1,265 £782	$1,265 £782
LEWIS, WILLIAM & SON	1	1	$611 £397	$611 £397	$611 £397
LOTTE, FRANCOIS	5	4	$428 £248	$860 £533	$655 £397

| Maker | Items | | Selling Prices | | |
	Bid	Sold	Low	High	Avg
LOTTE, ROGER-FRANCOIS	4	3	$1,373	$2,695	$2,252
			£960	£1,610	£1,393
LUPOT, FRANCOIS (II) (ascribed to)	1	1	$1,800	$1,800	$1,800
			£1,242	£1,242	£1,242
MAIRE, NICOLAS	3	3	$3,680	$7,222	$5,226
			£2,392	£4,600	£3,327
MALINE, GUILLAUME	5	0			
MARTIN, J.	1	0			
MARTIN, JEAN JOSEPH	5	4	$673	$7,499	$5,095
			£402	£4,629	£3,145
METTAL, WALTER	5	3	$96	$1,459	$853
			£57	£1,020	£558
MILLANT, MAX	1	0			
MILLANT, ROGER & MAX	2	2	$2,560	$10,971	$6,765
			£1,610	£6,900	£4,255
MOINEL & CHERPITEL	4	2	$712	$1,540	$1,126
			£437	£920	£679
MORIZOT (FRERES), LOUIS	3	0			
MORIZOT FRERES	2	1	$2,352	$2,352	$2,352
			£1,645	£1,645	£1,645
MORIZOT, LOUIS	6	3	$576	$2,248	$1,390
			£345	£1,398	£849
MORIZOT, LOUIS (II)	2	2	$1,328	$2,648	$1,988
			£805	£1,725	£1,265
MORIZOT FAMILY	1	1	$1,380	$1,380	$1,380
			£828	£828	£828
NAVEA-VERA, DANIEL	1	1	$2,070	$2,070	$2,070
			£1,325	£1,325	£1,325
NEUDORFER, RODOLF (II)	2	2	$894	$1,028	$961
			£552	£635	£593
NEUDORFER, RUDOLPH	3	1	$342	$342	$342
			£207	£207	£207
NEUVEVILLE, P.C.	1	0			
NEUVILLE	1	0			
NORRIS, JOHN	1	0			
NURNBERGER	1	0			
NURNBERGER, A.	2	2	$638	$3,353	$1,996
			£437	£2,070	£1,254
NURNBERGER, ALBERT	12	8	$690	$2,881	$1,548
			£421	£1,725	£966
NURNBERGER, CHRISTIAN ALBERT	1	1	$1,218	$1,218	$1,218
			£747	£747	£747
NURNBERGER, KARL ALBERT	1	0			
OUCHARD, E.	1	1	$3,523	$3,523	$3,523
			£2,300	£2,300	£2,300
OUCHARD, EMILE	5	5	$2,300	$5,750	$3,896
			£1,360	£3,491	£2,377
OUCHARD, EMILE (FILS) (attributed to)	2	1	$6,569	$6,569	$6,569
			£3,910	£3,910	£3,910
OUCHARD, EMILE A.	4	4	$2,881	$10,925	$6,881
			£1,725	£6,632	£4,389
OUCHARD, EMILE FRANCOIS	3	2	$2,708	$4,023	$3,365
			£1,725	£2,530	£2,128

Maker	Items		Selling Prices		
	Bid	Sold	Low	High	Avg
PAJEOT, ETIENNE	2	2	$8,228 £5,175	$12,334 £7,475	$10,281 £6,325
PANORMO (ascribed to)	2	1	$2,142 £1,323	$2,142 £1,323	$2,142 £1,323
PANORMO (attributed to)	2	2	$2,364 £1,459	$3,108 £1,955	$2,736 £1,707
PANORMO, LOUIS	2	1	$3,524 £2,300	$3,524 £2,300	$3,524 £2,300
PAQUOTTE, PLACIDE	1	1	$2,497 £1,495	$2,497 £1,495	$2,497 £1,495
PAULUS, JOHANNES O.	1	1	$960 £575	$960 £575	$960 £575
PECCATTE, CHARLES	6	3	$1,792 £1,093	$10,563 £6,325	$6,679 £4,006
PECCATTE, CHARLES (attributed to)	1	0			
PECCATTE, CHARLES & AUGUSTE LENOBLE (workshop of)	2	2	$5,589 £3,450	$6,427 £3,968	$6,008 £3,709
PECCATTE, DOMINIQUE	4	2	$10,689 £6,325	$22,356 £13,800	$16,523 £10,063
PECCATTE, FRANCOIS	3	3	$4,705 £3,290	$15,005 £9,775	$11,384 £7,422
PECCATTE, FRANCOIS (workshop of)	1	1	$3,073 £1,840	$3,073 £1,840	$3,073 £1,840
PECCATTE, FRANCOIS & DOMINIQUE	1	1	$13,476 £8,050	$13,476 £8,050	$13,476 £8,050
PENZEL, E.M.	1	1	$1,035 £628	$1,035 £628	$1,035 £628
PFRETZSCHNER (workshop of)	1	1	$489 £298	$489 £298	$489 £298
PFRETZSCHNER, G.A.	1	1	$920 £544	$920 £544	$920 £544
PFRETZSCHNER, H.R.	18	16	$489 £297	$3,110 £1,840	$1,713 £1,055
PFRETZSCHNER, H.R. (workshop of)	1	1	$920 £598	$920 £598	$920 £598
PFRETZSCHNER, HERMANN RICHARD	1	1	$1,986 £1,265	$1,986 £1,265	$1,986 £1,265
PIERNOT, MARIE LOUIS	1	1	$1,725 £1,047	$1,725 £1,047	$1,725 £1,047
POIRSON, JUSTIN	5	2	$570 £331	$2,865 £1,759	$1,717 £1,045
PRAGER, AUGUST EDWIN	4	2	$637 £379	$1,117 £667	$877 £523
PRAGER, GUSTAV	1	1	$705 £460	$705 £460	$705 £460
REICHEL, AUGUST ANTON	1	1	$1,353 £805	$1,353 £805	$1,353 £805
RETFORD, WILLIAM C.	1	1	$4,813 £2,875	$4,813 £2,875	$4,813 £2,875
ROLLAND, BENOIT	2	2	$2,852 £1,656	$3,562 £2,185	$3,207 £1,921
ROTH, ERNST HEINRICH (workshop of)	1	1	$1,150 £698	$1,150 £698	$1,150 £698

Maker	Items Bid	Sold	Selling Prices Low	High	Avg
SARTORY, E.	1	1	$12,775 £7,935	$12,775 £7,935	$12,775 £7,935
SARTORY, EUGENE	33	25	$3,749 £2,300	$23,046 £13,800	$11,780 £7,306
SCHULLER, OTTO	1	1	$188 £115	$188 £115	$188 £115
SCHUSTER, ADOLF	3	2	$978 £604	$1,035 £681	$1,006 £642
SCHUSTER, ADOLF C.	2	1	$1,294 £863	$1,294 £863	$1,294 £863
SCHUSTER, ADOLPH CURT	1	1	$1,233 £863	$1,233 £863	$1,233 £863
SCHUSTER, ALBERT	1	1	$1,150 £748	$1,150 £748	$1,150 £748
SCHUSTER, GOTHARD	2	1	$805 £483	$805 £483	$805 £483
SEIFERT (workshop of)	1	1	$431 £302	$431 £302	$431 £302
SEIFERT, LOTHAR	1	0			
SEIFERT, W.	1	1	$155 £92	$155 £92	$155 £92
SILVESTRE & MAUCOTEL	3	2	$1,845 £1,092	$5,654 £3,680	$3,750 £2,386
SIMON (attributed to)	1	0			
SIMON, F.R.	2	0			
SIMON, F.R. (attributed to)	1	0			
SIMON, PAUL	5	3	$2,103 £1,323	$7,452 £4,600	$4,838 £3,002
SIMON, PAUL (attributed to)	1	0			
SIMON, PIERRE	4	3	$6,006 £4,200	$7,941 £5,175	$6,763 £4,525
SIMON BROS.	2	0			
STEINEL, G. RUDI	1	1	$374 £262	$374 £262	$374 £262
STENGEL, V.	1	1	$159 £98	$159 £98	$159 £98
TAYLOR, DAVID	1	0			
TAYLOR, MALCOLM	2	1	$1,304 £805	$1,304 £805	$1,304 £805
THIBOUVILLE-LAMY, J.	4	2	$1,402 £828	$1,695 £1,012	$1,549 £920
THIBOUVILLE-LAMY, JEROME	2	1	$1,264 £805	$1,264 £805	$1,264 £805
THOMACHOT, S.	1	1	$3,697 £2,585	$3,697 £2,585	$3,697 £2,585
THOMASSIN (attributed to)	1	0			
THOMASSIN, CLAUDE	1	1	$2,185 £1,530	$2,185 £1,530	$2,185 £1,530
THOMASSIN, VICTOR	2	0			
TORRES, FRANK	1	0			
TOURNIER, JOSEPH ALEXIS	1	1	$989 £644	$989 £644	$989 £644
TOURNIER, JOSEPH ALEXIS (workshop of)	1	1	$1,955 £1,187	$1,955 £1,187	$1,955 £1,187

Maker	Items		Selling Prices		
	Bid	Sold	Low	High	Avg
TOURTE, FRANCOIS XAVIER	1	0			
TUBBS, JAMES	7	5	$3,882	$9,218	$6,823
			£2,530	£5,520	£4,393
TUBBS, JAMES (attributed to)	1	1	$1,714	$1,714	$1,714
			£1,058	£1,058	£1,058
TUBBS, THOMAS	2	2	$1,175	$10,018	$5,597
			£764	£5,980	£3,372
TUBBS, THOMAS (attributed to)	1	1	$2,120	$2,120	$2,120
			£1,380	£1,380	£1,380
TUBBS, WILLIAM	1	0			
VAN DER MEER, KAREL	3	1	$1,006	$1,006	$1,006
			£621	£621	£621
VAN HEMERT, KEES	2	2	$575	$805	$690
			£351	£476	£413
VICKERS, J.E.	2	1	$782	$782	$782
			£483	£483	£483
VIDOUDEZ, PIERRE	1	1	$3,353	$3,353	$3,353
			£2,185	£2,185	£2,185
VIGNERON, A.	3	2	$3,125	$4,298	$3,711
			£2,185	£2,673	£2,429
VIGNERON, ANDRE	2	0			
VIGNERON, JOSEPH ARTHUR	9	7	$1,035	$8,458	$5,146
			£681	£5,520	£3,313
VOIGT, CARL HERMANN	1	0			
VOIRIN, F.N.	3	2	$1,454	$6,721	$4,087
			£920	£4,700	£2,810
VOIRIN, FRANCOIS NICOLAS	24	14	$748	$7,498	$4,141
			£456	£4,600	£2,584
VUILLAUME, JEAN BAPTISTE	11	7	$768	$13,714	$8,602
			£460	£8,625	£5,404
WANKA, HERBERT	1	0			
WATSON, W.D.	1	1	$2,981	$2,981	$2,981
			£1,840	£1,840	£1,840
WEICHOLD	1	0			
WEICHOLD, R.	2	0			
WEICHOLD, RICHARD	3	3	$431	$671	$572
			£255	£437	£353
WERNER, ERNST	1	1	$1,380	$1,380	$1,380
			£838	£838	£838
WERNER, FRANZ EMANUEL (workshop of)	1	0			
WERNER, KARL	1	1	$1,190	$1,190	$1,190
			£738	£738	£738
WERRO, JEAN	1	1	$248	$248	$248
			£161	£161	£161
WILSON, GARNER	6	5	$1,147	$2,062	$1,464
			£698	£1,265	£906
WINKLER, FRANZ	1	1	$633	$633	$633
			£443	£443	£443
WITHERS, GEORGE	1	0			
WITHERS, GEORGE & SONS	4	1	$487	$487	$487
			£299	£299	£299
YAKQUSHKIN	1	1	$415	$415	$415
			£253	£253	£253

Maker	Items		Selling Prices		
	Bid	Sold	Low	High	Avg

XYLOPHONE

COSLEV	1	1	$556	$556	$556
			£368	£368	£368
PREMIER	1	1	$193	$193	$193
			£115	£115	£115
WARNE, REUBEN	3	1	$39	$39	$39
			£23	£23	£23

ZITHER

KIENDL, A.	2	2	$194	$495	$345
			£127	£322	£224
KIENDL, KARL	1	1	$354	$354	$354
			£230	£230	£230
PUGH, JOHANNES	1	1	$476	$476	$476
			£287	£287	£287
SCHUSTER, CARL GOTTLOB (JR.)	1	1	$575	$575	$575
			£345	£345	£345
TIEFENBRUNNER, GEORG	1	1	$112	$112	$112
			£69	£69	£69

ZITHER-BANJO

CAMMEYER, ALFRED D.	1	1	$339	$339	$339
			£207	£207	£207
DALLAS	1	1	$63	$63	$63
			£40	£40	£40
GORDON, GERALD	1	1	$97	$97	$97
			£58	£58	£58

Other Titles in the Backstage Books Series

Commonsense Instrument Care, $9.95
Violin maker and dealer James N. McKean, past president of the American Federation of Violin and Bow Makers, has written the essential reference on maintaining the playability and value of violins, violas, and their bows.

Violin Owner's Manual, $14.95
Read about the defining features of the violin and the evolution of the violin bow. Learn helpful tips on buying and selling, whether it is your first instrument or a major investment. Sound your best with pointers on violin setup, maintenance, repairs, strings, and amplification.

A Cellist's Life, by Colin Hampton, $12.95
One of the 20th century's most distinguished cellists, Colin Hampton is your guide to a bygone world of classical music and musicians. Through his witty, convivial, and candid narrative, you'll encounter such luminaries as Pablo Casals, Ernest Bloch, Igor Stravinsky, Arturo Toscanini, Béla Bartók, and Yehudi Menuhin.

21st-Century Violinists, Vol. 1, $12.95
An exciting collection of in-depth interviews with the world's preeminent string players including Corey Cerovsek, Sarah Chang, Pamela Frank, Kennedy, Midori, Anne-Sophie Mutter, Elmar Oliveira, Nadja Salerno-Sonnenberg, Gil Shaham, Isaac Stern, and Maxim Vengerov.

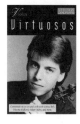

Violin Virtuosos, $12.95
This fascinating companion to Vol. 1 includes profiles of Joshua Bell, Chee-Yun, Kyung-Wha Chung, Jorja Fleezanis, Hilary Hahn, Leila Josefowicz, Mark Kaplan, Viktoria Mullova, Vadim Repin, Joseph Silverstein, and Christian Tetzlaff.